LIFE OF MY OWN

By Harley Flanagan
Introduction by Steven Blush
Edited by Laura Lee Flanagan

Feral House
1240 W. Sims Way
Suite 124
Port Townsend, WA 98368

10 9 8 7 6 5 4 3

Cover design: Dana Collins
Interior design: designSimple
Cover photo by Jay Nolan

CONTENTS

INTRODUCTION

BY STEVEN BLUSH

I t's a damn shame that Harley Flanagan even needs an introduction. The life story of this seminal musician is the total embodiment of the rock & roll lifestyle. He was a '70s pre-teen rock scene celebrity, growing up amid the sex and drugs of Downtown New York subculture, hanging out with punk legends like Richard Hell and Joe Strummer.

Allen Ginsberg wrote the introduction to a book of his illustrations and stories published when Harley was nine (1976's *The Shopkeeper and His Donkey*). At age 11, Harley found himself drumming in his aunt Denise Mercedes' New York punk band, the Stimulators, that ruled the fabled Warhol-connected scene at Max's Kansas City. The Stimulators' gigs inspired the rise of New York Hardcore, with young bands like the Bad Brains and Beastie Boys. Harley ran smack in the middle of that intense action, and was a primary motivator of the American Hardcore movement.

This all may sound edgy and exciting, but Harley grew up way too fast, and endured a childhood that no kid should've ever had to withstand. His father that he never knew was a drug addict always in and out of prison. His cool hippie mother, with baby Harley and little more than the clothes on their backs, hitchhiked across America and Europe, and eventually re-settled back in New York's perilous Lower East Side. They never had a pot to piss in. He never had a chance.

The only white kid of his age in what was then a hostile Puerto Rican neighborhood, Harley dropped out of school at age 13. Left to fend for himself like a feral animal among a jungle of knife-wielding street gangs straight outta *The Warriors*, he grew up to be a menacing street thug, a one-man wrecking machine that took down anyone who stood in his way (as well as many who didn't).

Harley first got exposed to Skinheads on a Stimulators tour of

Ireland, and returned to become the first American Skinhead. His lethal tattooed teen punk rock gang panhandled, robbed, hustled, and lived in dingy Downtown squats. Their victorious beat-downs on the hostile neighborhood thugs and street gangs made Harley the commander of the shock troops that unwittingly cleared the way for East Village gentrification.

Harley started much of the sound and style of modern music. He's the prototype for every shaved-headed tattooed nihilistic punker type to follow—he in New York, and his peer Henry Rollins in Los Angeles. When people today say "Hardcore," they really mean everything that Harley instigated and inspired. Back in the day, there was crude graffiti on Avenue A that read "NYHC = New York Harley Clones," which wasn't far from the truth. Untold generations of thug-core aspirants still attempt to emulate him.

Modern stars from Pantera and Hatebreed to Godsmack and Lamb of God have all paid homage to Harley. Too bad he never had the benefit of a publicist or a manager—or for that matter, responsible parental guidance—to help him reap the rewards. Harley's legendary band the Cro-Mags was the first to merge the Hardcore punk and heavy metal scenes on a major level, pioneering thrash metal and the punk/metal crossover. Their ferocious delivery spoke to tens of thousands of alienated kids of all persuasions.

The Cro-Mags' 1986 album *Age of Quarrel* is considered a bible to many. Songs like "Survival on the Streets" and "Street Justice" were not just allegories, but true-life tales of living on the edge in an urban hell. Heavy music would never be the same. The band's landmark tours with Motörhead literally changed the face of the music scene. Back then, Metallica played their rapid-fire music in tight pants and poufy hair. After *Age of Quarrel*, they never dared to again.

Cro-Mags had strong ties to the Hare Krishna movement, whose teachings made their way into the band's imposing imagery. Harley spent time in the temples. That uneasy juxtaposition of street brutality and Krishna consciousness made for a mutant strain of Vedic punk faith that still holds a place in the scene.

The Cro-Mags' breakup makes your typical rock-biz blood feud seem like *Romper Room* in comparison. They lived an unbelievably raw *Lord of the Flies*-like existence, and then got thrust into the limelight with no responsible supervision. It all devolved into a nightmare "quarrel" that 30 years later still offers no resolution.

Harley remains a notorious character of legend. People still quake in fear at the mention of his name—cuz they know they could still get their asses kicked. He held a scary Charles Manson-like sway over his followers, and upped the ante for the next decades of intense music.

Lots of people talk about being "real"—Harley Flanagan is the realest. He's the only person I've ever met who's never had to exaggerate a story because everything he's been through from day one is so intense. He never had a picket-fenced home or a warm hug from daddy. Most autobiographies tend to embellish. Harley wishes he can tone it down, but he can't.

Harley's precipitous late-'90s decline rates a book unto itself. As a 30-plus-year scene participant, I've personally never seen anyone take such mass quantities of hard drugs from such a young age over such a prolonged period of time—and then bottom out so badly—yet still now have their shit together. Like any classic rise-and-fall story, this one too ends with redemption. The Harley of today is mature, sensitive, erudite, and articulate, yet still sharp enough to bite your fucking head off.

I covered Harley's legal proceedings after his headline-grabbing "stabbing incident" at Webster Hall for *Paper* Magazine. The strange and sordid tale of the Cro-Mags founder going on a knifing spree against his bandmates for performing without him became one of the biggest rock stories of 2012. Only one problem: it looks like it wasn't true. We all know that dropped charges don't always mean innocence, but in the beginning there were dozens of eyewitnesses, yet as the DA's case unfolded, there were nothing but divergent, even bizarre, statements, rife with contradiction. The

ADA admitted they were unable to produce one credible witness for a grand jury.

Harley's personal exploration through Brazilian Jiu-Jitsu mastery, under mixed martial arts legend Renzo Gracie, has seen him competing since the '90s in Jiu-Jitsu tournaments and mixed martial arts events, and giving private lessons to wannabe ultimate fighters. One great irony of Harley's barbaric schism with the New York Hardcore scene, and his messy split with the mother of his children who took his two boys, is that through all this, he met the love of his life in his new wife—who has introduced him to impressive social circles, and has given him the closure offered by a happy and comfortable life.

If there's any justice in this world, one day there will be a shrine to Harley Flanagan in the Rock and Roll Hall of Fame. But we all know there isn't any justice in this world. Regardless of what the "experts" may say, Harley's cultural effects and musical legacies are still being felt over 30 years later.

— Steven Blush, author/filmmaker, *American Hardcore*,
New York City, 2016

LIFE OF MY OWN

HARLEY FLANAGAN
EDITED BY LAURA LEE FLANAGAN

S o there I was, handcuffed to a hospital bed with a nice stab wound in my leg, when I overheard the arresting officer say, "I'm here with the perp—the victims are in another room…" That's when it hit me—what the fuck is going on here, the perp? I'm the victim here: I got jumped!

I was being charged with four felonies: stabbing two people, biting one person's face and another person's arm; the shit was insane. But looking back, maybe what's insane is that nothing like this had ever happened before.

It was July 6th, 2012, and I had just come from teaching a kids' Jiu-Jitsu class; it was a beautiful day. I was going to see my old band, a band I started back in the early '80s—the Cro-Mags, or at least what was left of it. They were playing at Webster Hall—at the "CBGB Festival," for a club that no longer exists but has become a profitable trademark; a club I used to play at and went to my entire childhood in a city that no longer resembles that of my youth. Where there once was urban decay, gangs, crime, and lines of drug addicts at drug spots, there are now multimillion-dollar condos, John Varvatos, Whole Foods, and lines of yuppies at Starbucks.

I'd been hoping to see the singer and drummer. There'd been bad blood for a few years and I wanted to talk to them and try to put an end to it. I was thinking that if I went, maybe they'd even invite me up to play a song or two, and that we could talk about reaching out to the guitarists as well. Maybe do a show, a few shows, even a small tour, or if nothing else, at the very least we could publicly bury the hatchet. I knew it would benefit everybody involved to have peace, and truthfully the beef between us didn't mean anything to me after all the years that had passed compared to the significance of what we had done together and still could do. It's so funny when I think back on that now.

I went to Webster Hall that day in good faith—I was even gonna bring my kids! I went with VIP passes in hand and the belief, naïve as that may have been, that maybe we were all ready to squash the beef and the bullshit that had become as synonymous with "Cro-Mags" as the music itself.

Well, let's just say, things didn't go as planned.

MY CHILDHOOD

Chapter One

I remember a lot of things very clearly, and a lot of things are just kind of a blur. It's almost like a dream. You know how when you wake up and you remember most of your dream—or bits and pieces—but you can't make sense of all of it? Other things are as clear as if they just happened. That's kind of how my memory works at this point. I wrote it all down as best I can. Some of it might be a little out of order but that's about it. Now before I go any further, I'd like to say just for the record, if you work in any kind of law enforcement and you are reading this, everything in this book is entirely made up! If not, well then I don't really care what you want to think or believe.

I was pretty much raised by hippies and rock 'n' rollers from the start, besides the few years I spent living with my grandparents. So most of the people I looked up to early in life were fuck-ups and/or musicians and so on. I hit the streets pretty young, so it was kind of inevitable I would make a lot of mistakes in life. I don't want people to think I am proud of this life I lived. I am not. I am just amazed I lived as long as I have or did. Whatever the case may be by the time you read this.

Anyway, that having been said, I was born at San Francisco General Hospital on March 8, 1967 at the start of "The Summer of Love." My mom's name is Rose Marie Feliu and my dad's name was Harley Wayne Walker Flanagan. I have lived all over the world, but I'm a New Yorker at heart—that's where my mom was from, that's where I spent most of my life, and that's where I really grew up.

My mom was a hippie; my dad was a drifter. And somehow their paths crossed.

Before the hippie days, my mom was into all the early rock 'n' roll stuff—Motown, and pretty much all the music that was happening when she was young. Her father, Juan Feliu, came from the Dominican Republic. He came to America through Ellis Island by himself when he was in his early teens, and was one of the first Dominicans to join the United States Army. He served in World War II, where he played in the military band. That's how he got his citizenship, by serving in the military.

He was one of the funniest people I ever knew. He worked all kinds of different jobs, everything from a building super to a longshoreman. He was a charming guy; he had a thick Spanish accent. He spoke several languages, all with a Spanish accent, and he knew a lot about history. He was always reading; everyone called him "The Professor," and he loved to gamble. He'd bet on anything: cards, dogs, horses, even cockfights. One time he met Marilyn Monroe, and unbelievably, he brought her back to the house and she met the family—which just shows what kind of person he was.

Marilyn and then-husband Arthur Miller were at the Bohemian National Annex, or "Bohemian Annex," on 74th Street between 1st and 2nd across from where my family lived in Manhattan. It was a tiny local theater; my grandfather was working there as a janitor. He used to get all the kids in the neighborhood in to see the movies; my mom saw *The Thing* and *Bambi* there.

Anyway, at some point during the evening, my grandfather met Marilyn. He asked her if she would go across the street with him and meet his family, that he would be so proud if she met his kids and his wife. And, incredibly, she went. The buildings in the neighborhood were all poor and run-down, a lot of immigrants, tenement houses like you see on the Lower East Side. But she came over to the slum building across the street from the theater and went upstairs by herself. My grandmother, who was shocked and completely caught off guard, was in her nightgown and curlers, and my mom and aunt Denise, who were just little girls, were asleep in their beds.

As it turns out, they didn't have proper refrigeration in the theater for all the extra champagne that had been brought in for the event (after all, it was the '50s), so grandpa came to the rescue. They brought in buckets and buckets of ice and filled up the bathtub in their apartment, which was in the kitchen, with the ice, and had all the extra bottles of champagne from the event in the tub.

The neighbors had never seen anything like it. All the commotion from the theater running back and forth to the apartment to get champagne; again, it was just the kind of guy he was. It also goes to show how cool Ms. Monroe was—really down-to-earth despite all the fame.

He got her to kiss a napkin, and we had her lipstick print for years...'til my grandmother threw it out. I think she got sick of him showing it off to people. Yeah, he was a real character. I loved him a lot.

HARLEY AND HIS MOTHER, ROSE, IN ÅRHUS, DENMARK

My grandmother, Bea, she was my heart. She took care of me, and all the neighborhood kids. I miss her dearly. I really can't give them enough love in these few words.

I've got a lot of World War II vets in my family. My great-aunt Sophie was one of the first women to serve in the military in World War II. She was in the Women's Air Corps—she met Mother Teresa, and served with Captain Doolittle and remained good friends with him and his wife 'til way after the war. She told me some crazy shit—she said that she and Ms. Doolittle used to go out to restaurants from time to time after the war ended, and some of the restaurants in their neighborhood wouldn't serve Ms. Doolittle, 'cause she was an officer's wife and it was a German neighborhood. Believe it or not, there were a lot of Nazi sympathizers in New York City back then. You had shit like the German American Bund or German American Federation/Amerikadeutscher Bund, which was an American Nazi Organization established in the '30s. Have you ever seen the footage of the Nazi rally at Madison Square Garden in 1939, with Fritz Julius Kuhn? There were like 20,000 people there! But yeah, she was the rock of the family, the one who kept us all together after my grandmother died. She passed away on Christmas 2010, two days before her 98th birthday.

On my dad's side I have my great-uncles Jack and Gaylend, who both served in World War II and Korea. The people in my family have got a lot cooler stories than mine. But people have always told me I should write a book and I do feel like I got a story to tell.

My mom was friends with a lot of famous writers, poets and musicians, and freaks from the hippie era and the Beat scene like Allen Ginsberg, Harry Smith, legendary comedian Lenny Bruce, who she referred to as Uncle Lenny. And she was involved with the whole Andy Warhol-Factory-Velvet Underground scene. She was in one of the Factory films with Warhol when she was in her early teens, called Dirt, which was never released. Stills from the film have only just recently surfaced all these years later, with pictures of my mom with Warhol and others in the film. She was around a lot of crazy shit back in the day in New York and out West in San Francisco—hippies or flower children as they were called. She did a lot of hitchhiking and traveling back then, and at one point she told me she even met some of the Manson girls out West—they

HARLEY'S GRANDPARENTS, JUAN AND BEATRICE FELIU, AND HARLEY'S GREAT-AUNT SOPHIE KIEWLAK

tried to get her to come with them out to the Spahn Ranch to meet this guy called Charlie. But my mom thought they were a little too weird, so she didn't join them.

She was a go-go dancer—and like so many people, she was caught up in the whole drug culture of the '60s. And when I was a kid she was still a stripper. I remember going to work with her a few times when I was little; that was weird, looking back on it now. There was even a short period of time she was a dominatrix but that was much later. So if you wonder why I'm all fucked up, there might be a few reasons in there somewhere. And of course the alcohol was hard to deal with at times, but I loved her, and to her credit, she sobered up and got off alcohol for good in the '80s.

There's a lot about her life I don't know; I know my grandparents worried about her when she was off on her own. She had me when she was real young—she was 21.

When I was a baby and during my early childhood I traveled so much and saw so many things with her, from New York to Europe to Africa and more. She shared the world with me, and in a lot of ways she helped make me who I am.

We had an interesting relationship to say the least—with all its ups and downs and sometimes long gaps of time when we didn't see each other at all. But one thing is certain: I love her and she loves me, of that there is no doubt.

There were times that I had resentment and anger about my life, and I made it no secret. Sometimes I felt like I was living the life she wanted instead of the life a kid should have. Now looking back, I get it. She wanted to expose me to as much as the world had to offer, and I know I'm lucky I had her. As she approached the end of her life she told me one of her biggest regrets was that I grew up too fast.

My dad's name was Harley—he was from Texas. From what I have been told and what I found out over the years he's got Irish, Dutch, English as well as some Native American blood: Cherokee and Choctaw. I traced his family back to the 1800s in Oklahoma when it was still known as "the Indian territory." My dad's mother Wanda raised him after his dad left when he was just a baby. She was only 16 when she had him.

My dad left home for good around the same age as me, maybe 14–15, and started riding freight trains. But my Grandma Wanda told me the first time he left he was maybe six or seven: he rode off on a pig, and the cops brought him back from another town. She said when he got older, it always took at least two squad cars to take him in. Always a minimum of four to five cops, one for each limb. She laughed and said, "When he got older, there were states that he was banned from altogether. If he even showed up, they'd arrest him for even being there." That's my dad! He was a bit of a wild one—a "free spirit." He liked to live from moment to moment and from everything I've heard he had serious drug and alcohol issues most all of his life. He was always in and out of prison.

I found some hysterical letters he wrote my Grandmother Beatrice when he was in jail—complete with stories about escapes, recaptures, hiding from police dogs and the whole thing. It was pretty funny. He wrote about hiding in the mud and the weeds, listening to the dogs barking looking for him. At one point he said they walked right past him while he was hiding in the tall weeds, all covered in mud: "Them dogs ain't all they're cracked up to be!" He said they caught him the next day sleeping in someone's barn. I found other letters showing a softer, more, I dare say, poetic side to him—not the guy I heard about. My mom would probably say he got someone else to write that for him.

But from what I understand, he was *really* bad. On my birth certificate it says he was a "carpenter's apprentice," but he was pretty much a burglar/thief/hustler/whatever. One funny story I remember my mom telling me, she said, the cops came by our apartment one time when I was just a baby. He had all these stolen TVs and shit all over the place, a bag of golf clubs, and all kinds of shit. He used to break into people's apartments and cars. The cops looked in and said, "You got a lot of TVs, huh?" He smiled, and said, "Yeah, *I watch a lotta TV.*" Then one of them glanced at the bag of golf clubs and said, "You play golf too, huh?" He smiled and said, "Yup—*all the time.*" From what I have been told, besides being a total fuck-up, he was pretty funny.

My mom and dad met through their mutual friend Harry Smith at the Chelsea Hotel in New York. From what I understand, my dad didn't make a very good impression on her; he was drunk and stank of alcohol. He was obnoxious and threatened to rape her. How they wound up together after that, I will never know.

They were together on and off for a few years. From everything I have heard, it was pretty nuts; my mom split soon after I was born. I think he was in jail at the time. From what I understand, my dad wasn't the greatest person to be around. He was abusive and violent at times. The fact that he was kind of big—and my mom was kind of small—didn't help. I have heard from everyone who knew him that he was a charming guy when he wasn't all fucked up … but *by all accounts* that wasn't too often.

It's kind of fucked up but I remember, when I was in my early 20s, he sent me some letters. One was actually a cassette of him talking and playing guitar at some halfway house he was staying at. A halfway house for those of you who don't know is where you stay when you first get out of prison, and they are trying to get you used to living in society and the world again. But yeah, it was him playing guitar and basically talking to me and apologizing, and hoping that I could forgive him, and hoping that now that I was all grown up, I didn't want to kick his ass—but that he could understand if I did. It was sad.

The part that hurt the most was when he said that one time when I was a baby, he had left me with one of his junkie friends while he was out copping or robbing or something, and when he came back, they were nodded off in the corner while I was crying in my crib all covered in piss. He said he looked down at me and felt so bad for this little bitty baby all covered in pee, crying all by himself while his dope fiend friend was passed out in the corner. He picked me up, changed my diaper, held me, and rocked me 'til I fell asleep. He said that's the only time he ever felt close to me, and I must admit, it still hurts to know that. After I fell asleep, he said he stomped around the apartment cursing my mom for not being there. Meanwhile, as he put it, "she was only out trying to make some money dancing, 'cause [he] was too much of a sorry-ass motherfucker to take care of us or me."

He had a lot of regret and pain in his voice. He cried a lot on the tape. He would then turn it off, turn it back on and play some more little guitar songs he wrote and bluesy things. It was pretty hard to listen to, and is still hard to talk about. It's hard to accept that your dad chose heroin and alcohol over you. It really does kind of hurt even now. I guess that might be one of the reasons why I turned out the way I did.

From what I understand they'd break up and get back together. She'd go from one coast to another, and he'd track her down, until we finally moved to Europe in 1971. My mom and me did a lot of hitchhiking and stayed with a lot of different people. A lot of crazy shit happened on those trips. At one point, a friend of hers was going to Europe, and asked, "Do you want to come?" And my mom was like, "I'm getting the fuck outta here!" She did, and I went with her—I was probably around three or four. That was that; I never saw my father again. I stayed in Europe pretty much until I was about ten, but I'd come back to the States every year or so.

We settled down in Denmark in 1971. From what I understand, the guy my mom initially went to Denmark with was selling drugs when they first got there—I'm not sure if it was smack or morphine or what. I think there was a little bit of a dope scene going on there in the '70s. Some of it I remember, but not *much*, as I was real young. I do remember a few junkies here and there,

not many, but in all honesty it wasn't nearly as crazy as my life had been up 'til then with my mom and dad together. I lived in a lot of communes over there—one was Christiania, which is a famous hippie commune.

Denmark and Danish culture are very wholesome. It's a great place to grow up, but of course there's an underside there too.

In the '60s—and in my case, the late '60s and '70s—it was cool in certain respects, and wasn't so cool in others. You had all these people fucked up on drugs, and all the "free love"—everybody's fucking everybody. And that's not really the best environment for a kid to grow up in. And as cool as some of the things and a lot of the people were, a lot of them or at least *some of them* were just fucking lost. And yeah, all the kids were wild, what do you expect? I mean, we were just imitating the grown-ups.

So as a result, I was getting laid and doing all kinds of other crazy shit way before I had even reached puberty. You basically had a lot of little kids just going off. You've got all these hippie kids with their hippie parents, seeing all kinds of craziness; adults running around naked, people doing drugs, being insane. That shit rubs off on kids. I mean, Denmark wasn't as fucked up as like the "LES" or San Francisco or anything, but it was still pretty wild. People were still all in that "'60s mode," you know what I'm saying?

In Århus, we lived in a low-income area of town—at least it was then. It was near the docks. Lots of bars, hookers, a few porn shops, tattoo parlors and some local bikers—back then, they were called "rockers." It was pretty tame compared to a lot of the places I've lived and been; nonetheless, it was the "rough" neighborhood there... if you can call it that. We had one friend—he was our friend's cousin—his name was Helje, and he was like the first real thug I knew—*a fucking lunatic*. He was a really crazy biker, he used to come by our apartment and stash his weapons and shit in my room. He'd be like, "Harley, hide these for me. I'll get them back later." All kinds of shit, like motorcycle chains with handles on them, slapjacks, knives, and Nazi helmets. When me and the kids in my neighborhood would get into fights at the playground with the local Pakistani kids who used to come and try to fuck with us, I'd bring all his chains down and we'd chase them out of the playground! Last I heard anything about Helje, he had been convicted of some pretty violent robbery I think, and then broke out of jail and got recaptured.

I remember me and these kids, brothers Martin and Thomas and a few others, we used to climb up on the rooftops and break in to the backs of stores and steal stuff—stupid shit, like cases of bottles that were returnable. We'd return them through the front of the store and get the money. I remember a few times hanging out in cemeteries and shit, vandalizing stuff, stealing fruit from the farmers, and stupid kid shit. We once tried to do a heist at the local mall, but we got caught hiding in the store after closing. It was all stupid harmless shit, but I was definitely well on my way to becoming a juvenile delinquent.

HARLEY'S GRANDMOTHER WANDA, GREAT-GRANDMOTHER HAYS AND UNCLE JACK, PERSONAL COLLECTION

For the most part, my mom and me lived in Denmark, but we did do a lot of traveling. Usually it was my mom and me and my stepfather Karsten. But I remember a few times when just my mom and me were hitchhiking through Europe alone—and a lotta crazy shit happened.

I remember one time, some truck driver who picked us up in Spain tried to attack her and pin her down. I jumped on him and started hitting him and beating on him while she was fighting him off and screaming. I was screaming, *"Get off of my mom!"* He just split. The whole shit was pretty fucked up. Looking back, just being out there at all, me and her ... but I guess that's the kind of shit people did back then.

One time she and I went to England with a friend of ours from Denmark named Morten. He was going and he invited us, so we went. Well, he had a bit of a drinking problem, and pretty much as soon as we got to London he got real drunk and disappeared! We had no idea where the fuck he went or what happened. Weeks later, he turned up in Greece. He left mom and me there, broke and on the streets, with nowhere to go and no money. So here we are on the streets in London with our bags and shit—we'd walk the streets and go to pubs, meeting people, crashing at people's houses. Some crazy shit happened there, too. At one point some crazy English hippie-types who were fucking lunatic drunks took us in. But that didn't last long. After that, we wound up staying at this other hippie chick's apartment we met. I don't remember where we met her; I think we just met her on the street. She had a teenage son who was a Skinhead. I had no idea what a Skinhead was at the time, it was the early '70s. But yeah, somehow we made it back to Denmark.

When I was a kid in Denmark I had a lot of friends at school. I went to this really crazy school called Århus Friskole, "The Free School." A lot of hippies were on the staff. I remember they tried to help promote the kids' artistic skills. It was a "progressive" type of school—a lot of really cool shit was going down there, a lot of music programs and art. There was a school band that I played in; we did Santana covers and things like "Funky Stuff" by Kool & the Gang. When I was probably six or seven I used to jam on the streets with some of the other kids from school on Gå gaden, "the walking street" in Århus, and make money doing that.

That was like my first paying gig. I got really into drums and percussion. I was into all kinds of crazy stuff—funk, reggae, and rock. Some of the first records I bought were Herbie Hancock's *Secrets*, Stevie Wonder's *Songs in the Key of Life*, and Gasolin's *Live Sådan*. I was listenin' to all kinds of shit. I used to draw pictures of Jimi Hendrix and the Who. But one of the longest-lasting musical inspirations was Bob Marley. Even as young as eight years old, I used to pull his records out of my friends' parents' collection. And *The Harder They Come* soundtrack was really big for me. I was very into reggae.

I remember in '77 when Althea & Donna's "Uptown Top Ranking" came out—another big one for me, that and Dillinger's "Cokane in My Brain." I remember there was this disco around the block from where we lived in Århus where they knew my mom and stepdad. They used to let me come up and spin records in the DJ booth sometimes and run the disco lights. I was always rocking that Althea & Donna and Dillinger shit.

HARLEY IN DENMARK, 1978, BY JAN SNEUM

Music was in my blood—I came from a musical family. My grandfather played piano, flute, clarinet, etc., and my grandmother played piano. My dad played guitar, my aunt Denise plays guitar. She was the founding member of the Stimulators, which I'll get to later. I had a lot of music in my family; even the ones who didn't actually play were always going to shows and concerts.

My mom and my aunt saw the Beatles at Shea Stadium, the Stones, the Who, the Doors, Zeppelin—everything that was big or mattered. Denise was at Woodstock. Some of my first concerts are just vague memories. I was one of those little hippie babies in front of the stage, just running around—it might have been Jefferson Airplane or some shit, I don't know. I was at *a lot* of shows. I remember hanging out backstage at some big outdoor gig with Gentle Giant. Our friend, Mick Shepperd from the UK, worked for them and just about every other big English band that came over. I was breaking their balls, telling them they should change their name to Angry Midget! They were all laughing.

I remember my first reggae show—it was Steel Pulse in the '70s. That was awesome. I was always at shows my whole life, really. But my first real gigging experience was while I was living in Denmark. This guy, Jacob Haugaard, was in a rock band called Sofamania back in the '70s. He eventually became a famous comedian over there, and ran for office, and actually got voted into Parliament. He was a good friend of the family. He lived in the parking lot behind our apartment in like a gypsy wagon that he built himself out of wood. He was a nut. So yeah, at his band Sofamania's gig, Jacob and I would get up onstage and jam with other local musicians. I would for the most part play drums, and he'd play guitar and sing. That's how I started developing my "live chops," playing in bars. I have some pretty shitty memories of that shit too, because my mom still had an alcohol problem back then.

I remember coming off the stage one night, and these girls were there that I was hanging out with, and they're like, "You know that lady you came with? She's in the bathroom, she's not feeling too good." I went in the bathroom, and my mom was throwing up all over the place. That kind of shit was kind of a comedown, back to reality, to have to help your mom walk home. I don't want to dog her—she stopped drinking and was sober for the rest of her life. But it's really no wonder why I started being such a fuck-up so early in life. Between her and my dad, it was almost like destined or genetic for me.

So, Jacob, on Christmas Eve one year, he snuck into my bedroom, and set up an adult-sized drum set that he stole for me! He stole it out of a music store that had caught fire or some shit like that. Before I got that set, my "drum kit" at home was like a coffee pot, a phone book and a cardboard box, and I forget what else. I woke up to that shit in front of me for Christmas. That set it off—it was official that was the road I was on.

Another guy, Ed Jones, was my math teacher, and music teacher. I think he was one of the only two black people I knew in Denmark—and of course he was from New York, too. He was a jazz drummer and a standup bass player. Very early on, he recognized and heard "it" in me. We had great jam sessions at school. That's one thing that was great about that school: we had jam sessions all the time. I learned how to play all kinds of percussion instruments: timbales, cowbells, steel drums, and of course, a standard trap kit. He was a big musical inspiration to me; he really brought it out of me in a positive way. Between him and Jacob, those were two of my first big musical mentors.

Another one was a teacher in my school named Leif Falk. He was a music teacher who used to go to other schools and teach their music teachers music theory, and how to teach music to children. He would bring me along with some of the other students from school to teach them, and turn these people on to different styles of music. He was a freak, and we were visiting schools that were a little more conservative, and we'd break down "freakiness" for them. Stuff like funk and reggae and music that they were just not accustomed to teaching in Scandinavian schools back then.

One of my first drunken experiences was around that Free School period. It was at a party at this commune, where most of the teachers from my school lived. I was around eight or nine, and I think it was on New Year's. I got so fuckin' hammered on Jägermeister, I pretty much wreaked havoc on the entire commune! I got drunk with some of the older kids; most of them were like, "Don't give him any," and a couple kids were like, "Yeah, give him some!" So they filled me up a mug and I pounded it like it was juice. Well, I went completely mad once the shit hit me. I knocked over this chick's glass animal collection display case and dresser onto myself, and I threw up all over her room, all over the floor and the bed. The kids tried to put me in bed, but I climbed out the window, and was stumbling through the commune. I remember this kid was running toward me, I fell, and he tripped over my leg and knocked his teeth out. He was on the floor crying and bleeding. They dragged me back to the house, put me back to bed, and I climbed out of the window again.

At that point, I found my way to where the firework display was getting ready to go off. Well, my drunken ass went wandering through the rocket display set-up, and I got them caught around my ankles. I started tripping, I knocked all of them over, and they started shooting into the crowd! This chick's pants caught on fire—she had to strip down to her underwear in the snow. Then, my stepfather showed up, and he was pissed. He wanted to know who got me drunk, and he was ready to fuckin' kill them. All these kids that were the ones were shitting their pants. He scooped me up, threw me on his motorcycle, tied his belt around me, and did his best to hold on to me while we rode home. It was just a mess. There I was, this little longhaired hippie kid all fucked-up drunk on my stepdad's bike driving home from the party.

They tried sending me to another school for a little while, because they thought that my academic skills were being neglected, and only my creative skills were being addressed. They felt the staff was a little bit too loose. Their attitude was "well, if a kid doesn't wanna learn, then how can we force him?" The staff tried to cater to the interests of the kids not just academically but artistically and musically; the problem was my only real interests were music and art. But that doesn't always work in real life.

So they tried putting me in another school that had more discipline. It was so strict at the other school—it was an "old-school" Scandinavian school, really rigid. And here I was, a hippie kid, long hair, freaky clothes, and it sucked for me... the kids started fucking with me. I used to get fucked with at lunchtime in the yard and laughed at in class. That's when it started to really sink in that we weren't like all the other "normal families," we were different. I didn't really get it 'til that point, 'cause most of the people we hung with were like us "hippie freaks" and "counterculture" types. That's when my whole school-cutting shit started, 'cause I would cut school from there, go back to the hippie school, and hang out with my friends out in the yard.

Friskolen was in Stavtrup, way out in the country, so we'd run around in the fuckin' woods, run around in the fields, go nuts—it was great. We used to have "Viking battles" with wooden swords and shields that we made in woodshop, and rock fights. Every day, kids would wind up in the school nurse's office! I missed that place when I left—that was the last of my schooling 'til I moved back to the States.

I lived in Morocco for a short time; we went there twice. Both times, we stayed in the same actual village in Ourika Valley, at the foothills of the Atlas Mountains. Both times we stayed for less than a year, but it was long enough for us to become regular local residents in the little area. The village was literally a dirt road running up to the mountains, and there were four houses along the side of this road, one of which was ours. And then there were maybe 20–30 houses scattered throughout the hills, near that road.

They were stone houses, and the living rooms had no roofs, so you could sit in the open air and have your dinner. Most of the people that lived in the mountains there were called Berbers. We lived between two places called Arbalou and Setti Fatma. There was a guy named Muhammad who lived in Setti Fatma, who was a good friend of ours. He was our guide when we went all the way up to the top of the Atlas Mountains.

I saw caves and awesome carvings in stone that were hundreds of years old. A few miles from where we lived, there was a market-place in Arbalou, where every other week, all the people from all the different villages would come and bring their goods for sale. We were the only people in the village with a vehicle; it was a little orange minivan-truck-type vehicle that we had bought second-hand from the Danish Postal Service. We also had a van that we bought from them that broke down, which is how we got to Morocco the other time. So anyway, we would drive people from the village. There would be "standing room only" in our little mini-van; we'd have all the people from our village crammed in our vehicle, going to the market. And you'd have motherfuckers coming back with goats' heads and shit. The only store in our village was a mile down the dirt road, and it was this little stone shop with all kinds of goods.

I have a lot of memories from that time—memories that most people's imaginations could never grasp. We used to go to Marrakesh. I remember one time there was this huge festival, and these nomadic Bedouins would come down on their horses, and these guys had these crazy fucking rifles that looked like pirate rifles—like old sabers and turbans. I mean it looked like you were stepping back to Aladdin's time! Being there was really culturally mind-altering, to see that type of shit at such a young age.

While I was there with my mother and stepfather I wrote a few short stories that eventually got published, entitled *Stories & Illustrations by Harley*. One had just illustrations and the other one had a little bit of written stuff. One story was loosely written about this guy who lived in our village, but from there I took it to its own place where his mule and a bee were interacting; it was kind of funny. I wrote it when I was seven, I think in '74. Those trips to Morocco were great. I remember my folks smuggled a bunch of hash back to Denmark, a pretty decent-size amount, and Spanish rum or some shit in these extra plastic gasoline tanks my dad had. They had a major fuckin' party when we got back to Denmark—and that shit was nuts.

As I mentioned earlier, my mother was a friend of Allen Ginsberg, and for whatever reason, Ginsberg liked my book and he wrote the introduction. A company in Europe called Charlatan Press published it. They were friends of ours in Europe, who had a printing press. I might have been nine when it came out. But anyway, we used to go back and forth from Europe to the States all the time, just my mom and me.

I remember during one of my visits to New York while staying on 12th Street, Allen was very into Buddhism. He had Buddhist paintings all over his walls. One of my best Allen moments was with him trying to teach me how to meditate. We were sitting in the yoga position where you have your legs crossed, and he was trying to explain how to meditate on nothing. We were sitting there and chanting "Ohm." He would tell me, "Try to clear your mind of all thoughts. If you catch yourself thinking, try to think of yourself in a silent movie—stop yourself from thinking and just clear your mind." It was kind of hard for me to grasp at that point in my life, but it was a very cool Allen moment. Now, I can understand what he meant more. I should mention that Allen was the first person to chant the Hare Krishna mantra in the United States, before Prabhupada ever came here; most people don't know this. He'd met Prabhupada on one of his trips to India.

My aunt was friendly with a lot of pretty heavy people too. I met Bob Dylan through her when I was really young. I actually have a guitar he bought her, a really beautiful Les Paul. She toured with him on the Rolling Thunder Revue Tour. She played and jammed with a lot of really cool people, like Link Wray and others. She told me about a jam session she had with Iggy Pop back in the day at a party playing "I Wanna Be Your Dog." Imagine that shit!

Dylan came to one of my rehearsals, when I was working on preproduction for a solo recording in 1982. There was a big framed picture of him on the wall in the studio lounge along with other music legends, so the guy at the desk just about shit himself when he walked in and asked for me and Denise. It was funny to have Bob Dylan at my practice, me this little Skinhead. We were hanging out and talking, and he picked up my aunt Denise's MXR distortion pedal and asked "What's this?" Denise tells him, "It's a distortion box." He was confused— "a what?" he says.

Denise has always had a really strong personality. And she could really play. I'll never forget her on that black Les Paul rocking out at Max's Kansas City and all the clubs. She and Stimulators' bassist Anne Gustavsson were really something. Those were formative years for me, playing with them, and I learned almost everything I know about being a bandleader from her, both good and bad.

So my mom and me moved back to Denmark, and that's where I discovered punk rock. My mom went to London with a friend in '77. While she was there, she went into a record store and asked, "What are the kids listening to these days? I want to get it for my son." Well, she came home with the Sex Pistols' *Never Mind the Bollocks*, which had just been released, and a few others. She got me the first Damned album, *Damned Damned Damned*, and a few Stiff Records 45s like Wreckless Eric, Nick Lowe, and Ian Dury.

Well... that was that.

The next things I got my hands on were the Clash's first album, the Dead Boys' *Young, Loud, and Snotty*, Alberto y Lost Trios Paranoias' *Snuff Rock*—a fuckin' classic!—and then the Ramones. From there, I just tried to get my hands on anything I could. I was lovin' it. I'm hearing this nihilistic, chaotic insanity. Guys named Sid Vicious and Johnny Rotten, with fuckin' spiky hair and dog chains— it was great. It was awesome because you gotta understand, punk rock was very alien to what was mainstream back then, especially in Scandinavia, where they were into ABBA, and then on the other end of the Danish music spectrum, you had Gasolin', who were the big Danish freak-rock-stoner band of the day.

Until that point, I hung with all these little hippie kids. I had long-ass hair, so we were already little freaks. We'd walk around the streets, and people would give us looks and trip out on us. Our parents and teachers had long hair and beards and shit like that. But then, punk rock came about, and this was more appropriate for me. It wasn't all "peace and love." It was just more *me*. The music was raw, and the imagery and the craziness appealed to me. It was energetic, and a big factor for me was that you didn't have to aspire to be like Jimi Hendrix, you didn't have to be Carlos Santana, Mahavishnu, or whatever. It wasn't about technical skills or technique as much as it was about having fun. And you can do that with four notes. It was definitely a revolution—or a revelation—for me.

The Sex Pistols fucked it all up for me! I went to my first punk gig in Denmark—I saw Lost Kids, the Sods, the Brats, No Knocks, and a few other bands. The Brats actually featured a then-unknown, Rene Krolmark, later known as "Hank Shermann"—one of the founding members of the Danish metal band Mercyful Fate. It was great! The singer from the Sods had half an arm, and he would beat the mic stand with the stump and go off. They were awesome. I actually have a few pictures of me at that gig, stage diving and shit… stage diving *in the '70s*.

I was in my first punk band, Little Big Boss, that same year with these two French guys, who were in their early 20s. We did one tour: We played at a big anarchist festival, and at this one really big New Year's punk bash in Copenhagen, again with the Brats and the Sods, who were two of the biggest punk bands in Copenhagen at the time. And that was that; we fell apart after our first tour. I also went to England in 1978. I was hanging with Rat Scabies and his friends when he had a band, the White Cats. It was after the Damned had broken up for a little while, I think after "Neat Neat Neat." My Aunt Denise played with them for a while—she and this guy Kelvin Blacklock. He was an old friend of Mick Jones—I think he mighta been in one of the first Clash lineups, or London SS.

But yeah, Rat, his roadies, my mom, etc. used to sneak me into their shows in London. Early '78 in London, that was when I really saw some of the sickest shit. I was probably the youngest kid to ever get into or go to shows back then. I was younger than that kid Dee Generate from Eater, remember them? They had a great song called "Thinking of the USA." But yeah man, that was really back in the day.

It was a great experience, but after living in Europe for many years, I guess my mom felt out of her element and missed home. When it came down to it, my mom was a New Yorker, and Europe was not quick enough speed-wise for her. She never learned

Danish. I did. Eventually my mom and stepdad split up, and after bouncing back and forth between New York City and Europe from 1972–78, we returned to the States for good in '79.

Whenever we'd come to the States, I split the visits between my grandparents in Queens and the Lower East Side at 437 East 12th Street. I remember being back in New York City in 1973, 1975, and 1977. 1973 was the first time I went to CBGB. I saw a group called the Werewolves. I also remember the massive garbage strike during the summer of 1975 that practically crippled the city. I remember piles of garbage piled like seven feet tall. The whole fuckin' city *stank*. It was nuts. And of course, I remember the Blackout of '77, as well as the .44 caliber killer, Son of Sam, who at the time was killing people all over the city, and right in Forest Hills, which is right near my grandparents. So of course the three girls—my mom and her sisters—were scared shitless, as was the whole city at the time.

New York was just crazy back then—it seemed like people got pushed in front of trains all the time, almost as if it was the thing to do if you were a crazy psychopath. It was just a whole other place. After that trip to London in '79, we returned to New York City for good.

PART I: NYC — "HOWL" "LOW-LIFE" "HITMEN" AND "HELL" ON EAST 12TH

Chapter Two

HARLEY AND ANDY WARHOL, JOE STRUMMER, BY MARCIA RESNICK

t was 1979. I had been bouncing back and forth between Europe and NYC. But this time I was really back for good. My grandparents lived in Queens, and my Aunt Denise lived on the Lower East Side. She had a band called the Stimulators. She was all into punk, while my other aunt, Jean, lived in Queens with my grandparents. Aunt Jean spoke more Spanish than the other two, and hung out with a lot of the crazy Spanish dudes from her school and neighborhood, jewel thieves and shit. These guys were nuts; they'd do shit like go into stores in the Queens Center Mall on Queens Boulevard, and just walk out with whole racks of clothes and shit! The chicks behind the counter would be like, "What are you doing?" They'd be like, "Shut the fuck up bitch! What the fuck are you gonna do?"—and just walk the fuck out. They knew what time the guards changed shifts.

I remember she used to bring some of those guys to Stimulators shows back when we used to play with the Mad and the Bad Brains. They always had fun—they never started any shit. They were mad cool. They'd always steal bottles of booze from behind the bars. One time, they even stole a 15-foot brass banister from the One Under Club... I don't know what the fuck for. That was back when Hoffman Park on Queens Boulevard was known as "Dust-head Park." I remember back in the day her and all her friends would move all the couches out of the way in the living room, so they could practice all their disco dance moves for the dance contests at the clubs. It was still like *Saturday Night Fever* all the way.

When my mom and me got back, we stayed in Queens with my grandparents. But we soon moved in with Denise on the Lower East Side: East 12th Street. The Lower East Side—"the LES"—was mostly a total fuckin' Puerto Rican ghetto back then. East of First Avenue was where it started—it was kind of like everything east of First Avenue from like Avenue A, B, and C. The further east you got, the iller it was. Above 14th Street you had Stuy Town—that was kind of the border where it started to get a little better. And as you went further down it got heavier. The only way to get a feel of what I'm talking about is to look at some old footage of the LES in the late '70s and early '80s. Half the buildings were burnt down, and there were vacant lots that used to have buildings in them. It was really a run-down place. And that's where we ultimately wound up moving. We lived in a building with Allen Ginsberg, Richard Hell and one of the chicks from the Runaways. It was like the only building on the block with white people in it—mostly freaks, artists, writers, Punk Rockers, and poets. There were also a couple of Spanish families in the building; one lady, Susie, was real nice. Her son was a gang-banger and a real scumbag. Her other son was already in jail for murder, and the one I knew soon wound up in jail for murder as well.

"It was a rough neighborhood but there was a lot of good people there and a lot of good things too, but it was a dangerous place" — Rose Feliu, my Mom

12th Street and Avenue A—my block—was run by one of the local Puerto Rican gangs, the Hitmen. When you walked down my block, or anywhere in my neighborhood, all you heard was salsa and merengue—strictly Spanish music. And all the signs were in Spanish. At night, all the old-school cats from the block would be singing doo-wop and Motown classics, complete with all the harmonies and shit. You'd hear gunshots in the distance and roosters crowing at sunset, 'cause they used to do a lot of cockfighting in the neighborhood, as well as a lot of dogfighting.

Back then, they used to fight English bull terriers in basements all over the neighborhood, and they all had them; they were mean fucking dogs. The Puerto Ricans on my block weren't up on American pit bulls yet, but within a few years, every-fuckin'-body in the neighborhood had a pit bull. There was a legendary dog on my block named One-Eyed Kong. He lost his eye in a fight with his brother who died in that fight. And there was another badass little brindle pit on my block called Amadeus. He was small but he used to destroy all the big dogs. They used to fight him all the time in the basement of the building next to mine. He was real friendly and nice... but put him in a corner facing a dog and it was *on!*

You have no idea how that neighborhood was back then. The Hitmen used to have shootouts with another gang, the Allen Boys, on my block and down near Allen Street. It was all drug wars and fighting over streets where they would sell dope and coke. It was crazy. At least one apartment got robbed in my building every week. I'm not kidding—the cops were scared of the gangs in my neighborhood back then, so no one could really do shit. It was a drag.

I used to dread walking past certain stoops and certain buildings on my block when I was a little kid. I used to try to avoid them, so I wouldn't get fucked with and jumped. There were only a couple of other white kids in my area who were my age. There was one Irish family who lived in the projects down near my way, and they mostly all hung with the Ricans. I didn't really get along with them. One of the Hitmen was a friend of my aunt, this redhead Puerto Rican kid named Angel. So we didn't get fucked with too much in the beginning. But he got shot in the head one summer, and that was the end of that.

There were a few blocks in the neighborhood that had some Polish immigrants from back in the day, so there were a few Polish restaurants here and there. There were also a few Italian pizza parlors scattered through the area and all over the city, from when the mob was doing all the heroin smuggling back in the '70s and '80s. It was known as "The Pizza Connection"—look it up. There was also one old coffee shop down my block, closer to First Avenue, which the old Italian men—obviously gangsters—used to hang out at. They also had a spot at the other end of my block, where they sold cases of cigarettes and shit like that. But pretty much besides that, the whole neighborhood was Spanish.

Below Houston, there were still some Jewish family stores and businesses from back in the day—in the garment district area and by Katz's Deli, and there were a couple bagel shops and shit. But besides that, it was pretty much all Spanish. The neighborhood was full of drugs, dope spots, and gangs. I don't know what it was that made NYC and the LES the way it was. Back then, and historically, it had always been low-income—lots of immigrants, gang crime, drugs and gang culture. But from what I understand, it was pretty chill in the '60s, low-income, but cool. I mean, this was before my time, so I don't know if it was the "drug explosion" of the '60s that started its downward spiral.

NYC in the '60s spawned the Velvet Underground. So instead of peace and love and shit like "When you're in San Francisco be sure to wear flowers in your hair" type shit, here they were doing songs like "Heroin" and "I'm Waiting for the Man," Warhol and all that crazy decadent-arty-drug culture. There was a lot of crazy shit going down in those days.

42

Then, the end of the '60s happened. Everyone woke up from the sex-and-drug party with a bad hangover. Suddenly there was the post-Vietnam heroin era, the financial crises of the mid-'70s, the garbage strike in '75, and then the blackout in '77, and the looting. I mean, one thing after the next. It all kept adding fuel to the fire, and it all kept getting worse.

So when we finally moved to the LES, the city was kind of nuts and run-down. It seemed like every neighborhood and every block had a gang or some kind of organized crime. Uptown and in my neighborhood you had Spanish and Latino gangs like the Hitmen, Savage Skulls, the Nomads; you had gangs all over the city like the Ghetto Brothers, the Royal Javelins, the Supreme Enchanters, the Dirty Ones, and the Sex Boys. On my block the Hitmen used to have shootouts with the Allen Boys, from Allen Street. There were lots of black gangs, white gangs, and biker clubs, like the Hell's Angels over on Third Street, the Aliens, Nomads, and others. On the West Side, you had the Irish Hell's Kitchen mob, called the Westies, with Jimmy Coonan and his crew. Mickey Featherstone was a famous hit man for the Irish mob, and he was my boy Tommy's uncle—a crazy Hell's Kitchen motherfucker.

Tommy and me, we used to smoke a lot of dust together. Once, when he was a little kid, he walked in on Mickey and his dad cutting up a body in their kitchen. His dad was like, *"Go to your room!"* Yeah, they used to chop off their victim's hands before they dumped the bodies in the river, and saved the hands in the fridge so they could use them to put fingerprints on guns and at crime scenes to throw off the cops.

By the '80s, drugs were the big moneymaker for them and most of the gangs. If you don't know, and you have no clue, then picture that a lot of the gangs in my neighborhood back then looked literally like the main gang from the movie *The Warriors*—except the ones in my neighborhood were Puerto Rican, and not pretty-boy Hollywood/fake actors. It was ghetto and it was *real*. They all had cut-off/sleeveless vests, with patches on the back with colors and shit. That was kind of the look. And everybody either had a golf club, like a cane, and/or a 007 knife, which was this huge knife that from the handle to the tip was as big as your fuckin' forearm! Those knives were real cheap, like three bucks; they sold them at every corner store. They sold knives and glue at almost every corner store, so you could get your glue, get high, and get armed all at the same bodega.

There was one glue store on 14th Street and Third Avenue, where the dude would give me free tubes of glue if I ran errands for him. I remember a lot of the old-school Puerto Rican gangs looked like straight bikers back then, but without bikes. MC boots and shit—some rocked *F Troop*-style hats flipped up in the front and shit. This was before the B-boy era, back when cats still used to "up-rock."

I'll tell you, if you were a "white boy" back then, you were definitely prone to getting fucked with in my neighborhood and pretty much any ghetto. And you know, people can give you all the reasons for that—"Well, that's what happens from hundreds of years of whatever the fuck..." But y'know, when you're that white kid getting fucked with, that shit just doesn't matter. It was every day, guaranteed. If on my way from my house to school I accidentally made eye contact with anybody, they were gonna step to me for sure, and be like, "Yo, what the fuck is up? You got a fuckin' problem?" It was a given because I was small, and I was white, with spiky hair and a dog collar around my neck. So, I was pretty much set up for doom from fuckin' Jump Street.

There was a rhyme they used to sing at school whenever a white kid would get in a fight with a black or Spanish kid, it went like this: "A fight, a fight, a nigga and a white. If the white boy wins, we all jump in." Or, the other version would be "A fight, a fight, a Rican and a white. If the white boy wins, we all jump in." And that's basically how it was in my 'hood. I remember one time walking out my front door to go to the liquor store for my mom, and winding up in the middle of a shootout between the Hitmen and the Allen Boys. It wasn't that uncommon—to the point that locals on the block wouldn't even freak out, they'd just step into their doorways and poke their heads out. I specifically remember one time watching a van come down my block, the side door slid open, and a bunch of Allen Boys were in that van with all kinds of guns, and they just opened fire on a stoop that the Hitmen hung out on. Of course, they all dove off the stoop behind cars, cracked out their guns, and started shooting back. I was probably 12, and I was the only one that hit the floor besides the Hitmen. Everybody else knew they weren't the ones getting shot at.

JOHN T. DAVIS, HARLEY, DENISE, AND JERRY WILLIAMS IN FRONT OF 171A, BY PENNY RAND

I remember one time, when we first moved back from Denmark, when these kids from the block were fucking with me. I started muttering to myself in Danish, because that was the language I was used to speaking. First, I got punched, and then they started fucking with me more: "What are you saying? What's that you're speaking?" And then I'd get hit for that; it really didn't matter—no matter what you did, you didn't win. The gang on my block would be hanging out with their golf clubs, listening to the radio, smoking dust, and their little sisters would be following me from the corner all the way to my house—spitting at me, smacking me, pulling my hair, and talking shit to me. Meanwhile their older brothers, who were straight gang bangers, were laughing and waiting for me to do something, so they could just stomp my ass into the ground.

Now, this was before I started fucking people up and before I became a Skinhead—this is when I was still just a little kid. But you do this type of shit to a little kid long enough and you're going to create a really angry, frustrated kid. I really had nowhere to turn. What was I going to do, tell my mother? What the fuck was she going to do? Was I going to tell her English poet boyfriend who's probably never had a fight in his life? What the fuck is he going to do? No, I'm going to lie there at night, in my bed, gritting my teeth, wishing death on every-fuckin'-body.

I went through a lot of shit and it made me violent inside. So when I finally did blow up, I fucking *exploded*. When I was young, I did get a bit racial. But that was a direct reaction to all the negative shit I was going through on a day-to-day basis in my neighborhood and in my school—you either go through it or you get through it, or you don't. I did. I got fucked with so much for being a white boy in a non-white neighborhood, it was nonstop, every day; but I always had close black and Spanish friends ever since I was a little kid, and even during the worst of it. Funny thing is, I never even really knew what racism was until I moved to the Lower East Side. I'd never experienced it. Everyone I grew up around was a hippie—all into peace-and-love shit. And on the punk scene back then, all that racism and discrimination shit wasn't really accepted either—that was just something I never knew, even as a little kid.

A lot of my heroes were black: Muhammad Ali, Pelé, Bob Marley, and Jimi Hendrix. I didn't know what it meant to discriminate against someone's color or race; all that shit was new to me. And all of a sudden, everybody on the Lower East Side was fucking with me for being white. And here I am with all kinds of blood in me: Dominican, Spanish, Polish, Irish, Dutch, and American Indian... It's not like I was this Aryan white boy. But in my 'hood, I was definitely the minority because of my race.

I became very antisocial. I got fucked with a lot. So to me it was always "us against the world." "Us" meant whoever I was down with—punk rockers or whatever. Years later, when Eric J. Casanova and I became best friends, he was straight-up Puerto Rican. They even used to fuck with Eric on my block too, 'cause they didn't think he was Puerto Rican because he hung with us and dressed like us. So he got fucked with a lot too. My neighborhood was mad thugged-out. And this was just the kind of shit I had to deal with.

HARLEY PLAYING WITH THE STIMULATORS AT MAX'S KANSAS CITY, PERSONAL COLLECTION

So yeah, you'd see the gangs on my block practicing "The Spiderman" to get up the fronts of buildings and into apartments. They'd practice on one of the burnt-out buildings down the block. They'd scale the wall on the first floor to the fire escape, and then the window next to the fire escape, and sometimes all the way up to the roof—right up the side of the building, using the bricks and windowsills as footholds and any cracks or crevices to grab onto. They would take turns. They had a storefront down the block, where you'd see all the TVs and other stolen shit—a lot of it from my building! They'd break into the building at least once a week; it was true ghetto old-school LES style.

But even with all the crazy shit—people doing the Spiderman in broad daylight, loud-ass music blasting, people playing congas, getting high—it just was business as usual. Just a normal day in the 'hood: kids playing in the open fire hydrants in the street and a lot of "ghetto charm." In our building, the "white building" on the block, it wasn't uncommon to wake up with somebody on your fire escape, trying to get into your apartment. There wasn't much you could do about it, because maybe they'd leave when you started yelling… or maybe they wouldn't. Maybe they had a gun or maybe there was a bunch of them. And we didn't have a phone a lot of the time.

I remember one night lying there, hearing some chick down the street getting raped, and knowing there was really nothing to do. It was like a helpless feeling. You knew that if the cops got called it wouldn't matter because they probably wouldn't show up, and if they did, it would be too late and they probably wouldn't find her. One night, my mother's then-boyfriend got the tip of his nose almost shot off by a zip gun—he has a scar to this day—just because he was white, looked a little freaky, and was walking down our block. I remember coming home one night with my aunt and Anne Gustavsson, the Stimulators bassist, who got jumped by six dudes with golf clubs and shit, trying to pull her guitar out of her hands. You don't really think about groups of guys jumping two chicks and a kid, but that shit happened. They didn't give a fuck. You've got to figure, a lot of these guys would hang out and huff glue and shit. And when you huff glue and you smoke a lot of dust, you get pretty grim and lean toward violence.

My next-door neighbor, Luc Sante, author of *Low Life*, recalls: "The first time I met you [Harley], it was at a party for the Clash, after their first show in NYC at the Palladium. Happened before I moved into 437 East 12th, I think in maybe September '79. It was in a loft on the top floor of the Provenzano Lanza Funeral Home building on Second Avenue. It was supposed to be for the Clash, but the drummer was the only member of the band I remember seeing there. Met your mom, and remember you stomping around in big boots. And then it was amazing when I moved in and found that I was across the hall from you all on 437. I keep thinking that someday, somebody will write a book about the building. I moved in November '79. Lots of famous people lived there besides the poets; Richard Prince, who lived in #5, between my apartment and yours, is now one of the richest and most famous artists in the world, and music people I know are always impressed that I knew Arthur Russell, who died 15 years ago but, like Tupac Shakur, has put out a lot more records posthumously than he did in life. But nobody who lived there then, besides Allen [Ginsberg], had a dime. Another common feature of the landscape—our block was a favorite for dumping and torching cars that had been stolen for a joyride. There always seemed to be at least one parked outside."

So yeah, when I was young I was kind of a loner in my neighborhood. I was just a freak that got fucked with. They didn't understand the spiky hair, the dog collar, the combat boots. They didn't like me at all. I was always a target. Anybody who was into punk back then knows what I mean: you were a walking target. Depending on the neighborhood, you really took your life into your own hands if you were a punk rocker and you walked the streets alone.

So inevitably I started getting into a lot of trouble in and out of school. I had a lot of pent-up anger and frustration over all of it, and there really wasn't much I could do with it. When I started going to public school, that's where even more trouble began. There were fights every fuckin' day, lots of hassles. People nowadays, especially these "Hardcore kids," don't realize what poverty is. They don't know what really "roughing it" is. We lived in a two-room apartment with a small kitchen. I slept on a chair that opened up into a bed. It was a small room with no door, and it also served as the closet. I had all the coats and stuff hanging over where I slept. Our bathtub was in the kitchen, and it had a piece of wood over it as "the kitchen counter." It was tiny and there was no privacy.

It didn't help that when you took the wooden countertop off to take a bath, there were always tons of roaches in there. In the winter, it was so cold that we all had slept together in our clothes and with every blanket in the house on us 'cause our scumbag landlord wouldn't fix the boiler and or give us any heat. We were broke. We got our clothes from second-hand stores and my mom would find stuff on the street and bring it home, be it clothes or furniture. It was embarrassing as fuck. But that was life.

Over the years, I lived in different apartments in that building. The first apartment my mom and me lived in was Allen Ginsberg's apartment, with my Aunt Denise. Allen also had an apartment next door to his, and soon we moved into that one. Then we moved down to the second floor, with my mother's then-boyfriend and soon to be ex-husband English writer Simon Pettet. Then, I wound up living in another apartment in that building with Donald Murk, the manager of the Stimulators.

I started drinking really young, and then doing drugs. And it didn't help that my mom still had a drinking problem at that point, and was completely oblivious about what was going on in my life. She worked little bullshit minimum-wage jobs and I pretty much raised myself out in the streets. As far as me joining a gang, it wasn't something I was into, and wasn't even so much an option in my hood because I was white. The gang thing never appealed to me so much because I always received the shitty end of bullying.

I was probably like 11 or 12 when a bunch of the dudes on the block just surrounded me and made me huff glue with them—or they were gonna fuck me up. I mean, what do you do when you're a little kid and a bunch of dudes from 14 up to 17 surround you and tell you to? "Put this over your face and keep breathing until you can't breathe no more, or we're going to fuck you up. Don't worry kid, you'll like it." It's like, what are you gonna fuckin' do?

There were lots of burnt-out and abandoned buildings in my neighborhood that sold smack, and there would be lines out the building down the block and around the corner going all the way up to the top floors, where they sold the shit. The dudes running those spots were like Puerto Rican Gestapo—smacking dope fiends up, talking mad shit, making bitches give 'em blowjobs right there. It was nuts. I had friends who used to work as lookouts for some of those spots. When the cops would roll down the block, you'd hear one warning cry after another, "Bajando, bajando!"—*coming down, coming down*—and people would scatter. Then you'd hear, "Tato bien, tato bien!"—*it's all good, it's all good*—when they'd pass and business would go back to normal. I remember seeing garbage trucks pull up and sanitation workers jumping out to cop drugs; I even saw firemen, businessmen in suits. All kinds of crazy shit—cops pulling up to take their payoffs. A lot of the old-school punks were all fucked up on dope, too, so I'd see people I knew there.

Up until that point, as far as New York punk rock shit, I experienced the late '70s between Max's Kansas City and CBGB. There were a lot of drug and dope fiends in the New York scene. The New York Dolls had broken up, but Johnny Thunders was still playing a lot. One of my first memories of Max's was Johnny Thunders stumbling down the steps from the upstairs dressing room, with a syringe still hanging out of his arm, going up to the bouncers, "*Are we up yet?*" As a kid, you don't realize the level of wrongness in that.

There was a punk band called the Blessed—they were in their late teens, which was really young on that circuit. Back then, there really was only one other kid even close to my age, his name was "Excessive." He was like 15 or 16. But he pretty much stopped hanging out around that time. Some other bands around back then were this black punk band, Pure Hell, and also Shrapnel. Before the younger kids started hanging out and coming to Stimulators and Bad Brains gigs, I used to hang with a lot of the old-school punks and some of them throwback junkie-punk types. There weren't that many punk rockers back then. It was just people who knew what was up with the music, the clubs, and *the scene*. This was back before the Luscious Jackson girls, the Beastie Boys, and that whole crew started hanging out. Neneh Cherry and her friends used to hang with us back then, too. I used to chill with a lot of the fuck-ups that were around.

From Howie Pyro: "I lived a couple doors down from [Harley] for a bit in '79 when we were playing together a bunch at Max's. I remember talking [him] out of running away from home on the stoop once. [He] was incredibly well informed and I could always have an honest conversation with him, much like I could have a similar conversation with someone like Johnny Thunders who was eight or ten years my senior.

"There was a time when my band, the Blessed, were the youngest people on the New York punk scene. It was unheard of for people 14, 15 or 16 to be in a "nightclub." Not only unheard of, but illegal. And then Harley came along, way younger than us; we were pissed!

"People may define Harley as simply a "Hardcore guy" because they are slow and closed-minded and can't see beyond their fantasies of what they want him to be, and they'll never ever understand that he was totally well versed in music and culture LONG before any of that happened. Not punk, hardcore, but all kinds of music and culture. He would have to be as he fucking invented so much of it!"

One friend of mine who used to work at Max's as a busboy, John Watson, was only a few years older than me, and he would check on me, see if I needed a soda or some shit. He was always cool. I think he was mostly "buggin' out," like why is this little kid here? But yeah, he was part of that first generation of New York Hardcore kids, before it was even called "NYHC." He used to write graffiti, his tag was "JOHN 13"—you used to see that shit every-fucking-where.

John remembers those mad Max's days:

"I came from the Bronx. I went down one night with some friends, we wound up at Max's—the guys I was with were total mooks. I was maybe 16—I was fucking up real bad in school, so it was like a turning point in my life. The Bronx was real crazy, race riots and shit. We weren't even up on real punk rock at that point—we knew about DEVO and the Talking Heads. So yeah, one night I went down to the Village and we went to Max's Kansas City. We stuck out like sore thumbs. The next day I went back. I was hanging out in the restaurant downstairs, and I had like three bucks on me. I got some soup. It turned out they needed a busboy, and I got hired on the spot. I came back the next night, and that was it.

"I remember telling my dad I got a job at Max's, and he was impressed. He knew what was up with Max's—he was a biker and used to hang out in the Village. I met Harley like a month later—he was like the only little kid in there. The Stimulators and Harley pretty much introduced the Beastie Boys and that whole crew of young kids to that whole scene. That was before Hardcore. People like Robbie CryptCrash, Doug Holland, Jimmy Gestapo, Reagan Youth—all of them. That was like 'the beginning.' The Bad Brains came to town, and that was kind of the beginning of New York Hardcore."

A few years later, like 1981 or '82, me, Watson, Little Chris and a few other "Heads" started "The Church of Herb's Quest." That's where Murphy's Law got the song "Quest for Herb," because we were always on the "quest for herb." That was like our saying, our motto—the eternal quest for the "burning bush."

We used to all get together at John's apartment on Eldridge Street. Everyone had to bring a 1/8 of an ounce of weed to get in the door. Watson, Little Chris, and I would get really cheap shit from our friend Manuel, this crazy like 6'5" Colombian dude. He also sold fat spliffs for like two bucks as well. So we'd have all the dirt weed, but then we had a few friends, who were dealers

and growers, and we'd invite them, and they'd always bring the killer bud. So we'd have *major* smoke-outs. This one grower, Ron, me and John Bloodclot used to call him "Ron the Kali Man," 'cause he always had the good shit. He and his wife were like old-school '60s-'70s freaks that used to go to A7 and CBs in their hearse with tons of weed and blaze us all out. They brought us a nice pot plant, and that was the altar at the church over at Watson's house. We had a green light bulb behind it, and there were just green lights, smoke, and reggae. Man, that shit used to get ridiculous—we were some straight-up Cheech and Chong-ass motherfuckers.

But like I was saying before, in the Max's days, before New York Hardcore, I used to hang with an older fuck-up punk rock crowd. I remember one party back in the day at Joey Ramone's house. He was away on tour, and this chick was watching his apartment for him, so she threw a party there. I was there with all these older punks, and they were all getting fucked up...but at least they were shooting their drugs in the other room so I wouldn't see it. I wasn't even really aware of what was going on at the time... I mean, I was just a kid. There was also the art scene, with bands like the Contortions and Teenage Jesus, Bush Tetras and shit like the Talking Heads and the B-52's. They were all lumped together as "new wave." And people like my friends and me were like, "This is *not* the same shit!"

From the late '70s to the early '80s there were so many clubs, and there was always something going on. Like I said, we had Max's Kansas City, which was one of the first places I started hanging out. It had been there since the '60s, and when I first started going there Tommy Dean ran it, and Peter Crowley booked the shows. Max's and CBs were the beginning for me as far as New York punk.

Max's saw the beginning of Hardcore, but closed in 1981. The bouncers there were legendary—I know James Kontra from Virus ate shit going down those long-ass stairs leading to the front door face-first quite a few times at Stimulators shows. Sid Vicious used to gig there after the Sex Pistols fell apart. All the freaks hung out there. We had CBs, and the Mudd Club over on White Street. My friends and me all fucking hated the Mudd Club. There was also a little spot, TR3, down on West Broadway that did gigs for a while. My mom worked there as a bartender for a minute, and I saw some great shows. The Stimulators played there with the Bad Brains, and I saw D.O.A. play as a three-piece—Joe Shithead, Chuck Biscuits, and Randy Rampage—on their first U.S. tour.

The Rock Lounge was another great place near TR3 and the Mudd Club, down by Canal Street. The Stimulators played there a few times, and I saw Suicide there, as well as the Plasmatics and lots of other bands. It eventually changed its name to the Reggae Lounge. There were other places that had punk and hardcore gigs from time to time, like the Peppermint Lounge up on West 45th Street, which was a famous club back in the early '60s. Like most of the big clubs back then, the Mafia ran it. In 1980, they started doing punk and hardcore gigs there once in a while. That was the first place that I played after I left the Stimulators, with me on bass, Dave Hahn from the Mad on drums, Dave Stein from Even Worse on guitar, and John Berry from the Beastie Boys on vocals. We did the gig under the name Disco Smoothie. I remember meeting Billy Idol there when he was still in Generation X. Black Flag did a great show with Henry Rollins. I even saw the fucking Anti-Nowhere League there.

REIGNER, BY FRANK WHITE

Club 57 at Irving Plaza, a Polish community center at Irving Place and 15th Street, that place was a big deal to play. The Stimulators gigged there with the Cramps in the summer of '79. That was the first time I met Henry Rollins; he bought a Stimulators "Loud Fast Rules" 45 from us at the merch table. He still has it! We also played there with the Circle Jerks and the Necros. We even played there on my birthday: it was billed as "Harley's Birthday Bash," and Joey Ramone's brother's band, the Rattlers, played as well as a bunch of other bands. Joey came up and sang "Happy Birthday" to me.

There were a lot of little places on and off throughout the years, like Trax, One Under, and Botany Rocks. The Stimulators played at most of those places—we played every-fucking-where.

We even did a gig at a deli, called the Chew and Sip Deli. Johnny Stiff booked the gig. It was a deli during the day and they let him do shows there at night. I remember parties in basements on the Lower East Side that would get so crazy—pogo dancing and spilt beer everywhere—that you'd be covered in mud by the time you'd leave the fuckin' place.

Danceteria, which as much as it sucked 'cause there were so many club freaks and shitty music, was great, 'cause it was huge with like four floors of different types of shit going on. That place moved to a few different locations over the years, but the most famous one was on West 21st Street. It was in the club scene in the Madonna movie *Desperately Seeking Susan*. That place was nuts. You had the early days of B-boy shit going on one floor, you had the shitty new wave on one floor, and on the top floor there was the pre-goth shit, like "Bela Lugosi's Dead." I used to run into people I'd known since the Stimulators days there, like Martin Rev from Suicide. In the early '80s, they had a few hardcore shows there, but it didn't last—there were too many fights, and people didn't really know how to deal with the slamdancing.

I remember back when Madonna used to hang there, back when she was just a dirty club skank. She was living at the music building on 38th Street at the time, before she was a rich-and-famous dirty skank. Yeah, that was a long time ago. I was just barely in my teens; the shit was pretty crazy.

I played there with the Stimulators a few times back around 1980. We gigged there once with the L.A. band X, on their first trip to New York. But yeah, that place was a lot of fun, and there was so much shit going on in all these secret hidden little rooms with everybody fucked up out of their minds. We'd leave there so late, the sun would be on its way up, and people would be getting up and on their way to work around us. It was run by Rudolf Pieper and

Jim Fouratt; Jim used to book Hurrah. The Stimulators played Hurrah with the Damned on 1980's *Machine Gun Etiquette* tour.

As far as I was concerned, when Sid Vicious died, that was the death of punk rock—that era was done. Hardcore was the next phase: the rebirth of it. I remember when different people turned up with shit that belonged to Sid and Nancy that had wound up missing from the room at the Chelsea Hotel, after Sid's girlfriend Nancy Spungen's murder.

I actually have the key to room 100, the infamous room. This punk rock couple I knew were the first people to stay in the room after they reopened it and the police took the "Do Not Cross" tape off the door. I stayed with them, and kept the key after we stayed there. I know it was one of the keys that Sid and Nancy used 'cause there were only two of them for each room and they didn't replace that shit back then.

Things were so much sloppier as far as police investigations and collecting evidence. And besides, they were so sure it was Sid who killed her that it was pretty much an open-and-shut case from the get-go. I remember the night my friends and me stayed in the room. We were crawling around on the floor trying to find any bloodstains they might have missed during the cleanup. I found what I thought was one on the rug, so in true punk rock form, I licked it. I also remember lying on the floor under the bathroom sink so I could see what her last view was. A lot of people think there were other people involved in all of that. Sid was such a fuckin' mess at that point, who knows? Dee Dee Ramone said he thought Sid did it, but everybody else I know doesn't agree. A lot of people say they have a good idea who did, but that's another story.

But yeah, NYC was hard back then. Within its lawlessness, there was also a sense of total freedom and anarchy, kind of like the Wild West. You did take your chances back then if you were any kind of freak or punk. But I was lucky to be part of the generation that saw the Ramones, Dead Boys, Blondie, Dolls, Suicide, etc. I was on the scene before this whole Hardcore thing was even a thought. So, I'll tell you the actual evolution of it—or rather, the "de-evolution" of it.

PART 2: HARDCORE DE-EVOLUTION

T he first show I saw at CBGBs was in late 1973. It was a band from Texas called the Werewolves. They were pre-punk/proto-punk. The owner of CBs, Hilly Kristal, used to reminisce about that, and say: "You were just a kid." I remember they weren't going to let me in because I was so young, but my Aunt Denise was with me, and she hung there, so they let me in. From that day, I never paid to get in, ever. But the first *real* punk show I saw in NYC was at CBs—the Dead Boys.

Back then, there were seats bolted into the floor all the way to the front of the stage, Years later, my friends and me would rip them all out. Yeah, the Dead Boys... it was sick! Stiv Bators came crawling out onto the stage, and then he threw a jar full of live "roaches and water bugs" into the crowd of people all seated in the front! Of course, they freaked. It was hysterical. They were mostly normal people who just went to a nightclub to see some live music, and had no fuckin' idea what they were getting themselves into.

As it turned out they weren't roaches, they were crickets Stiv had bought earlier at a pet store, and for months after you could hear crickets at CBs.

Later in the set, Stiv hoisted himself up to the ceiling with a noose around his ankles, and dropped repeatedly on his head into a pile of broken glass, over and over again. Well, needless to say, they had to eventually take him to the hospital to sew him back up before the second set—which they did do. Their guitarist called me "a young Sid" 'cause I told him to go fuck himself.

Years later, I remember Cheetah telling me about walking into A7 one night in like 1980. He was like, "Man, I went in and some band was playing. There was like no one there, it was just like you and two of your friends, beating the shit out of each other on the dance floor! I remember thinking to myself, 'These motherfuckers are crazy. Damn, I'm outta touch, I must be getting old.'" I also remember running into him one time in the '90s, back when I was really out of control, and he was like, "Damn Harley, you're

DEBBIE HARRY AND HARLEY, BY MARCIA RESNICK

fucking crazy, man. I thought we were bad back in the day, you're *fuckin' nuts!"*

That was after a weekend I had at the St. Marks Hotel doing dope, smoking dust, and fucking my dominatrix girlfriend, literally all at the same time. The St. Marks Hotel was a total shithole back then—hookers, drag queens, drugs, one shower on each floor. You could rent the rooms by the hour or by the night. We had just copped, we got our room, I had my dope set up on the table next to the bed ready to be done. I was smoking dust while she was blowing me, then when I was fucking her I did the dope right as I was getting off and totally high on the dust.

Not long after I overdosed. I woke up in the shower with her beating on my chest screaming, "You're not gonna die on me!" Then my crazy ass got all horny and started trying to fuck her again even though I could barely function and had just been at death's door. I eventually passed out. She was fuckin' traumatized. When I got ugly, I got ugly.

And if Cheetah fuckin' Chrome says that you're nuts, you know you're fuckin' bad, 'cause those dudes were crazy! But yeah man, the Dead Boys, those guys were fucking great live. I was lucky to see all that. As far as punk rock history, that shit was real.

But like I said, when Sid died, the way I saw it, it was kind of the end of that original punk rock era. Which is funny, 'cause at the time, the late '70s, major labels had started to sign punk bands like the Clash, Generation X, and Siouxsie and the Banshees, and so many other bands that had been considered "punk" back then.

But then the Sex Pistols fell apart, Nancy got killed and Sid died. It was like "the end of it." All the labels started dropping the punk bands. I think the negative press scared off a lot of labels. Then all the British press like *NME* and *Melody Maker* declared, "punk rock is dead." But for us, it wasn't at all. And that's when Hardcore started to happen in the States and also in the UK; the real like-minded bands over there like Discharge and the Exploited and Crass and so many others kept it going.

You had a few hardcore old-school punk bands that kept it real, like the UK Subs and Cockney Rejects and a few other pre-Oi! bands happening overseas. In the States, it morphed from punk to hardcore punk, and then to be called straight-up Hardcore. The music got faster, the dancing got harder, the whole imagery got more intense.

But it was a *gradual* change. It happened on the West Coast, the East Coast, the Midwest—everywhere—all at once. These bands had their own sound and style, their own identity. Everyone came in as an individual, but we were all part of the same scene. It wasn't so conformist; there was still a pure connection to punk. 1979–1980 was when it started making that change from the original punk rock scene to the newer generation of kids. There was a whole crew of bands who proved that the spirit of punk wouldn't die.

In New York, it had a lot to do with the Stimulators, who were by no means a Hardcore band, but who had a large young fan base. The Mad were another very influential New York punk band, as well as the Bad Brains, whose sound would forever change everything.

A lot those kids who used to come to those shows started the first New York Hardcore bands: bands like th' Influence, Reagan Youth, and the Mob. There were so many great bands in the early '80s. We all kept it going when the old punk heroes were either dead or had sold out. The Pistols were done. The Damned broke up many times and had gotten weird. The Clash were getting "lost in supermarkets" and "rockin' the Casbah," and shit like that. Billy Idol was "Dancing with Himself" at a "White Wedding." The original punk scene was just about gone.

But we were still way into it, playing punk rock music and living that lifestyle. We were part of a new generation of punks. Pogo-ing turned into slamming, moshing, stage diving, and whatnot. It was a natural progression. The music got faster, the dancing got crazier and more violent. My friends and me, meaning the kids on the West Coast and in D.C., were all doing it at the same time. And I don't think at first any of us were aware of it being what'd become known as "Hardcore," 'cause the term hadn't spread nationwide yet. But the first generation of Hardcore kids came out of that late '70s punk scene.

From the late '70s to the mid-'80s in NYC, there were a lot of little places that booked these Hardcore shows, but most of the places didn't last long. Of course, A7 was the real home of NYHC, 'cause it was "ours." Jimmy Gestapo, Doug Holland, and Ray a.k.a. Raybeez worked there. But CBs was basically the only place that lasted from the original punk days through the entirety of Hardcore, 'til the end. That place was literally like my home; I practically grew up in there.

One great show back in the day was UK Subs, a classic punk band from England. Their singer Charlie Harper is a punk legend. He's been a good friend since I was a little kid. One of the best shows I ever saw at CBs was when their guitarist Nicky Garrett climbed up the light rigs, and was hanging upside down from his feet while he was playing leads! It was the illest shit I'd ever seen. They had this mesh army shit that they hung behind them when they played. Yeah, they used to come over almost every year to play, which was awesome.

Another band that used to come down and put on some killer shows at CBs was Negative Approach from Detroit. I remember one show where you couldn't even see the band, there were so many people dog-piled on the stage. The guitarists were pressed up against their amplifiers, and the singer was under this "mountain"—all you could see was his head and a hand holding a mic, and a pile of humans, just diving on each other, getting higher and higher, diving off the stage and back on the stage. Negative Approach was such a great band. There have been so many bands over the last 30 years that have gotten over on just the strength of being poor imitations of them.

To me, CBGBs meant one thing: freedom. Hilly Kristal had one criterion when he opened that club: anybody could play there, as long as they played their own material. He didn't even like most of the bands he had playing in there, but he let them play anyway. To me, that sums it all up. We owe Hilly a lot for that.

CBs was the place that gave bands like the Ramones a place to play, which in turn sparked the punk rock explosion, which in turn sparked the Hardcore explosion, which in turn sparked the punk-revival/Green Day/whatever-the-fucks. CBGBs gave freaks and bands that were not mainstream a place to do their thing. It was the only place you could do that. So if it weren't for CBGBs and Hilly, none of the things that people take for granted today would exist. *Period.* There have been a million shitty dives in every state and every country that contributed to their local scene and kept the underground going. But there is only one CBGBs, and that place will forever go down in history as not just the birthplace of punk rock, but the place that spawned all of the shit that followed.

But yeah, prior to all that, back in the late '70s through early '80s, New York was a pretty fuckin' tough city. The LES was not the weak-ass touristy bullshit you see now. Back then, anything east of First Avenue was "ABC Land," and you didn't fuckin' go down there. To me, I thought anything above 14th Street was Uptown! Where my grandparents lived in Queens was like another state. But like I was saying, it was rough down there. The city was hard back then: the LES stood equal to Spanish Harlem, Brooklyn, or the Bronx. It was all ghetto—gangs, drugs, and crime. There were a lot of things that led to me becoming the violent teenager that I eventually became. And a lot of it was because of my neighborhood.

Besides all that punk rock, regular life sucked. Going to school was a really bad experience for me in many ways. I would cut school a lot, and go up to Forty Deuce/42nd Street, and hit all the arcades—they were all over the place—and go to Kung Fu movies. They were like two or three bucks, and they showed them continuously back-to-back, and all kinds of ill horror films—all the crazy classic shit.

Back then, Forty-Deuce was all live sex shows, pimps, hookers, peep shows, hustlers and drug dealers. It was a crazy place that if you hung out long enough, you were bound to see someone get pickpocketed. I used to hang out and just watch all the madness go down—it was fun.

New York just had a different vibe all together—a certain street vibe and hustle. I also used to go down to Chinatown and go to all the Kung Fu movies there, too. Chinatown had all these movie theaters that were really cool, in these big-ass warehouses, and only Chinese people were there. They didn't serve popcorn; they served noodles and other Chinese food. The subtitles were in different types of Chinese. Four or five different types of subtitles were underneath, and one of them would be in English. It was great. Sometimes, I'd take my lunch money, leave the house, buy a fifth of vodka, drink it, and go find a place to pass out for a few hours until people that I knew would wake up, and I would go hang out with them. On the Westside by NYU, there's this one building with a circular wall, on the corner of

Waverly Place and Mercer, where you can't really see into the center. I used to crawl into it and go to sleep. A lot of times that was how I started off my day.

I remember when I was really young, I would "explore" all the buildings around my neighborhood. There are always steps leading down into the buildings on the LES, leading into the cellars. Usually, if you go down those steps, you can go through the back of the building and out the back door, and there are all kinds of alleys that run through behind most of the buildings. I'm sure most of that shit is shut now, but back then all that shit was unlocked, and I would go explore. I knew how to enter one building through the basement, and come out a half a block away on the other side of the block—all kinds of escape routes. I would walk all the way to the river, and all the way to Chinatown.

A lot of crazy shit happened during those childhood years of cutting school and exploring the city. I found two bodies: I found a dead chick who had O.D.'d in an abandoned building, and another time, I found a dead bum who had already started to bloat and decompose—all full of bugs and shit. One time I walked under one of the bridges downtown toward Chinatown. I got to one of the dumpsters, I remember I looked down and saw all these ripped-up porno magazines and shit with blood all over them, and all over the ground were drops of blood; I looked up, and there was this really freaky dude standing there behind the dumpster looking right at me. I'd have to describe the guy looking like something out of a Rob Zombie movie. I don't know what the fuck was in his hand—he had ripped up pages from the magazine in his fingers and he was holding something bloody. I swear to Christ he looked like he had just killed someone or something. He had blood on his fingers, on his clothes, smeared on his face. He was seriously fucked-up and scary-looking. I just took off running as fast as I fucking could. I didn't look back; I just kept running. I will never forget that fuckin' weirdo. Yeah, I came across a lot of crazy shit roaming those streets back then.

By that time, I'd been skipping school for months at a time, and my school was sending truant officers to my house. This eventually led to me living on my own, in the squats. I was 14 when I really left home for the last time. From that point on, I was more or less living in abandoned buildings with other "squatters." I did that for years.

When I was a kid and I started smoking weed, there was a spot on 14th Street that was down a little staircase, and it looked like a little candy store. It was called Paradise Plum. Except when you went in there, there was just a wall of fiberglass with a little bank teller window cut out of it. You'd stick your money in there, and they'd pop out your nickel bag or dime bag, or back then they had "trey bags," which was a three-dollar bag of weed. They didn't even come in plastic baggies back then—they came in little manila envelopes.

Anyway, there were these spots all over the city, and there was the one that I used to go to when I was in fifth or sixth grade. A friend of mine used to work at one of these places, and he hooked me up with a gig for a minute. It was down on Avenue D. I'd basically sit back there behind the "tell window," and serve people. I only worked there for a day though, before the cops came and busted it. I was there with this black kid they called "Stubby"—he had real short stubby arms and everyone used to fuck with him. I kinda felt bad for him—the dude's hands were basically at his elbows. But as it turned out, he was a real dick, so I was like, "Man, fuck this dude. Fuck you, Stubby."

They handcuffed me to the doorknob and they fucked up Stubby. They were screaming at him, "We told you we'd be back, motherfucker, and we better not catch you here!" They uncuffed me and said, "If we catch you here again, you're gonna get what he got." Needless to say, I didn't work there anymore. My friend who got me the gig did, though, and he had a shaved head too, so they thought he was me when they raided the place again, and beat his ass! The whole time they're screaming, "We told you not to come back!" He's like, "It wasn't me!" They're like, *"Bullshit, motherfucker!"*

Meanwhile, right in the middle of LES was this punk and Hardcore scene spreading out into the neighborhood: all these crazy, freaky-looking white kids. We were in the gangs' neighborhood, and they didn't like it. They even thought we were some kind of gang. They didn't know what the fuck we were. They didn't understand that it was all about music, and that we just had nowhere else to be.

But this was where I lived. At the end of the night I was still there, and the next day I was still there. I still had to deal with all these fuckers—unlike so many of the kids on the scene who hung out, but didn't really live down there. Even most of my friends were "bridge and tunnel." Then as time went on, the scene started moving down further into my neighborhood.

Back in the old days, punks used to hang out by all the stores on St. Marks, but didn't really go much further east. But as time went on, the cops kept chasing punk kids further and further east, 'cause all the store owners and tenants were complaining. So we all just started hanging further and further down in ABC Land and Tompkins Square Park. There, the cops really didn't care what happened. It was "off limits."

We just had to deal with the locals. But it got a little crazier and harder for me, 'cause it wasn't just me anymore. I couldn't just come and go anymore; there were a bunch of us. It was the beginning of the Hardcore scene on the LES. To a lot of the young locals, it was kind of an invasion—and in a way it was, 'cause to those that came after, we had opened the doors to gentrification. But at the time, it was still rough. I mean, like I said, I couldn't just come and go anymore by myself—there was a group of us. We stood out, so we became a bigger target. I was part of a group. I wasn't just a lone freak anymore. And in a way, it kind of started opening the door to more problems.

By then, around 1980, the Bad Brains stayed at 171A. Eventually, Doc and Earl moved into a squat on Avenue A and 10th Street the next year; a few other dreads lived there and in the neighborhood too. Nowadays, no one who lives down there is really "from down there." They're all rich kids and yuppies from somewhere else, fucking thousands of dollars to live in little bitty-ass apartments that went for just a couple hundred dollars back in the day when I grew up. The people who are from there are gone. Those days are over.

The only things left are all the ghosts from the years of craziness down there. They still roam up and down those streets, but most people can't see them—except me. Sometimes it's weird to walk down there, now that it's a high-dollar thriving neighborhood. No one today could ever imagine what the LES of NYC was like back then. You could really never explain it or describe it in a way that would do it justice. It just can't be done. To me, it's a cemetery of ghosts from the past—a time of so much danger and creativity that is now gone for good.

PART I:
THE STIMULATORS — THE CLASH — THE BEASTIE BOYS

Chapter Three

HARLEY AND MICK JONES OF THE CLASH BACKSTAGE AT THE PALLADIUM, NEW YORK CITY, BY PENNIE SMITH

"If I ever had a li'l brother in this 'rock shit,' it's Harley Flanagan. From the very start we would fuck with each other all the time, wrestling at sound check, slappin' each other in the head. Kid could destroy a drum set with the purest form of this 'punk shit.' After I witnessed the Stimulators wreck a stage with the real punk rock—watching Harley literally dancing on his drums—we knew we had to step up our Bad Brains game. Harley is a key component to the early years of my bass style and approach. I was so blown away by his drumming that I sometimes forget his bass playing, which reminded me of Lemmy. Kid is the real deal. As a rock 'n' roll youth he was iconic in my eyes."

— Darryl Jenifer, Bad Brains

My Aunt Denise, founder of the Stimulators, had been in several rock bands in the early and mid-'70s.

Denise did so much for the New York underground music scene. She could outplay most of the guys, and yet still never got the respect she deserved. Even though the Stimulators were a significant band in the evolution of the New York scene, and have made it into one or two history books, I don't feel she or the band got the credit they warranted.

As a kid, I would jam with her on my visits to the States. We did Ted Nugent covers and some originals. I remember Denise and Stimulators bassist Anne Gustavsson played briefly in a band with the noted British drummer Bryson Graham, who played with Spooky Tooth and Alvin Lee, among others. They had a power trio: Bryson sang and played drums. I saw them open for the Dictators at Gildersleeves in the '70s; it was great!

By the time I moved back to the States, Denise had gotten fully into the whole punk rock thing. She had been to London and played in a band called the White Cats with Rat Scabies from the Damned and this guy Kelvin Blacklock who sang with Mick Jones before the Clash in a band called London SS. She saw a lot of classic punk shows in both New York and London.

Anyway, it was 1979, and I was almost 12 years old. My mom and me were living with Denise, and I was going to all the Stimulators gigs and practices. And before I knew it, I was in the band! I replaced Johnny Blitz of the Dead Boys, who had replaced Bob Wire.

What happened was, Blitz just bailed out the day of a show. I knew most of their material from having seen them play and having been at so many of their practices. So I jumped in. They had a gig that night at the Hott Club in Philly, and I learned all the material in the back of the van, listening to a cassette and drumming on a phone book. We played that night with the Autistics, and it was great. No one had ever seen a kid my age in a real band. It was hysterical, and people loved it. Plus, we had two girls in the band, and this crazy little bleach-blond dude on vocals, Patrick Mack, who was all over the stage.

Patrick had never been in a band before. Denise and Anne met him at a club and asked him if he wanted to sing and he said "Yes!" He was a poet, openly gay, and lived down the block from CBs, which was a really bad neighborhood back then. The Bowery was no joke: bums, junkies and scumbags. There was like one or two little stores near St. Marks Place that sold punk rock stuff, records and clothes. There was CBs, there was a halfway house and a homeless shelter and like one bodega, and that was it. It was pretty desolate. One time, Patrick told me he got jumped three times in one day going and coming from his apartment: the first time he was mugged, the second time they tried to mug him but he had no money left from the first mugging, so they beat his ass anyway, and the third time he just got jumped, with no mugging attempt.

Patrick was really into Iggy and Bowie, so he was a crazy frontman. He would dive across tables on his face, knocking people's drinks all over the place, do flips onstage, spazz out, and go nuts. He was a really cool guy. Honestly, I was never a huge fan of his voice, but hey, at the time everybody was doing their own thing.

At one point, we started blowing up a little bit on the club scene. Everybody knew about us. I even got mentioned by name on some stupid sitcom called *Square Pegs*. I made it into the September 1980 issue of *Whole Earth Catalog*—which was like the equivalent back then to Google but in paperback; it was the Who's Who world book of information, so it was kind of crazy I made it in there.

We were getting all these big write-ups. There was an article about me with interviews and full-page pictures in Andy Warhol's *Interview* Magazine. It was funny; I was being hailed as some "wonder-kid drummer" although I was far from that. We weren't a typical so-called "punk band." We didn't really fit into any of the categories, but we were good. Looking back, my drumming needed work, but hey, I was 12. But we were breaking ground, not just musically, but because there weren't many females in heavy bands and there definitely weren't any little kids in bands and hanging out at clubs! Jesse Malin of Heart Attack, and later D Generation, who was around my age, told me, "When I first saw you, that's what inspired me to start a band. I was like, 'If *he* can do it, so can I.'"

The Stimulators were a kind of a transitional thing in the evolution of the New York scene, between punk and hardcore. The band helped create a scene for the young kids that weren't the throwback-junkie-Sid-wannabe punk rockers that were floating around, or the arty Contortions types. All the bands of the time, the whole English movement, and American stuff like Iggy & the Stooges and the Ramones, all influenced us, but we really had our own thing going on. Back then, everyone was doing their own thing. It was all new. There were no rules.

Eugene Robinson from Whipping Boy, now a noted writer, wrote me: "One night, I went to see this band called the Stimulators... with some crazy ten-year-old kid drumming. I was thinking 'novelty act,' I was thinking 'cute factor.' I was thinking some sort of sideshow appeal. But then they started playing, and the kid, who I later discovered was Harley, beat the fuck out of his drums. He was the most committed-looking ten-year-old I had seen. And while I thought the band was a little too 'New York glammy' for my tastes, I knew I'd see him again. And I did."

Everyone on the scene before had been older and from that whole burned-out punk rock era. The young kids started breathing life back into it and made it fun again, instead of just the high and jaded leftovers that the Max's, CBs and Mudd Club scenes had become. This was before bands like Minor Threat came to town or Circle Jerks or Black Flag. This was the pre-Hardcore era, on the tail end of punk—late '79 into early '81. It was a short period of time but a lot was happening.

A lot of bands were coming over to the States at the time besides the Clash. Bands like Siouxsie and the Banshees, the Buzzcocks, the Undertones, 999, and Stiff Little Fingers. It was a transitional time for music and because of it we really played with *everyone*. We played with the B-52's, Suicide, and the Stray Cats at Max's, back when they were called the Hep Cats, and with Madness at their first U.S. show, at a club called Privates. We played with Levi and the Rockats, another popular rockabilly band from the time. We did that great show with the Damned at Hurrah on their *Machine Gun Etiquette* tour. I remember breakin' Dave Vanian's balls backstage at sound check. He was trying to bust on me 'cause I was a kid, and I was like, "Oh shut up, you stupid vampire." Captain Sensible started pissing himself, so I had the whole band rolling. Rat Scabies still remembers that night. They were such a great band.

We played with the first-wave Hardcore bands, like the Bad Brains and Circle Jerks when they did their first New York show, Black Market Babies in D.C., and lots of other New York and D.C. Hardcore bands. Glenn Danzig told me the first time he ever saw me play was at Max's Kansas City with the Stimulators. He was in the back at the bar. He looked up, and he was like, "Is that a fuckin' midget on the drums, or is that a little kid?" He made his way up to the front of the stage, because he had to see for himself.

It was kinda funny, the craziness of my day-to-day life on the LES and in school, and then I had this whole other life as like a child star on the club circuit. It was really weird—it was these two separate lives that somehow collided somewhere in the middle.

A lot of really young kids started coming to our gigs. Maybe because they felt like they had something in common with us besides just the music. My age probably had a bit to do with it, and a lot of them figured if I could do it, they could too. We also had a lot of girls at our shows probably because there were two girls in the band. But I think there were just more girls on the scene back then.

Because I was in the Stimulators, I got into most of the clubs for free, and so did whoever I was with. So my 13-year-old ass would walk up to like Danceteria or the Peppermint Lounge, with all these young kids, and they'd be like, 'Are they with you?' and they'd let us all in.

I knew Adam and the Beastie Boys since before they were the Beastie Boys. Adam Yauch was always at Stimulators gigs when he was young, that's how we met. He was only a couple of years older than me. I don't know how many, but a little older. Him and John

OUTSIDE OF A-7, BY RANDALL UNDERWOOD

Berry, who was the original singer, were best friends; they used to come together.

We became fast friends. I used to crash at their apartments all the time. John lived uptown, I can't remember where exactly. He had a big-ass bedroom. I remember there were windows all around the room with a view to the street, and there was a shelf that went all the way around the room above the windows up near the ceiling and wrapped around all four walls. It had empty beer bottles of every kind you could think of from one end to the other. I used to think that was so cool. You gotta remember I was like 12 or 13. We used to get drunk, listen to music, jump around on the bed, beat each other up, and just freak out. This was before I'd even smoked pot or anything. I think I may have started popping a pill now or then around that time. But yeah, the first time I ate acid was with those guys, too, and that was a crazy night. We went to see A Clockwork Orange with Jill Cunniff and Kate Schellenbach from Luscious Jackson and a bunch of other girls. John, Adam and me were tripping our faces off. After the movie we wandered all over the Lower East and West Sides until the sun came up.

We all used to hang out at this record store on the Lower East Side, Rat Cage Records. This guy Dave Parsons owned it; him and his girlfriend Cathy ran the place, he also sold weed and LSD. Dave eventually started a record label with the same name. He only put out a few records. The Beasties recorded their first single and released it on Rat Cage. I was supposed to put out a solo recording of "Don't Tread On Me" and a few other songs but never did. Rat Cage also put out The Young and The Useless, Adam Horowitz's first band's first and only single, as well as Agnostic Front's first record. Rat Cage was where you could get all the newest punk and hardcore; I even got Venom's first single and most of my Motörhead there.

We were at Jill Cunniff's house when Adam Yauch and John Berry first conceived of the name "Beastie Boys." It wasn't even for a band, because they didn't have a band yet. They were referring to themselves as "the Beastie Boy Crew." It was really just the two of them. But soon after, Kate Schellenbach and Mike Diamond joined. I remember like it was yesterday. We were all sitting around, customizing our combat boots and drawing skulls and shit all over them with white Magic Markers. They came up with some stupid logo, like, "This is our logo for the Beastie Boy Crew!"

I tell you, some of my best memories of being a kid were with them, before the Beastie Boys and before the Cro-Mags. And not for nothing, Yauch was one of the funniest kids I ever knew. Berry and him, we'd be laughing and goofing and giggling for hours; it was just that young dumb energy, getting drunk for the first time, eating acid the first time, and being retards. My best memories of the Beastie Boys will always be the silly ones, like Adam teaching me how to play Dungeons & Dragons. Adam and John were some of my best friends when I was a kid.

Back then we used to have to sneak a lot of our fans into our shows 'cause they were all underage. We'd sneak them inside our road cases, and through back doors and windows! The only reason I could play these shows was because my aunt was the guitarist. So I had a legal guardian. Soon after, we started doing all-ages

ROGER MIRET, VINNIE STIGMA AND HARLEY, BY AMY KEIM

shows, a tradition that continues. That became a regular thing at CBGB, and that's how the "Sunday Matinee" was born.

Adam had a real nice Fender bass. We both used to write songs on it. He was a huge Bad Brains fan; we all were. How could you not be? I think that may have been in some ways one of the biggest influences on all of us.

I remember them getting all into Sugar Hill Gang and all that early rap that pretty much created their style. I remember Adam jumpin' around his room out in Brooklyn doing his best Grand-master Flash impersonation, and it was fuckin' great. I would've never known then if you told me what would have happened to them. I think they would have laughed too. I stayed friends with them through the years. Although we lost touch, I'd occasionally get invites to their gigs and go backstage. They'd always give me a shout-out onstage.

I remember going uptown to Mike D's house one time when I was a kid, when he lived with his parents. It was on Central Park West—huge fuckin' place, big staircase leading up to the second floor. It looked like a museum. It was in a very fancy, expensive building. They had two floors and the elevator opened into their place. I felt very uncomfortable, I knew I was out of place. I never knew anyone with that kind of money. It was definitely not the life I knew. It was definitely not "Hardcore." To be honest, at the time I never understood how rich kids even found their way into Hardcore or punk or even rap for that matter. As far as I was concerned, that was "street music"; that's what gave it its integrity. But a lot more kids on the scene had money than I realized. I just didn't know.

One night at the Rock Lounge, or it might have turned into the Reggae Lounge by then, I was with Adam, Jill, and that whole Beastie Boys/Luscious Jackson crew. I was really fuckin' drunk. I remember I was trying to catch a rap with this chick. She had to be 18 or so, which to me was an older chick. All I remember was mad cleavage, blonde hair—*totally hot*. She said something like, "I really like you." And I remember looking down at her tits, and I'm like, "I really like you too..."—and then I just fuckin' puked right down her front, right down her tits! She was screaming, crying, freaking out. The next thing I know, I'm puking in every fuckin' corner of this club, vomiting in ashtrays. Then I staggered outside and puked in someone's convertible. That shit was a fuckin' mess. It was hysterical.

But yeah, those were good times: young and goofy, early teens— that awkward stage. But those kids all lived a little outside of the madness. They had good families and/or a bit of money. I lived among the chaos that was the LES, and I had been in it a little while longer. But I remember when they all started coming around and I loved those guys a lot.

I later saw them at Madison Square Garden with Run-DMC; that was a crazy show. A bunch of other rappers were doing little walk-ons onstage through the course of the show, Whodini and a bunch of others. It was a mixed crowd: all the white kids came to see the Beastie Boys, and all the black kids came to see Run-DMC. I saw one white kid get knocked the fuck out while walking past a group of black kids; one of them just turned and clocked him and he dropped. It was fucked up, but the whole shit was almost funny.

When I was backstage at one of their big gigs in Cali in the '90s, Green Day was on the bill and the singer was backstage in their dressing room. I was chillin'; well, not really chillin', I was a mess at the time, and I was a little drunk. There were all these Buddhists running around. Billy Joel or whatever his name is from Green Day kept asking me "Don't I know you from somewhere?" I kept blow-in' it off, and he kept asking, and I was like, "I look like a lotta people." I'm laughin', and he's like, "No, seriously, I think I know you from somewhere." I'm all like, "I used to be in a band a long time ago but I doubt you ever heard of us." I just kept laughing it off, but he keeps looking at me the whole time. A few years later I saw a story about them on MTV or VH1 or some shit like that and his wife was wearing a Cro-Mags shirt.

Eventually, a lot of the kids who found their way to our scene would come to define New York Hardcore. Dave Insurgent who founded Reagan Youth came from that scene; so did Robby Crypt-Crash who started Cause for Alarm, and Doug Holland from Kraut. They all started out going to Stimulators gigs at Max's. Of course this was before bands such as Agnostic Front. Vinnie Stigma says he was the first punk rocker in NYC, but I don't remember meeting him until 1980. He told me he had a band called the Eliminators, but I never saw them play; I don't know if they ever did. Doug Holland told me, "I remember meeting Vinnie on the dance floor at a Stimulators gig at TR3. That was late '79. With a mohawk, black eyeliner, and two needles and a tourniquet wrapped around his arms on his leather jacket. Remember, I was 17."

The Mad was another really cool band similar to us but with all kinds of crazy stage antics and props. Blood, gore—all kinds of crazy shit. It was punk rock meets psycho Alice Cooper-style madness, with projectors and screens and all kinds of horror shit! They had these two crazy Japanese guys, Screaming Mad George on vocals, Hisashi Ikeda on bass, this chick Julien Hechtlinger on guitar, and Dave Hahn on drums. Dave wound up managing the Bad Brains for a little while, and was also one of the first Cro-Mags drummers, which I'll get to later. The Mad's singer, Screaming Mad George, went on to do special effects in Hollywood. He was a really amazing artist, painter, and sculptor. That was kind of the beginning of it. We became instant friends with the Bad Brains, who had just come to NYC from D.C., through our close friend and then-roadie/future Stimulators bassist, Nick Marden. They were really the fire that changed everything musically forever. It was a kick in the ass for everyone.

The Stimulators helped the Bad Brains get some of their first New York shows. Darryl Jenifer was like a big brother to me, and he was the only person besides Anne Gustavsson to show me how to play bass. But he's the only person who actually gave me a lesson. I learned everything else from listening to records and watching people live. He taught me about proper usage of the power chord on bass, and how to pick properly. I was already a drummer, so that instinct was already there. The style of songs that I would later write throughout the course of my "Hardcore journey" was very influenced by the Bad Brains.

The Bad Brains spent Christmas at my grandparents' house back in '79. They lived in a one-bedroom apartment, and you don't have that many people to your family gatherings when you live in a one-bedroom apartment! The Bad Brains became like family to me: Earl, Gary, Darryl and H.R. I love those guys and I always will. Every time Darryl would see me, he would jump on me and attack me and wrestle me to the ground, like the way an older brother does. You've got this gigantic black guy and this little white kid, and we were just rolling around in a ball. One time, at 171A, he must have made me surrender 10 or 15 times, and then I finally got him one time. I got him in a choke, and I made him beg and promise he wasn't going to do anything when I let him go. There were all these girls sitting there watching. He's like, "I promise, I promise!" And of course, when I let him go, he started fucking me up twice as good.

One time, the Stimulators played with them at the 9:30 Club in D.C., and we stayed with them at a house in Herndon, VA. It was the early days of their Rastafarianism. There was such a music vibe going on, it was great. You hear a lot of crazy stories about H.R. But as crazy as H.R. can act at times, back in the day he was inspirational beyond belief. He and the Bad Brains had the entire NYHC scene talking like fuckin' Jamaicans for the longest time. Everybody was like, "Fireburn!" "Bloodclot!" It was hysterical. Bands like the Mob were so heavily influenced by them that the bass player started growing dreads and wearing a Rasta hat. A whole contingent of white Rastas started popping up on the Hardcore scene. They took things to such another level. It was impossible not to be inspired by the Bad Brains.

The only way to describe H.R. would be like James Brown-meets-Johnny Rotten-meets-Bob Marley. He was such a dynamic frontman. H.R. could do a standing back flip, and land right at the end of the song, nail it right at the last beat. It was like, "Oh my God! Did he just plan that?" I remember one time at A7, which was such a tiny club, within the first two minutes or so of their show he had already knocked the sheetrock ceiling out and bent the mic stand in half. The amount of explosive energy that would come out of that motherfucker, you couldn't help but be blown away. Especially since we were all young, and here was this guy that was "in shape." He used to be a javelin thrower back in school. He was always athletic. So you had a bunch of scrawny punk rock motherfuckers, and then this dude up there that was an athletic powerhouse, going completely apeshit—and he could sing his ass off, he could hit the notes.

H.R. came out there with purpose, like he was on a mission. Every show I saw of theirs back then was amazing. But then they got to a point where they started playing almost exclusively reggae, and that started pissing people off. People started talking lots of shit, but you know, people go through their phases. And that's the right of the artist.

Because of the way I grew up, I was never starstruck. Even when I met the Clash, I felt like we were on the same page as punk rockers. As much as I respected them and was a huge fan of their music—they were like "punk rock royalty"—I still felt like we were one and the same.

I saw the Clash on their first two trips to the States, both at the Palladium, a beautiful old theater. I actually saw a few bands at the Palladium back then, like the Buzzcocks and Siouxsie and the Banshees. But very few punk bands played the Palladium. I remember when Blizzard of Ozz played there, walking under the awning every day going to school, and going, "Blizzard of Ozz? What the fuck kind of stupid name is that?!" I didn't even know what the fuck it was. I was a punk rocker. That's where I was at.

I remember the excitement of that first Clash gig. It was a really big deal. The Cramps opened, and after they were done, my aunt and my mom went up, and we were hanging out with the Cramps in their dressing room. The Clash's dressing room was upstairs above theirs. As soon as I realized that, I was like, "Fuck this, I'm going upstairs!"

One of my favorite bands of all time was upstairs, and I was a local punk. I felt like it was my duty to represent New York punk and introduce myself, and tell them about the local bands, the good ones—the Stimulators, the Mad and Bad Brains—and not the bullshit that was out there: the wannabe-Sids and the new wave assholes, posers that the press were just catching on to. I wanted to tell them about the real New York.

So I ran up the stairs, walked down the hall, and into their dressing room. I met Paul Simonon first, and then there I was in their room with all of them, meeting Mick Jones and Joe Strummer and Topper Headon and their tour manager. They were all getting a kick out of how young I was, I mean I was only 12 and I had my plaid bondage pants on with zippers all over them and straps and like a plaid shirt. My hair was all spiked and I wore a dog collar, and I was like, "I'm in a band." Mick smiled, and he's like, "What's the name of your band?" I was a little embarrassed 'cause I didn't like the name that much. I think he could tell 'cause when I said "the Stimulators" he smiled and said, "Say it like you mean it—you gotta say it with pride like you're proud of it, that's your name." He was all smiles and shit, laughin' and grinnin'. I think he was stoned. It was cool; they treated me so well right away. They gave me the all-access pass so I could go wherever I wanted and watch the show from the side of the stage.

I hung out with them before the show and then again after the show. There was so much commotion. I think De Niro was backstage and Warhol was there. It was the Who's Who of whoever the fuck I didn't know and honestly didn't care. I was a punk rocker and I was there to see the Clash. Their road manager Johnny Green mentioned me in his book *A Riot of Our Own*—"I made a point of barging into the glitterati, spilling their drinks, as I tried to clear the dressing room. Harley sat grim-faced. He wasn't glitterati, he was gutterati. He looked like he was in the band. He looked like it was his dressing room, his theatre. He didn't respond to pleasantness or threats, so for sheer bottle he was allowed to stay. He was 13. More streetwise than the whole of Glasgow."

There were a lot of cameras going off and at one point I remember someone said, "Hey kid, turn around," and that's when about 20 camera flashes went off—I was standing in between Joe Strummer and Andy Warhol. I didn't even realize Warhol was in the picture or give a fuck who he was. And in the Clash photo book, *The Clash Before and After* by Pennie Smith, there's a picture of me and Mick Jones backstage and Joe Strummer brushing his teeth in the sink.

When it was time for them to go on we all hustled down the stairs and to the stage. I'll tell you this: it was one of the greatest shows I ever saw. They opened with either "Safe European Home" or "I'm So Bored With the USA." I'd listened to those songs so many times and to see them live rippin' them up only a few feet away from me was incredible.

It was such high energy; it was amazing. I was standing there with all their friends and roadies. But as soon as they started playing—they barely got halfway through the first song—I ran out to the edge of the stage, and jumped right into the front row. I was just a little bit left of center stage, kind of between Joe and Paul.

I wanted to see it right from the front, not from the side of the stage. I wanted to be in front of the stage so I could see and hear the whole show. They were running all over the place. It was great. I remember Mick kept running over to where I was and I felt like he was making eye contact with me—yeah, me and everybody there felt that way I'm sure. But seriously, I really felt like he was looking at me, and I really do know what it's like to be onstage and make eye contact with people you know in the crowd.

That photo for the *London Calling* album cover was shot when I was standing in that front row, like four feet away. I remember when the flashbulb went off. I know it was that flashbulb, because it was from that angle, and it was the only flashbulb that went "*pow!*"—right when the bass made the impact, the neck broke off, and the body split in half. Every time I see that picture, I remember it as if it were yesterday.

At the end of the first night, they were like, "Do you need a ride back to your house?" They were offering to drive me home in their tour bus. I'm sure most people would have jumped at the chance. But I was like, "It's cool man, I live a couple blocks away. I'll walk home." You gotta remember this was on 13th Street and like 3rd Avenue and I lived on 12th and A, so I was always on these streets. I had friends who lived on 13th Street. I was on that block all the time. One day it's all normal, the next day the Clash are just a few blocks from my little one-bedroom apartment where me, my mom and her boyfriend lived, and here is the fuckin' Clash and I'm hanging with them.

They did two shows, back to back, two nights. Joe gave me the shirt he had worn the first night for my birthday. I still have it. Ian Dury was there and he gave me a silk scarf and a Blockheads watch.

At sound check on the second night, after I'd been running all over the place with my VIP pass during the day—upstairs, to the store, backstage, on the stage, running errands for the band—I wound up on the stage, standing by the drum riser looking out at the place. All those seats; it was empty except for the few people walking around who worked there and the band crew. It just seemed so huge, and I was like, "Wow, imagine playing a show on a stage this big in front of that many people..." It seemed unimaginable to me. Of course, years later I would play at lots of shows on even bigger stages. But who knew?

By the second time the Clash came to the States, *Sandinista* came out. I felt they had lost their edge, and that they were selling out. I felt they were catering to a broader American market, and that they were losing the rawness and edge they'd had. I was disappointed. I took it personal, not to me, but to punk rock.

By the time they started doing those huge shows with the Who, I had completely lost interest. I had no idea that Joe replaced Mick, and got new guitarists and a new drummer. I was busy living on Avenue A and dealing with the day-to-day craziness of my life and my 'hood. They no longer represented anything that had anything to do with me or my life or what I was going through. But I'll never forget those few encounters with those guys.

By that point I was creating what would be known as New York Hardcore. The original punk rock, those days were gone, that era was done. It was dead and over.

PART 2: IRELAND '80

The Stimulators recorded a 45, "Loud Fast Rules." We recorded a few other tracks that didn't wind up making it. We eventually wound up doing our last show, and recorded it in North Carolina. When we recorded the single, one of the problems I encountered was the drum set was huge, and it was really hard for me to reach the toms. So I wound up standing. Even live, I would stand up when I was playing a lot of the time. I'd be rockin' out almost Keith Moon-ish, and most of my shows ended with me wrecking the drums. Keith Moon and Rat Scabies from the Damned were some of my early drum influences, just real destructive and chaotic.

Eventually, the Stimulators' intention was to tour England. But they wouldn't let us get working papers because I was a minor. Since we weren't able to get into England, we said, "Fuck it. We'll go to Ireland. That will be even more fun anyway."

In 1980, the Stimulators went to Ireland, which is where I became a Skinhead. The New York scene would never be the same! We went over to do a small tour, and play the first-ever Irish punk festival in Belfast called "The International Festival of Punk and New Wave" at Ulster Hall. We stayed with film director John T. Davis and his family. John made a great movie about the Irish punk rock scene called *Shellshock Rock*.

We hung out with lots of bands: the Outcasts, Rudi, and many more. We also hung out with Terri Hooley, the owner of Good Vibrations Records, a record store in Belfast. He also produced some of the local punk bands. I think he might have put out the first single by the Undertones. He was hysterical. He would get drunk as shit, and then pull out his glass eye and shake it at everybody while he was talking to them!

There were a lot of good local bands—this was when the Oi! movement just started in England and Ireland. While I was there, I was in one full-on riot, two bar brawls, one fight in a chip shop, and a melee on the streets between two rival factions of kids, one Catholic and the other Protestant. Bottles crashing, bricks and whatnot, immediately after which we had a shotgun aimed at us from a second-floor window, and some guy screaming "orange bastards!" "Not me, I'm from the Shankill!" Fallsy from the Outcasts yelled back. They exchanged a few more words and we went on our way.

The first real riot I ever saw was at that festival at Ulster Hall, with Aussie punk legends the Saints, us, the Outcasts and a bunch of other Irish punk and Skinhead bands. It was huge. I remember meeting John Peel, the legendary UK radio DJ and record producer at the show. He introduced the event and some of the bands at this two-day event. It was the first time I had ever seen any punk event of its size and as extreme. I had never seen so many mohawks, spikes, and Skinheads in any one place in my life. When you went into the bathroom, you got a fuckin' contact high from all the glue that was getting huffed! I was just walking around, meeting people, mingling, and soaking up the vibe.

The end of the second night is when I was in that first full-on riot. It was a big-ass hall, the capacity was around 1,000 and it was more than half full. It started with just a little fight, and then another one broke out, and then it just spread from little skirmishes here and there to all of a sudden, *everybody*. The bouncers got a huge metal ladder thrown at them from the balcony, and chairs started flying. All the while, we're onstage playing! As we ended the set, our manager Donald was onstage, trying to make sure none of us got hit with the chairs that were flying at the bouncers—who were running past us and hiding off to the side of the stage, while getting pummeled by Skinheads! Then the Royal Ulster Constabulary came rollin' in all the doors at once, shields up, and clubs comin' down hard. They circled the kids, rounded them up and out, all the while getting pelted with shit. It was nuts. Then the kids ran amok in the streets as they dispersed into little groups.

The first Skinheads I met in Ireland were the Black Catholics, in Dublin. I almost got jumped. They were all kids just a little older than me. The rest of the Stimulators and the people we were with were in a pub, so I was hangin' outside and walkin' around, looking in store windows. And these Skins came walking by, a crew of five or six. They were like, "What are you? You've got punk hair, a

mod jacket, a dog collar, and a Sham Army badge." By now, they'd totally surrounded me, with my back against a wall.

I started getting nervous. I was used to this type of shit from back home, but just from Spanish dudes, black dudes, and jocks. I didn't know what the fuck a Skinhead was. I was sure I was about to get a beating, but I wouldn't show them any fear. I said, *"I ain't no fuckin' mod!"* And they were like, "A fuckin' Yank!" And they all started laughing, imitating me and my American accent. They kept saying, "I ain't no fuckin' mod!" And then just left me alone and kept walking. Boy, was I relieved. But that was my first encounter with the Skinheads in Ireland.

The first time I got my head shaved was in Belfast was by a Skinhead they called "Fallsy," who roadied for the Outcasts, and eventually became their drummer when their original drummer Colin Cowan, rest in peace, died in a car accident. He gave me my first pair of braces, or suspenders as we call them, and a Ben Sherman shirt, which was the traditional Skinhead shirt. He also trimmed up my pants and rolled them up. He got me decked out properly like a "boots and braces" Skinhead. The punks and Skinheads all hung out at this place, the Harp Bar. They were all really nuts. That's where I saw my first slamdancing, if you could call it that—it was more just drunken wrestling to music and people throwing and pushing each other around again. Colin Cowan comes to mind.

We got in fights in chip shops, on the streets, and at shows. When I say "we," I mean my newfound friends that I was running with, not the other Stimulators members. One time, I went into a chip shop with this one punk, and these assholes started talking shit and fucking with him. He just laughed it off and they kept talkin' shit. So we went around the corner, and next thing you know, the whole fucking Harp Bar full of Skinheads came running in the chip shop! You should have seen these dudes' faces, they were shittin' themselves. The Skinheads started kickin' their asses, hittin' them with chairs and whatnot. Then they all bailed out, door slammin' behind.

One time, two or three mods accidentally walked into the Harp Bar, and they didn't know it was a Skinhead pub. They walked in, and got their asses beat. It said "Skins Rule" in the corner—in their blood! And the Harp Bar had chicken wire up front by the door, so people couldn't throw Molotov cocktails in the place. People think Ireland is all fuckin' Lucky Charms now that everything is all chilled out, but back in the day, it was no bullshit. Anybody that grew up in Ireland in the '70s and '80s will tell you. That shit was *a warzone*. You used to have to go through checkpoints, get searched, guns in your fuckin' face; riots could happen at any moment.

Ireland was also where I saw people fucking each other up with cue balls and cue sticks for the first time. And of course, years later, I would incorporate the cue ball into my arsenal. I introduced the New York scene to that weapon. I used to carry one in a sock. People started callin' it a "madball," and that became quite popular over the years.

That cue ball in the sock thing, the reason I put it in a sock was because I could use that motherfucker like nunchucks or a mace. The sock gives a little bit, it stretches, and I could do circle-eights with it. If somebody was trying to fight with me and they had their hands up in a boxing stance, I could whip that thing, and it would wrap around their wrists, and crack them in the head. There was an art to using this thing—I was bad with those motherfuckers. But you'd have to double-sock it, because a lot of times you'd whip it at somebody, and the ball would just rip through the sock. It was a great weapon; they are so hard, you can throw a cue ball at the cement as hard as you want, and it won't scratch or crack. So imagine what it will do to a head, face, wrist, hand, or shoulder!

I remember in one Irish town we played in, for some reason there were tons of Skins in the streets. I don't know if a football game had just been played or what, but there were tons of them: an army of bomber jackets and Doc Marten boots. They were terrorizing this little beach town and chanting "Skinhead! Skinhead! Skinhead!" They were picking me up and carrying me around on their shoulders. It was a rush—the feeling of taking over. That's where I saw the Skinhead movement on a large scale. And I was so inspired by the fact that "Damn, these crazy white boys don't take shit from *nobody*." I thought that was awesome. It made me feel like us punk rockers don't have to take anybody's shit. I felt that in numbers, we could take care of our own. And that never entered my mind before. We had always been such a small scene that it felt like it was just "us against the world." But when I was over there, I was like, "Damn, this shit is worldwide!"

They told me, "Teach America about Skinheads!" So I came back to New York with a goal: I was gonna teach everyone. I wanted my own crew within the scene, that didn't have to take no shit from no one in our neighborhood.

After returning from Ireland, I had this whole new outlook on the possibilities of the movement, with these new sounds and new bands happening around me. And at the same time, this whole Hardcore thing started to happen. I wanted to split from the Stimulators—it was time. Music was getting faster and harder, and I was getting into all the D.C. and West Coast shit, and I was heavy into all the Skinhead/Oi! stuff, and the English punk shit like Discharge, GBH, and the Exploited, etc. I was up on everything that was coming out at the time, and the Stimulators were from a different time. They did their thing and they served their purpose well. But now, it was time for something new. It was time for me and my friends.

I started writing songs and learning bass while I was in the Stims. There was so much different stuff going on musically around me, I had started blending it into its own thing in my head. First, I learned how to play Sex Pistols, Dead Boys, and Black Flag songs. Later on, once I got good enough to learn most of the Bad Brains' ROIR cassette, Motörhead's *Ace of Spades*, and eventually Black Sabbath's *Master of Reality*, I knew I was ready to write my own shit, and that learning other people's songs was no longer necessary. I started coming up with all my own riffs and ideas, some of which turned into Cro-Mags songs. The sound of the Cro-Mags was coming together. I was starting to develop my own songwriting style. I was musically on fire. But not just that—I was a little older, and I wasn't taking shit no more.

PART I: THE LOWER EAST SIDE — A,B,C LAND

Chapter Four

Life on the Lower East Side was not easy. Growing up there was rough for me; a lot of gangs, a lot of drugs and crime. I got no respect in school. I got jumped all the time and I had no friends. That's just how it was day in, day out—until one day I finally snapped.

It was one of those days when you just had enough. There was this one big white kid, this bully that no one fucked with, this fuckin' oaf. Not even the hard-rocks in school messed with him, 'cause he was just too big to fight. All he had to do was grab you, and you were fucked. He was a dick, the one who'd smack people for no reason, take people's shit, steal people's homework and make people do his. He'd tell people to move and they would. He was the size of an adult and we were all kids. And like I said, it was just one of those days. I had had enough. And I was having a shitty day as always. I'd already been to the guidance counselor, the school shrink, and I was hating life as usual.

Anyway, the teacher stepped out of the room for a second, and I got nailed in the back of the neck with this big wet spitball. I stood up and spun around with rage in my eyes. He stood up, got right up in my face, and looked down at me. I could smell his fucking breath, and I was getting heated. He was smiling and said, "What are you gonna do?" Everyone was already laughing, and the teacher was still out of the room. Now they're all going, "Fight! Fight! Fight!" I looked to my left, to my right, I looked down at the chair with the table attached to it in front of me. I picked it up and crashed him with it. He went down but I just kept hitting him in a frenzy. Then I threw it at him; then I started kicking him. I really fucked this kid up. I picked up a regular chair and started beating him with that while he was scrambling away. No one had ever seen that kid get fucked up! The whole fucking class was on their feet and on their chairs chanting "Harley! Harley! Harley!" I didn't even know they knew my fucking name until that point.

And then I won all the respect in the world at school. The teacher came back in and goes to send me to detention, and everyone came to my defense. All of a sudden, I was the man. I guess it was like the victim-turned-aggressor thing. Once I realized I could fight, and I was good at it, I finally found a way to get respect. Like I've said, everyone in my neighborhood was in a gang and everyone was a fucking hard-ass. You were just supposed to be tough. And after that incident in school, I was done getting fucked with.

So, I started fighting a lot. I was at the top of the food chain. And all the Puerto Rican kids at school left me alone, and all of a sudden, all the black kids in my class loved me. It's funny, I was the only white kid they let sit at their table. They had their own section in the cafeteria where they'd meet up at lunch from the different classes. The first time this one kid, Marc, called me over to them. Him, Melvin Hicks, and Timothy, man, they were the three biggest kids in my class. And these two other guys were sitting with them. It was that same day I fucked that dude up. I was walking through the lunchroom to get my tray and food, and they were like "Yo, Harley!" I was still all heated from the shit that happened in class. I was thinking, "What the fuck is this now?" He was like, "Yo, relax you crazy motherfucker! Come grab a seat when you're done getting your food." I came back over, not knowing what to expect, and sat down. And they were like, "Yo man, this is one *crazy motherfucker*." They started telling the other guys what happened in class, and all of a sudden, I was in. They were the funniest motherfuckers in school, they were bigger than everyone else, and pretty much the hardest motherfuckers around. A few of them had been left back and had mustaches and facial hair.

Yo, even the black chicks in my school were feared! They'd get into fights that'd turn into mini-riots. They were worse than the dudes. But anyway, these motherfuckers used to sic me on people. "Yo Harley, go fuck with that dude," and they'd all stand, watch, and giggle. They were the real hard-rocks of the school. I mean, the Puerto Ricans ran shit and outnumbered everyone, but the black kids didn't get fucked with at all. And now, I was down with them, after I had proven that I was "the crazy white boy," as they called me. They also called me "Boulder Head"—after I head-butted a kid in the face and broke his nose—and "Popeye," 'cause I had a tattoo. I was the only kid in school with a tattoo—you gotta figure this was like fifth grade.

The funny shit was that I was already in a band, and no one else my age or in my school was. Even the "rock heads" who wore Rush and AC/DC shirts were like, "You're in a band?" It was inconceivable to them, like I might as well have said, "I'm from fucking

Mars." But then when these punk rock chicks, Stimulators fans like these girls Artificial and Nowhere, these Russian punk rock chicks May and July, Gabby Glaser and Jill Cunniff from Luscious Jackson, and all these other friends of mine who were a lot older than the kids at my school would show up to pick me up from school, all the kids would be like "Oh shit! Who are they?" It's funny, 'cause I went to school with Huey Morgan of the Fun Lovin' Criminals, obviously way before he was doing music. But yeah, I bumped into him and Everlast on Houston Street in like 2000, and he started telling Everlast—who I'd gigged with a few years back when he was with House of Pain—"Yo, I remember when we were in junior high and Harley was talking about being in a band and shit. It seemed so insane, we were like, 'What do you mean, you're in a band?' We were little kids and he's talking about doing gigs at Max's Kansas City and touring."

Up until that point, I had been the only punk rocker in my school. And then in 1980, I was the only Skinhead. Anyway, it didn't matter. I was done with school, I never went back: I quit school for good in the seventh grade. At that point, I had been left back a few times already. I only went back once in a while during lunch to hang with my friends, drop acid, and fuck with the high school students from Stuyvesant High. And of course, to rob kids from time to time like I had grown up seeing all the kids on my block and in school do. That was just normal pecking order. That's how shit was.

In those days, there was a serious rift between rock and disco. It was the white boys that listened to rock, and everyone else listened to disco. Those *Saturday Night Fever* days still lingered. Rap didn't really exist yet. My point being, the lines were very drawn. And then you had this little fuckin' pocket called punk rock. We were like the shit-stain on the wall. Everybody fucked with us.

Back then, if you were into rock, you were part of the Rush and AC/DC T-shirt-wearing crew. I remember some of the kids were just starting to get into Van Halen. But I could never get past the striped spandex and big hair. I grew up on punk rock—Johnny Rotten and Sid Vicious, motherfuckers who looked chaotic. Dudes with chains around their necks, spiky hair, and scowls on their faces. I was into the Bad Brains and Minor Threat: fuck all these guys in fuckin' spandex, their inflatable dragons, and heavy metal puppets.

Even as a kid I couldn't get into it. I'm probably one of the few people that never liked KISS. The whole idea of being "larger than life" was phony and pretentious to me. I was dealing with real shit—like my mother buying my clothes at the Salvation Army and finding furniture off the street that didn't look so bad. That was my reality—my mother, her boyfriend, and me, all sleeping in the same bed with our clothes on, and under every blanket in the house just to keep warm, 'cause we had no fuckin' heat in the middle of winter. When you live the way I lived, you'd rather listen to shit like the Dead Boys, Sex Pistols, and the Clash. Van Halen has no interest to you when you have Puerto Ricans shooting at you 'cause you're funny-looking and it's dark out, and they don't give a fuck.

At that point, I had pretty much become a full-time truant. I used to go on trips to school to hang out with some of my friends at lunch. On one of those trips, I met Chris Wandres or "Little Chris." This little-ass kid a couple years younger than me was singing a Clash song. I was like, "You like the Clash?!" "Yeah man, they're fuckin' great!" I was like, "You gotta come hang out." And that was it. You gotta understand, back then, if you met someone who was into punk rock or hardcore, there was an instant connection and bond.

Soon, Chris' head was shaved and we were inseparable—me, him, and Eric Casanova. The three of us were little maniacs, huffin' glue, trippin', gettin' wasted, and gettin' in trouble, shoplifting like crazy. We were fucked up, but we had a great time. We used to kick out subway windows, vandalize—stupid kid shit.

We'd hang out with other kids from my junior high school who'd cut class, including "Puerto Rican George Olson"—the only Puerto Rican I've ever met with a Swedish last name. I met him when we got into a fistfight in the fifth grade when I was having beef with the Puerto Ricans. Now we were best friends. Also this Filipino kid, Florencio, who was a master thief. He was tiny and had a filthy fuckin' mouth on him. And Aram Abraham, this kid from England, who was a fan of the British soccer team West Ham. He loved me 'cause I knew about the Hammers and Skinheads.

We were little delinquents. If one of us got caught shoplifting, we'd all attack the storeowner. We'd all start knocking over stands

LOWER EAST SIDE, OUTSIDE OF C-SQUAT, ALPHABET CITY, BY BROOKE SMITH

of food and chips, and throwing shit in the air and at them. We'd all beat on the storeowner until he'd let whoever he had caught go, and then we'd run like fuck. We'd go down to Chinatown or up to Central Park—always in trouble. We were like the Bowery Boys, a bunch of little maniacs shoplifting, writing graffiti. And these kids knew nothing about punk rock, except for Little Chris.

Up until I came back from Ireland, there were no Skinheads in New York. By this point, there was maybe between five to eight Skins in New York, and two of them were from England. At first, it was just whatever of my friends I could get to shave their heads. That's how it began. I always remembered what the Belfast Skins told me: "Teach America about Skinheads." The first few friends of mine to shave their heads included Adam Yauch and a few others who weren't really Skinheads in the stereotypical "thug" way. They just liked the look and the music. I mean, we were all into the early Oi! style music, Cockney Rejects and bands like that, even though it wasn't really called Oi! yet. The Two Tone thing was happening, with all the ska bands jumping off like the Specials, Selecter, Madness, and they were all popular with Skinheads early on. But there still wasn't a Skinhead scene in New York, just a few friends of mine who were up on it. But within a couple years, that would all change.

In like 1980, there was a loft party in the West 20s, where I was tripping my face off. Some of the Beastie Boys cats were there, and it turns out Richard Birkenhead from Underdog was there, too. Anyway, there were some pseudo-rockabilly cats there playing all sorts of Stray Cats shit, and these dudes were dancing, snappin' their fingers, shakin' their legs, and tryin' to look like Elvis or some shit. You've got to remember, I'm tripping my balls off, so they looked even more ridiculous to me. It's totally comedic and I start breakin' balls, I couldn't help it. My mouth was flyin'. I got my hands on a pre-mixed big-ass bottle of Kamikazes—like a fuckin' gallon bottle—and a friend and I are suckin' this thing down. So, I'm fucked up beyond recognition. Eventually, one of the dudes, an Italian kid from Little Italy, Anthony, gets the balls to say some shit to me. He was kind of a big guy, and older than me. So I got up, and my gravity knife comes out, blade to his face. Needless to say, he backed the fuck off. So I went back to suckin' down this bottle of Kamikaze.

The rockabilly dudes get on the horn and called the Thompson Street Boys, from Little Italy. At least that's what I heard. I needed to get some air, so I left the party—in the elevator and trippin' my dick off. The elevator gets to the first floor, and all of a sudden, all these dudes come flying past me—with baseball bats! They get in the elevator and start going up. I was so high, I didn't even make the connection that they were coming to fuck *me* up! So I get outside, just hangin' out, leanin' on a car with my boy Chris Jones, bullshittin' with this other guy, T, who stole a big bottle of vodka from the party. All of a sudden all those guys start piling back out from the building, and in the front is the guy who I held the knife to—holding a baseball bat. He goes, *"There he is!"* I turn just in time to see a bat and all kinds of "trails" because I was still tripping so fuckin' hard, as the bat came cracking down on me.

I got fucked up pretty bad. I got my knee broken and got cracked across the face. I took an ass-beating. My friend T knew some of the guys and tried to stop them, and got blasted with a baseball bat a few times. For some reason I remember vividly T holding that bottle of vodka and extending his other hand, going, "No!"—and then just getting cracked across his other arm, the bottle shattering, and him doubling over; and then, another crack across his shoulder. It was a bad scene. The Beasties dudes ran like fuck right away. Me, I've never run and left a friend to take a beating; I've taken beatings for them. But I'm not talking shit; they weren't fighters, and never were. They were scared and ran. I've had motherfuckers who claim to be hard-asses do the same shit, so like I said, it's no big deal.

One of them guineas actually pulled out a fuckin' whip, and was about to start whipping me with it! And this chick, Tanya, jumped on him, and then a passing cab driver yelled out the window, "I just called the cops on my radio, they're on the way," so the guys jumped in their cars and bailed.

At that point, I was fuckin' destroyed, blood everywhere. Me and my friend Chris hobbled off to his house. He had run away from home, so his father was not too excited about him showing up, especially since Chris had stolen money and the TV the last time he was there. But I was like, "Dude, we've got to go there, I'm a fuckin' mess. We'll deal with his bullshit tomorrow." So he let us in, looked at me, and says, "What the fuck happened to you guys?!" "Dad, I'm sorry, I'll explain it tomorrow." The next morning I woke up, and we had spilt a 40 oz. of brew in the bed—so I woke up in this beer-soaked bed covered in blood, my leg was swollen and all sideways, and my head was swollen. And Chris' father was standing at the foot of the bed, screaming at me. "Where the fuck is he?! Where did that motherfucker go?!"

It turns out Chris woke up first, stole his dad's wallet, and his dad had company over, and he stole their wallets too, and split! This is what the fuck I woke up to. I'd never met this kid's father before in my life. It was such a bad scene. And his father had let us sleep in *his* bed. I tried to get out of the bed. I stepped on my leg, and my leg just gave out. My knee was broken. So he had to scrape together what little bit of change he had around the house to hook me up with the five or six bucks to get me in a cab to my mom's.

It didn't get too much better for me. I got home, hobbled up the stairs to the second floor, and let myself in. I was around the corner in the apartment, and called my mom. I'm like, "Mom, it looks a lot worse than it is." I just remember her looking at me and going, "You motherfucker! What the fuck did you do?!" Just when you need a little bit of love! Of course, I went to the hospital and had all the emergency room drama, where I was there all fuckin' night, and I've got cops up the ass trying to get me to tell them who did it. And I didn't want to say shit, because I knew who he was and I was going to get him back on my own time. So fuck it.

Needless to say, that was a pretty fuckin' rough night for a young kid. I was still in junior high at the time. The kid that it had all started with went to high school a few blocks from my junior high. I wanted to fuck his ass up. I remember like a week later, I approached him. I was still walking with a cane. He was leanin' against a car with two friends lookin' kind of nervous. I walked up, smiled and handed him an ace of spades, and told him, "Every dog has his day," and then I limped away with my cane and left him standing there holding the card looking scared as shit. But time went by, he graduated, I dropped out, and I never saw him again until like 20–25 years later, and he was like, "Are we cool?" I honestly didn't recognize him! Then when I did finally realize who it was, I was like, "Ah fuck it, who cares? That shit was a million years ago. We were kids, stupid shit happens." But it was a fucked-up night for a 14-year-old.

A few weeks after that shit there was a gig at Irving Plaza, with Kraut opening up for the Misfits. I was still walking with a cane at the time, so me, Jimmy Gestapo, Paul Dordal and a few others spent most of the show onstage sitting on the drum riser. I remember every time someone we didn't know would try to stage dive, I'd hook them around the ankle with the handle of my cane, Jimmy would shove them real hard in the back, and they'd bust their ass! It was hysterical. There was only maybe a dozen of us Skinhead types there, but we were totally running the show.

I remember at one point a fight broke out in the crowd, and all of us jumped off the stage. I remember hobbling to the edge of the stage with my busted knee, hopping into the crowd, and beating the shit out of some jocks with my cane, while Jimmy and my boys were laying an ass-beating on them. By the time the Misfits

HARLEY, BY JEANIE PAWLOWSKI

came on, Paul and me were up onstage on Jerry Only's mic, calling out the entire audience. Paul whipped a beer mug into the crowd, we were like "Fuck you, we'll fight all of you!" We were all drunk onstage while the Misfits were playing, singing backup and talkin' shit to the crowd. It was a great show.

One of the first to shave his head after me was Eric Casanova. I first met Eric through Jimmy Gestapo. Jimmy was like a brother to me, one of the people I have known the longest, and I can't for the life of me remember how or when we met; it seems like I've just known him forever. Maybe I met him at Max's. I think Doug Holland brought him there when he was still in his first band, Apprehended.

I met Eric through Jimmy on St. Marks Place. Jimmy and him were walking east, and I was walking west. I was already good friends with Jimmy, and Eric had spiky hair, a dog collar, and brown construction boots with nails in them. We became best friends right away. I was like, "Yo, we gotta do something about that hair." We went by my house, out came the clippers, and the next time I saw him, he had on combat boots. That was pretty much how we all looked in the beginning—shaved heads and combat boots. Eric's mom Eva flipped on him when he shaved his head.

You've never seen or heard the rage of a Puerto Rican mother like that in your life. She went fuckin' ghetto-rage mad. The shit she was yelling at him: "You motherfucker! You think you're gonna shave your fuckin' head?!" And then she launched into some shit that I still can't believe she screamed at us and him—it still makes my jaw drop, it was so ill. Launching back into "You motherfuckin' son of a bitch!" Then all kinds of shit in Spanish, then back to English, and then Spanish. Yo, this woman was hard. She was an old-school New Yorker. She didn't take any shit, but she had a huge heart. She treated me like a second son.

I remember one time she pulled a fuckin' knife on our friend Bubby 'cause he showed up at her door with a mohawk and black nail polish, looking for Eric. She didn't give a fuck about the mohawk, but she flipped on him for the black nail polish! Bubby was just coming to see if he could get the drums back he'd loaned Eric. She was like, "Fuck that! I don't know this motherfucker, and he ain't taking my son's shit!" She was great.

Eric lived with his mom, stepdad, and two sisters out by Ocean Avenue. His mom told me that Eric's granddad used to collect bets for the guys who worked the numbers in their neighborhood back in the day, and for that he got killed. Some fucking scumbags cut his throat over like $30. She found him bleeding to death; this was when she was a little kid. She went through all the gang and drug shit back in the day, she was old-school, when New Yorkers had character. Now that New York ghetto charm is gone. It's been yuppied the fuck out. There are so few real New Yorkers left or even people who remember what it was like.

So Eric and me became best friends. I finally had a kid my own age to hang out with. Prior to him, everybody was older than me. We'd meet at Chock Full O' Nuts across the street from Max's Kansas City, which by then had already closed down. But it still had an arcade underneath it, where the old soundman worked. And he used to hook me up and give us free games. We'd hang out with his sons and fuck around all day.

Eric, like all young people, would go through a bit of an identity crisis from time to time. He'd be hanging down on the LES with us, dressing like a Skinhead, then he'd go back to his neighborhood with all the Ricans and they'd be like, "Why are you dressing like that and hanging out with those white boys?" And the next time I'd see him, he'd be rocking his blue sheepskin, gazelles, and fat laces and shell toes. I guess like so many kids at that age, he really didn't know how he fit in—especially back then, 'cause the lines were pretty drawn. He was Puerto Rican, hangin' with all these crazy punk rockers, and all his old friends from the neighborhood were B-boys. Sometimes he'd get jumped with me, mistaken for being a white boy by the Spanish kids. That shit used to fuck with him, 'cause it was like, where did he belong?

I know people who went through that shit even years later. Jorge from Merauder would get into shit 'cause he looked more white than Spanish. SOB got into shit, too. But the irony was that the New York Hardcore scene had always been more diverse than most Hardcore scenes. There had always been some Spanish kids, black kids, and Asian kids. I mean yeah, it was mostly white, but our scene was more open and diverse than some people might think. A lot of the early NYHC Skinheads were Spanish. Roger from

Agnostic Front is Cuban, Diego was Puerto Rican, as was Jose from the Mob, and so were a lot of the Skinheads that came around later on. Even back in the Max's days, you had the Bad Brains, Pure Hell, Th' Influence—who were one of the first real NYHC bands—and they were all black.

When Eric first started singing with the Cro-Mags, it was so great, 'cause he was like "the B-boy-Hardcore-kid." He'd come out screaming the words, then bust into some ill B-boy shit, break dancing and working the floor—do like a head spin into a pose or some shit—and then spin back into Hardcore. It was off the hook! He would have become such a great frontman if he could have stayed with us. He had too much energy, he never stopped moving. He'd be sitting on a bench doin' B-boy shit—poppin' and lockin' even while he was sitting down. He was so much fun to hang out with.

The first people I can think of mixing those influences were Eric Casanova and Mackie Jayson. I'm just trying to give credit were it's due. When I came back from Ireland with my head shaved, no one "got it." Even Vinnie Stigma still had a mohawk back then. You said Skinhead over here, and people thought of the Fordham Baldies from the '50s, if that.

Back then, I put out a fanzine. I only did a few issues. I did interviews with bands like the Circle Jerks and Madness. I also did show reviews of whoever was in town: Siouxsie, 999, Buzzcocks, Undertones or Stiff Little Fingers. When I became a Skinhead, I wrote an article compiled from a bunch of newspapers I got in Ireland and from England about Skinhead history—violence, hooligans, and music, to teach my friends and the scene. I was on a mission.

Every day, I kept recruiting friends, bringing them to my house, and shaving their heads. As the Hardcore scene grew and grew, it really started to take on a life of its own. Like I said, at first it was just me, and then like maybe five of my friends—me, Eric, Jimmy, Little Chris, Paul Dordal, Vinnie Stigma and the Agnostic Front crew, and Diego, a fuckin' crazy redhead Puerto Rican Skinhead who roadied for the Mob. We started shaving up whole bunches of our friends' heads. We would have "head-shaving parties," music blasting, everybody slappin' each other in the head, and giving each other "red necks." Before you knew it, Skins were the biggest

HARLEY IN FIGHT OUTSIDE CBGB, BY DREW CAROLAN

part of the New York scene. And we were getting known all over the States and the world—thanks largely to *Maximum Rocknroll*, and the lies and rumors they spread about us.

In those days, there was no Internet, so *Maximum Rocknroll* kind of became the global link for Hardcore kids and punks. And people would anonymously send in letters and "scene reports," talking mad shit about people on the scene—especially about me and my friends from the NYHC scene. People who didn't know any better took it as the truth. In the beginning, we laughed it off. But over the years it got annoying.

I remember when Raybeez first got his head shaved. The first few times I saw him, he was so quiet. He was probably high on dust. Raybeez had duct tape wrapped all up and down his pant legs, and a chain around his waist. He had this crazy bushy mohawk, a big-ass nose, and big bushy eyebrows—he looked like some kind of crazy big bird!

When Agnostic Front got together, Vinnie and Raybeez got into the Skinhead thing.

They went through a few singers in a short time before Roger got the gig. Raybeez was on drums, and they got this kid Adam Mucci on bass, later in Murphy's Law. At one point, Vinnie offered to buy anyone an Agnostic Front "Skinhead Army" tattoo. And would you believe people jumped on it? Hey, a free tattoo was a free tattoo, especially back then. All of a sudden there was a whole ton of Skinheads on the scene. You had the so-called Agnostic Front Skinhead Army, the Warzone Crew, the Lower East Side Crew or Lower East Side Skins. But the truth is, most of these knuckleheads weren't even really from the city. We all just wound up there together on the Hardcore scene.

My mom wasn't happy about the whole Skinhead thing, especially in the beginning. When I first got back from Ireland, she kind of freaked. And my mom's husband Simon Pettet, the poet/writer from England, didn't dig it at all. Him and me had always gotten along well, but when I came back from Ireland as a Skinhead, it freaked him out. They had no idea how much trouble I was getting into at school or in the neighborhood. I was drinking a lot, huffin' glue, takin' pills and lots of LSD, and whatever else.

PART 2: THE BEGINNING OF "NEW YORK HARDCORE"

It was around that time that the D.C. guys started to enter the picture. The Stimulators played D.C. with the Bad Brains several times, as well as with Black Market Babies and others. I had met Ian MacKaye, Henry Rollins, and the whole gang there, bands like Void, Scream and Iron Cross. For the record, not everyone in D.C. was straight edge back then. Every time I went to D.C., I had a great time, especially when we played the legendary 9:30 Club.

A few of those D.C. guys had been to Cali, and adopted the "Huntington Beach thing"—the whole look and style of stage diving, slamming, skanking, or whatever you wanna call it. In New York, people kinda stage dived, but it was more like get onstage, sing along as long as you can, and try to jump off before the bouncers get you. The D.C. guys were more launching themselves off the stage, with boots, spurs, chains with locks, and fists flying. The whole thing looked violent as hell, but really, not too many people got hurt. Unless of course assholes got on the floor, or fools who didn't know made the mistake of hitting someone who was "down with the crew." Then it got ugly very quickly.

The first shows that made a big impact as far as kicking off New York Hardcore were when bands like the Circle Jerks and Black Flag came to town. Things like that were big events, even bands like Flipper—it was always a big deal when West Coast bands would make it all the way east back then.

Circle Jerks' first New York show was the first time New Yorkers experienced real slam dancing. It was Circle Jerks, the Stimulators, and the Necros, and a lot of the D.C. kids came up on a "road trip," and some of the Necros' crew from Ohio. They made it a point to really go apeshit. They wanted to leave an impression on New York, and they definitely did.

That gig was a huge moment for me 'cause it was the end of one era and the beginning of a new one. We played our show, we did our thing, but I'll never forget how that show really changed everything. There were the Necros, just raw and fast. And then the Circle Jerks; they were fuckin' sick, they just ripped. The songs were so fast and tight, the dance floor was insane. It was a pivotal moment for me. I knew it was time for me to do some new shit. That whole gig really made a big impression on New York. Even though most of the D.C. dudes weren't that tough, they weren't like thugs or hard-asses or nothing, but they were goin' crazy. They were tearin' shit up on the dance floor. That experience left a tremendous impression on me and NYC.

Some of the New York people were intimidated at first, especially the old punk rockers. The "New York Hardcore sound" didn't really exist yet. New York is now considered to be a home of real Hardcore, but it wasn't that way at first. There was lots of great stuff, but the New York scene consisted mostly of girls and really young kids, the few leftover punk rockers, and a handful of dudes who were, for the most part, kind of soft. I don't mean that in a bad way, they just weren't thug types or tough guys. The Beasties, Luscious Jackson, and Neneh Cherry crowd, who'd been coming to see the Stimulators, disappeared as it turned into full-on Hardcore.

All the West Coast bands and D.C. bands started coming through more regularly as it officially turned into Hardcore. I remember after the D.C. guys came to a few shows, even Stigma was at first annoyed about these "Skinheads" from D.C. He pedaled by on his bike one day by Tompkins Square Park with his mohawk, plaid pants, and bum flap, sayin', "Who the fuck do all these Skinheads think they are, comin' and startin' shit?" Meaning all the D.C. crew that had started to come up for some of the big shows.

A lot of those D.C. guys are very PC now, but back then, they would fuck shit up on the dance floor! Henry and Ian and all of them, from what I recall, there was a point when people started getting jumped on the dance floor, or at least singled out and targeted for cheap shots, back fists, and all that dirty shit by some of those guys. Not all of them, but it got out of hand from time to time. Some of them dudes were pretty fuckin' nuts on the dance floor and fights would break out. I mean, not as much as it does nowadays, but they weren't as "peace-loving" as they claim to be now. But it seemed more pure and unrehearsed and spontaneous. Back then, punk rockers of any kind and "Skinheads" got fucked with so much in regular life, we didn't really fuck with each other on the scene at shows. It was only when outsiders would come in and get in shit. But things started to change; I think it had a lot to do with the whole straight edge thing, and New York was so *not* straight edge.

In the beginning, the D.C. guys would come up and go nuts for some of the big shows. Then the Boston guys—who were just fake jocks and middle-class dweebs all on D.C.'s dick—would come try to do the same.

D.C. had pulled off some kind of hard-rock shit two or three times as far as intimidating the crowd a little with all the slam dancing, and Boston maybe once or twice.

It's fucked up—a lot of these guys that had been cool turned into a bunch of dicks. The first two or three times they came down, they were almost timid—'til the music would start, then they'd slam and go off. They all came down with this attitude that they were gonna "mosh New York" or something—like they were gonna come down and fuck shit up, and make an impression. I still haven't figured out what that was all about or what they were trying to prove, but those Boston kids had this grudge with New York as a whole.

I guess they were all frustrated and pumped up 'cause they didn't fuck and they drank too much Coke and Pepsi. We were all getting laid and getting high. Of course, I'm just kidding, but it was all just stupid kids' shit.

They tried that shit again at A7, but by then, me and my friends were "growing up," and for shit-sure we weren't gonna take no one's shit anymore, especially not from a bunch of fuckin' suburban middle-class jocks pretending to be Hardcore—*fuck that*. We were used to getting jumped by Puerto Rican gangs who would stab us or shoot at us. We took shit to another level—that's just the way it was. They started it, and we finished it.

That last time they came down was to A7, that's what fucked it all up. Al Barile, the guitarist from SSD, was rockin' this "Kill New York" T-shirt. I remember his big-nosed ass wearing it, written in marker. I don't know if it was just some jock mentality carrying over into Hardcore, like some Red Sox/Yankees rivalry or whatever, but it was some really dumb shit. My boy Paul Dordal went up to him and said "You wanna kill New York, motherfucker? Start with me!" Al didn't do or say shit. He just stood there looking stupid. His friends were not tearing up the pit that night—we were. A lot of those Boston kids got hurt on the dance floor that night; by the end of the show, none of them were in the pit, they had their tails between their legs, and they packed up and left.

Let's just put it this way: they never came down again. I heard some bullshit story about how a bunch of Boston straight edge cats came to New York, and they all had X's on their foreheads and hands or whatever, and they were punching everyone on the dance floor who didn't have X's. I don't know what universe that happened in, but not this one.

One time, Jerry's Kids and the FU's and a dumb band, the Fucking Assholes, played at CBs. At that point we were still chill with the Boston cats. Then the Fucking Assholes came on, which was a joke band made up of those other bands wearing ski masks, so no one would know it was them. They started playin' and talkin' mad shit about New York.

Well, I wasn't having that shit. So, I came running from the back of the stage and tackled the singer around his waist right off the stage, and a bunch of friends of mine started kicking him. He was lucky he made it back onstage. They cut their set short and got the fuck off. Backstage, they were all cowering like bitches. I walked by and looked in on them. One of them was like, "I thought they were gonna kill us!" They were all realizing that it wasn't as funny an idea as when they had it back home. They later said one of the Boston guys got cut with a knife on the dance floor. I don't know, and I don't care.

One guy that inspired me a lot, and that I respected the most, was Ian MacKaye. He is one of the few people that I can say has never lost his integrity; he has always maintained a high standard for himself. I was really tight with those D.C. guys, before they got on their "Fuck New York" kick. I discussed that with him one time, and he said he never thought of it so much as a fuck New York attitude, as opposed to more of a D.C. pride thing, like they were putting D.C. on the map. And they really did. They came in, and they really left their mark, at least on our scene.

I became friendly with a lot of the D.C. kids. A lot of them weren't straight edge—cats like Bill and Jay McKenzie and others who were fucking messes; I mean, pill-popping, beer-drinking, and getting-fucked-up motherfuckers. But when fights would go down in D.C. with some drunken jarhead Marines or whoever, pretty much all of them cats would get down. Guys like Henry and Ian, when push came to shove, those guys would scrap. They all had chains around their waists with padlocks on them—they'd all tie heavy locks or those lead sinkers that you use for fishing to the corners of their bandanas. So if they got jumped or got in a fight, they could use those things to beat the shit out of them.

Back then was when I first met John Joseph, a.k.a. John Blood-clot. I met him when I was in the Stimulators. I remember seeing him on the street around 1980. I mistook him for Rob from CFA. He was walking by a restaurant where everybody was eating, and he blew a snot rocket at the window!

John used to come up from D.C. and Virginia, where he was stationed when he was in the Navy. His family lived in a middle-class neighborhood in Queens, but since he was stationed in Virginia, he used to go to shows in D.C. He wasn't a Skinhead, but he had his head shaved, 'cause he was in the military. He'd dress like the D.C. guys, with spurs on his MC boots, bandanas around his ankles, and a chain around his waist. Most of the D.C. guys looked like the drawing of the dude in the Circle Jerks logo. Most of the D.C. guys also wore black trench coats and wool caps, so they kinda looked like a crew when they rolled in together. But John didn't wear the trench coat—he wore a leather jacket.

My mom never dug John. She was like, "Why is this dude hanging out with my son? He's older than my son, and he's not really a good influence." And I guess in a lot of ways, he wasn't. But then, look at what other choices were around me. I mean, here's this guy who showed me how to roll better spliffs. He taught me how to be a better get-over.

My mom always used to say that she thought John was gay, or someone who didn't yet realize he was gay. She used to say, "He's in his 20s and my son's in his early teens. This guy should be at an age when he's trying to get girls. He shouldn't be hanging out with little kids." That shit used to drive me nuts. I was like, "Mom, c'mon!" You don't want to hear when you're a teenager that your best friend is gay. But that shit cracks me up now looking back on it. It didn't help that he used to wear a T-shirt that said in Magic Marker, "Fuck off bitch, I'm celibate." Now, straight edge is one thing—"don't drink, don't smoke, don't fuck"—but there's definitely some unsettled business in that dude's mind, or some kind of sexual tension or something that I still don't get.

John says that he lived in all kinds of foster homes and foster care. Some of that is probably true. All I know is that when I met him, I went out to his mom's house in like 1980, and it was a nice apartment in Queens. It was bigger than where I live now or did then. It had pictures of him and his brothers, all over the house, like any family. He even cooked me a steak! Can you believe that? John and me eating steak at his mom's. I know his brothers Eugene and Frank quite well, too. I never heard as much of a hard life story out of either of them. I mean, I know they went through a lotta hard shit, like all real New Yorkers did back in the day, but it ain't all like he spins it.

But yeah, it was a pivotal time for music, and bands that were happening around that time were setting the standard for what would become Hardcore. Black Flag had recently played in town with Dez Cadena singing. It was around this time that I came up with the idea for the Cro-Mags. I was so inspired by all the intense new music. I came up with the name while hanging out with a friend from L.A. that everyone called Mugger, who roadied for Black Flag. We were at a friend's house on 12th Street and Avenue A, where UXA was staying, down the block from my mom's apartment. Mugger and me wanted to start a band—or at least we were talking about it. He suggested we called the band the Cave Men, and then the Ape Men, the Neanderthals, and so on, 'cause we both had shaved heads and both looked very caveman-ish. I came up with the Cro-Mags, and that was that. I thought it symbolized modern man as a modern primitive. Black Flag split back to the West Coast and that was that. But the name stuck.

I was on a mission. I was gonna start my own band, and I had the name. While I was trying to put together a working line-up of the Cro-Mags, me and Roger from Agnostic Front started calling ourselves "Cro-Mag Skins." When I'd get really drunk at shows, I used to run around with "Cro-Mag" written in marker on my forehead. Jimmy Gestapo still has pictures of that shit. Roger nearly wound up as the Cro-Mags' singer, and I gotta say, looking back, I wish he had. But I guess it all happens for a reason—instead of one great New York band, we got two.

Before long, everyone knew of the Cro-Mags, even though they didn't know what it was—a gang, a graffiti crew, or a band. I wrote that shit every-fuckin'-where—all over town, at all the clubs, up and down St. Marks, the LES, and Uptown. At that point, I don't think Jimmy had shaved his head yet—probably 'cause his dad would have killed him if he did. And if you knew Jimmy's dad, you didn't want to piss that man off in any way. He was a scary moth-erfucker to have as a dad. I remember one time, Jimmy's dad al-most smacked me for cursing in front of him at the table. Jimmy was like, "Bro, are you crazy? I thought my dad was gonna kill you! I saw him give you 'the look.'"

I used to crash at Jimmy's folks' house in Astoria. We'd ride the train in the next day to play chess, and drink Southern Comfort on the ride. That was our ritual when I crashed there. By the time we'd get into the city, we'd be shitfaced, and would have forgotten all about the chess game!

Me and Jimmy started Murphy's Law together. Jimmy's like, "Dude, I got a band. We've got practice!" It was their first practice. I was like, "Oh yeah? Let me come down." It was Jimmy, Uncle Al, Adam Mucci and some kid on drums, and I was like, "Jimmy, I'll smoke this motherfucker, are you kidding me?" So I got on the drums and ripped the shit up. Afterwards, they were like, "You're in." So we were sitting at Uncle Al's a few days later, trying to think of a name. He had a poster on his wall that said, "Anything that can go wrong will go wrong, Murphy's Law." So I was like, "Yo, we should call the band Murphy's Law!" It was instant.

We didn't have any songs or anything. It was New Year's 1980, and MDC was playing at this place, the Loft. A bunch of bands were playing. Me and Jimmy were zooted out of our minds on moun-tains of blow from Dave A7, 'cause it was New Year's. We were dusted and trippin' our balls off, and at one point, we were like, "Let's go up there and play!" We went up and basically took the stage over from MDC. We started playing, and made songs up on the spot. Some of the songs that wound up on the first album were sort of conceived in that mess. I don't remember much of the performance, except afterwards someone coming up to me and going, "Man, that was the greatest shit I ever saw in my life—look, I broke my arm!" That was the beginning of Murphy's Law.

We had a reggae song, "Who's Got the Bong?" and part of the ritual was everybody would bring weed—spliffs pre-rolled and bongs—and during that song, everyone would crack out the weed. So there was no human way you could be in the club and not walk out stoned. If you were straight edge, you were fuckin' doomed. Chris Charucki, who later sang for Cause for Alarm, would be running around onstage, dosing everybody with acid. Half of the time, we'd already be tripping when we started the show. So he'd be dripping liquid acid into our eyeballs. I'd be up onstage drumming, with liquid acid running down my face as if I was crying. My friend Eric and Chris would be wiping it off my cheeks and licking their hands to get the residual acid.

One night we did a gig at Rock Hotel, I dressed like David Lee Roth; before we went on some of my friends almost jumped me, because they didn't recognize me! At that same gig, Warhol was there on the balcony getting harassed by me on the mic and several Hardcore kids in the crowd. Jimmy dedicated "Wild Thing" to his stripper girlfriend. She stripped down to her G-string, in front of this sold-out crowd of mostly fucked-up-on-acid-drunken-tripping-messes, and she basically lap-danced the shit out of him—all over the stage, all over the club. It started a ritual that continued for years afterwards: during "Wild Thing," she'd go up there onstage and strip.

Murphy's Law was madness when we started. It was total savagery. There'd be kegs, bongs, and Jimmy's half-naked girlfriend onstage! It was always more about the party than it was about writing songs, or really even being a band. Every night, we'd be doing this one song, "Fun"—and I hated that song. I'd get sick of playing it, and sooner or later, I would get up and knock over all the fuckin' drums and walk off the stage. That's how the Cavity Creeps formed, which was basically Murphy's Law's roadies and friends picking up the instruments and making noise. So you'd have a bunch of tripping idiots onstage, none of who were musicians, all making noise. So you can only imagine that this shit would be atrocious!

I played with Murphy's Law during a two-year period, and I was always trying to quit so I could form my own band. I was a musician, and I was serious about wanting to play. Jimmy is a great entertainer and one of the best front men around, but as a band, they were into goofing around, and I wanted to write some hard shit. Every time I'd quit the band, Jimmy would be like, "I just booked another week's worth of shows. Come on man, you've got to do this!" So it just went on and on, until eventually they got Petey Hines on drums, who kicked ass.

Another important musical discovery for me around this time was Motörhead. I was fortunate enough to see their first New York show at Irving Plaza. There were only two hundred people there, but they kicked so much ass. I was there with Darryl from the Bad Brains; Darryl and Nick Marden were the first cats to turn me on to Motörhead.

I actually wound up meeting Lemmy and Phil Taylor that weekend, and hung out with them at the Mudd Club. I was this young kid, and there I was doing mad rails of crystal meth with Phil and Lemmy! The funny thing was, back then nobody knew who the fuck they were over here. Nobody was paying much mind.

I told Lemmy, "I just started a band called the Cro-Mags." Meanwhile, I didn't have a full band, and I barely even had songs yet. But I was a huge fuckin' Motörhead fan. I said, "I'd love to gig with you guys. How can I get on tour with you?" He told me, "Well, the first thing you've got to do is you've got to get a record deal. Then, you've got to get a record out. If everything goes good, get it to our manager. That's how you get on tour with us." Little did I know that years later, the Cro-Mags would actually go on tour with Motörhead!

I think Phil dug me 'cause I was a Skinhead and back in the day, he was too. He was telling me all kinds of funny stories about old-school Skinhead shit, how they used to go to shows and not even go inside. They'd just hang out front and beat people up.

At the bar, I wound up picking up this new wave chick. I took her outside and found an unlocked car in a parking lot right around the corner from the club and "got to know her a little better." Then I went back upstairs to the bar and continued where I left off with Phil and Lemmy. Phil asked me what happened to the girl, and

I stuck my fingers under his nose and said, "Smell my fingers!" He laughed and bought me a drink. I think they were kind of impressed—I mean, after all, I was only like 13 or 14. I went to their hotel the next day: the Iroquois, this grimy hotel that all the English bands would stay at when they came to the States. Phil came down and gave me a little care package of speed.

There was a lot going on in NYC and on the LES back then. On Avenue A there was our club: A7, on Avenue A and 7th Street. It was two small rooms connected; there was a couch and a bar in the back, and a tiny little stage in the corner that was like six inches off the floor. It was real small, and we would jam a fuckin' ton of people in there. Doug Holland was the bartender, and he got Raybeez and Jimmy G jobs working the door; there was this crazy black dude Dave, a total cokehead, who ran the joint.

I was such a mess back then that even on nights when there was no one at A7 except for Doug and maybe one or two people, I used to end up on that couch in the back of that club, passed out, usually with a pool of vomit between my legs. Doug hated it because he'd be working the bar, and he'd have to clean it up at the end of the night, and send me home or bring me back to his place on 3rd Street to crash. Man, A7 was a fuckin' trip.

Across the street there was the Park Inn, where a lot of us would hang and get drunk, even though we were all minors. Tompkins Square Park was right there, and there would always be a small handful of us out every night. Me, Eric, Little Chris—we were on Avenue A and 8th, or in the park, every single night, all year 'round. 171A on Avenue A was a rehearsal studio and four-track recording studio where the Bad Brains' ROIR cassette was done. They had gigs there as well. It was a great place; a lot of really cool shit happened there. Jerry Williams and Scott Jarvis who ran the joint always let a bunch of people live there, including the Bad Brains. Rat Cage Records was down in the basement.

Back then, there were big shows at different places. Irving Plaza, the original Ritz on 12th Street, Rock Hotel, Great Gildersleeves, etc. Everybody came through town. Me, Jimmy, Watson, Eric, Diego, Paul—all the fuckin' lunatics—we pretty much dominated all the shows in the pit. Even the big shows, there was always a crew. Hell, I remember bands that we had a beef with, or that talked shit from the stage, that wound up getting beat down right there onstage! On weekends and in the summertime you could get anywhere from 50 to two hundred kids just running wild all up and down St. Marks Place, in the park, up and down Avenue A, and down to B. In the winter, we'd break up park benches and burn them in garbage cans to stay warm. There were always people huffin' glue, trippin', drinkin', smokin' dust or weed or whatever else anyone could scrounge up.

It was still completely lawless down there, but it was really busy. There were a few other clubs and bars in that area as well as all the drug spots, so it was pretty jumping. It was still a very bad neighborhood, so you definitely were taking your chances. There were tons of gangs and drugs and crime. We were way outnumbered when it came down to it, and the Hardcore kids and Skins would get jumped a lot.

On the other side of Tompkins Square Park, on 9th Street and Avenue C, we had C-Squat. Then we had Apartment X down on Norfolk Street, where there was always a ton of kids staying. We had a few people who had their shit together enough to have their own apartments that were like crash pads, like the old drummer from Cause for Alarm had a place on 2nd and Avenue C that housed a bunch of us.

C-Squat was one of the many early-'80s squats on the Lower East Side, but this one was mainly taken over by Skinheads and Hardcore kids—along with "chaos punks," not really "peace punks." Back then, there was a real distinction in New York between the two. The chaos punks used to hang out more with the Skinheads; the peace punks were into Crass, and into getting together and being like hippies with mohawks. The other guys were more into slam dancing, getting fucked up and into fights, more like the Exploited.

Me and John Joseph lived in one apartment in this burned-out building. There was an old Puerto Rican dope dealer on one floor, who had been there from the start; we were never really able to get rid of him, 'cause he had a lot of pull in the neighborhood. The building was really gutted—you basically had to find a door and attach it to the doorframe, and hold it up with chains to keep people outta there when you weren't around. It was a half-demolished building, but somehow, in everybody's minds, we were gonna live there, fix the place up, and eventually get control of it. That was the mentality back then. The Lower East Side was a very different place. So yeah, Skinheads were living in that building. Raybeez lived there a long time. For the most part, it was "party central."

When we moved in, the building didn't have anything—no windows, missing stair steps. We'd be stepping over openings in the staircase, walking on the metal frames where there used to be steps. There were no lights, so depending on how fucked up you were, it would be a treacherous trip to your apartment. And the one that me and John lived in, the walls were down to just the wood framing. You could see into the other rooms. We had blankets we stole and mattresses that we found on the street that weren't too filthy. We used to bathe in the fire hydrants with buckets in our shorts, even in the fuckin' winter with ice on the ground. People thought we were nuts. The shit was as real as you could get.

Apt. X was nuts, too. It was a building's basement turned into an apartment. It had all the pipes from the building running over our heads. It was completely illegal; it violated like every building code. There were so many people living in there. Mattresses everywhere, sheets hanging up as wall dividers, a bunk bed in the living room—if you can call it a living room. It was a fuckin' cave/dungeon, a grey cellar with Hardcore kids everywhere. Little Chris and me always crashed there, Steve Poss lived there, Rob Kabula and the rest of them. One time, John was trying to sleep on the bottom bunk, and the top bunk collapsed on top of him! Raybeez, Kabula, and like three other motherfuckers were up there smokin' dust, and they were so high that they didn't realize that he was under them when it collapsed! He was all screaming at them trying to climb out of the wreckage. It was funny as hell.

Another time, they were fucking with John and burned all his Hare Krishna books and pamphlets. He freaked the fuck out. John was a fucking nut. Some chick who stayed there for a minute had this really expensive furry cat. And one night, John shaved its head with clippers! We were really stoned and laughing, and he was like, "Yo, wouldn't it be funny if she came back and her cat was all bald and skinny and shit?" I mean, this cat was mad fluffy, in fact, I think that was its name. Anyway, he only got the cat's head shaved, 'cause the fur got caught in the clippers. The cat had no claws so it couldn't do much.

We were living some urban Road Warrior reality. This chick Nancy had a car. We'd be high as hell on acid, mescaline, and whatever, and drive real fast up and down Houston Street and Avenue A, "surfing" on the hood. If we'd see a cop car in the distance, she'd slow down and we'd hop off real quickly. Nancy eventually became an ambulance driver.

One night, I remember hanging out on Avenue A by Tompkins Square Park. We were drinking beer, smokin' joints, and huffin' glue, and this guy walked through the crowd—no one really noticed him, but I couldn't help but notice there was blood all over his hands. I was so used to seeing crazy shit, it didn't really faze me. About 40 minutes later, we realized that this fuckin' wino that had been sitting on the same bench with us all night long, who looked like he was asleep, had his head on his chest because his throat had been sliced from ear to ear! That also tells you about what the neighborhood was like.

Another time, we had a fight with a bunch of Puerto Rican dudes in Tompkins Square Park. We started getting the better of them, and we began chasing these dudes down Avenue B, toward the projects. I'm hauling ass, and I'm ahead of the pack. We get to the projects, and we're screaming mad shit and throwing bottles. All of a sudden, lights start going on, doors start opening, guys start coming out, and shit starts crashing next to me. I turned around and realized all of my friends had stopped running a while back! There were only two or three of us, where there had been ten or more. It was like right out of the movies: all of a sudden you're running for your fucking life, being chased by dudes with fuckin' pit bulls and golf clubs.

Almost every night was some sort of high-action drama on the LES back then. Because I didn't go to school, I was out all night long. I could go on and on with stories about fights and crazy shit from that neighborhood back then. Every night, someone got fucked up. In my neighborhood, we all knew the folklore of the neighborhood gangs, and what gangs ran which blocks.

One of the neighborhood hitmen was a dude known as "Pig Man." He was Pig Man because he wore a pig mask when he'd pull up alongside people in his blue Nova and blow 'em away with a shotgun! This guy was infamous; he was the boogieman of the neighborhood, except he was real.

During my "wilding days," there was a time when I was targeting a lot of the people that hung out at trendy clubs like the Pyramid. One night, I beat up someone who was friends of one of the owners of one of the clubs around there. I never really got the exact lowdown on what happened, but I heard that about $2,000–3,000 was paid to put a hit on me, because back then, things like that got done pretty cheap.

It didn't help that the local Puerto Ricans were getting pissed because me and my friends were fucking up a lot of their coke business, since a lot of the club fags were buying coke from all the little coke and dope spots around there that were run by the local gangs and we were scaring off their customers. So they put a hit on me through Pig Man. There were instances where Pig Man pulled up next to some Skinheads who were walking down the street—in his blue Nova, with his pig mask on—and aimed a shotgun at them. He drove alongside them, and then just drove off when he realized it wasn't me, or he was sending a message. There were a few instances like that, and one time, at the squat where I was living, someone got grabbed and dragged into an alcove with a knife to their throat, and asked, "Which apartment is Harley in?" During that same week, someone kicked in the door at a Skinhead apartment on Stanton Street, put a shotgun and a .38 snub nose to someone's head, and was like, "Where's Harley?"

The shit got hairy for a while. I even had local Puerto Ricans from my block say to me, "Yo man, you need to watch out. There are people after you, and this isn't even personal, this is about money." I'd be like, "But what about my mom? We live on this block, what am I supposed to do?" And they'd straight-up tell me, "Everybody likes your mom, don't worry about her, everything's cool. But you should disappear for a while." The shit was real. That's when I started to realize the violent repercussions of my lifestyle. Even H.R. said to me at that point, "You live by the sword, you die by the sword." That's when it started sinking in. It was not too long after that that I wound up heading out West.

When I left home and was squatting, it was no big deal. In fact, I had more space, more freedom, and more privacy. So what if it was in burned-out buildings? Having been raised by hippies and always being on the move, it was nothing new to rough it and just get by. Like I said, I had more space, more freedom; I was on my own. It was cool. By then, I guess I was almost 14. But the state was still giving my mom problems, 'cause I wasn't going to school and I was fucking up a lot. They wanted to take me away and send me to Spofford, a juvenile institution, like a prison for kids. I was not with that program. Soon after that, I was like "Fuck it!" and went to Cali.

HARLEY AT THE COMPOUND, SF, 1981, BY AMY KEIM

Chapter Five

GOING OUT
TO CALI

January 1982. I had been getting into so much trouble: doing a lot of drugs, drinking heavily, and fighting all the time. One night in Tompkins Square Park, eight or nine Puerto Rican dudes almost stabbed me. They walked up to us with golf clubs and 007s, which were these big-ass folding knives that everyone carried back then. They were talking mad shit. It was Tony T-Shirt who sang for Ultra Violence, and me, and these three chicks. They were all huffing glue, and probably dusted. Those were pretty much the neighborhood drugs of choice for gang bangers and street kids—glue and dust.

We were immediately surrounded. Two of the punk rock girls that were with us were actually Puerto Ricans, and the other was black. One of the girls, Bernadette, was getting all up in their faces 'cause they were talkin' shit to her: "What're you doin' hanging out with these white boys?" And she was like, "Fuck you! You make me ashamed of my own race!" All of a sudden, I've got knives at my neck, chest, and eye, and it's like, yo, even if you're a bad motherfucker, you're still a dead motherfucker. Or you're gonna catch a golf club in the back of the head, and then you'll get stuck by everybody fuckin' else. I think they just started laughing and walked off, and we went back across the street to A7.

That night, I was like, "Yo, I can't take this shit anymore. I live in a squat with no running water, and I bathe in a fuckin' fire hydrant with a bucket." I was doing this in February. People would be walking around in down coats, and me and John Bloodclot would be out there with liquid soap, doing sponge baths in the freezing fucking hydrant water. It was such madness for me here, I didn't have anything to lose by leaving.

So across the street at A7 were two Cali bands, Whipping Boy, and another called Hammer Slag with a girl singer, Lucille, who was a crazy Dutch chick, and this cat Dave Burks, who was only about 16 or 17 himself, and two other guys. I asked them, "Do you think I can hitch a ride with you?" They said, "Sure. There ain't much room, but okay."

The sun was coming up, and right in front of A7, I jumped in the car—five of us in an old beat-up car, with hardly any money: a chick with a reverse mohawk, my skinny little 14-year-old shaved-headed ass, and the three skinny Hardcore dudes. We were heading out West, eventually to San Francisco, against the protest of my friend John Watson, who was now Agnostic Front's first singer. He kept saying, "Yo, don't go! Yo, let him out at the bridge! He doesn't know what he's doing! You don't know nobody out there!" I left anyway, with nothing but the clothes on my back and less than a dollar in change.

It was five of us in a four-seater, and one of the back windows wouldn't roll up, which sucked when it rained—which it did for days. I was the only good shoplifter of the bunch, so I had to steal all the food and drinks at truck stops along the way. We'd split all the candy bars, chips or whatever I could steal, five ways. And that was dinner. I was walking around shaving my head with a Bic razor, but every day I'd miss spots, so I was this totally mangy-looking thing. It was really a wild trip—it's its own story.

Dave remembered: "Since this badly planned tour was a bust, we of course had no food and just enough money for gas home. At the gas stations Harley saved us from starvation...he would have the band members distract the clerk while he would load up his shirt and pants with frozen burritos and candy bars. We would cook the burritos on the car's metal dash in the sun while the car overheated."

We looked like a fucking mess wherever we rolled in. At one point, we had to detour from the trip to visit one of their family members and hit them up for gas money. Nobody was there, so we broke into their house, stole change, raided their fridge, and left a note. A week or so later with a few stops and minor mishaps along the way, I finally wound up in San Francisco. I envisioned getting to California and it would be nothing but beaches, sun, and chicks in bikinis. I thought everything in California was going to be like a Sunkist commercial or a Beach Boys song. We pulled into San Francisco, and it was freezing cold and foggy. The first place we got to was the Castro, and I was just like, "Damn, this ain't nothing like the commercials!"

Fortunately, I was able to get an address and phone number of my friend Kirsten, who had lived in New York, and had introduced me to Mugger and a few other people from the West Coast before I went out there. She was originally from the West Coast, and was friends with Darby Crash, the Germs, the Avengers, and most of

CRO-MAGS AT CBGB, BY KIM GRAF

the old-school West Coast bands. She had moved to San Francisco. So I showed up at her door in the middle of the night, standing in the rain. She's like, "Oh my God, what are you doing here?!" I stayed there for a few weeks. She lived in a big-ass house with these dudes. I don't know if they were college students or what. They weren't punk rockers or anything.

I never really got to know any of them, but one of them had a grow room. He said, "Dude, help yourself. Pinch a little bit every once in a while if you want." Well, he should never have said that 'cause I smoked almost his whole fuckin' room before it even fully matured! I didn't know shit had to mature. I was just throwing shit in the microwave and smoking it. By the time I moved out, he had twigs with a few buds left on them.

Kirsten introduced me to the Lewd, the Undead SF, and Terry Sergeant, who roadied for the Undead SF and some of the other locals. I remember the first show I went to on the West Coast; I almost got into a fight on the dance floor. I stepped to the dude that was beefing, and I let them all know right away: "People might think you're a badass around here, but I'm from New York, and I don't give a fuck who you are. I'll kick your fucking ass!" And that was it, no one jumped me. Me and the kid that was beefing made up, we became friends, and I had made a name for myself pretty much right away.

After I stayed with Kirsten, I jammed for a minute with a band called Murder, with Bobby Clic or "Bobby Lewd" from the Lewd, who had a great record called American Wino. Murder wasn't really a Hardcore-type band, they were kind of the first punk/metal "crossover" band in SF. But they were too early, so the punks had a problem with them, and the metal bands out there like Exodus still sounded like Priest or Maiden. The singer of Murder was this chick Nyna, who came from a punk band called the VKTMS.

It was during that stay in San Francisco that I discovered Black Sabbath. While I was jamming with Murder, I moved in with their bass player, Ju. He was a freak who played an eight-string bass. I had been tripping for a week or so, and my man put Black Sabbath on. He's like, "Dude, really, you gotta check these guys out." I was pretty uninterested. He was a lot older than me, and I thought it was just some hippie band from back in the day, I really had no idea what the fuck was up. He put on Master of Reality, and started with "Children of the Grave." That intro started, and I had this LSD-induced vision of barbarians with horns on their helmets coming out of the speakers, on horses with axes, ready to kill screaming villagers! Then I heard "Into the Void"— the whole thing blew me away. To this day, Sabbath is still one of my all-time favorites.

After I played with Murder for a while, I pretty much crashed everywhere and anywhere I could. And like everyone else, I was doing tons of drugs—lots of speed and acid. I started meeting a lot of kids on the scene through Bobby Lewd, Ju, Terry Sergeant, the singer from the Undead SF, Sid Terror and all of his bandmembers. Terry had a mohawk then; actually, he had three—one big one in the middle and two little ones on each side. Sometimes he just had the one. His jacket was all studded up old-school like Discharge. Years later, he became one of the most legendary and notorious San Francisco Skinheads.

Terry and me became good friends. We were always fucked up and running wild. He was all into crystal meth, while I was more into acid, alcohol, mescaline, and whatever. But as far as drugs went at this point, I was dead-set against shooting and heroin.

Being from New York and seeing that whole Max's-era scene, I knew better. And even when I experimented with speed for the first time like a dumb fuck, it was almost like a dare. I was always hounding Terry about the fact that he used to shoot speed all the time. Everyone out there did. I'd bitch him out for it, and he once gave me the, "Man, fuck you. You've never even done it. Quit trying to preach to me about shit you don't know." He pretty much shut me the fuck up. As a 14-year-old, I didn't have the intelligence to be like, "You know what? If this dude wants to kill himself, then that's on him." I felt like in order for me to actually speak about it from a point of knowledge, I had to at least experience it one time. So I could say, "Bullshit. I have done it..." Real smart, huh?

Anyway, I did it, and I enjoyed it—that shit is fuckin' evil. I wound up doing a lot of it for quite a period of time while I was out there. The first time I did it, it was at a club called the Tool and Die, at a Mentors gig with this Mexican dude with a green mohawk named Carlos. He got us some speed off one of the local dealers. I told him if he got me some I'd share it with him. We went in the bathroom, split it, and he shot me up.

I had seen it done, but I had always been against that shit and had never done it 'til then. He prepared it, tied my arm off and injected me first. I tasted it in the back of my throat, and right away it hit me. I'm lucky I didn't have a heart attack right then and there. It was zero to a thousand in one second, an instant rush of adrenaline: jet fuel, heart pounding, fuck, it was insane; and then he did his. I was just a kid. He was an adult. When I think back on it now it makes me sick. If I could go back I'd kick his fuckin' ass, but I was a dumb kid and he was a scumbag punk rock speed freak so he didn't give a fuck.

Fortunately, I didn't stick myself with needles for more than a few months. But I guess I was that kid that gets asked by their parents, "If your friends all jump off a bridge, are you gonna do it too?" At that point in my life the answer was "Yes!" That was the beginning of my unraveling.

Prior to that shit, me and Terry ate so much acid that it's amazing I can still talk. We had been dosing pretty regularly, and one day we were walking down Haight Street. On the corner of Haight and Ashbury, we found a baggie of acid. And we ate all of it. He ate

14 hits and I ate 19 hits. It wasn't like we ate 'em all at once, but we might as well have. First, we ate two or three each. We had been tripping a lot that week so we figured to feel it, we had better eat a couple. Time went by and we didn't feel anything, so we ate more. After a while, we started getting a mild sensation, but it was really weak. So we figured it must've gotten rained on or something, so we just split the whole fucking bag, thinking if we eat it all, we'll get a buzz. Well, we're walking down Haight Street from Golden Gate Park down toward the Mission and as we're walking by that store, the Compound, all of a sudden we start getting serious rushes, slow and heavy. My man looks at me and says, "Dude, that was good acid, man. We better get to my friend's house."

By the time we got to his building, we were starting to trip severely. It felt like the Earth was made of marshmallow, like we were walking on a big soft marshmallow, and things were getting more and more confusing. We got there, and I remember sitting on the floor. I was there for days, I have no idea how many, but I was trippin' my balls off. I could not see or function. A lot of times I was in the fetal position; sometimes I'd lay around, roll around, and say weird little things. But I didn't do much except fry. Terry was a mess, too. When I eventually came down, one of the weird quirks that came out of it was I felt like I didn't have to wear shoes anymore. I wanted to "feel the ground beneath me." I didn't wear shoes for like a month after that. For some reason, it made sense. But acid does some crazy shit to people. I mean, my mother thought she was a fuckin' snowflake back in the '60s, taking all her clothes off and running down the street.

Around that time, I started hanging at a place called the Compound. It was a punk rock store that sold second-hand records in the back, and punk clothes and boots on the second floor. They also sold tea and coffee. It was like the total DIY punk rock mini-mall, on 16th Street near Mission not far from La Cumbre. The drummer from the Avengers was working there. I was hanging out there a lot when I first arrived, and would meet people, bum food, and panhandle on the street. I was just a kid and very far from home.

Another friend of Kirsten was Richie Detrick, the singer of the Nuns. We were hanging out one day. I had picked up some acid from this crazy fuck who hung out by the On Broadway, this red-head dude who looked like an evil version of Jesus. He dressed in all black and had a pentagram necklace, and said he was a disciple of Anton LaVey. He used to fuck with the Christian preachers and Jesus freaks handing out the pamphlets by the On Broadway. But anyway, Detrick hadn't tripped in years, so I gave him some. But after a long night of partying, we both fell asleep on the couches before it hit us, and about an hour or so later, we were both tripping our fucking faces off. We just crawled around on the floor, unable to get up. The walls looked like a H.R. Giger painting from *Alien*. It was a bad experience. Finally, we came down enough to get our shit together.

After having such a bad trip, I actually went and bought more of the same acid, 'cause I figured, "Man, that was some good shit. Maybe if I just put myself in a better head before it hits me, I'll have a good trip." So the next time I ate that shit was with Terry. He ate some and freaked. He tried jumping out the window, 'cause he said there was a stainless steel butterfly doing circles around the building, and he wanted to jump out the window and grab a ride. We had to physically restrain him from leaping out the fucking window. LSD is one hell of a drug. I don't recommend it.

The San Francisco scene was total fuckin' debauchery. It was like New York but even crazier and bigger. Back home, it was just me and my boys that were fuckin' maniacs. Out there, it seemed like they all were. There were way more of "us." Like Berserkers, they didn't give a fuck: drinking, drugging, fighting, fucking, and taking no prisoners. I started hanging with the Fuck-Ups and a few other bands: Verbal Abuse, Code of Honor, Sick Pleasure, Bad Posture, MDC, and Crucifix. I was a friend with the Dead Kennedys.

They were no Nazi-type Skinheads in SF at the time, at least not like Oi! boy boots-and-braces types. I saw so many great shows out there, like at the On Broadway and the Tool & Die. The On Broadway was great. Almost every band that rolled through I knew from having met them in NYC, so I always managed to get in on the guest list as someone's kid brother. Dirk Dirkson, a legendary San Francisco promoter who put on shows there, would say, "You sure have a lot of brothers, don't you? You're 'related' to every fucking band that comes through!" If I didn't know who was playing, we'd

HARLEY AND DARRYL JENIFER, BY KAREN O'SULLIVAN

climb up the back of the building and in through the window in this back room where they had a piano.

One night, some chick who was like new wave or something got into an argument with these two little Hardcore girls, Heather and her sister. They were 13 and 14 years with their heads shaved, black lipstick, crazy eyeliner, and spike dog collars, and always tripping. Well, next thing you know, they ripped that new wave chick's fucking dress off! She was standing in the middle of the club butt-ass naked, freaking out, getting spit on and laughed at, 'til the bouncers covered her up and dragged her out.

Another time, there was a gig going on and outside there were tons of Navy guys all up and down the strip in uniform, getting drunk, going to titty bars, and starting shit. Of course, shit popped off. There was a mini-riot: Navy guys in their white uniforms fighting everywhere, brawling; and then, white uniforms covered in blood, running down the street. A few punk rockers got fucked up, but not many. It all began 'cause they started a fight with this punk chick called Monster. I think she was panhandling and they thought she was a dude 'cause she had a mohawk and tattoos and rings in her nose and ears and shit. They were fucking with her. Next thing you knew, it was a full-on riot! A lot of those old San Francisco boys were pretty hard. There were a lot of crazy motherfuckers out there who would throw down, like Bob Noxious and a lot of other crazy fucks. That was a wild night: Punk Rockers 1, Navy 0.

At that point, I was crashing all over the place. I stayed at the Mission A House for a little while, along with about a dozen speed freaks, including the singer from Bad Posture, Four Way, who sold speed at the time. I was so fucked up on speed at one point that I remember sitting in a chair for about a week straight, playing bass. I pretty much only took breaks to do more speed. I wrote about a hundred songs and forgot them all. But I learned how to play real fast. By the end of the week, the bass was encrusted in blood, and my fingers were all ripped up and raw. I actually wound up staying in that same fucking apartment years later in the '90s, with Flipper drummer Steve DePace.

This guy Sweet lived there since the first time I was there in '82. He died while I was there in the '90s, and no one even knew he died. He was in his room, in bed, and it was days before anyone knew—he had like melted into his electric blanket. That place was insane; everyone was fucked up on speed, trippin' balls drunk. Those Bad Posture guys were a mess—everyone was.

I also used to hang with the guys from the local skater crews Jak's Team and Eb's Team; there were all these crash pads and party houses everyone used to bounce between. I don't think they had ever heard of straight edge in San Francisco back then. I swear, they were all fucking savages.

I eventually wound up moving into an infamous San Francisco squat called the Vats. It was an abandoned Hamm's Brewery that was turned into a squat/party-central/living quarters for tons of Hardcore kids, punks, runaways, drug addicts, and freaks.

I first lived in one of the building's air vents. You had to crawl down these vents, then up some small ladders, and down other vents; it was a total maze. Some of them you could stand up in, but not all of them. Where I was, I had about enough room to lay down. I had my sleeping bag and some flyers on the wall. I eventually got taken in by this chick Spike and her boyfriend, Marc Dagger, and moved into an actual vat, where they used to store the beer. I think she felt bad for me, 'cause I was so young and on my own.

The Vats themselves were big, square, rubber-coated rooms, with no electricity, and a manhole with a chain on it as a door. We had hot plates, lights, radios, and whatever else, all running into a big cable down the hall. There were like 20 or more Vats on each floor, and a few people living in each one—sometimes up to like five, sometimes six or more. We called ourselves "Vat Rats," and can you believe people used to actually pay rent to live there?! There was this scumbag speed freak dude that had moved in first and had it on lockdown with security and shit. It was like some kind of apocalyptic chaos zone, in a very desolate area by train yards and train tracks. On the first floor of the Vats there were rehearsal studios, but on the fifth floor, it was nuts. The parties there would be insane. People would be fucking right there in the middle of a room full of people walking around, drinking, and getting high. There was even a family with a baby living there!

Anyway, Marc and me became like brothers. We'd have to steal together to eat, and we fought back-to-back all the time. It was a bad neighborhood, and the cholos, blacks, and the white-boy rock 'n' rollers were always jumping us back then. It was always a brawl, just like NYC, but it was a new environment, and I was having a ball. We eventually moved up into the yeast culture room of the building, which was on the top floor. It was like "the penthouse." It was the only room in the building with windows. It overlooked the train yards and it was covered in tile. We got it rent-free, 'cause me and Marc were now doing security for the building.

A lot of crazy shit happened with Terry, Marc, and me. After I left San Francisco, they became two of the most notorious Skinheads out there. But it wasn't always that way. I always used to break their balls about their mohawks, and tell them to shave their heads. The funny shit is, after that one serious acid episode with Terry where I stopped wearing shoes for a while, I actually let my hair grow into a mohawk. At first it was just 'cause I ran out of razors. But the acid probably had something to do with it. I also had an "X" carved in my forehead. It really was crazy; we were kids in our teens and on the streets, trying to eat, get high, and just basically survive. We were into music and drugs. We had nothing, and had no hopes for what the future was gonna bring. It was just day-to-day madness and chaos.

While I was living at the Vats at one point, the three of us were trying to get work, any kind we could. There wasn't much available for teenage runaway punk rockers on the street. But there was this company that delivered newspapers and hired anybody. It didn't matter who you were; you didn't need ID. You didn't need shit, and they paid cash. They just needed people to walk paper routes and deliver papers and ads. So we delivered papers in the outskirts and suburbs of San Francisco. The shit was pitiful. You'd go there at like 5:00 in the morning. There'd be all kinds of illegal aliens, bums, and homeless freaks. It was in this big parking garage, with all these trucks, newspapers and bags. You'd stand around in a big group, and hopefully they'd pick you to work. So we would try to dress down a little. Marc and Terry would flatten down their mohawks and put on baseball caps, so we wouldn't look too crazy—leave all the chains and spikes at home, and try to look a little more low-key so we'd get picked.

If you did get picked they'd put you into different groups; different trucks drive you out to drop-off spots, and then you had a certain amount of time to walk fucking miles and miles—up and down hills, dropping off papers. You'd be getting attacked by dogs the whole fucking way in the hot-ass sun. It was hysterical. One dog would start barking, and then all the neighborhood dogs would start barking. They knew it was time to attack the paperboy! After getting attacked by like three dogs, I got attacked by this little poodle. I was like "Fuck you!" and I chased it back to the house. Then this fuckin' Doberman came running out the door at me, but it had a cast on its leg, so it didn't catch me.

We'd usually still be fucked up from the night before. It was funny but it sucked. It was illegal work too, so they only paid like three bucks an hour, and then they'd charge you money as well for getting picked and for rental of the bags to carry the papers. It was a total fuckin' scam. We were better off panhandling or stealing food. The shit was a joke, but we tried. There wasn't much a runaway street kid could do for work. A lot of the fucked-up things I did, I did because desperation will cause people to do desperate things.

I remember one time Spike sending me and Marc out, saying, "Motherfucker, if you don't come back here with some kind of food or some kind of money, you fuckin' better not come back!" I guess she was getting pissed 'cause we weren't bringing any money in. We had nothing. We were living in an abandoned brewery, what do you think we had?

The one time I tried to grab anything from somebody older, like an old guy, was once when we were panhandling and trying unsuccessfully to get some dinner. We were starving. We hadn't eaten in days, maybe some Top Ramen noodles the day before at best, and this guy was walking out of a restaurant with his leftover doggie bag. We were so desperate that we ran by him and tried to snatch it out of his hand and run—and we dropped it! The leftover rice and little bit of leftover dinner went all over the street. He just looked at us like, "You assholes." We could have probably just asked him if he could spare it, but no one had hooked us up all day and we were desperate. I guess we didn't want to risk him saying "No."

I am still ashamed of that one. It was just so pathetic. We were such unsuccessful crooks, we couldn't even pull that off. We were never the kind of people that would do something to old people or women—that was really as low as we ever went. But we were hungry. It was straight-up strugglin' on the streets. After a while, we got to know what bakeries and restaurants were throwing out their food which nights. We'd go grab all the old bread and cakes and shit, and bring them back to the Vats and feast.

There was the occasional mugging, mugging attempt, or "fag bashing" as people would later call it. But that's not really what it was. It was usually just a crime of opportunity, not a hate crime. I guess at the time we didn't have as much of a problem with robbing a fag because half the time, we were the ones getting "approached." When you were young homeless kids like us, especially living on the streets in San Francisco, you'd have creepy men hitting on you all the time on the street, and offering you money, drugs, and food, to try and get you to go home with them. So when we had the opportunity to rob someone who's trying to taunt you with money, when you don't have shit, that's what you're going to do. Some of my friends would let them think they were taking them into the alley to suck their dicks, go back in there with them, and then they would rob them.

It's like, this motherfucker is trying to "chicken-hawk" on you, 'cause he thinks you're lunch. It's like, "All right motherfucker, we'll see who's going to be lunch." And not to justify my actions, but a lot of my predatory behavior at that point was directed toward people who were trying to be as predatory with us. We were young-ass homeless kids. I was 14, but I was a hard-ass 14. I wasn't a 14-year-old little fake punk, I didn't play that shit. So yeah, me and my friends did rob a lot of fags; it's just the way it was on the street. But it's not like there was this big homophobic thing going on, 'cause I had so many friends who were gay. A lot of people used to try to be like, "Oh, Harley and all his friends are Skinheads and homophobes." I guess some people were, but that wasn't it for me. The Stimulators' singer was gay, the Stimulators' manager was gay—I mean, Christ, Allen Ginsberg was a close friend of my family. Me and my friends were just criminals, and a vic was a vic.

At one point, I hitchhiked to L.A., and stayed with Black Flag for a few days at their infamous SST offices. It really was how it's been described—very small, complete chaos, where people slept anywhere they could, under desks or on reclining chairs. It was as insane as you could maybe imagine. I just found a place on the floor and stayed there.

I had a run-in with an L.A. cop along the highway before I showed up at SST. I was walking along the highway trying to find a bus stop, and I saw a cop car pass on the other side of the highway. He made a U-turn, came back my way, pulled me over, and started searching me. He had me on the hood, and then he started pushing me around with his nightstick and talking shit: "So what are you into, punk rock? What are you, some kind of a punk? Some kind of faggot?" And right when I was sure the cuffs were going on, he got a call on his radio, jumped in his car, and split. I told Henry, Mugger, and the guys about it when I got back to their place. Henry was fucking pissed. They had a genuine hate for the cops, and with good reason. The L.A. cops fucking sucked.

The Bad Brains toured California during my stay in L.A. I showed up at their sound check. They were surprised to see me, and not too happy to see the state I was in. I was turning into a bit of a mess. Darryl especially was like, "Harley man, you've got to come back home with us!" But I wasn't really ready to. They did one show at the Santa Monica Civic Center; it was them, Discharge, Circle Jerks, Bad Religion, and Duff McKagan's old band, the Fartz. That was the first mega Hardcore show I ever saw. It was like going to a "rock concert" except there were like five mosh pits going.

At that show, I got into some shit with the bass player from Suicidal Tendencies. I don't even think Suicidal was a band yet, but they may have been a crew. It wasn't really a fight; I got sucker-punched by Louiche Mayorga, and went down. I had a little buzz on. I'd been drinking and smoking some weed and was walking around, just looking at everybody, checking out the scene. I accidentally made eye contact with this dude; I didn't make anything of it. All of a sudden, I'm looking up at the sky like "What the fuck just happened?!" I got up, and I'm like, "What the fuck, man?" And he's like, "What's up?!" Suddenly it dawned on me that I was not dealing with this one guy; he was with several people. This punk rock dude and his girlfriend were walking by and said to me, "Let it go! Let it go!" I heeded their advice as my senses started to gather. I looked around and I was like, "I'm going to get my ass kicked. I'm outnumbered, and this dude is three times my size." So I tried to save face by talkin' some shit, and I kept walking.

For the rest of the show, I noticed him on the side of the stage. I watched him all night, and I really got a good image of his face. I wanted to fuckin' punch him all night, but he was with all these people. Years later, our paths would cross again.

But I was having too much fun to really care, the pit was insane. I was stage diving into the biggest mosh pit I had ever seen, cannonballin' across people's heads, rollin' across the crowd and taking people down with me, and hanging out backstage with the bands. At one point that night, either at the end of the night or between bands, I remember being outside the venue in the parking area standing with H.R. watching the sun setting. The sky was red and he said something about the sky being red like blood and that it was a sign, and then started quoting Bible stuff. Later there was some big police riot, but that was so normal out there back then. That was pretty much the way shows ended in L.A.

All in all, my trip to the West Coast was pretty nuts. But by going out there, I fucked up one of my greatest opportunities—one of my biggest regrets. I'd just started jamming with the Misfits on drums before I left New York. So I was kind of poised for that slot. To tell you the truth, it came down to the fact I was eating too much acid at that time. I split, got out West and called Glenn and Jerry. They're like, "Dude, what the fuck. Where are you? We've got to fly you back out here!" I was too fucked up. I don't know how many acid casualties are going to read this and relate, but I was just too lost in my trip to really give a fuck about much else except riding it out. In my head, I had some mission to complete: I had to get some shit off my chest before I could focus on being a functioning musician in a band. Like Frank Sinatra said, "Regrets, I've had a few." That's one of the few that I've always kicked myself in the ass for—I coulda been in the Misfits, and drummed on *Earth A.D.* Eventually, after almost a year on the West Coast, it was time for me to go home.

Not long after I got back to New York, there was a surprise birthday party for me at the Park Inn. I found out they were having it, but I didn't want to go. I had eaten acid, and I knew my mom and her boyfriend Simon and other family and friends might show up. I remember being at Jerry Williams' house on 11th Street, smoking weed and dreading going over there. Finally, I knew they were all expecting me to show 'cause that's where I hung out pretty much every night. But by that point I was tripping pretty hard.

I remember walking in and heading to the back of the bar. I didn't see anybody yet and the acid was really kicking in; everybody's faces were starting to distort. So I got to the back of the bar, and all of a sudden everyone turned around and screamed, "Surprise!!"

They started singing "Happy Birthday" and my mom came out with a cake and candles. I was peaking on the acid. The candles were giving off this glow, my mom was holding the cake, and her teeth were glowing from the candlelight. The whole thing was quite an experience. Everybody's faces were looking all cartoon-like.

The pitchers started flowing and they called open bar. At some point someone gave me some crystal meth, which was a rare thing in New York, and I snuck off and did it in the bathroom. I was wired, tripping, drunk and stoned. I vaguely remember Ginsberg stopped by and wished me a Happy Birthday.

For the next hour or two it was open bar and everybody was getting drunk. The crazy thing wasn't just that I was barely in my teens and tripping my face off, but that I was having an underage birthday party in a bar—one of the craziest bars on the Lower East Side—full of drunken freaks, half of them high on drugs, and my mom is there with a cake.

But I didn't stick around long in New York. Soon after I got back, I would head to Canada.

VOID SHOW, HARLEY, BY NEIL SCHWARTZFARB

SKINHEADS — AND THE GREAT WHITE NORTH

Chapter Six

Now before we get into this next chapter, I'm gonna try to give you a brief explanation of how and when the Skinhead scene started to turn ugly. It's just my opinion, and I only give it so you can get a better sense of what was happening at that time. I'm not trying to give you a full-on history lesson; that's not what this book is about.

In the early days, the Skinheads were into ska music, and a lot of them borrowed their style of music and dress from the Jamaican "rude boys." So in the late '70s, when the Skinhead revival started, and the whole "rude boy" Two Tone scene blew up, you had both white and black kids into it. In those days you had punks, mods, rockabillies, and whatnot all going on at the same time.

But then you had your Skinheads that were into rock 'n' roll and punk rock. They were less about fashion and "dancing" and more about street fighting and just being hooligans. When the football hooligan scene blew up in the late '70s and early '80s, Skinheads were a major part of it. That's when the National Front and the British Movement started making its presence felt. That's when shit really started to change. I was into reggae and ska in the beginning, but I was definitely more attracted to the other end of it.

Some of the bands that started attracting Skinheads during the punk years were Sham 69 and the Cockney Rejects—one of the best bands, if not the best band, of that style as far as I'm concerned. These were punk bands minus the ridiculous safety pins and colored hair. It was a more down-to-earth rock 'n' roll, but with street attitude: hooligan rock.

Then in 1983, a late-'70s punk band called Skrewdriver formed by Ian Stuart Donaldson, by then a Skinhead band, came out with the 45 "White Power," and the Skinhead scene started taking a turn for the worse. They put out a few records, but that 45 brought them attention from the media and the right wing. Most Skinheads I knew back in the day were into Skrewdriver. But up until that infamous single, no one in the States knew they were Nazis. As far as we all knew, they were another punk rock 'n' roll band. I had all of the earlier Skrewdriver records, and I was surprised when "White Power" came out 'cause up until that point, they had never expressed those types of sentiments in their lyrics.

"Oi!" was a term created by the press, specifically journalist Garry Bushell. In some ways, Cockney Rejects may have been the first Oi! band. They had so many singalongs: "Running down the back streets, Oi! Oi! Oi!" All their songs were street-type hooligan anthems, such as "Fighting in the Street" or "Sitting in a Cell with You." But they were also quite funny, like "Where the Hell is Babylon?" They even covered Motörhead.

Roi Pearce of the Last Resort and Micky Fitz of the Business both told me that Cockney Rejects was the band that made them start their bands. They said if Stinky Turner could do it, they could too; he was just a fucking kid! Cockney Rejects was a great fucking band. And just for the record, they were not right-wing or racist. In fact, they mockingly referred to the British Movement as the "German Movement." Turner's autobiography, *Cockney Reject*, describes an incident where the bandmembers and their supporters had a massive fight against British Movement members at one of the Rejects' early concerts.

So when "White Power" came out, that changed everything. Bands like the Last Resort, another one of my favorites from that era, started coming out with extremely violent, Skinhead-type lyrics about fighting. The Rejects had football hooligan-type lyrics, but now bands were singing songs about straight-up Skinhead violence.

Oi! music caught on and the Skinhead scene started to grow, and with it, a lot of racist Skinhead music. Many of the bands really sucked—it became less and less about the music, and more and more about the imagery, the violence, the politics and the ignorance. The media loved it and fed into it, and me, being a street kid always into fighting and huffin' glue and drinkin', I could relate to the street-fighting aspects, and I loved it.

The change in the music influenced my lyrics in a sense. But the fact is, I wrote about my life: hard times, street justice, survival on the streets, show no mercy, etc. But over time it became a fashion statement on the NYHC scene. People that weren't even hard would try to act tough and sing about Skinhead fighting. Meanwhile, they weren't living it. They never had a real fight or had to steal food; they had never lived the life I was living.

In 1982 I returned to New York from the West Coast. When I left, there were hardly any Skinheads at all, maybe a dozen—just a few

friends of mine. But when I returned, it was as if Skinheads had taken over; there were tons of new kids I didn't know hanging out. I called them textbook skins 'cause they were all good at dressing the part but they had no heart. They were full-on Skinheads with bomber jackets starting trouble and raising hell on Avenue A and St. Marks Place. But when shit would go down with the locals, most of them would either run away or get their asses kicked. They'd go back to wherever they came from until the next weekend, and then it would all start again.

The Bad Brains did two back-to-back shows at CBs for Christmas that year. Shit was already getting stupid; motherfuckers were practically knocking the band off the stage, even during the Reggae songs. Motherfuckin' new jacks were more interested in being onstage with their friends than they were in the music. Some total "Hey, look at us" Romper-Room shit. I mean sure, looking back, those days were great compared to now, but to me that was the beginning of the downhill slide; everyone was trying too hard to be "hard."

Around that time, I went to Canada, "The Great White North." I met this punk rock chick Manon; she and a girlfriend Lucy had hitchhiked to New York, and were checking out the scene. I was like 15 and she was 18. We started going out. I lived with her for a while

151

at different squats, and wound up hitchhiking to Canada with her one day on a whim.

I remember walking down the highway in the snow getting rides from truck drivers, and when we got to the Canadian border, they denied me entry. And they were not letting her back into the States either. They told her she had to return to Canada, on the Canadian side of the border where I was getting rejected. On that little stretch of highway between the two borders, there's probably about a few hundred feet between the two checkpoints. That's where vehicles go from the American checkpoint side to the Canadian checkpoint side. So, as I was hugging her goodbye and she was crying, I told her real quietly, "Just start going toward Montréal. When you get to the first truck stop on the way there, wait for me, I'll meet you there." So I took my bags, and started walking back toward the American side of the checkpoint. And as I walked, I sort of veered slightly toward the edge of the highway, where the fences are. But I was doing it real casually, and everybody was so preoccupied, they weren't really paying attention.

Right as an 18-wheeler passed me, I threw my bag and myself over the fence: just up the side of the fence and over, commando-style. I grabbed my bag, got real low, and started running—straight into the woods, parallel to where I was, to get distance between me and the checkpoint. For some reason, I had it in my head that if I stayed real low to the ground, if they had radar, then they wouldn't pick me up. I ran as fast as I could, probably a good half a mile deep into the woods, took a left, which was toward Canada, and kept running. I hustled through a stream, and ran until I was very confident that I was deep into Canada, and that I was nowhere near the border. Then I banged another left, to get back to where I figured the highway was, because that was the direction I came from. I got to a little fence, climbed over, and sure enough, there was the highway a little ways down. I started walking down the highway, found a sign that said "Montréal," walked in that direction, and saw a truck stop not too far up ahead. I went in, and she was sitting there reading a paper. She looked up, and there I was in Canada.

When we first got there, we stayed at these squats that were really rehearsal studios, but people used to rent the studios and live

HARLEY, BY KAREN O'SULLIVAN

in them. They were called the Locales. This was in Québec, not too far from St. Catherine.

I met a guy called Yob, a Skinhead who was best friends with a guy that Manon used to go out with called Orbit, as well as this fucked-up kickboxer Bruno. I started hanging out with those guys, and they turned out to be extremely psychotic, violent Skinheads. People whose idea of "going out" would be "Let's go out and fuck people up." It wasn't "Let's go out and have a few drinks," it was "Let's go out and hospitalize people and steal shit." There I was, 15 years old, and I was hanging out with violent cats in their early 20s.

We wound up moving in with those guys. It was a very fucked-up situation. On one hand, those guys were fucked-up and we knew it, but at the same time, we looked up to some of those cats because they were a bit older, and were into the same music as we were. They were covered in crazy tattoos on their arms, heads, and necks. They were hardasses and they fought a lot. But there was also a really sadistic side to them that I wasn't down with. Eventually it started to come out in me too, as if I was being pulled into it.

153

I think it was egged on by them, and by my upbringing, but I ain't blaming no one else.

I eventually learned what cowards they were. They would turn on anybody, even each other. Their message to me was: "The strong survive, the weak do not." They were into all kinds of satanic shit, *The Satanic Bible*, Nazi shit, and crazy amounts of porn.

They were some crazy fucks, but we did have a lot of fun. These guys more or less indoctrinated me into the world of *A Clockwork Orange*-style violence, as if it was an integral part of Skinhead culture. Up until that point, Skinheads and Oi! music were just extensions of punk rock; in my mind, Skinheads were just the harder punk rockers with a different look. But these dudes took it to another level.

In the apartment where we lived, they'd take on a tenant, usually a friend or someone off the scene, and after stealing their rent money, they'd kick the piss out of them and throw them out. Seriously violently boot-stomp the shit out of them. You don't typically do that to friends! It's just not normal. But that was the rule of that house. That was normal.

In Montréal, there were two Skinhead gangs. You had your French-Canadian Skinheads, I think they were the NDG Skins; and then you had all your English-type Skinheads who were not down with the French. The guys I hung out with were the English-speaking dudes, who would scrap with the French ones. But because Yob and Orbit were such ill motherfuckers, pretty much everyone hated and feared them. These guys would take tacks off golf shoes, that are basically like nails, and put them in the lace holes of their boots, down in the bottom few lace holes so they'd have anywhere from four to six little spikes coming out of their steel-toed boots. So picture: you're getting kicked full-force with a steel-toed boot with fuckin' spikes coming out of the lace holes.

Some of the worst things I truly regret as far as beatings I have given to people happened around that time. We were taking a lot of acid and a lot of mescaline. It really was like *A Clockwork Orange*, when they'd sit around doing psychedelics all night at the Korova Milk Bar, and then they'd go out and fight. That was more or less the life we were living.

The worst number of beatings I gave out in one night was in New York, not long after that Canada trip: I put 19 people in an ICU in one evening. It's weird, I know, because I talk about these things so casually, but it's so distant to me at this point, it's like another time, another place. It's so fucked up, I can't believe it was me. I do have a lot of regrets about the early part of my life. But those guys were fuckin' savages. All those dudes did was work out all day, stretch, spar, eat acid, and prepare for the fights and beatings that would take place later in the evening.

We'd practice kicks. We used to love grabbing people by their hoods or jackets or hair and kick them in the face, so we always practiced those kicks; it was like our signature move. One time, Yob, Orbit, and Bruno started a fight on the street, and this one dude started fucking them all up. They picked a fight with the wrong guy. He was with his girlfriend; it was just extra wrong. I didn't even know it was coming. This guy basically turned around and picked Bruno up off the ground, slammed him into the concrete, and started beating the shit out of him. Yob and Orbit grabbed the guy, tried to hit him, and he just reached over his shoulders and slammed them to the ground, too. This was a really big man; I don't know what these dudes were thinking. One of them had a little club that rolled out of his pocket. I was watching two of them get pounded, and the other one was going, "Harley, give me the club!" Because they were supposed to be my friends, I grabbed the club and I cracked the guy a bunch of times. My adrenaline was pumping.

I feel really fuckin' horrible when I think back on it, I always have. He rolled off of them and yelled to his woman, "Go get my brother!" So these guys took off running down the block like the cowards that they were, laughing the whole time, going "all right Harley, did you guys see him, good job." And me being a kid tripping my face off with nowhere else to go, ran right along with them. What the fuck was I supposed to do? It was a bad scene.

Another time, we were riding the bus, going to a club. Yob's girlfriend liked some dude's earring, a dagger-type earring, and the guy was with his girlfriend. They were rock 'n' roll or new wave types. So when they got off the bus, we got off the bus. Yob and Orbit walked up to the dude, and high-kicked him across his face.

It turned into an assault. That dude got stomped out over a fuckin' earring, while his girlfriend stood there in shock.

Afterwards, we all walked away laughing. But that was nothing; it was common to say, "Whoever knocks somebody out first to-night gets a six-pack!" I remember one time they said that shit in a cab, and Bruno said, "Pull over," got out, punched some old dude in the face, and got back in the cab. That was really where I got "desensitized." And it's where I saw white boys who were as ill as the dust-smokin', glue-huffin' Puerto Ricans from my block on the LES; the same dudes I had witnessed assault my aunt and other women, shoot at each other, and beat people with golf clubs. And all of a sudden, I saw a bunch of motherfuckers who were acting like that, but more sadistic. The only difference is that they were into the same type of music I was into, they were white boys, had their heads shaved, and looked like me and all my friends. But they were all completely psycho.

I don't know if anyone's ever heard of a Satanic Nazi Skinhead, or if there even is such a term, but that's what these dudes were! Or-bit had a big-ass pentagram tattooed on his chest, Yob had a giant swastika on his forearm, a big spider web running down his neck, a skull with a knife through it on the top of his head; his head and eyebrows were shaved. His bedroom was painted black with a big red pentagram painted over his bed, and there were pictures of Hitler everywhere. But as insane as they looked, they looked cool in a crazy way—and if you were a Hardcore kid and you didn't know what kind of sick fucks they were, you might be impressed. They were very fashion-conscious, always had their boots super shiny, the right Skinhead jacket, pants and shirt, the whole nine. But if you got to know them, you'd know they were just dangerous, psychotic fucks.

Like I said, I lived in this apartment with them. I don't remember if there were neighbors upstairs, but it was like a two-family type house. I mean, shit, I don't know how we got away with half the shit we did there. When you think of Canada, you think of a nice place with nice people, but these were some violent, crazy fucks! We'd be getting into fights in these nice, quiet neighborhoods. It's really got to make you wonder why we never got caught. But then again, there weren't cops anywhere. If you called the cops, it took them a half-hour to get there. Those dudes used to kill stray cats and dogs, and they'd kill rats in the alleys with hockey sticks and play "rat hockey."

I remember the first time I saw them kick a friend of theirs out of the apartment. It was when this guy Griffin and his girlfriend moved in. This was a guy they knew for years. It was then I realized these guys had no fuckin' remorse. They moved him in, collected the rent, and waited 'til he got all settled. Then one night, we were all high on acid, and they just stood up and said, "He's got to go!" I guess they'd been planning it but I didn't know anything. They were like, "Harley, go knock on his door." I went and knocked, and they were standing on either side of the door, and Griffin was like, "What's up guys?" And I'll never forget it, 'cause there was this big Skinhead dude with a griffin tattooed on his neck, standing there in leather underwear! And his girlfriend was lying naked in bed with the blanket pulled up to her neck, looking a little concerned. They started beating his ass mercilessly.

Now mind you, we used to wear rings that had spikes in them, like little half-inch nail-type things that you'd barely notice. A jeweler friend of theirs used to custom-make them for us and they would rip someone's face as soon as you punched them. So that Griffin literally got the shit beat out of him in front of his girl. They didn't do anything to her. They told her, "Get dressed, we want you both out of here right now!" She got dressed while her boyfriend was getting fucked up, and they kicked them out. They told him to take what he could carry and leave, "but," they said, "not your Doc Martens—they're staying here!" That was the thing back then, stealing people's boots.

At one point, Yob and Orbit wanted to start a band with me. I was gonna play bass, Orbit was going to be the guitarist, and Yob was going to be the singer. They wanted to call it The Last Reich. The idea, musically, was to create a Skinhead version of something that sounded like Discharge. They loved Discharge. They would tune out all the lyrics that were about peace and anarchy, and just focus on lines like "The blood runs red!" and "The nightmare continues!"—all the one-liners that described visions of destruction and violence. That was when I wrote the music to the song "Everybody's Gonna Die."

The Exploited was one of the first shows I went to in Canada. It was me, Yob, the chick I was with, and this one other cat who was nowhere nearly as psycho a Skinhead, but trying to be "hard" nonetheless. So we went to see the Exploited, and we got into like two or three fights on the way to the gig. That's just how it was with those motherfuckers.

Anyway, we were at the show, and no one in Canada had ever seen slam dancing; they were not up on it at all. It was still a fairly new phenomenon, even in the States. And I was drunk as a motherfucker by the time the band went on. I had on a ski mask, so no one knew who the fuck I was. There was a group of NDG Skinheads, and I was "New York" all the way. So I was slam dancing, takin' motherfuckers' heads off, doing spinning back fists. I'd creep up to the side of the stage where nobody could see me, and I'd go running across the stage and just dive into this pretty much stand-still crowd. I'd spread my arms out all the way and take down four or five people with me, get up, and start goin' apeshit. So in my ski mask, trench coat, and boots, no one knew who this motherfucker was, and everybody was getting real aggravated, because they'd never seen shit like that before.

Then I did it again. I dove right into the mob of French Skinheads. The main dude of the group was named Norman. He was an older Skinhead and covered in tattoos. I actually landed on Norman the first time, and all these motherfuckers started looking at me all hard. I think a couple of them were ready to jump on me, but Norman held one of them back while he was looking at me all pissed and like "who the fuck is this guy." And then I stage dived another time! At that point, I was purposely antagonizing them, because I was drunk, and I was like, "Fuck these motherfuckers!" I landed on them again, and that time I landed on the biggest dude of the bunch, who was probably in his early 20s. I don't remember his name, but I remember his reputation; he never lost a fight. He pushed me. I got up, and I was like, "What's up?!" We didn't even get to exchange more than two words—he didn't speak English anyway—and he blasted me.

I don't remember much except that he really fucked me up. He out-boxed the shit out of my drunk ass. I never stood a chance, he was way bigger and stronger. Within two or three shots, he opened up my eyebrow, and blood was gushing down my face. I got back up and I was like, "What's up motherfucker?!" He looked at me like "Are you crazy?" I went after him again, so he busted me up again, and opened up my other eyebrow. So at that point, I've got blood pouring down both of my eyebrows. I still have the fucking scars over 30 years later! So I was still talking mad shit, I just totally didn't give a fuck. So he was ready to fuck me up again, but at that point Norman puts his hand on him to hold him back, while all the younger ones were ready to jump on me.

Norman pushed me in my chest, and tried to see what my problem was. Then Yob came in and was like, "He's drunk, he's only 15, he doesn't know what he's doing." So for the rest of the night, I was going up to Yob like, "Yo, you got your knife on you? I wanna fuck that dude up!" I'm going up to strangers like, "Yo, do you have a knife I can borrow? Does anybody have a knife? I'm going to stab this motherfucker!"

Finally, I made it home. But yeah, I got my ass kicked royally that night. I've only had my ass really kicked a handful of times and that was one of them.

I'm ashamed for having been that person, and for having known and been around people like that. But that's the problem when you're a kid on the streets—you can't always choose the situations you're in. You're living here and there, and you sometimes wind up around some really fucked-up people. Those were the first times I was involved in acts of violence that I knew were wrong. But as a kid, I didn't always know what to do. Back then, you didn't really question how shit started. You just watched your friends' backs. To me that was the code of the street.

I had talks with those assholes about it, 'cause the shit just didn't make sense to me. I would tell them, "I don't mind a good fight as much as anyone else, but beating up somebody just for no reason, that shit is just wrong." And those guys were like, "No man, it's just a beating. That's what you do, you give out beatings—we're Skinheads!" And they totally tried to brainwash me into that insanity.

Of course, I have paid for that throughout the course of my life, time and time again. I have suffered some serious ass-beatings myself, getting jumped for no reason. And you know what? That's karma. Bad things come back to bad people. I know a lot of the shit

I've done in my life was caused in part by my influences and my surroundings, but you can't blame everything on everyone else—even though you may want to.

I'm a changed person in a lot of ways. As I've said, I was 15 years old at the time. As ashamed as I am to talk about it, when most people are 15, they aren't exposed to the shit that I was exposed to. So I've got to excuse myself a little, although not too much, and hope that God can forgive me.

Things eventually and inevitably went bad with those two assholes. Orbit tried to make moves on the girl I was with on the sneak tip. She was not having it, so he got pissed. So they were like "Fuck this kid," and got it in for me one of the nights they were trippin' on acid. My number came up. It could have been anyone staying there, and I got stomped out by both of them and another guy. I received a serious ass-stomping from the three of them with steel-toed boots. I basically curled up into a ball, covered my face, balls, and stomach as best I could—tried not to get stomped anywhere that mattered—and hoped the storm would blow over. When they were done beating me, they were like, "We're going to the store. You better be gone when we get back."

I scrambled, packed up my shit, and got out on the streets. Some Good Samaritan in a car picked me up and drove me to a hospital because I was completely covered in blood and my face was swollen. They put me in the hospital pretty badly. It was also the same week I got my chest tattooed with The Devil grabbing the world. I got it done by a tattoo artist in Québec named Norman DeMeers. It was actually my third tattoo.

I remember seeing Yob and Orbit on the street one night a few days after I got it. My face was still a fuckin' mess. They were like, "Hey, what's up?" Acting like nothing happened. I was like, "Man, you guys are fucked up." And they're like, "Oh man, you're still mad about that? Come on man, you guys can come by the house." I was pissed, but I kept my space. I wasn't ready to fight those guys; I was alone and I just had my chest tattooed. It was still healing, and so was my face. After that I didn't see those guys again for a while.

A few months later, I would cross paths again with Orbit in New York, but that's another story. So in 1983, I finally returned to NYC.

But as it turns out, it was not the same place I remembered. When I came back from Canada, it was almost like I had blinked for a second and the Skinhead scene had blown up.

PART I: CRO-MAG — SKINHEAD — BREAK OUT — NOW!

Chapter Seven

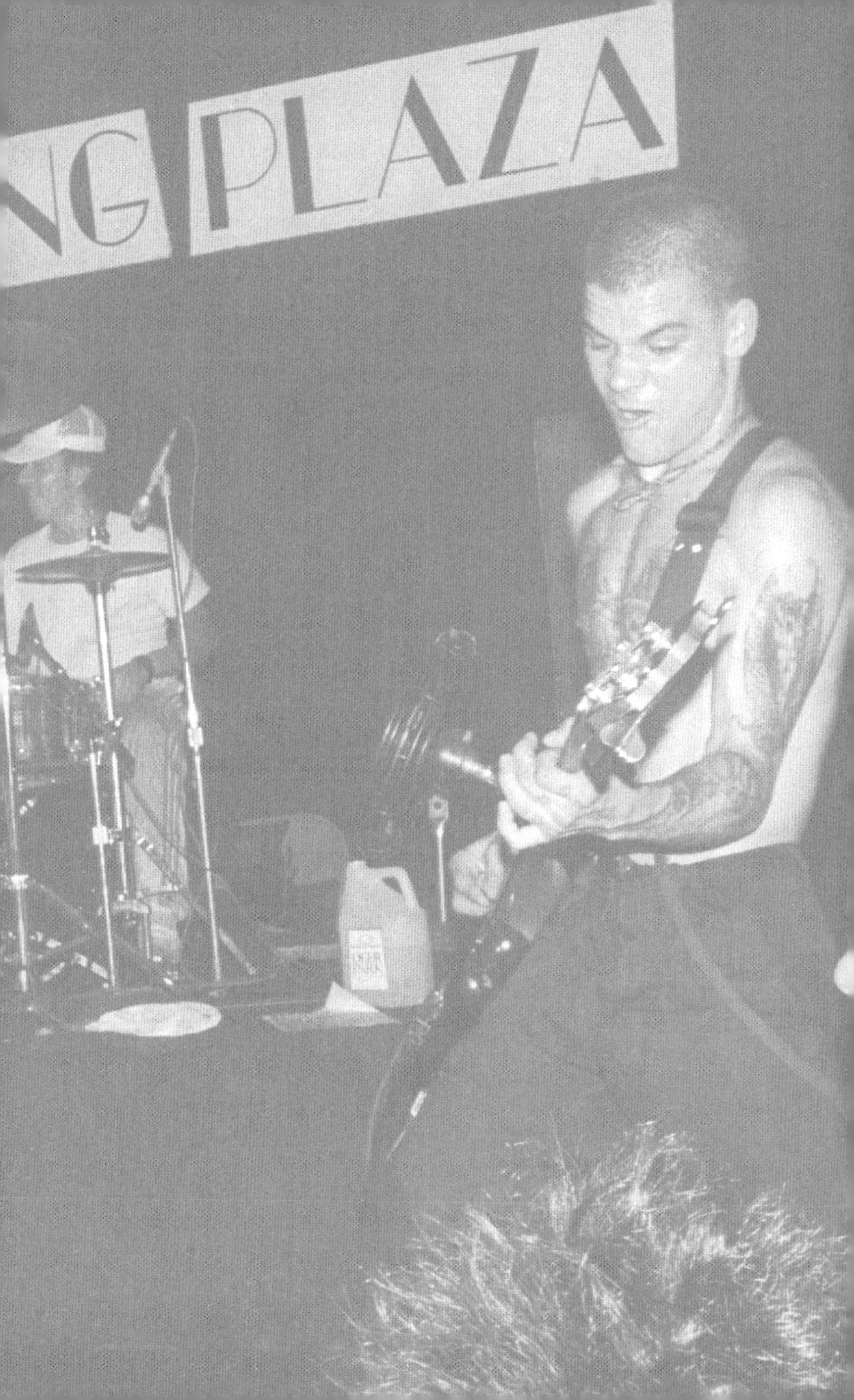
NG PLAZA

NG PLAZA

Before I get started about the Cro-Mags, let me just say, I do have a lot of good memories of all those guys. I had good times with all of them. I mean, how can you spend years around people, making music, touring, and growing up together, if you truly hated the motherfuckers?

Everyone can now play all self-righteous and point fingers. The fact is that all of us were freaks. John and me were some raw motherfuckers, while Parris was more on the down-low about it, but everyone in that band had issues.

If I had it my way, the band would have never broken up. It's really too bad that a band that had as much influence couldn't get our shit together and put the past in its place. But old beefs die hard, and people don't want to let go. Sometimes anger is all you're left with.

A band isn't made up by one or even two people, it's made up by a group of people playing together, and the chemistry they create together.

Like I said, I tried putting a band together before I hitched out to California; I came up with the name Cro-Mags in 1981 hanging out with my friend Mugger who roadied for Black Flag. They had just done some gigs and they were auditioning Henry Rollins around that time at 171A. We were hanging out at a friend's who lived down the block from my mom's on 12th Street, where a band from L.A. called UXA was also staying. Black Flag left town soon after that, so Mugger and me never did start that band together.

I started writing songs and jamming with guys like Dave Stein, the guitarist from Even Worse, Dave Hahn, the drummer from the Mad, and John Berry. We even did one gig at Danceteria with John on vocals, opening up for the Stimulators. We did Black Flag's "Nervous Breakdown," Dead Boys' "Ain't Nothing To Do," and a few originals. I also jammed with other guys while trying to put the band together, including one or two times with Louie Rivera from Antidote, and John Bloodclot for a quick minute.

I used to practice at 171A when I was trying to get the band together. I jammed there with the Bad Brains, who lived there at the time. I was on drums when they wrote "We Will Not." A lot of jam sessions went down there.

John lived there on and off also. Louie crashed at 171A, and this other guy Tomas; a lot of people stayed there. It was Jerry

Williams and Scott Jarvis who ran the place. And right outside of 171A, next to the front door and under the metal cellar doors in the sidewalk and down the steps in the basement, was Rat Cage Records. Rat Cage was the hangout where everyone could go and listen to new records.

People forget that you couldn't get these records in most places; you pretty much had to be into the music to even know how to find the stuff. Dave Parsons at Rat Cage turned me on to a lot of good music, not just Hardcore but jazz and other cool shit. He was very into Motörhead, and he turned me on to Venom's first single the week it came out. He also sold skateboards and acid. He used to have a fanzine back in the Max's days called *Mouth of the Rat*. At one point he started dressing in drag, which was funny especially since he was married. We had all known him for years and he'd never worn a dress, then one day he was in a dress and makeup. He'd be skateboarding down the street in his dress and his combat boots. Everyone was cool with him even though it got a bit strange toward the end, to say the least—great artist and photographer. He eventually moved to Switzerland and supported himself as a Charlie Chaplin impersonator, got himself a sex change, and died of cancer.

It was around that time when I really started to learn how to play bass from Darryl of the Bad Brains, with power chords and all that Motörhead-style picking. Darryl helped break down a lot of that for me, back when I was first switching from drums to bass. Shit, I remember one time the Stimulators jamming at 171A with Rat Scabies of the Damned, a lot of good times. But anyway, nothing really panned out for the Cro-Mags—yet.

I met Parris Mitchell Mayhew around that time, through my crazy-ass Skinhead friend Paul Dordal, back in like 1980. Paul introduced him to me as "Kevin," and that's how we all knew him when we started playing together. He never told me his name was Parris. I didn't find that out 'til *The Age of Quarrel* cassette came out, and I saw it in the credits. Paul wrote a lot of lyrics on the first Murphy's Law album. He told me, "Yeah, this kid Kevin, he ain't a Skinhead, but he can play guitar! He's really good, he can play Rush songs and shit." Well, I didn't give a fuck about Rush, but I was having little luck finding people on the scene to play with who were any good, or who could cut it. So I figured, "Hey, if he can play Rush songs, he'll be able to play my stuff with no problem!"

As it turned out, Parris used to go to Max's and he was a huge Stimulators fan, as well as of the Bad Brains, Motörhead, Sex Pistols, and other stuff I was into. I think he was pretty excited about playing with me, 'cause he'd seen the Stimulators many times. We became friends and started talking about jamming, and planning to do a band together.

We had little in common in terms of our lives. I was living in and out of squats on the Lower East Side, getting high and eating acid like it was candy. He lived with his mom on the Upper East Side and didn't do drugs. I was a dropout. He was in high school. I was always in fights. He was never in fights. One night we were all sitting in the Park Inn drinking pitchers of beer, and me and Paul were telling him about a robbery we had tried to commit earlier in the evening, and years later Parris told me he was thinking to himself "What am I getting myself into?" But I think he liked my brashness and craziness, at least back then he did, and on music we clicked. We were both good artists, we were both into different kinds of music, and we were both serious about playing our instruments.

Me and Parris would always hang out at the Park Inn, and sit at our table in the back getting hammered with our friends and all the regulars and local freaks. The place was always packed. "Ike the Dyke," this old black ex-con former pimp, loved fuckin' with people who'd walk in. His line was, "I catch you in jail, I'll make you my girl, candy hips." He'd hit on people's girlfriends right in front of them even though he was mad old. Then he'd look them dead in the eye and say, "What, punk, don't you fear me boy?" He'd get right up in their faces and start yellin' "Don't you know niggas carry knives boy!" He'd pull out his 007 folding knife all crazy: "I'll cut you boy." But it would always end with "You know I'm just fuckin' with you boy. You know I love you, candy hips"—always smackin' everybody on the ass when they'd walk by. "Candy hips" was about all you could understand from him half the time; the rest was just mumbling sounds and shit-talk.

One time, Eric Casanova went after Ike with a knife for talkin' shit 'cause he didn't know I knew him. The place erupted in a half-second, but ended as quick when the bartender, Aid McSpade, this really cool dreadlock Vietnam veteran who played guitar in the New York Niggers, came flying over the bar and yoked Eric by his neck and dragged him up, then out the door sayin' "You fucked up tonight boy. Go home and sleep it off." Eric was completely shit-faced, and Aid looked out for all of us, so it was no big deal. Eric was so bombed that I think he fell asleep on the steps next door.

Usually, if there was a fight in or around the Park Inn, it was pretty bad 'cause shit would go on and on. The cops wouldn't come, plus everyone from the block and/or in the park would get involved 'cause it was on Avenue A. There was a lot of action on that strip 'cause there was literally no police presence. The streets were wild, and they were ours.

We'd be drinking all night, even though we were just little kids, talkin' about our band and shit. I'd stay at Parris' house uptown with his mom, and when I'd be staying with my aunt, he would come over and jam with me there. When I was living in squats. I'd call him up and hum him riffs over the phone or leave them on his answering machine.

Eric Casanova joined the band. We did our first two shows with him. Eric was only like 15 when he got his girlfriend pregnant and left to try and do the right thing. That's when John Joseph joined. Those early days were the best, that's all I can say—crazy but fun. Fortunately, there are some photos from those days.

Before we even really got the band off the ground, when we were still just in the planning stages, Parris asked me if he could do a school project about me. He wanted to follow me around with a video camera and shoot a short film about me for a class he was doing. He asked me, if he bought me a bottle of whatever I wanted to drink, could he just follow me around with a camera for the day.

I wanted a bottle of Bushmills Irish Whisky. So he bought me a big-ass bottle and started filming me. It was me young as hell on the old Lower East Side, hangin' on St. Marks and in Tompkins Square Park, all wild and shit, my head shaved, already tattooed down. I remember in it, I ran into some old friends, some of whom are now dead. Parris always said he was gonna give me a copy, but of course he never did. Years later, I would beg him for that shit—he always held it over my head.

AT CBGB, BY ALEXANDER HALLAG

When we finally started playing and writing together, there was instant chemistry. But we were having no luck finding other players. And before anything really happened with the band, I wound up heading out to Cali and then to Canada. When I came back to New York after all that madness, I really wanted to get a band going.

It was around that time I did solo recordings of "Don't Tread On Me," "Wake Up," "Dead End Kids," and "Why Don't You," which Denise helped produce. Soon after that, I started jamming with Parris again. But we still couldn't find the right players. So in the meantime me and John—who was fresh out of the Hare Krishnas—formed a band for a quick minute called M.O.I. (Mode of Ignorance). John had been in a band called Bloodclot with some of the guys who hung out with the Bad Brains—and did sound for them. It was Alvin Robertson on drums, Jerry Williams on guitar, and Ted "Popa Chubby" Horowitz on bass. John also roadied for a little while for the Bad Brains.

The band Bloodclot didn't last long, but the name sure did—for a lot of reasons. M.O.I. was John on vocals, me on drums, Nunzio, the guitarist from Antidote on bass, and Doug Holland on guitar. Doug was still in Kraut at the time, and 'cause Doug worked at A7, he had keys, so he used to let us practice there during the day on the club's gear. He also let Raybeez practice there when he and Vinnie Stigma were putting Agnostic Front together.

Doug quit after maybe our third gig and Nunzio switched to guitar, and this kid Elroy, or "Ill-Roy" as we called him, got on bass. M.O.I. didn't last long. We only did a handful of shows, and then John split town to go back into the Hare Krishnas.

John wrote lyrics like, "In a bar or butcher shop/Eating flesh and drinking pop/Can't take it no longer/Mode of ignorance gets stronger." Doug would always look at me and start laughing and say, "Drinking pop?!" He also had this one song "Six Ounces Less," about the weight of the female brain; it was so sexist and fucked-up. It was stupid, but he was funny and none of us took him or it very seriously. M.O.I. sounded like a D.C. Hardcore band, but with a New York vibe, like Void and Faith meets Agnostic Front: real fast two-minute songs, with slow breakdowns at the end.

When I got back to New York, I was still going nuts on the streets, and getting in lots of trouble. Parris and me hadn't yet fully gotten our shit together. I was still kind of wilding too much. By that point, I had tattoos on my chest, my arms, and my head. I had the devil grabbing the world on my chest, a skull on the back of my head, a skull dagger and top hat that I got from Bob Roberts when he was on 23rd and 3rd Avenue, back when I was 14. I had the letters spelling "Skinhead" written across my knuckles with stars over them, 'cause the last thing you'd see were "stars" when I hit you—get it? I was living the ultraviolent lifestyle.

From what little I can remember and from what people tell me, I was a fucked-up little bastard. I was a glue-huffing-dust-smoking-drug-taking-fighting-all-the-time nut. If you read A Clockwork Orange, Alex is only in his early teens in it. And here I was, basically the same age.

I was always armed. As a kid I'd been jumped so many times in the 'hood, I didn't give a fuck about fighting more than one person—you just take one out quick and then go for the other one. Weapons and/or surroundings always helped and are always there. When I say "surroundings," I mean, weapons are everywhere, you just have to have the eye to see 'em. Like a garbage can, a bottle, a brick or a piece of rock; you can roll up a newspaper, fold it enough

HARLEY AND DARRYL JENIFER, BY KAREN O'SULLIVAN

times and make a "millwall brick." I didn't care about jumping on people. If someone was beefing with me or my friends, to me it was one-on-one/all-on-one!

That's how I was living. A lot from that period I don't remember very well; it was just a lot of getting high and street fighting. I was completely belligerent. I really had nowhere constructive to put my energy until I got the band going. And a lot of that bad karma kept following me from the early '80s 'til way into my *Best Wishes* Krishna consciousness days. Even when me and my friends were no longer seeking out trouble, it seemed to find us.

Parris and me finally picked up where we had left off. So there we were, it was 1983. I was in full-on Skinhead mode. But this time I was serious about starting the Cro-Mags. When we started jamming, I'd already written "Do Unto Others," "Don't Tread On Me," "Everybody's Gonna Die," and "By Myself," as well as the songs that wound up on my solo recordings like "Why Don't U," "Wake Up" and "Dead End Kids." That became the template for the sound and the direction we were heading. Parris had a lot of riffs for the songs. Eric Casanova co-wrote a lot of the words that ended up on *The Age of Quarrel*.

In the beginning, we were kind of basing our style around Motörhead, Bad Brains, and other stuff we were into. But it already had its own sound. We just needed a drummer who could cut it. We wound up recruiting Mackie Jayson from another local band, Frontline. He was also playing in this other band, Urban Blight. He was definitely one of the best drummers around. He was a huge Bad Brains fan; I remember he used to sit and watch Earl Hudson at every show they did back then. And I have to say, next to Earl, he was definitely one of the best drummers—if not the best—on the Hardcore scene.

Mackie was into a few punk bands like the Damned, but he was into all kinds of crazy fusion stuff too, like Lenny White, and all the D.C. go-go bands. He turned me on to some good shit back in the day. One of my favorites of that time was Lenny White's *The Adventure of Astral Pirates*. I bought it off the sidewalk in front of Gem Spa on St. Marks in like '84. He pointed it out and said, "That album is badass!" He was right! We used to bug out on Al Di Meola and Return to Forever *Romantic Warrior* and shit. Even though I was a Hardcore Skinhead, I was into music. We were all serious about playing—we weren't just a strict Hardcore band that couldn't play. I was listening to all this crazy stuff 'cause I wanted to become a better player. And with Mackie, the rhythm section was complete.

Eric would have been such a great frontman if he would have stayed. He was so hyperactive; he had too much energy. He never stopped moving. We'd be hanging out on a stoop or a bench, and he'd be "popping and locking" even while he was sitting down. It was hysterical.

Eric would get so pumped up live. The songs would start, and he would just bust right through all the words at once, and finish all the verses and choruses in the first verse before the parts would even come up. Then he'd get done with the words and we'd look at each other like, "Huh?" We'd be playing the rest of the song and he'd already have sung all the words, so he'd either start repeating parts over again, or break dancing and doing B-boy shit onstage. It was funny, but it used to drive me nuts though, 'cause me and Parris took the shit real serious. He'd be blasting through the songs quicker than the rest of us, and Mackie would be forgetting parts and laughing at Parris and me. I'd get all flustered and he'd just laugh.

But despite all of that, we were pretty tight, especially for our age. I was always writing songs and coming up with riffs. I mean, even when I was living in the squat and had no electricity and no way to record song ideas, I would bum a quarter and call Parris' house. When the machine would pick up, I'd be like, "Don't pick up the phone! I want you to learn this riff!" Then I'd hum a whole fuckin' song or a riff to him. Next time I'd see him, he'd fuckin' know them! That's how possessed we were about that band and the music. We had tons of riffs and song ideas. We'd weed through them and keep the best ones, switch parts around, and combine parts with parts from other songs. "Malfunction" started as a song called "Back to Square One" 'til we took it apart, thus the line "Now it's time to go back to square one."

Unfortunately, Eric would leave the band pretty early on, 'cause he had a kid. After he left the band, he moved to Canada with his girlfriend. They both got into Krishna consciousness and he eventually wound up going to India and so on.

After Eric split, we auditioned John Bloodclot—who had just split the Krishnas for like the third time—as well as Roger Miret. John wound up getting the gig. Not 'cause he was better, he was just more persistent. He was always hounding Mackie and me about the gig. Mackie and him were pretty tight, and besides, Roger was already in Agnostic Front. I guess things worked out the way they were supposed to. But I still always wonder what would have happened had we got Roger. There would have been less headaches. And the band might have stayed together.

The last one to join the band before we recorded *The Age of Quarrel* was Doug Holland. When he joined, the album was already written. Doug was the most experienced one in the band musically besides me. His first band was the Apprehended. Doug also formed Kraut, and their first gig was with the Clash—what kind of a first gig is that! They had also gigged with a lot of the early bands that came to New York, like the Exploited when they first came over in like '82, and they did a bunch of shows with GBH in '83.

Doug introduced a lot of the Queens kids to the LES; that whole '80s Astoria scene was pretty much brought in by him, and then by Dave Insurgent from Reagan Youth. Doug used to drive into the city in this big 1969 International mail truck with all these kids from Queens. He used to see the Stimulators at Max's and gave us a lot of the credit for inspiring him to start the Apprehended and then Kraut.

Doug moved to Norfolk Street with Jack Rabid, who had moved to the city from Summit, NJ. Jack was a huge Stimulators fan, a DJ, the publisher of the fanzine *The Big Takeover*, and the drummer for Even Worse. Then Doug moved to 3rd Street, the Hell's Angels block. Back then that area was still really nuts.

Doug was friendly with Steve Jones of the Sex Pistols, who stayed with him for a short while. He became a bartender at A7, and then he got Jimmy Gestapo and Raybeez jobs working the door. When the Cro-Mags started, Doug used to tell me, "You guys sound really good, you just need a lead guitarist." Then finally one day after the gig we did with the Bad Brains at the Rock Hotel on Jane Street, I was walking off the stage, and there was Doug on the side of the stage with his usual smirk. I walked off and again he was like, "You guys sound really good, you just need a lead guitarist." I laughed and said, "Fuck you motherfucker, you wanna play lead guitar or what?" And that was pretty much that. He left Kraut and joined the Cro-Mags.

Back in those days, John and me lived in squats together, and did whatever we had to do to get by. He kinda took me under his wing in the get-over/hustle department. He was a good hustler. His nickname, Bloodclot, came from a few different things. He had been in a band called Bloodclot, but that ain't why the name stuck. It came from the fact that he was a big-time get-over, that's why it stuck.

Not long after my return to New York, I bumped into one of my "old pals" from Canada, Orbit. Right here on the streets of NYC, on St. Marks Place! I was with Bloodclot, who knew about those guys who fucked me up in Canada. So we walked up to Orbit, right by Gem Spa. He looked a little nervous, and put his hand in his pocket, like he might have a knife or some shit. I said, "What's up, Orbit?" He was smiling all nervously, like, "Hey Harley, how you doing?" We started fucking him up right there on St. Marks Place. I blasted him and John threw a kick at him. He started backing away, trying to act like he had a knife. He had an empty sheath in his hand. We started closing in on him to go in for the kill, and the fuckin' cops came rolling down the block. As they got to us, they bleeped their sirens, got out of their car, and basically broke it up. They told him to go one way and us to go the other way. We went running around the block, and while we were running we saw our friend Louie, the original singer from Antidote. John yelled, "Yo! We just saw this dude that fucked Harley up in Canada!" We started running to catch up to him and we did, on 10th and 3rd.

Louie ran up behind Orbit, jumped up and kicked him with both feet—I had never seen any shit like that! He landed with both feet on the dude's back, like some crazy WWF-type shit, and put him to the ground. Hard. I ran up behind them and kicked Orbit square in the face as hard as I fucking could, like I was trying to kick a fucking field goal. I kicked that fucker so hard, if his head wasn't attached to his neck, it woulda wound up like fuckin' blocks away! But since it was attached to his neck, it just kinda flopped around while I kicked it. We started laying an ass-beating on him. And he was trying to cover up his face and half-assedly rolling around. He was like, "I thought we were all cool?!" And I was like, "Yeah, well… welcome to New York, motherfucker!"

By then, we got his bomber jacket pulled over his face so he couldn't really see or defend himself, and he was getting kicked and hit by all three of us. He was getting the shit beat out of him, and I was saying shit like "Let's cut his fucking ear off, and send it to Yob!"

Again, a cop car pulled up, bleeped its siren, pulled over, and said, "Break it up. What's going on here?" John immediately launched into the cops, "Yo, him and his boys jumped my little brother when he was 14." Louie is all flipping out too: "Yo, they jumped my little brother!" They're both going off, and Orbit was just standing there all discombobulated and fucked-up looking. They saw the knife sheath and were like, "Where's the knife?" Orbit said, "Some cops confiscated it earlier today, officer. I didn't know it was an illegal knife." The sheath was for a double-edged old-school-style commando knife; you know, with the button snap on the sheath for your thumb. The cops were basically like, "All right you guys, break it up. You guys go this way, and you guys go that way."

See, that's how it was back then. So they sent us on our way. The funny thing is, if you get into a fight on 3rd Avenue now, there will be like fuckin' 12 cop cars, everybody will get taken away, and there will be a big scene. People don't get it. Street justice, that shit was real. It was NYC. Needless to say, that was the last I ever heard of Orbit and Yob.

PART 2 – THE SCENE / NYHC / NY SKINS

I n the early '80s, there was a lot of violence coming out of the Skinhead scene in NYC. Anywhere there was a Hardcore scene, you had a Skinhead scene. And it was starting to get pretty ugly. Shows were starting to get crazy. But it didn't start out that way. In the beginning, it was really all about the music and the style.

For instance, even though all the Skinheads that got attention from the media were white-power Nazis, in New York some of the worst Nazi-type "Skinheads" were black and Puerto Rican! This one black chick, Lefty, used to come up from D.C., covered in swastika tattoos. I guess we were all just crazy, with an ironic, twisted sense of humor here. Half of the Skrewdriver fans in New York were Puerto Ricans, Jews, and blacks. None of us took it very seriously. Most of us were high on drugs and just bugging. It was people from other places that took that shit seriously.

I remember one time, the singer from this band Genocide getting his ass kicked at A7 because he was talking some Nazi shit, and he pissed off this chick Lazar. So we were kicking this dude's ass for being a "Nazi," meanwhile I was beating him with a swastika belt buckle! It was all just completely stupid shit. No one really gave a shit at first—it was just nihilism, chaos, craziness, and aggression. The funny shit is, Lazar got knocked out by my friend Djinji Brown for calling him a nigger. I was like, "Well, you kinda had that one coming, Lazar."

It was a totally dysfunctional scene, and for the most part—at least in the old days—it was like one big dysfunctional family. I feel that the bad rap and the bad write-ups about Skinheads generated more of the racist stereotype. Maximum RockNRoll caused that shit to catch on with the dumbasses, who really didn't know shit—motherfuckers in the 'burbs and bumblefuck middle-of-nowhere. In a lot of ways Maximum RockNRoll was at the root of that so-called Nazi scene blowing up in America, 'cause of the shit they were always writing about us—and it spread. How ironic, huh?

The more shit they talked, the more we laughed. We kind of enjoyed being the bad guys of Hardcore. But we didn't know the effect it was having, or that people were reading this shit worldwide. And not only that, they believed in it. For a while, there was a Skinhead problem on the scene in NYC with fighting and shit. But there was no "Nazi problem." There were only a couple of real Nazis on the scene, and they got their asses kicked off—like this one schmuck we called the Nazi Garbage Man. The real white-power guys, they didn't last too long here. I mean who? Bobby Snotz? C'mon, nobody beat him up 'cause he was like what, 90 pounds soaking wet and five feet tall? I mean, we used to have scraps with the local Rican gangs all the time, and we were mostly white boys, but not all of us, that's for sure.

There were Spanish and black and even Jewish Skinheads here. Back in the day when Sid Vicious wore a swastika, no one freaked out; it was just for shock value. We didn't take all that shit so seriously. If it freaked people out and pissed them off, it was punk! That was the punk rock attitude. I mean, I once wore an SS uniform to CBs 'cause this dude loaned it to me, and I goose-stepped up and down St. Marks Place with 20 or so Skinheads—but it was just to freak people out. It was more for shock than anything else.

Maximum RockNRoll was really the only monthly publication that was about Hardcore. A lot of the editors then were ex-hippie radical leftovers. It was San Francisco-based, so everything was politically correct. Everything radical, anarchist, pro-everything, against-everything—you name it. So on the scene, you had people that didn't like me, Roger, or different New York Skinheads, and you'd have motherfuckers writing letters in, talking crazy shit about us. In all honesty, a lot of it was complete and utter nonsense. Some of it was based on a little bit of truth—they'd write about fights that happened—but they'd always get their facts all screwed up. And a lot of people wrote in letters in our defense, but somehow those never got printed. It was always the ones condemning us and talking shit that got printed. They seemed to like having us as a scapegoat.

It was usually such total bullshit that we didn't take it seriously. But then as we started getting out of the city with our bands and touring, we started realizing people in other cities and countries who didn't know any better took that shit like it was CNN. But the fact is, you never saw Nazi Skinhead rallies in New York or any of that shit. I mean, I ran around with a Nazi flag as a Superman cape one time—it was more just to piss people off then anything else, and to spite *Maximum RockNRoll*. All the real Nazi skinheads and all that Klan-type shit mostly went down in the middle of fuckin' nowhere, not here.

I always used to crack up at that shit—a bunch of goons out in the middle of the woods somewhere Sieg Heiling at trees! Motherfuckers didn't have to deal with or know any black or Spanish people. New York was too mixed and diverse for that shit.

But me and my friends weren't like the punk rockers of the past or the peace punks who used to get jumped. We used to fuck people up.

One night, 33 of us—it's funny that it was exactly 33, but 33 of us Skinheads from the LES and C-Squat, uptown, Jersey, and some visiting from Maryland and D.C., were all piled into two vans, cruising around and getting into shit all night long. All of us tripping balls. At one point, we pulled over by Danceteria, and everyone was in the vans except Lefty from D.C. and this big dude Skinhead Mike from Maryland who was always with her; they were nuts and were both covered in swastika tattoos. They were standing in front of the door to Danceteria next to the doormen, the bouncers, and all the people on line that were trying to get in, when all of a sudden, out of nowhere, Mike spun around and lays out one of the doormen with a pair of brass knuckles! Immediately, we all jump out of the vans and start fucking people up. The bouncers all ran inside the club and pulled the doors shut and we all jumped back in the vans and peeled out.

We were like, "Yo Mike, what happened?" He was like, "I don't know, I think someone said something about Skinheads, so I hit him. I think it was him, but it might have been someone else." He was so fucking crazy. We were all high on windowpane gel acid and tripping our balls off. So we all went up to Central Park, it was the middle of the night, and we started robbing drug dealers. It was a crazy night.

By this time, the New York scene was a lot bigger—more and more people from other areas and the suburbs started coming around. Some of them were super cool, but some of them were real assholes, coming to the LES acting like hard-asses and fronting like they were from here. They'd start shit with the local Puerto Ricans and make us look real bad to the neighborhood, and usually get their asses kicked by the locals anyway.

I remember Billy Psycho got himself shot in the leg one night running his mouth on Avenue A. He called some black guy a nigger, and, well, shit happens. It was still a tough neighborhood, and sometimes these new cats would act up thinking they were running shit, and they'd get fucked up.

People still got shot and stabbed in that 'hood back then. For instance, I remember there was this crazy homeless-type dude that used to hang out, named Juan. He didn't really talk, he just whistled and made weird sounds. But he was really funny. He always had a plastic cup, and he'd ask people for beer in his cup by whistling, doing little dances, and then handing out his cup and signing that he wanted some beer. Then he'd bow! He was harmless. Darryl always got a kick out of him. One night, he was being his usual crazy self, and someone shot him in the chest. He died right there. The guy just walked off, and didn't get caught or anything.

But as for the number of people hanging out, the scene was jumping. There was A7 on 7th Street and Avenue A, at the corner on Avenue A and 8th Street there was a pizza parlor where we all used to hang out and play pinball and Spy Hunter (that years later became the bar Alcatraz), and all up and down Avenue A and B. There were bars that we drank at like the Park Inn, the Holiday Lounge; I can't even remember all of them. There was C-Squat, Norfolk Street, Apt X, Robby CryptCrash's place on Second Street, Natz from Virus/The Undead/Cop Shoot Cop's apartment, and a few other spots where we all hung.

That neighborhood was full of freaks. There was this one dude who used to hang out around St. Marks/Avenue A area on weekends who used to pay punk rock chicks to walk on him. The harder they walked and stomped on him, the more he liked it, especially when they had combat boots on. He used to do shit like roll himself up in dirty rugs, ones he would find on the street, and lay them across the sidewalk by the garbage cans in front of buildings—vertically across the sidewalks, so when people would walk down the street they would step on him thinking he was a rug that had been thrown out. So on busy weekends people would be all drunk and there'd be all kinds of people walking up and down 8th Street, and he'd be laying there all night getting walked on in the rug, unbeknownst to the people walking on him. So whenever I'd see a rug laying across the sidewalk, me and my friends would kick it real hard as we'd walk by.

One time he was hassling some punk chicks I knew that I think may have walked on him in the past and he was trying to get them to do it again. They didn't feel like it or whatever, so we started having words. My boy Mark Dagger walked up and said a few words to the guy, and he responded in a way Mark didn't like. So Mark blasted him in the face; the guy got stomped to a bloody mess. I actually had to pull Mark off after a while. That asshole didn't enjoy it that time.

I didn't see him again for months after that. Then one night, I was walking west on 8th Street with a friend of mine. It was late, maybe 5:30 in the morning. The sun was almost coming up and the streets were empty. We were all the way over by West 4th Street and we saw a carpet rolled up lying across the sidewalk near the garbage cans. I laughed and said that I wouldn't be surprised if that asshole was rolled up in there, so I gave it a good couple of kicks, jumped up and down on it a few times, and kept walking. Sure enough, as we were walking down the block, I look back and I see the rug moving around and this fuckin' asshole wiggling and crawling out of it, and he's all running up to me, "Hi, how are you? What's going on? How are you doing?" Bullshit nervous small talk. We just laughed and kept walking.

By the mid-late '80s, there was a whole influx of new Skinheads. Some of those guys would beat up winos and shit like that, then they'd head back out to the suburbs or their middle-class families in Long Island or wherever. Even when me and my friends were at our most belligerent, *A Clockwork Orange*-style, we were never the type of guys who'd set fire to a bum or something like that. But some of these cats would do shit like that, fucked-up cowards with no balls. Those were the cats that we'd eventually run into shit with—the so-called Krishna Skins. So I started fucking up the new Skinheads.

See, I wasn't in it to impress people or to make friends or to be liked or loved. I didn't care. I was there when Hardcore began, I didn't "come to" it. Me and my friends started it; I didn't give a fuck about all the new-jack bands. What should I care about new kids who were all in awe of me and my buddies? Not to sound like a total dick, but I just didn't give a fuck.

In the '80s, one cat I used to see around the 'hood from time to time was Jaco Pastorius—an amazing bass player. He played with Weather Report and a lot of famous jazz cats. He was one of the greats, but he was also a fuckin' maniac, and a bit of a mess as well.

I was tripping my face off on mushrooms when I had my first Jaco encounter. I was in Washington Square Park under the arch and I was just peaking off these 'shrooms. This old black guy always used to walk around with a speaker on a little luggage-type cart, and he'd push it around playing jazz. He'd sing songs for money on the street with a mic through his speaker to instrumental tracks. And this time, he happened to be walking by and was playing "Teen Town" by Weather Report. Now mind you, I had already started getting into some "out there"-type music. Darryl from the Bad Brains and Mackie turned me on to Return to Forever and other jazz fusion, and Parris was into shit like Rush, Yes, Brand X, and Dixie Dregs. I was already into Miles Davis and John Coltrane from when I was a kid, so I had an open mind to music. But I wasn't really up on Weather Report.

So there I was, tripping my balls off and just starting to really peak, and that old dude was playing this crazy fuckin' song, "Teen Town." I'm listening, going to myself, "Damn, this is like the craziest shit I've ever heard!" Again, remember, I was tripping under that arch, and the music was blasting and echoing. The sun was shining in my face, and I was bugging out on that song. All of a sudden, this crazy fucking drunk dude with no shirt and no shoes comes running up. He started jumping around, and he was all "This is me! I wrote this!" He started air-bass-playing along with it, and I don't know if it was 'cause I was tripping or what, but I could almost see the bass in his hands. It was fucking note for note. It was insane! I was sitting there tripping balls, and Jaco—who I had no idea who he was at the time—was going off, playing air bass. That old black dude just sadly shook his head.

I had other encounters with Jaco over the years. I actually wound up with one of his basses: I bought it off my friend, Twilight, this Jamaican cat from my neighborhood, who used to sell coke. I think he traded Jaco some blow for it. Anyway, one time he was naked in the street, pouring a Foster's over his head, while these two chicks were unsuccessfully trying to get him to get into a cab with them. This bartender chick I knew was a good friend of his. I remember after he died—this was back when I was still wilding—she told me, "I can't hang out with you. You remind me too much of Jaco," meaning my behavior, not my bass playing, I'm sure! "I already lost one, I don't want to lose another."

Darryl had a couple of funny Jaco stories, too. One time, Jaco told Darryl he was gonna give him a free bass lesson. Well, of course Darryl got all excited. Darryl showed up to where they're supposed to meet. Darryl had his bass with him and Jaco showed up, and he had no keys to get into the building. So he made Darryl climb up the fire escape with him into some apartment. And when they got in, he broke out a crack pipe, and he was like, "Are you ready for your freebase lesson?" Darryl almost cried! But yeah, poor Jaco—another sad story; a great player and a tortured soul.

Another great bassist I knew was a guy named Hayward Peele. He was so nasty. You never heard a cat like that. He used to play a lot on the street in the city, with different musicians, by the Cube at Astor Place and in the parks. But he also played with a lot of famous cats. He was one of my favorite bassists to just watch and listen to. And he was super cool. But he also sold a lot of "weight," both weed and other shit. He liked me and my bass playing for whatever reason. I think he felt I had potential as a player. He took me into his world, and the shit was nuts; homeboy had safes that were the size of rooms, and crazy shit was going on. He was one of the first really serious rollers I knew. I guess he got into that game when he was younger, hustling and shit. It's a hard life to get out of.

That was some sad shit—he got set up by some of his own friends. They tortured him to get him to open his safe, but he wouldn't, 'cause supposedly from what I heard, he owed a lot of money from having been robbed years back or some shit. So he couldn't afford to get robbed again. His life was kind of on the line for it. From what I heard, they cut his fingers off, shot him in the chest, and he died. That was really some of the saddest shit; it really bothered me a lot, and still does. Two other people also got killed in that home invasion, a couple that happened to be there at the wrong time. From what I heard, they were coming up the stairs of the building, and they got bum-rushed by the scumbags who did it. They used them to get into his apartment, and then they were shot. That's another reason I say "Trust no one," 'cause you never know who the fuck is gonna set you up.

HARLEY, BY DAVID SORCHER

Chapter Eight

NEW YORK "KRISHNA" CORE

n the early '80s, people on the Hardcore scene didn't take the Hare Krishna stuff too seriously; people made fun of that shit a lot. John Bloodclot had been away for a while—he had left the Hardcore scene and he was doing the Hare Krishna thing. But I guess he couldn't really shake his "material desires." He came back and wanted to start a band. We'd be hanging out and he'd be trying to talk Krishna consciousness to me, while we'd be burning spliffs or sitting there panhandling change for weed. It was funny as shit: "Hare Krishna" one second, then the next second, "Spare some change for some weed?"

Yeah, John was funny like that: always up to some no-good shit, but preaching all kinds of holy righteousness. One time we jacked this dude up for his weed. I was still in "street mode," so it was no big deal to me. But here's Mr. Hare Krishna. We brought this dude back to our squat 'cause he said he had Hawaiian bud and he was gonna smoke a joint with us. He was trying to sell us some shit. Meanwhile, we didn't have any money. So we brought him back to C-Squat, and he cracked out this shitty-ass bag of dirtweed, and tried to sell it to us. We were like, "Are you kidding? Where's the Hawaiian?" The dude tried to tell us that shit was Hawaiian, and he pulled out a big-ass sheet of Bambu.

John looked at me and started laughing. I was like, "Fuck this asshole." I grabbed him by his shirt and dragged him to the door of our squat to throw him out. I started dragging him down the stairs. Then I said, "Fuck it, gimme what you got, motherfucker!" John's all like, "Yo, you better give it up! You better give it up!" So I start pounding the guy out, with John yelling at him, "Give it up! Give it up motherfucker! He's gonna fuck you up!" John was egging me on and all the while he was going through the guy's pockets.

He was just a fuck-up like me and everybody else. The only difference was that he was on his self-righteous religious kick. That dude got me into more trouble than most people ever did. Like I said, most cats I knew when I was young were trying to steer me right. The Brains woulda checked me quick for that type of shit. Their old roadie Pip, every time he'd see me, he'd always hook me up a fat spliff or some buds, just so I'd chill out instead of running around, getting into mischief and fighting. John didn't give a fuck, as long as he was getting over.

It's funny 'cause besides John Bloodclot getting into the Krishnas, a few other friends of mine got into it too—like John Watson, who I had known since the Max's days. Then my best friend Eric got into it too. It was that dude Tomas who got them all into it. He was living at 171A with Jerry Williams and the Bad Brains. That's how John got into it too. Even cats like Googie, who played drums on the classic Misfits *Walk Among Us* album. Googie later changed his name to Bliss and founded Antidote, with Louie Rivera and Nunzio. I knew Louie since the Stimulators days. He used to bounce at TR3, and all the old clubs: Reggae Lounge, Mudd Club, Berlin, Danceteria, and Peppermint Lounge.

I remember being really freaked out by it for a minute, like, "What the fuck is going on? Why are all my friends turning into fuckin' Hare Krishnas?" As far as I was concerned, they might as well have been turning into Jesus freaks or Moonies or something. I even wrote lyrics about it: the original words to "Do Unto Others," which was called "Wake Up," were about not bowing down and being subservient to religion.

I couldn't figure out why the fuck my friends were all being lured by this religion. I was really unimpressed with the whole thing. But here's the kicker: when I was a baby, I was in the presence of A.C. Bhaktivedanta Swami Prabhupada, the founder of the movement, both at the Second Avenue preaching center and Ratha Yatra in San Francisco. That's a big deal if you're a Hare Krishna. It's like being in the same room as Jesus or something.

Allen Ginsberg knew Prabhupada, and that's how my mom wound up hanging around the devotees. My mom almost named me Harley Krishna. She said she didn't 'cause she was afraid I'd wanna kick her ass when I grew up. Ain't that funny though? I actually have a few drawings she did of Krishna from before I was born, and I have vague memories of the devotees. And of course, that George Harrison record with "Govinda Jaya Jaya" and "Bhaja Bhakata-Arati" I remember from when I was a kid.

I used to make fun of John in the beginning and break his balls about the whole Krishna thing, especially 'cause he was such a hustler and he was using the philosophy to justify it half the time—him and the rest of them like Bliss and Louie. It was hysterical, 'cause it was all the dudes with the shady reputations that were getting "religious." I don't know, maybe it was 'cause each of them had a guilty conscience or something.

One reason that John was so good at his Hare Krishna shtick was because he was such a good bullshitter. He was good at convincing people whatever the fuck he was trying to convince them, 'cause he was a hustler. So he was real good at doing their gig, which was basically panhandling—what they call Sankirtan, which is when you sell books and stickers. A lot of times, you'll see guys dressed as clowns or Santa Claus, selling stickers for charities and children's food programs. The ones he used to collect for usually didn't even exist. That was John's gig when he was with them. He would go to concerts and sell stickers in the parking lots. He had different scams that he'd do and tell me about. We'd be sitting there smoking spliffs, and he'd be laughing his balls off, telling me all kinds of stories about different ways he used to hustle money and scam people.

As far as I'm concerned most people who make spiritual claims and are self-righteous are usually full of shit. People who claim to be "spiritual" and criticize others often turn out to be total hypocrites. People who truly are spiritual don't proclaim it, they just live it.

But anyway, John couldn't shake his "material desires." He was all into the Bad Brains, and he wanted to do his own thing. He split the temple and started pursuing the idea of starting or joining a band. One morning, some Hare Krishnas came to C-Squat looking for him, to try to get him to come back to the temple.

John told me he was making thousands of dollars a day hustling for them; so when he split, they sent the Hare Krishnas' Secret Service, as he called them, to the squat looking for him, 'cause they wanted him back! At least that's what he said. He said it was 'cause he was making them so much money, and that's why they were there looking for him.

One morning, these Hare Krishna devotees, dressed undercover without their robes and with hats covering their haircuts, showed up at the squat looking for his ass; it was hysterical 'cause he was totally ducking them. My ass was asleep on my dirty-ass mattress and I woke up to "Excuse me, have you seen Jayananda?" I'm like, "John?" and they're like, "Yes, John." They were looking around at the broken walls and debris all over the place. One of them said to the other two, "This is what he wants over Krishna?" The other one said, "He's in maya." I was like, "I have no idea where he is." The first one who woke me up said, "Tell him we stopped by looking for him," and then they said "Hare Krishna" and left. When I told him, he freaked out. He had snuck out of the temple a few days earlier. He pretended that he was taking out the trash, but he had already packed his stuff and tons of merch and stickers that they would sell and had hid it outside, planning to sell the stuff himself to make some money, and then split.

It had been three years since Parris and me hooked up and started writing together. On November 2, 1984, and on February 16, 1985 the Cro-Mags went into High Five Studios on 27th Street and Park Avenue and recorded 12 songs—*The Age of Quarrel* cassette, which is released on CD called *Before the Quarrel*. Jerry Williams and his brother Tim Williams engineered it. It took us just a few days to do the tracking and mixing. It was my favorite recording besides *Revenge*, which didn't come out till 2000.

That first recording was so raw; it was high-energy. There was an urgency to it. We were young as hell, and we just blasted it out. There were a few mistakes here and there, but it was great. I played my old semi-hollow-body Guild Starfire through an old Vintage Acoustic. It was just me, Parris, Mackie, and John—no so-called "producer." The original singer of Warzone, Tommy, and Ill-roy, and possibly Carl sang backup vocals. The pitiful shit is that we only pressed like five hundred cassettes. But since Parris' father paid for it and he used to be in the music business, he kind of fucked us. Even though we only pressed a small number, he was still the "publisher." He looked out for his own interests, meaning Parris, who held that over our heads years later since they "published" the material.

Anyway, looking back, those were good times, Parris and me; the musical chemistry we had was undeniable. It was fun and we really did get along in those days, even though me and him were never as close as me and Eric or even me and John. We were all a lot wilder and way more street than Parris; in that sense the rest of us had a lot in common, and we were kind of the image of the band.

CRO-MAGS, BY STACIA TIMONERE

Around that time, we did a benefit to raise some money to do some work on C-Squat at Danceteria. Cro-Mags, Reagan Youth, and Agnostic Front played; it was a successful show. Well, a day or two days later, the building burned the fuck down! Three people died in it. To this day, I'm convinced that it was the slumlord that was trying to get us out of the building for a long time. He had hired local gang members to jump people and try and scare people out of the building—we got into serious battles with them, with two-by-fours, flying bottles and bricks, and people getting stabbed. He hired dirty cops to come and fuck with us and intimidate us out of the building. We fended for ourselves—which was kind of pathetic if you saw what a mess the building was. One dude was walking up the stairs one night and two steps broke out from under him, and he had to go to the hospital to get his balls sewn back together, 'cause the rusty fuckin' metal almost cut his balls off!

It was a fucked-up building. There were no lights, no running water or plumbing. John and me used to have to shit in paper bags, 'cause there was nowhere else to go. We'd throw 'em out the window at the building across the way in back, and try getting them in the window! There were shit stains all over that building from us throwing paper bags. Despite all the madness of that building, me and John were like the only ones who tried to maintain some standard of cleanliness. We bathed in the fire hydrant in front of the building with buckets and liquid soap every morning, no matter what it was like out. Even in the freezing cold, with slush on the ground. People thought we were fucked up.

At one point, a lot of people's shit started getting stolen. There was a Spanish dude named Angel who lived there, and one night Raybeez and a few others busted him. Well, that dude got beat down in the hall of the building with baseball bats by four dudes that were high on dust; it was bad. The only light in the hall was from a penlight someone had! Imagine that: in the dark, with a penlight, a bunch of dudes stomping that motherfucker and beating him with a bat in a staircase of a squat—fucking crazy.

That building was a mess; it could be a book in and of itself. There was this lunatic old homeless dude named Three Star and his hillbilly wife who wound up there for a minute right before it burned down. They used to steal dogs. He had like four dogs at one point; he was like in his 40s. John beat his ass one time; it was one of the only fights I ever saw John have. He was beating the guy's ass, dragging him through the water running from the fire hydrant. I was laughing, saying, "John, you want me to throw him some soap while you got him in there? Let me get the Dr. Bronner's for you." His wife was all screaming at John, and John's all "If you don't shut the fuck up bitch, I'm gonna keep fucking up your husband." It was hysterical; that whole place was pure fucking madness.

So, by this time in early '84, the Cro-Mags had formed, and I had become a vegetarian, influenced by the Bad Brains, but also by John and by Vinnie Signorelli, who was later the drummer for the Unsane. Vinnie worked at a vegetarian restaurant on 9th Street and 1st Avenue. Between him and the Hare Krishnas giving out free food, that's how we'd survive—that and stealing. Vinnie used

looked through the peephole, and opened the door. John and me kicked the door in and we all bum-rushed through the door—inside there was a whole fuckin' room full of people doing blow. I grabbed the motherfucker by his throat and pinned him against the wall and said, "Where's my shit, motherfucker?!" He's like, "I don't know what you're talking about!" I looked around—not only were those assholes doing blow, but the guy's got kids there. Louie's like, "Damn, you're doing drugs right in front of your kid?" I said, "Y'know what, motherfucker? I'm not going to beat your ass in front of your kids."

So I dragged him into the kitchen. Meanwhile, one of them ran to grab the phone to call the cops. John ripped the phone out of the wall and threw it at one of them—Navy Dave, I think—and just missed his head as the fuckin' phone exploded against the wall. We had the whole room in check. I dragged Marshall into the kitchen by his throat. The whole time I was looking around because I knew he had a gun somewhere in the house, and I didn't know where he kept it. We got into the kitchen, and the first thing I saw was a rolling pin. So I grabbed the rolling pin, raised it over my head, and was ready to start smashing his fuckin' head in with it. I was like, "Motherfucker, I'm going to give you 'til three. Where's my shit?! One, two..." "Here it is, here it is!" and he went and got me all my tattoo equipment.

So we split and got into my boy Stig's car. This was near Central Park. We pulled out on the west side of the park to head downtown, but it was the day before Thanksgiving. So they're blowing up all the fuckin' balloons for the parade. We got stuck in traffic, Rich was driving, John was next to him, and I was sitting in the back with all this tattoo shit on my lap in between John's brother Eugene and Louie. All of a sudden, I see a cop talk into his walkie-talkie. He turns, looks at our car, and points at us. Now you figure, the street is lined with cops, 'cause they're all setting up for the parade. So within a matter of seconds, it looked like the Blues Brothers movie—the car was surrounded by 50–100 cops! They all got the call at once: "There's been a home invasion, assault, robbery." And then there we are, right in the middle of them. They pull us out of the car. This is when we were all vegetarians, so Marshall and those assholes are out on the street going "That's them! I eat meat! I eat meat!" So we got locked up.

John's nickname was Squid. The Bad Brains gave him that one, because he used to be in the Navy. But a "squid" is actually a UDT SEAL, so that's how John started his whole "I was a Navy SEAL" rap. So we get locked up, and one of our boys was like, "Yo, Squid." And one of the cops came in who happened to have been in the Navy, and he was like, "Which one of you is a Squid?" We were like, "Oh shit…" 'cause John was AWOL. His brother was in the Navy too, so Eugene said, "Uh, I was, officer." And he started grilling him about a bunch of military shit that only a military person would know. Eugene had got out of the military properly, so he was cool. But they were going to arrest us all for that assault, so Stig and me immediately jumped up and said, "No, man, it was us, we did it." We took the rap, 'cause we knew that if they fingerprinted John, he'd go down. But because it was Thanksgiving weekend, we didn't get to see the judge for about a week.

We ended up spending eight days bouncing from cell to cell, precinct to precinct. What they did was keep us in a cell until right before it was time to feed us, and then they'd move us. And then they'd keep us in the fuckin' truck handcuffed to everybody, until right after they feed everybody who's in there, and then they'd bring us in. So they were basically torturing us for days.

We didn't eat the ham in the sandwiches they eventually gave us, so there Stig and I were, trading the ham sandwiches for cheese sandwiches with other cats in the cells. And we were trading the cheese because it had rennet in it, which is an enzyme from a cow's stomach. We were really serious about our vegetarianism, so we would trade the cheese for some sugar, so we could put it in our tea, which was horrible.

So we were living off bread from the cheese sandwiches and tea. It had been a few days and nights, and at one point they had like 30 of us in a big holding cell, and this one dude cracked out some weed! He only had like a little bitty pin joint, but everyone was like, "Oh shit!" So they lit it up. Me and Stig were standing at the other end of the cell, and within about 40 seconds, you could hear the cops coming. They were like, "Who the fuck is smoking weed?!" Like four of them came in and went, "Hold out your hands!" So they lined everyone up. "Let me smell your fingers!" They started smelling everyone's fingers to see who was smoking. They got to one guy who had been puffing and they smelled it, and boom—body shot, right in the solar plexus! He dropped to the floor and they dragged him out.

As they worked their way around the cell to get to me and Stig, I'm like, "Fucking pigs," and I stuck my hands down my pants and rubbed my hands all up and down my nut sack, so when they got to me and smelled my fingers, all they smelled was ball sack sweat! Mind you, we hadn't bathed in days! You shoulda seen the look on that pig's face when he smelled my fingers! Fuck him.

One of those nights, everybody was in their individual cells and everyone was pissed off—hungry, irritated, just mad at the world—and getting ready to go to Rikers Island. So everyone was talking shit. There was one Puerto Rican guy talking mad shit: "Yo, when we get out to Rikers, my brother's already out there, we're gonna be fucking shit up! All you niggas better know, don't fuck with me!" And everybody's like, "Shut the fuck up!" Everybody was getting ready for Rikers, so everybody was being a dick, letting everyone know not to fuck with them.

Every now and then, the cops would come by and say "Shut the fuck up!" and start slamming their sticks on the cell doors. We were in cells with no bars, so we couldn't see each other, we could only hear each other screaming and talking shit. At one point, the cops started getting real pissed. They started talking mad shit to the inmates, and cats were talking shit back to the cops. Then, out of nowhere, the whole fucking row of cells started singing, "We will, we will rock you!"—in defiance of the cops. It was awesome. For a minute, there was unity. Nobody knew each other, but everybody starting singing it, just to piss off the cops. No one knew the words except for that part, but all of a sudden this one metalhead white boy started rapping the lyrics. I got goose bumps—all of a sudden, we all united through this fuckin' song, and then this timid white boy who hadn't said shit the whole time, starts, "Buddy you're a boy make a big noise..."—it was just beautiful! It was one of those moments when you were just like, "Fuck authority."

Eventually, we went before the judge. We didn't have any major priors, so they let us go. The only people who didn't start talking shit were all my craziest, illest Skinhead friends from back in the day, cats like Dagger and Spike, who came to New York around that time. Dagger fucked up anyone who talked shit about me; same with Bags. All the most violent ones still had my back 'cause they were my boys. But the rest of the NYHC scene pretty much started talking shit when I got into Krishna consciousness. All the fake Skinheads thought I was getting soft or something, and even motherfuckers I didn't know—'til I put a bunch of them in the hospital.

I kept hearing about this one Skinhead named JP that had supposedly kicked my ass. It was all over the place: "Yeah, I heard that JP kicked Harley's ass!" Meanwhile, I didn't know who the fuck JP was. When he was finally pointed out to me by this kid Yoko I knew, I was like, "That motherfucker!" I got pissed and started walking up to him. I said, "Hey JP, lets go for a walk." He started saying some shit about not going anywhere with me, and before he got it all out of his mouth, I started punching him, then I head-butted him in his face. That's what really fucked him up. He bent over wobbling, holding his face, with blood dripping through his fingers, both his hands over his mouth. I started picking shots and kicking him in the head and face at will. It went on for a while, right in the middle of the park, in the middle of the day. I had this big, pointy ring John gave me with a big silver lion's head on it, so whenever I punched his bald head, it would just bubble up and blood would start running out of it. Yeah, I fucked him up good; turns out I knocked out eight of his front teeth, his top four fronts and then his bottom four with the head-butt. It all happened right in broad daylight. You could never do that shit now.

After I fucked him up, I split for a while. When I came back, I walked up and the motherfucker was sitting there on a bench with his back turned to me and he was telling someone he'd been jumped by eight Puerto Ricans. I was like, "What, motherfucker?!" I was gonna fuck him up again. I grabbed him by what was left of his toothless face and instead of punching it with my fist, I looked him up and down and said, "Take off your boots," 'cause that's how we used to do shit. I took my punch knife and cut them off him. All these Puerto Rican dudes were laughing their asses off. The funny shit was I didn't wear leather anymore as I was already vegetarian, but I guess it was an old habit. So I held them up and said, "Who wants these?" Some chick said, "He stole them from my friend." So I gave them to her and said, "Here, give them back." Some comical shit all of it was.

So after I beat down a lot of the new-jack Skinheads for talking shit, quite a few people started following John and me down that Krishna path. "Krishna-core" and "Krishna Skins," that shit is laughable to me now. Those were terms given to us by the other idiots on the scene; we didn't come up with such dumb shit.

So, when John and me both got into Krishna consciousness, the devotees embraced what we were doing, because we were turning on a lot of Hardcore kids to it. They didn't say "Renounce Hardcore." They said, "Go out and preach Krishna consciousness," and that made total sense to me. I don't think Parris knew what to make of it; a lot of people didn't. But for a minute, it seemed like half the New York scene thought about moving into the temple. Of course I'm exaggerating, but a lot of people started getting into it.

I guess the whole non-materialism aspect appealed to people like us who had nothing. The spiritual thing was attractive to people who were disillusioned with everything around them, the material world, etc. It felt like here were some answers in such an uncertain world. And at one point, as we started getting more popular, we had all these Cro-Mag fans and groupies going to temple, trying to hang out with us and shit.

One night, me, Bloodclot, Watson, Crazy Dave, Todd Youth, and Louie, all ate a shitload of mushrooms. We freaked out, and decided everything was bullshit—that everything we were into and all the Hardcore shit and the material world was all an illusion—and we had to all move into the temple that night! So we all did, except for Louie. Well, that didn't last long. Bloodclot, who was always moving in and out of the temple, left that same night. So did Todd. They both snuck out separately at different times. Todd left when he saw they had no toilet paper in the bathrooms. They just had a little thing of water. He was like, "Fuck that, I ain't wiping my ass with my fingers!"

A few weeks after that, I went looking for John, and found him at the squat—sitting in our old pad, smoking a spliff, and listening to the Bad Brains. I went off on him, telling him, "Man, what happened to Krishna consciousness, dude? You still stuck on your false ego trip, bro?" He got all pissed. Eventually, I started to question if I was there for the right reasons. I had a meeting with the devotees and the temple President. They told me I would do more good for the spreading of the philosophy and the movement if I stayed out in the world, playing music and spreading the word. God gave me the gift of music for a reason, and that it was a blessing and that I should use it—that I would do more for the movement that way than by standing on a street corner handing out books. So with that in mind, I listened and left.

Of course, the Bad Brains had a lot to do with that whole shit by introducing religion and spiritualism to the New York Hardcore scene with Rastafarianism. With their influence, it just started a spiritual fire. Tomas, who lived with Jerry Williams at 171A, got into Krishna, and in turn got John Bloodclot and Watson and all those cats into it. Around that time, people on the scene were getting very political—left-wing/anarchy/peace/hippie Crass-holes, or right-wing pseudo-Nazi Skinhead, or straight edge, and everything else. Then there was John, trying to instill Krishna, vegetarianism, and good karma, but still always up to no good.

One time John talked me into trying to rob one of the weed delivery services. He was a grown man talking a 15-year-old into laying in the snow and hiding with him for like three hours—with fake guns—to try to rob a pot delivery service! He was like, "I know what room their safe is in, we've just got to grab somebody, put the guns to them, and force them to open it"—with our plastic-ass fake-looking guns. That's the type of shit this guy would do. Anyway, the robbery didn't wind up happening, because we ended up laying there all night, didn't get in, and we wound up abandoning ship. It was ridiculous: "the Hare Krishna criminal." He was so hypocritical that it was funny—it just added to his character. We were definitely the two most unsuccessful criminals as far as that went. I mean, he'd always manage to pull one scam or another and get by. But there were some really dumb moments. However, one thing that we were really good at was shoplifting.

Besides the free vegetarian food from Vinnie, it was up to what we could steal throughout the course of the day to survive. We were total kleptos when it came to that shit. I had a jacket with a pocket that was missing, so I could walk around looking like my hand was

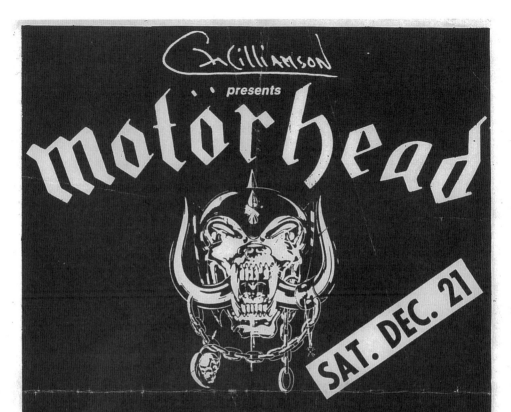

motörhead

SAT. DEC. 21

THE
CRO-MAGS

Doors Open 9 PM

Show starts 11PM
prompt
New York's Only

ROCK HOTEL
AT THE
RITZ

Doors Open 9 PM

Show starts 11PM prompt

11th St. bet. 3rd & 4th Avenues

INFO
279-1984
254-2800

in my pocket—meanwhile, I'd be filling my jacket full of shit, and they couldn't see it. We'd go into stores and walk out with over $100 worth of groceries! It was survival, you do what you have to do.

But like I said, some of the moral values that this dude was propagating—someone who was trying to live "the spiritual path"—were pretty ridiculous. He once told me, "Dude, you can convince anybody anything, if you convince yourself first." Then he gave me an example of a time he completely bullshitted his way on a cross-country bus or train or flight; just ask him, I'm sure he'll be happy to tell the story. He got a free ticket 'cause he accused the person next to him of stealing his wallet! First, he started looking through his shit, making a big stink. "Yo, where's my shit? Yo, where's my wallet? That shit was right here, in my jacket pocket!" Everybody started noticing; people started to help him look for it. He started flipping on the dude sitting next to him, threatening to kick his ass and to call the cops! He flipped out so hard. It was like, "Yo, how could he be lying?" It got to the point that the person next to him was so freaked out and panic-stricken from John freaking the fuck out on him that the passengers chipped in to pay for his ticket! Everyone was trying to help him find a ticket he never had!

Listening to him tell the shit, he was laughing his ass off the whole time: "You just gotta believe your own bullshit." I guess he's right, 'cause to this day people still believe the bullshit that guy says. But in his defense, he went through a lot of crazy shit growing up too. I don't blame him for being who he is. I mean, despite it all, I still have love for the guy—he was like a brother or as close to one as I had at the time.

Ultimately, the Hare Krishna influence was positive for me. Even Roger from Agnostic Front has said he credited that influence with saving me from prison or death. It helped turn me on to vegetarianism again, and over a period of time it definitely mellowed me out. It got me more philosophical. But since I had been a Skinhead and a hard-ass for so long, a lot of people on the scene started feeling a need to test me, to see if I still "had it."

Even people that I thought were my friends turned on me a little because of the whole Hare Krishna thing, people that I had been down with for years. It did bother me a little, but what can you do? I understood. I mean, I was confused and upset when Bloodclot,

Watson, and especially Eric got into it; I felt they were being brain-washed or something. I just didn't want to see my friends go—that's really what it was. And I guess some of my old friends felt that same way. But for the most part, it was the new jacks talking shit. That's when lines started getting drawn: who's down with Agnostic Front-Warzone-Murphy's Law, and who is down with John and Harley, etc. It was fucking lame as fuck.

Basically a lot of the new kids that we didn't give a fuck about—simply 'cause we didn't know them and didn't care—thought John and me were stuck-up, or aloof or some shit. Like we were better than everybody else or some shit. Maybe in some ways we thought we were. I know John always did, 'cause he talked shit about everything and everyone, like if you ate meat or if you didn't believe in the same religion. Whatever it was, I never really gave a fuck; I just didn't care what people thought of me.

Some of the guys who became Cro-Mags' roadies and some of our tight friends were also kind of following that spiritual path. Ironically, trying to spiritualize themselves, were some of the hardest motherfuckers you wouldn't want to fuck with. My boy Bleu was a black belt.

Bleu and me just had this weird chemistry. It seemed like every time we'd get together and go somewhere, we'd get in a fight. Not just a fight—we are talking serious beatings, where people would go to the hospital. It wasn't like we'd seek them out, but we had some weird karmic connection. Shit would fly, and people would get fucked up. It always happened, on the street, at parties, at shows. Him, me, my boy Stig, and Squint, they were vegetarians, too. It was funny, we wouldn't even wear leather; we were trying real hard to follow this path that we thought would lead us to a higher place. But at the same time we also had these beliefs that justified our violent streak, because we were somehow of the "warrior class," and were not meant to take shit from nobody. We had this weird idea of how we fit in philosophically into the whole thing. These guys were meditating and practicing yoga all the time, but we were also getting in fuckin' crazy fights all the time, and somehow it all made sense.

But in reality, I don't think I'm really that tough. There are plenty of people that could kick my ass. The only thing is, I grew up on the streets and around ill shit, and I just didn't give a fuck. If I got in a fight with someone big, I'd grab something off the street, like a bottle, something out of a garbage can, or throw the garbage can at them! And I did train a lot and spar hard with my homies, who were all either black belts or great street fighters. We'd work on combinations, kicks, stretches—even weapons. We'd wrestle each other and do full-contact shit; we'd beat each other's asses training.

But as far as being a badass, it comes down to heart. If you ain't got heart, you ain't got heart. It don't matter if a motherfucker is 90 pounds—if they are really "hungry" they're gonna eat you alive. If motherfuckers are soft, no matter how big they are, no matter how many people they're rolling with, they're still soft inside. When you wind up dealing with a crazy motherfucker who's got heart or who has no remorse in life, it doesn't matter how little they are. Trust me, I've seen big motherfuckers get their asses kicked by little ones.

But yeah, we were always getting into shit. If we didn't find it, it found us. One night, we were in D.C., and we were getting ready to go to the O Street Hare Krishna Preaching Center, to eat and hear the lecture. We were standing on the street, and two rednecks drove by in a pickup truck and said some crude shit to this chick that Bleu and Squint knew. We were about eight or nine feet away, so they didn't know that we were with her. So, being the assholes that we were, we had to make sure that they got reprimanded severely for their insults. We were probably just jonesing for an excuse to get in a fight or fuck somebody up, to be 100% honest.

So we jumped in the car, and we followed these motherfuckers for like three or four miles, until we caught up to them at a red light. We jumped out with shovels that this chick had in her car—I guess it was her dad's car—and we started smashing in their windshields and taking out the side windows. My boy Bleu wails a brick through one window. Then Richie Stig picks one up, hurls it through the broken window, leans in, and screams in the guy's face. Richie's brother David was there too, and he's smashing the car with a shovel the whole while. This one redneck is in his friend's lap, bleeding and cowering, while we're crushing their windows and the shovel is ripping holes in the hood of their car.

And then we just hopped in our car and drove away. Meanwhile, the chick that got insulted, it was her dad's car, and she doesn't want any part of this. The whole shit lasted three to four minutes tops. It turns out the shit happened not more than two minutes from a police station. So some passerby took down our license plate. After this shit goes down, we go to the O Street Preaching Center for dinner.

So we were at the Krishna Temple, having prasadam—food that has been offered to the Lord. All of a sudden, we hear walkie-talkies and see cops coming through the front door. We snuck through the temple room, where they just finished reading from Bhagavad Gita and everybody was eating. We tiptoed through the room, climbed out the back, down the back wall, and snuck out the back of the Hare Krishna Temple. Krishna Skinhead thugs—it sounds like something out of a Mel Brooks movie!

The thing about Bleu was, like myself, he wasn't a very big dude. He was under six feet, about 160 pounds maybe. He didn't look like a tough guy. He sounded like the kind of guy that you'd be like, "I will fuck this dude up." He just wasn't very intimidating. And that was the problem—he was kind of a magnet for people who thought that they were hard. And they would get fucked up.

One time, also in D.C., there was this big black Skinhead acting all hard, fucking with people in front of our show at the 9:30 Club. My boy Bleu looked at him like, "Who the fuck does this guy think he is?" The dude walked up to him and said, "You've got something to say? What's up, faggot?" And my boy just looked at him, like, "Yeah, all right." But see, Bleu would always try to be discreet about when and where he'd bust someone's ass. Usually, he'd wait 'til the end of the night, when our show was over and the gear and merch were packed up, and then he'd approach whoever had pissed him off, and basically take them the fuck out big-time. You have no idea how many shows we left peeling out of town with a bloody mess twitching behind us.

So anyway, he saw that guy again later in the club. The guy had made his way downstairs to the backstage and was walking toward the dressing room in a little hallway. And I walked up right as Bleu was pulling on his SAP gloves, which are police gloves—they have eight ounces of powdered lead in the knuckles. We used to all have those gloves. I saw him pulling the gloves on, and I knew someone was about to get laid the fuck out. So I ran up behind him and put my hand on Bleu's shoulder, and I'm about to stop him. I'm like, "No!!" And right as I said that—quicker than you could see it happen—he spun around, kicked this dude right in the temple. Mind you, this dude was like 6'4". The dude's head just cracked and tilted to the side. He was out before he hit the floor. And before the guy dropped, Bleu caught him with an overhand right while the dude was still frozen, with his head tilted to the side, a trickle of blood running out of a crack in the side of his skull. The dude dropped and hit the floor. He had plasma coming out of his head, and was twitching. Those were the kind of cats I was rolling with.

I moved into the temple for a brief period of time. I really did believe there was a higher purpose in life, and I knew I was missing it. That was one of the phases of my journey; I was trying to "find myself." One night on Avenue A, a bunch of the new-jack Skinheads made the mistake of starting a fight with Bleu, and John Watson and some other Krishna Skins. Bleu wheel-kicked one guy in the face, Watson bashed another dude's head in with a skateboard. The "attacked" became the "attackers." I got wind of this in the temple, that a bunch of my friends had gotten jumped. Even though these new-jacks lost, I still felt like they were attacking me and Krishna consciousness.

So that Sunday I left the temple, and I went to CBGBs with the intention of fucking those dudes up. I remember vividly the stoop across the street, right around the corner from the deli—eight or nine of those cats were hanging out on the steps. Billy Psycho was one of them, this kid Eugene, and a few others. Anyway, I picked up a quarter-piece of a cinderblock and wrapped it in a T-shirt. So basically it looked like I had a T-shirt in my hand, but I had a good-sized piece of rock. This big black English rude-boy Skinhead friend of ours, Errol, told me that he asked John Bloodclot, "Should we go give Harley a hand?" John just laughed and said, "Nah, he can handle this."

I started walking over. I walked up the steps, right up into the middle of them. Everybody moved a bit away from me, and I stepped right up to the main one who had instigated the whole fight the previous weekend. I said, "So what's up, Billy? You want to start some shit? You've got a problem? You want to fuck with my boys? What's up?" He wouldn't make eye contact with me—he was all stuttering, "Nah, nah man." I smacked him in his face, and all of his friends got up and started backing away. So I smacked him again, and he started tearing at the eye—you know how when you get smacked real hard, your eye tears up? He had a big old nice imprint on his face of my hand, and I was like, "So what's up motherfucker? You want to fuck with my boys?" At this point, he was backing away from me, and up the steps into the doorway. I was like, "What? You've got nothing to say now?" And right then, my boy Squint comes running past me and screams, "You lying fat pig!" It stuck in my memory—it was such a funny choice of words! He came flying up the stairs past me, and started pounding on this dude's face like he was working a speed bag. He hit him so many fucking times that this guy couldn't even raise his hands to defend himself; he was just getting pummeled.

So he scrambled and jumped off the stoop past us and started running. Squint chased him across the street and down Broadway. I turned to one of the other guys who was one of the main instigators. And I'm like, "What's up motherfucker? You want some?" Right as he made eye contact with me, one of my friends comes behind me with a sweatshirt with a brick in the pocket, holding it by the sleeves. He swung it over my shoulder, and caught the dude in the temple. The last thing the dude saw before he got knocked into a coma was me standing in front of him. So of course, he thought I did it to him. It was a bad scene. He hit the ground and blood started coming out of his ears and his nose. He hit the ground with such force that the impact caused his head to bounce back up, into sitting and then back down. He started doing "the fish" on the floor. When I say somebody's doing the fish, it's what we called it when they started twitching uncontrollably on the ground from getting fucked up real bad. Kind of like a fish that's not in water.

I've seen a lot of people do the fish over the years, but at that point it just turned into a really bad beatdown. I don't remember if I kicked him first, but I remember my friend Errol blasted him in the face with a 40-ounce bottle, and then Squint ran up and blasted him with a brick in the chest. It was overkill. This guy was getting fucked up, and he wound up in a coma for a while. Everyone at the matinee was all freaked out and upset. I just looked around at them all as they gathered around us. I was like, "What!? They started that shit!"

All those motherfuckers who thought they were badasses were crossing over to see what happened. They were looking at this kid in shock. I don't think most of them had ever seen that kind of a beating. I started looking at all the assholes and yelled at them, "See what happens when you fuck around!" I wanted all these fuckers to know, "Don't fuck with us or you will get fucked up!" That kid had to learn how to talk and walk again, but the way we looked at it, there were eight or nine of them sitting there. And when they jumped my boys, they outnumbered them. So, payback is a bitch. That's why we went after them with such intensity. Besides, at first, I went after them by myself. They started it that past weekend when they jumped my friends, so fuck it. But they all punked and scattered, then it turned into me and maybe three friends of mine taking on the whole bunch of them, and pretty much laying them to waste.

The rumor was I delivered the damaging blow that put him in the coma. But that wasn't the case. Anyway, no charges went against me. There were some retaliation attempts, but nothing that amounted to shit. After the dude finally got out of the hospital and learned how to talk again, we did a gig in Long Island like a few months later. It was at the club Sundance. Doug's friend Steve Jones from the Sex Pistols was hanging there with us. It was a great show, and we had a blast. I think Steve missed most of our set 'cause he was getting a blowjob in the dressing room.

But anyway, we were driving home from the show. We were speeding, trying to get home because it was late. We were doing like 70. All of a sudden, a black van pulls up next to us. The window rolls down, and a fucking cinder block comes flying at our windshield! It just bounced off the side window. We swerve, but our driver was able to recover quick. Steve Jones was in the van with us, and he was freaking, "What the fuck?! Who the fuck is that?" And me and Bleu are like, "Drive! Drive! Get after them! Step on the gas!" Steve is like, "No, no! Just let them go, let them go!" Anyway, they hit the gas, and just peeled away, so we lost them. But it was funny listening to Steve Jones freak out.

A month or two later, I was in the city near Houston and 2nd Avenue. I was sitting on a stoop in front of this bar talking to Petey Hines. All of a sudden, a van slowly pulls up, and the door slides open. A bunch of guys came piling out, with ball-peen hammers and shit, and came running at us. I jumped up and used my momentum to drive forward as I jumped up from the curb. I grabbed the first guy, and drove him straight into a parked car, and then spun around and whipped him in front of me. I was still holding him, so while everybody was trying to hit me with hammers and tire irons, I was using this guy as a human shield! I had him by the sides of his jacket, and I was just swinging him from side to side, keeping him completely off balance. So he was taking most of the shots. I had my back to the car, so no one could really swing on me. As soon as I saw a chance, I punched one guy in the face as hard as I could. His knees buckled as he dropped and I ran through the hole I'd just created. I ran about 30 or 40 feet, and turned around to see who was coming. That's when I realized that one of them was the kid that had been put into the coma. He had grown a goatee so it took me a minute to recognize him and figure out who he was. They were walking toward me spread out, through the middle of the avenue.

There was a little bar there on 2nd or 3rd Street near Houston, so I was backing away, trying to see who was coming at me. And as they started to make their move toward me, I turned around and just hauled ass. They jumped into their van and sped after me, so I started running the wrong way down every one-way street I could. I started zig-zagging, cutting a left on this corner, a right on the next one, so the van couldn't follow me. Then I ducked down and hid behind a bunch of garbage cans.

Right when I did that, I was like, "Oh shit, Petey is still back there!" So I picked up two 40-ounce bottles and ran back, not knowing what the fuck I was running into. I went back, still in "stealth mode." I actually lost one shoe in the fight, so there I was running with one fucking shoe on. My adrenaline was pumped: I was ready to bounce this fuckin' bottle off someone's head and smash the other one across someone's face. I was fully fuckin' ready, running up quietly. I ran up and found Pete in front of the bar—they were already gone. Pete had only been hit a few times, because really they were after me. A few people I knew were sitting in a car and saw it happen, but panicked and didn't do shit. It was over so fast. My boy Doug Crosby was in the bar; he was so pissed he wasn't there to help us, he was flipping. I had a knot on the back of my head from one of the hammers that got through and a trickle of blood running down my neck, but other than that, I was fine. I went over to Doug Holland's apartment and spent the night there.

It's one of those things that for years after, there were a few other people I was convinced had something to do with it. And I was gonna go after them. But enough years went by, the shit didn't happen. If it was meant for me to get back at them, it would have happened 30 years ago. It would have happened when it mattered. And as it turned out, a couple of the guys who I thought were in on it weren't, so it was a good thing I didn't act out on it. I might have fucked up the wrong people, so all in all it's a good thing.

For years, John had me believing Paul Bearer from Sheer Terror had something to do with it. Of course when I eventually confronted him about it, he nearly shit his pants, the fuckin' coward that he is. He denied it and denied it and pleaded and nearly fuckin' cried. The whole shit was fucked up. It was a hard time for me in some ways. Getting involved with this Krishna consciousness thing, it was sort of saving me from myself on one level, but on another level it was causing a new type of problem within the NYHC scene.

Chapter Nine

'THE AGE OF QUARREL'

CRO-MAGS, BY STACIA TIMONERE

et's talk about *The Age of Quarrel*. Some would call it one of the most, if not the most, influential NYHC and "Crossover" albums. It was recorded and mixed in under one hundred hours, over a 14-day period in January/February 1986 at East-side Sound by Steve Remote and Chris Williamson, our manager and so-called "producer." But it was really Steve.

We loaded in our gear and set up January 11, started tracking the next day; we recorded all the basic tracks in two days. That took us about 16 hours. Additional overdubs and mixing were done over 12 sessions, and we were completed by February 21.

Me, Doug, Mackie, and Parris all played together live in the same room, and John was in a different room tracking scratch vocals. Then he did his vocal tracks over in the main room. No click tracks, totally old-school. We just played like it was a gig or a rehearsal.

I blew out my bass amp the day we started recording. So rather than getting another amp for the session, Chris Williamson said "Play direct, and we'll overdub your bass later." Against my pro-tests that's what we did; I wound up playing direct and I got a real shitty bass sound, which made me play my runs and fills real half-heartedly. They claimed I would do the tracks over or that they would re-amp the direct signal. Of course that never hap-pened, so the bass sound sucks. I never got a chance to re-record my parts. I think I played better on the demo. John was sick when he was doing his vocals. He didn't even sound like himself.

Nonetheless, *The Age of Quarrel* is considered by many to be a classic album and I am grateful and proud of that. But I know it could have been better.

Most of the songs on *The Age of Quarrel* were written either at my aunt's house on 12th Street and Avenue A, at the building where Richard Hell, Ginsberg, and all those people lived, or at my aunt's house on Staten Island, where she moved later. Parris would come out there. I'd also go up to his house on East End Avenue on 82nd Street. I only stayed on Staten Island with her for a short time, 'cause I got in a fight with her then-boyfriend, and went after him with a machete! The cops came and it was a big problem, so need-less to say I had to move.

One time while I was still staying there, Eric Casanova and Little Chris came out there to hang, and they were all drunk and probably tripping or high on glue. But either way, they started kicking out windows on the Staten Island Ferry. They didn't put cops on the ferry back then—they got them a few years later when some dude freaked out with a machete and started fucking people up. But anyway, when the ferry arrived on Staten Island with Eric and Chris, they just stayed in the water until the cops arrived, and they arrested Eric and Chris. I was still kind of a fuckin' nut back then. The three of us were terrible, it was like the Little Rascals had grown up and gone bad—real bad.

When I was out on Staten Island, I'd sit in my room all fucked up, huffing glue, and blasting Venom, Skrewdriver, Cockney Rejects, and Hardcore shit. One time, I was high on glue and I tried to walk into the store across the street where I used to buy the shit. I walked in and grabbed the entire box of glue from behind the glass counter. I remember thinking, "They won't notice me if I just do it and don't pay them no mind." But there was no one else in the store but me, the Pakistani guy behind the counter, and his wife!

I just walked over, walked behind the counter, slid the glass case open, and grabbed the whole fucking box. He started yelling some shit like "Hey you, what are you doing?!" I turned around and said, "What the fuck are you gonna do?" and threw the entire box at his face, besides the few tubes I kept in my hand. The glue tubes went flying everywhere when the box hit him in the face. He started screaming at me and his wife was flipping out. I told him, "Shut the fuck up—I'll burn your fucking store down!" And I walked out. I went back upstairs and sat on my fire escape, huffing glue and blasting music. The whole while, I was taunting the storeowner, who I could see from my fire escape through his store window—giving him the finger, and huffing my bag.

I was a belligerent maniac, and didn't care. I mean, there was a police station just a few blocks away, and I just didn't give a fuck. I was so high already, I honestly thought that if I walked in there casually and just grabbed the whole box right in front of them, that they wouldn't notice me, even though there were no other customers in the store. Damn, glue really fucks up your brain and makes you do some evil and stupid shit.

I wrote some of my favorite riffs around that time period—it was just from the level of intensity in my life, I guess. The songs had

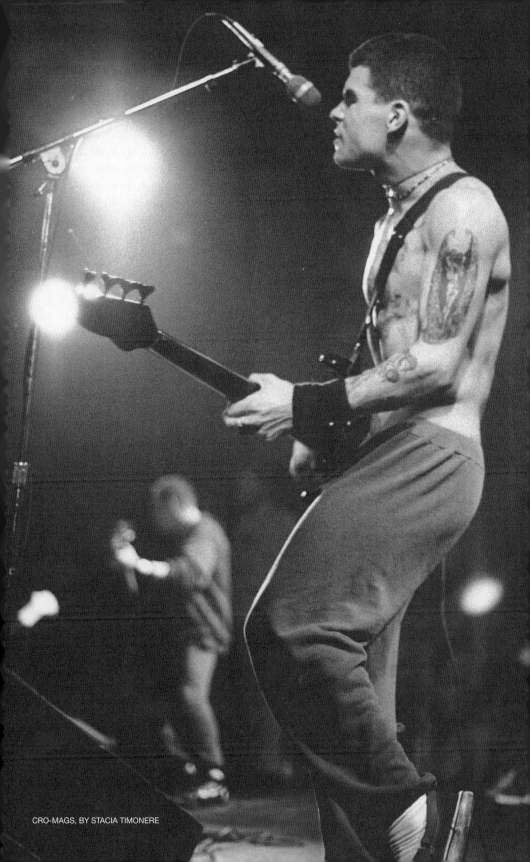

CRO-MAGS, BY STACIA TIMONERE

most of the ingredients that would be used in future Cro-Mags songs, the same kind of chromatic chord progressions—a Discharge-meets-Motörhead with maybe a bit Venom kinda vibe to it.

Most of that album's songs, Parris and me worked on together. We were the songwriters of the band. But honestly, I have to say that none of the songs would have sounded the way they wound up sounding had it not been for a little bit of everybody. It was just the chemistry of all those people. I mean, I've played with a lot of people over the years. I can play with almost anybody, and I write songs that sound like the Cro-Mags. Just like Lemmy can play with anybody and write songs that sound like Motörhead. But that initial sound, as far as the standard that was set, came from that group of people together.

The title *The Age of Quarrel* comes from *Bhagavad Gita*. This age we're living in is referred to as "the iron age of quarrel and hypocrisy." It's the final age of the four ages, before the annihilation of the universes.

One day, I was going in to record the album, and I was coming from a matinee at CBs where there had been a major brawl, and my friend Bags had bitten this dude's thumb off! He looked up at me, with blood all over his face, and screamed, "Harley! Get me out of here!!" I'm like, "Oh great, everybody knows my name, and I'm attached to this mess." So I grabbed the asshole and started running down the street.

He was pulling pieces of fuckin' skin out of his teeth. He literally bit the dude's thumb off in a fight, and spat it in the drainage pipe on the side of the street right in front of CBs, so that shit was gone. It wasn't even a sew-it-on type job.

We were running and I got him into the 2nd Street apartment of Robbie CryptCrash and his then-wife, Michelle. I ran him in there, and I said, "Do not let this fucking asshole out of your sight! Do not let him outside, the cops are everywhere." You can't miss the motherfucker—he's got a scorpion tattoo all the way up his neck to his ear, on his back he had a big skull made out of naked bitches, on his arm he had "Worship Shit" tattooed backwards, and on his chest he had "I Eat Pussy" tattooed. The guy was a fuckin' mess. I think he got out of jail just prior to that. He was drunk, and the guy he fucked up started trying to gouge his eyes, so the thumb came off.

PHOTOS BY KEN SALERNO

When you're fighting, shit happens; I almost bit a guy's finger off once. Fortunately for the guy, I have a missing tooth on that side of my mouth, so his thumb slipped into the missing spot, and I just kind of gnawed all the meat around the bone off. But like I was saying about my friend, I was like, "Don't let this mother-fucker out of the house." He was being so belligerent. With what just happened, I knew the cops were looking for him all over the neighborhood. So I left him there and I went from that back to the studio to finish recording.

It was just another day in my fucking life. Of course, they were not able to keep his out-of-his-mind ass restrained, because every-body was so afraid of him except for me and a few of my friends. He went back out on the street, got caught, and went to jail for a considerable amount of time.

This kind of shit made the lyrics on The Age of Quarrel raw, real reality. "We Gotta Know" had some of the first lyrics that John con-tributed, those and "Face the Facts": "Strugglin' in the streets just trying to survive/Searchin' for the truth is just keepin' us alive"— that's pretty much where John and me were at that point. He was just beginning his spiritual quest. You've got young people that are confused, making mistakes and looking for the truth, looking for answers. The lyrics are powerful. "We Gotta Know" was written when we were practicing at Westbeth, a big tenement and artist complex on the Westside highway where a lot of our friends lived, including the Ice Men, Front Line, and Gabby Abularach, who years later would play on Alpha Omega.

It came together like this: the Bad Brains had not played the song "I Against I" in years; this was before it was on their I Against I al-bum. But my friend Dave Hahn, their old manager, had a copy of it on tape. When I'd go to his house, I'd listen to it, and I still remem-bered the song. But I didn't remember it well enough to cover it, which I wanted to do. So I wanted to write a song that was as nasty and vicious. At the time, Mackie and the Bad Brains had been turn-ing me on to a lot of fusion shit, and I had started picking up on a lot of it on my own, whether it was Return to Forever, Mahavishnu Orchestra, or Weather Report. A lot of it had big open chords with crazy drum fills over them. Though some of the parts sounded re-ally complicated, sometimes they'd actually be very simple.

CLOCKWISE FROM TOP: HARLEY, ADAM YAUCH, AND FRIEND,
PERSONAL COLLECTION; HARLEY, MOM AND FRIENDS AT MAX'S, PERSONAL
COLLECTION; PHOTO BY DAVE PARSONS MIR.

Stories &
Illustrations by
Harley

Introduced by
Allen Ginsburg

Barbaran Press

CLOCKWISE FROM OPPOSITE:
HANGING ON ST. MARKS PLACE,
PHOTO BY DAVE PARSONS MIR;
TRIPPING ON LSD, PHOTO BY
DAVE PARSONS MIR;
HARLEY AND GRANDFATHER,
CONEY ISLAND, PERSONAL
COLLECTION; *STORIES &
ILLUSTRATIONS BY HARLEY*,
ORIGINAL COVER.

people who app...
and roll, who understand it
and have it as their own.
But I do not want the kids
who go into Central Park
with a can of beer in their
hands."

★ ★ ★

The Stimulators are a
new wave band with a twelve-
year-old drummer who usu-
ally plays places like Hurrah,
Max's and CBGB's, but last
night they performed at the
Rainbow Room for Lynette
Widder's Sweet Sixteen party.

★ ★ ★

Governor Jerry Brown

CLOCKWISE FROM LEFT:
HARLEY PLAYING WITH STIMULATORS,
PHOTO BY GLEN FRIEDMAN;
STIMULATORS NEWSPAPER CLIPPING;
OLD EAST VILLAGE LANDSCAPE,
PHOTO BY BROOKE SMITH.

LOUD Fast Rules!
Run Run Run

STIMULATORS

STIMULATORS RULES!

TR3

W/ BAD BRAINS
THURSDAY, DEC. 27
225 WEST BROADWAY

CLOCKWISE FROM TOP LEFT:
HARLEY PLAYING WITH STIMULATORS,
PHOTO BY GLEN FRIEDMAN;
SID VICIOUS STIMULATORS POSTER,
PERSONAL COLLECTION; TR3 FLYER,
PERSONAL COLLECTION; STIMULATORS
LOUD FAST RULES, PERSONAL COLLECTION.

max's kansas city

213 PARK AVE SOUTH AT 17th STREET

THUR. SEPT. 28

SID VICIOUS
PURE HELL

FRI. & SAT. SEPT. 29 & 30

SID VICIOUS
THE VICTIMS

TUE. OCT. 3

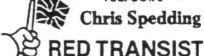 **Chris Spedding**

RED TRANSISTOR
STIMULATORS

24 HR SHOW INFORMATION

777-7871

STIMULATORS

CHEW'N'SIP DELI

FRI. SAT. JAN 25, 26 AT CLUB X

$3.00

5th AVE OFF 17th ST

Noisy World

CLOCKWISE FROM TOP LEFT:
HARLEY AND NICK, PHOTO BY GLEN
FRIEDMAN; DENISE AND HARLEY AT
MAX'S, PERSONAL COLLECTION;
HARLEY AND LITTLE CHRIS WANDRES,
PERSONAL COLLECTION; PHOTO BY
DIANE GOLDNER; STIMULATORS FLYER,
PERSONAL COLLECTION.

CLOCKWISE FROM TOP LEFT:
CRO-MAGS AT CBGB, PHOTO BY DAVID
WALLING; HARLEY WITH LEMMY, PHOTO BY
FRANK WHITE; CRO-MAGS AT THE RITZ, NYC,
PHOTO BY JJ GONSON; JORGE ROSADO AND
HARLEY, PHOTO BY STEVEN J. MESSINA;
PHOTO BY NAKI.CO.

GOOD VIBRATIONS & SESSION MUSIC PRESENT

BELFASTS 1st PUNK & NEWWAVE FESTIVAL

ulster hall   fri 15th aug

STIMULATORS STAGE B
OUTCASTS   STARJETS
ENPRODUCERS BIG SELF

sat 16th aug

STIMULATORS SAINTS
SHAPES PROTEX   RUDI

TICKETS £2.50 per Night : £4 for both nights *available from:*
SESSION MUSIC, York Street, Belfast
GOOD VIBRATIONS, 102 Gt. Victoria Street, Belfast

CLOCKWISE FROM TOP LEFT:
C-SQUAT, PHOTO BY STEVE BUTCHER;
GARRY SULLIVAN, PHIL ANSELMO,
HARLEY, ROCKY GEORGE AND JEFF
HANNEMAN, PERSONAL COLLECTION;
SAMSARA STICKER; WHITE DEVIL
FLYER; HARLEY AND ROCKY GEORGE,
PHOTO BY BJ PAPAS; BELFAST
FLYER, FEATURING THE SAINTS, THE
OUTCASTS, ETC...

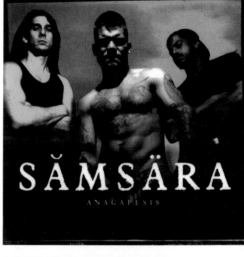

SĂMSÄRA
ANAGAPESIS

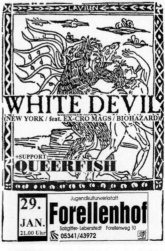

WHITE DEVIL
(NEW YORK / feat. EX-CRO MAGS / BIOHAZARD)

+SUPPORT
QUEERFISH

29.
JAN.
21.00 Uhr

Jugendkulturwerkstatt
Forellenhof
Salzgitter-Lebenstedt Forellenweg 10
05341/43972

CLOCKWISE FROM TOP LEFT:
PHOTO BY BJ PAPAS; RENZO GRACIE, HARLEY
AND BOYS, PERSONAL COLLECTION; HARLEY AND HARLEY
JR., CBGB, PHOTO BY JOHN GIUSTINIANI; L'AMOUR,
BROOKLYN, PHOTO BY FRANK WHITE; HARDCORE SAMURAI,
PERSONAL COLLECTION; BLACKBELT CEREMONY WITH
RENZO GRACIE, PERSONAL COLLECTION.

TOP TO BOTTOM:
HARLEY AND THE BOYS
JUNE 2016, PERSONAL
COLLECTION; PHOTO BY
FRANK WHITE; IF YOU'RE
NOT BLEEDING, YOU'RE
NOT PLAYING HARD
ENOUGH, PERSONAL
COLLECTION.

The intro to "We Gotta Know" was my dumbed-down version of a fusion idea: holding a few big notes, and filling up that space with those big drum fills. But if you really listen to the main chunk of the song, it's inspired by the end part of "I Against I" that Doc does the lead over.

The guys were on a piss break during practice, everybody was out of the room. It was like a maze in there—Westbeth is a huge building with rehearsal studios, recording studios, and art studios—so it took a while. By the time they came back, I was like, "Yo, check this out guys." I played the opening chords to Mackie, and I said, "Do some crazy shit over this; just fill it up." Mackie always had a funky bounce to his playing, so that on top of my chords made for an inspired attack or groove. That was one of our most famous songs, and it came together in five minutes! And even back then, we had parts with double kick drums, which had never been done ever on a Hardcore record at that point.

"World Peace" was one of the first songs me and Parris collaborated on. He came up with most of the riffs and we arranged it together. It was a Cro-Mags version of a Motörhead-type song; we just repeated all the parts twice, and had the breakdown at the end. It was probably the fifth or sixth set of lyrics I ever wrote.

"Show You No Mercy" is another song about LES street fighting. John wrote most of the lyrics to that one. In that song are lines that referred to people and situations that were happening at the time. "Show you no mercy at all/Gonna kick you when you're taking your fall" had a lot to do with that fight that took place in front of CBs.

"Malfunction" I always felt was like a peek into John's psyche. He says in the chorus, "I'm tryin' and I'm lyin' but I just can't get through to you." But that's him—he tries, and if that doesn't work, he lies! It's such a Freudian slip. It's such a great song; it's one of the first metal-style songs from a Hardcore band. It has a bit of a "Sabbath Bloody Sabbath" influence in that particular part of the song.

"Street Justice": "If it really doesn't matter why do you care?/ Don't turn around if it's not your affair." One night on Avenue A, Eric Casanova beat on Matt from this band called Hellbent. I think it was over a girl. Either way, Eric was real drunk. At some point in the night, he had ripped his pants all the way in half from like right under the belt loop in the back to right under the zipper in the front. While he was beating Matt's ass, he ripped the last shred of material holding his pants together. So Matt started running, and Eric was chasing him up 8th Street toward 1st Avenue. His pants were ripped in half, so they balled up around both his ankles! He had on long johns, his combat boots, and his suspenders that were on his jeans, dragging behind him leaving sparks as he ran. He looked like a fucking maniac. He was chasing after Matt, who begged him to stop. Jimmy and me were tagging along, just to keep an eye on Eric, 'cause he was so shitfaced.

As we got around the corner, a group of college-type yuppies were standing there. They didn't know what the fuck was going on, but they saw Eric chasing Matt. So one of them said, "Hey dudes, don't fight..."—all like trying to intervene. Eric turned around and cracked that guy in the face, at which point the guy's friends had no idea what was going on. Matt kept running, and Eric kept beating up this guy. Jimmy and me came running up. I grabbed a milk crate from in front of the store and started beating those people with it. Jimmy knocked some dude down the stairs into the basement of the store, and started kicking him as he was trying to come back up. So in a matter of seconds, me and Jimmy are fucking up like five people!

Eric fucked up the one guy, and Matt got away. All of a sudden, the cops pulled up. I ran, and Jimmy ran around the corner and dove under a parked car. They drove right past him, while other cops were coming on foot. They ran past him, and I got away. Needless to say, Eric got popped. I saw them pulling away with his drunk ass in the car, in his fuckin' long johns and combat boots! The shit was fucked up, but it was hysterical. So that's where that line "Don't turn around if it's not your affair" comes from.

The line "Overpower—Overcome" came from one fight we got into at a party in Canada. Bruno, after he kicked the shit out of a dude, picked the dude up over his head, and yelled, "Overpower! Overcome!" before he threw the dude down the stairs. "Survival of the Streets" included memories of living in C-Squat. Two lines in particular: "Wake up with the gun on my head" and "If the beast pulls the trigger, I'll wind up dead." The lyrics were real; it wasn't made up. That's how we were living.

We woke up one morning, and the first thing we saw was the cops kicking in our door and throwing guns to our heads! They were looking for a dude who was wanted for multiple murders, who had been staying in the building on and off. We'd just woken up, and we were getting ready to light up a spliff of Hawaiian purple bud. Louie, the singer from Antidote, was there too, and he threw the joint out the window in a panic. Once the cops realized we weren't who they were looking for, they were like, "Don't worry. If you see this guy, let us know."

Sure enough, a few days later, I was lying there, and out of the corner of my eye, I saw something glimmer through the window. I backed up, and said, "Who the fuck's out there?!" I backed up and I picked up a stick. I saw this shape come into the window, and it was the guy they were looking for. Turns out I knew the kid from the neighborhood. The glimmering/shining thing turned out to be scissors in his hand.

In a lot of the songs, the messages are the same: the "don't fuck with me" outlook on life. Like "It's the Limit": "Why you messing around with me/Pushin' me around/Values changing, But I can't get caught in it today/We won't lose with what we've got/'Cause we'll just sit and watch it all rot." Then "Seekers of the Truth" was more of a metal song than it was a Hardcore song. We never intentionally tried to write anything metal or Hardcore. We just tried to write songs that we liked and were up to a certain standard.

A lot of the lyrics had undertones of spiritual knowledge, because the materialistic aspects of life are all going to crumble, and then we're going to be left with nothing. "As this age progresses, and gets more and more degraded..." wasn't just inspired by our street experiences, but also from reading the *Bhagavad Gita*.

The lyrics in "Hard Times" speak for themselves. It gets redundant to keep writing about that shit, but at that point in life, that's how me, Eric and John were living. Again, that was the difference between Hardcore and metal; we wrote about real-life experiences. More or less, the whole album's about the same goddamn thing! But the line "Cro-Mag, Skinhead, Breakout, Now" had particular meaning to me, 'cause I was a Cro-Mag evolving. I was a Skinhead and I knew it was time to break out of the life I was living.

227

John wrote the lyrics to "By Myself" but I went over them with him at the end. It was kind of one of the Cro-Mag "template songs"—one of the musical blueprints. "Don't Tread On Me" was on those solo demo recordings that I did. It was one of the few songs that carried over from my days before I started playing with those guys. "Face the Facts" was one of our most Krishna consciousness-type songs. The first album didn't have a lot of those overtones, but that song was leaning that way. It was one of the first songs that me and Parris wrote together.

The music for "Do Unto Others" was very Minor Threat-inspired, but with a New York style. It was written before I started down the road toward Krishna consciousness, and whatever other spiritual paths that crossed my way. So a lot of those songs were still rooted in my street experiences and my Skinhead-ness. "Do Unto Others" was written right as we were crossing those roads. John and I put that song together.

"Life of My Own" was one of our first songs. I feel that lyrically, it's one of our most significant songs. Eric and me wrote it. The riffs came together when we were practicing in one of our early line-ups with Parris. We didn't have a full band, so I was switching between drums and bass while we were auditioning others. I remember this guy Steve Psycho, who we started calling Stevie Love almost as a joke, because he really was a psycho. He tuned up his guitar and hit three notes. Those three notes sounded good to me, so I added another note, and turned it into "Life of My Own." The album's last song, "Signs of The Times," is some Motörhead-style shit, but with our own unique twist. But you can definitely hear the influence.

For the cover, we wanted to use this painting from the *Bhagavad Gita*. It's a mushroom cloud with all the "sinful" activities going on inside of it. When I say "sinful," I mean as according to Hindus, Buddhists and so on—acts of violence against animals, children, and humanity, drugs, illicit sex, gambling; all the actions of man that are causing the world's turmoil. Alex Morris, the original guitarist for Murphy's Law, updated the art a little for us. He added dogs fighting, pornography, a punk rocker shooting drugs, a doctor dropping a baby in a garbage can, and a father beating his kid with a belt. And one part of it had two gay guys in it. Some people at the label who were gay got all pissed off but it also had straight people, pornography as well, strippers and so on. But it was too offensive for Profile Records, who distributed Rock Hotel Records. Too offensive for a hip-hop label, can you believe that?

It goes to show how long ago it all was. We insisted that they use the artwork, but they wouldn't let us, so we said, "Fine, use it as the inner sleeve, and we'll put a photograph of a nuclear explosion on the cover." So they did. Profile printed the "controversial" art on the inner sleeve, like they said they would. But instead of printing the color art we'd given to them, they printed it in red—a color that completely blurred all the stuff they found offensive. It was so obvious that it was intentional. So we were like, "Yo, fuck that. If you're gonna censor our shit, you better print 'censored' over it, so people know you censored it." So after a short stalemate, that's what they did. We ended up with that classic photo on the back cover, which was the most appropriate cover for that album.

That controversial artwork did get used on a 10" bootleg of the original demos that this kid in Switzerland made off the original cassette. It came out on a limited pressing; the cover was in black-and-white and it had a Hare Krishna mantra etched into the vinyl. They are hard to find: there were like five hundred with the Cro-Mags written in red, and five hundred with it written in green, and they're numbered. I was pissed at first that it was bootlegged, but when the kid found out that Profile never paid us, he sent me all the money he made, as well as copies. He said he just loved that original recording so much, and it wasn't available for people, so he wanted to make it available. I wish everyone who pressed my shit without telling me was that cool. Like I've still never seen a check from Profile, but that's another story. I think that was Chris Williamson and Rock Hotel, or as we called it, "Rock Hell."

One of the reasons we were one of the first Hardcore bands to break through, or cross over, was because MTV played our "We Gotta Know" video. That video turned on much of the country to Hardcore and/or slam dancing and mosh pits. Suicidal Tendencies was the only other Hardcore band that had a video on *Headbangers Ball*. People who were not involved with the Hardcore scene had never ever seen that kind of shit before.

I don't think people realize just how many doors that video opened for other bands. When *The Age of Quarrel* came out in 1986, rock videos kind of sucked, and all of a sudden you have an MTV video with people throwing their bodies off stages, swinging fists around, kicking each other, people covered in tattoos with their heads shaved, screaming about really heavy shit. It was exciting to watch.

It started to sink in that the Cro-Mags were beginning to make some waves when we started meeting big bands that were into us. Metallica came to see us at L'Amour in Brooklyn, and came backstage to hang out. That was the early stages of "crossover," when metal bands started noticing Hardcore. Once again, it goes back to the "We Gotta Know" video. Jason Newsted had just joined the band, and James Hetfield was still a complete maniac. In fact, James walked up to some kid that was wearing a Megadeth shirt, ripped it off of him, and walked away! He grabbed it by the collar, ripped it down the front, and the kid was like, "I just had my shirt ripped off by James Hetfield!" It made his fuckin' night.

We were selling out clubs like the Ritz—and that was as big as you were going to get for a Hardcore band. I was on the "house guest list." I had a reserved table, and all that fake rock star bullshit you get when you're halfway hot shit. I remember going to see Alice Cooper. After the show, I was upstairs, and he came walking through the crowd at the end of the night. I walked up to shake his hand and pay him respect—he's a legend. So I was going to just give him his props, and as I walked up to him, he says, "I recognize you—you're in the Cro-Mags." I was shocked. But I was in all the metal magazines at the time. You'd open up a *Kerrang!* or whatever, and it would have Ratt on one page, and you'd flip it over, and there would be me with no shirt on, lookin' like a fuckin' gargoyle.

Bands like Pantera, years later, they gave us mad props. That shit meant a lot to me. When you live the life I've lived, take the little bit of skill that you have developed and get some recognition from that, it does feel like some kind of accomplishment because Dimebag Darrell was one of the sickest guitar players of our time, and he gave us mad props. Phil Anselmo came up and sang a song with us in Norway. Phil goes to me, "I feel like we were twin brothers, separated at birth. Without you, there would be no me." We did have a connection, and Pantera is and was one of my favorite metal-style bands.

David Bowie was also very cool. I was on a Tin Machine music video shoot; me and a few of my friends got recruited on the street to be extras, offering us some money to be in the audience. I ended up doing a lot more at the shoot than just being in it; I helped with crowd control, and this and that. It was a good time. We hung out for the whole day. He wound up getting in touch a few times after that through my grandmother 'cause I didn't have a phone. I'd give her number out if people needed to reach me. On MTV he actually said, "I'd like to say 'What's up' to Harley of the Cro-Mags and his grandmum."

Whenever he called, he'd stay on the phone with her for a while. I'd come out to see her, and she'd be like, "Oh your friend called, David." I'm all, "David who?" "David Bowie!" she says, like it ain't no big deal. One time he called and told my grandmother he was getting married before the media knew about it. The guy's really down-to-earth.

So, when I got heavy into Hare Krishna, I showed up at Profile Records, where Chris Williamson's Rock Hotel Records office was, and it happened to be on the day they were throwing a surprise birthday party for him. At that point, I got it into my head that I was done with music, the whole "material thing." I showed up in my Hare Krishna robe, with a tilock on my forehead, which is the mud from the Ganges River that the Hare Krishnas wear on their foreheads, my head shaved, and bead bags. Chris was like, "What's up?" I was like, "I have to tell you something, Chris. I'm renouncing rock 'n' roll." Our record just came out, and he was like, "What?!" I was like, "I can't do this anymore. I can't be around this type of lifestyle." All the things that someone who was on that path would say. He was like, "You can't! You're kidding me?!" He started having a panic attack. He was watching his golden goose take flight, right out the fuckin' window! I was like, "I'm sorry. I hope you understand—maybe someday you will."

By that point, I was walking toward the elevator, and he was like, "Harley, come on man, be serious!" The elevator door started closing, I looked at him, and I said, "Hare Krishna." It couldn't have been better timing, because they had just sung "Happy Birthday"! It was great, I dropped a bomb—on his fuckin' birthday.

Mike Schnapp worked at Profile, and he remembers:

"I first met Harley when I worked for Rock Hotel/Profile Records from May 1986 through February 1987. I was hired to be the 'promotion guy' for Rock Hotel Records, kind of like Artie Fufkin from Spinal Tap.

"When they came back from opening for Motörhead for six weeks, Harley was not quite the same. I realized he spent a real lot of time with Lemmy on this tour. He really looked up to Lemmy, and I think Harley saw in Lemmy a man that lived his life like he wanted to—by his own rules and took no shit from nobody. The influence of Lemmy made Harley the tough guy even tougher.

"Another time, the Cro-Mags came back to New York from a six-week van tour, and as was customary, they all piled into the record label's tiny office to tell us all the crazy stories that happened on the road. At the end of the workday, like 7 p.m., I was getting ready to go home, and I noticed Harley still hanging around—way after the rest of the band went to wherever they were living at the time. I told Harley I was going home, and asked if he needed a lift to wherever he was staying. He said that he didn't know where he was staying. Whoever the last person he was living with was, he was not getting along with them and was out on his own, so he had no destination.

"I was living two blocks from the beach in Long Beach, Long Island at the time, about an hour drive from the Downtown streets. I told him that he could ride home with me and sleep in the extra room in the house. I lived with a few roommates and there was a really tiny extra room with a mattress and a window on the side of the house. Harley accepted the offer and we drove out to the beach. Harley didn't know me very well, on a trusting level. A few days later, I found a big knife under my car seat. I guess he'd lived a life where he never knew if someone was going to try something on him, and needed protection.

"I came from a different place—a happy home with parents and no fears for my safety. He did not. I learned this, and came to appreciate that I had it easy and Harley didn't. So with the way I learned that he grew up, he had to always be on the lookout for anybody who was going to fuck him over or harm him. Once we got to the beach house and sorted Harley out with a place to sleep I remember him going right into the room and shutting the door. The next morning, there's Harley, standing in the living room looking happy, rested, mellow, chill and happy. Harley had always seemed to be the angriest person.

"He told me it was his best night of sleep ever! I didn't get it at first, in a tiny room with just him and a mattress? I guess that for once, he wasn't bothered by anybody, could just sleep in total privacy—as opposed to living in tight quarters on the Lower East Side, and also just coming off of a six-week van tour with no privacy. I asked him how he was feeling, and he just smiled and was so relaxed. He said that he left the window open and heard the waves from the beach, and said he never had that before in his life. That's the way I lived. But for Harley, it was paradise for one night."

Touring really was an escape for me. It was easier than regular life: I had food and a place to crash. But even when we were starting to gain a certain level of popularity, there was always all kinds of crazy shit going on—some of it I didn't even know about. I had fucked up so many people in the past, I mean, I could tell you so many stories. I still had a reputation for being crazy. Motherfuckers used to threaten people with me and shit; there were even times when John and Parris pumped me up to go after motherfuckers, and a lot of time, it was straight-up bullshit.

'THE AGE OF QUARREL' TOUR

Chapter Ten

PHOTO BY JJ GONSON

The Cro-Mags played with everybody back in the day—almost every Hardcore band that was around, and as the shows got bigger and the whole "crossover" started, we played with tons of metal bands too, so many that I can't even remember.

One of our first tours was with GBH; we did like a half a tour with them, then Agnostic Front picked up the other half. I met GBH on their first trip to the States when they were playing at Great Gildersleeves with Agnostic Front and CFA in 1983. They told me when they first arrived in New York, they didn't leave their hotel for days 'cause they were too scared! When they finally did, they met Eric, me, and this punk rock chick from Canada, Lisa Bat. We saw them walking down St. Marks Place, so we walked up and started talking to them. Within a few minutes, a photographer came up and started snapping pictures of us. Lisa started protesting, but he kept snapping away like we were on display, like some fuckin' zoo animals. After a few seconds of this, I grabbed the guy by his collar and kicked him in his face and knocked him to the ground. Me and Eric and proceeded to beat his ass for taking our pictures. It was a pretty bad ass-beating: stomped on him, field-goal kicks to the head. It ended with his camera smashed over his head and his face getting bounced off a fire hydrant. This was on 8th Street and Avenue A in broad daylight! GBH were shocked.

As we walked off, the photographer was still rolling around on the ground, trying to get his brains back together. Jock from GBH told me, "If you lived in England, you'd have a fucking Army!" Later that evening, they saw a Hell's Angel stab someone on 7th Street and Avenue A, so between me and Eric laying an ass-beating on that photographer and then that Hell's Angel, New York really lived up to everything they expected, I guess.

One night on that tour with GBH, me and Mackie and busted into a jam of Jimmy Castor Bunch's "It's Just Begun." Doug started ripping into some sick leads—some of the sickest shit I ever heard him play—and we just jammed out for a good 15–20 minutes. There was hardly anyone there, so I could see clear through to the bar at the other end of the club. I could see GBH sitting there with their jaws open, drinks still in their hands. It turns out Lars from Rancid was there. He told me years later it was one of the sickest things he had ever seen—it was a straight-up funk-punk-metal-fusion jam.

We were so broke on tour, I don't know how we did it. It was a very different world. We didn't have ATM cards, no cell phones, no GPS. John and me were out of control with the shoplifting, 'cause we had no money. We literally had pocket change between shows until we'd get to the club and got the buy-out money from the clubs for food, unless they were cooking for us or buying us a pizza. But me and John didn't have a place to live half the time. So at least when we were on tour we knew we'd get a hotel room with a shower, and a few bucks for food. But we were so broke, so we'd steal at truck stops and shit.

But John would take shit to a whole other level. One time, we were at a restaurant and we had our buy-outs from the club. We went to eat at this place nearby that the club had recommended. So John finished before the rest of us and split in a hurry. We didn't think anything of it; we paid, left and started casually walking back to the club. All of a sudden, the waitress came running up screaming, "You motherfuckers! Give me back my fucking tips!" And we were like, "What are you talking about?" She was screaming at us, and she was pissed. She was like, "One of you motherfuckers stole my tips off that table next to yours. I don't make shit working here; one table left me a good tip and one of you fuckers stole it!" We looked at each other like, "That motherfucker!" I was so pissed at John. We were so embarrassed—I went off on him when I got to the club. He just stood there not saying shit, looking stupid. Twenty minutes later, it was back to burning spliffs and preaching Krishna. It was ridiculous—but it was all part of his wacky personality.

Besides little bullshit like that, he was my boy—and we really had a great time. He was a funny motherfucker and we were friends. I mean, who doesn't have at least one friend that they've known forever who even though you know they are a dick, they are still likable. They make you laugh, and it's like you almost can't believe what they do.

On tour in support of *The Age of Quarrel*, we played with a lot of metal bands when all the "crossover" started—even stupid shit like Lizzy Borden, bands with huge castles set up onstage for drum risers and props. Our crowd would come and terrorize the shit out of theirs. It was funny some of the bands we would play with. But our first big break came touring with Motörhead on their *Orgasmatron* tour. That was cool as hell, and a big thrill for me. I loved Motörhead since I was like 14. I watched every set they played on that tour, and every sound check as well. I think my ears are still ringing from that shit 30 years later.

We used to gig a lot with Carnivore. That shit was hysterical 'cause they'd be out there in fur, throwing meat at the crowd; me and John were both vegetarian, so we were not down with that, but it was funny. Actually, at one point Pete Steele shaved his head. I remember him showing up at CBs with his head shaved, his jeans rolled up, and big-ass combat boots. He looked like a total skinhead, but he soon grew his hair back. I was always cool with Pete; I liked him a lot.

When we initially started going out with metal bands, there was always lots of drama, fights and chaos. I remember when Pete was in the band we played with Helloween or some shit, and it was a fuckin' comedy. That was in Minneapolis, I believe, and we were big there as far as Hardcore. We were supposed to be headlining, so the majority of the place was Skinheads and Hardcore kids. It was our gig; there was no question about it. We showed up and the whole stage is a fuckin' castle! The drums are set up on top of it, and we're like, "What the fuck!" So anyway, we show up for our sound check, and we all have our heads shaved and tattoos; we have no stage props. But these guys got their fuckin' 12-foot boa constrictor, and their mother's their manager, and she's being a real fuckin' douchebag—she's acting like, "Who the fuck are these bald-headed dudes? They're opening for us!" We were like, "Fuck this."

So there was a Laundromat/bar across the street from this place that also used to have concerts. We were like, "Fuck this, our contract says you still have to pay us whether we play or not. We'll play across the street for free, you'll still have to pay us, and everybody that came to see us will go across the street!" We called our manager and he looked over contracts. They finally came to terms: "Technically, it was a co-headlining bill."

They wanted us to set up in front of this castle, 'cause it was already set up, which left us with no room. Now, if you've seen John and me play, we were all over the place onstage, and running into each other. There wasn't a big enough stage for us. And these guys wanted us to set up in front of Castle Grayskull! It was fuckin' pitiful. So, I started doing spinning back kicks at the walls of the castle, trying to take the shit apart. We had to play with Pete on their drum riser, and I couldn't see him. It was fuckin' hilarious. He was scared of heights, so he hated it. And the best part of it was after we played, pretty much everybody left. There was like one row of people standing in front of the stage for them.

One thing about that night was there were a lot of Skinheads; they dominated the show. They were huge fans of ours and they were there to kick some ass. I remember looking out at the crowd and seeing a longhaired dude get beat up. After he got beat up, this one Skinhead kicked him in the face, and made sure to lift him up by his hair and look him dead in his face. I could see his lips move, and he said, "I did that!" As much as you don't see anything from the stage 'cause you're so wrapped up in your playing, you still see a lot of things in the crowd. I don't think people in the audience realize how much you observe and how many things catch your attention. That was one of those things that bothered me; it was fuckin' disturbing. Especially because back then, people had a lot of ideas about what they thought the Cro-Mags represented or were about. It did start to bother me that people were doing these things at our shows. It got to a point where we'd always have to stop during songs to stop shit happening in the crowd. It wasn't like that in the beginning.

It's hard 'cause you don't want to turn against your fans, or make it seem like you're turning against them. But when they're emulating you or "honoring" you in some way you don't want, it's just so not cool. With the Cro-Mags, there were so many mixed signals coming from that band: a Hardcore band with a Skinhead past, and then to top it off, Neo-Hindu beliefs. It was a strange mix. And being one of the first Hardcore bands to cross over into the metal world made for a big mess, and led to a confused fan base.

We gigged with Venom a few times here in the States, and once in Europe. But the first two with them were in *The Age of Quarrel* days. The first night in Chicago was one of my best memories I

have of a gig. We were getting ready to go on, and the show was packed with metalheads. The paper had described us as "Skinheads gone heavy metal mad." So we were getting ready to go on, and the crowd already hated us. We walked out onstage, and the whole place starts chanting, "Skinheads suck! Skinheads suck!" I walked out, plugged in, and my bass wasn't working. "Skinheads suck! Skinheads suck!" turned into "What the fuck! What the fuck?" Finally, Cronos loaned me his bass, and we start with "We Gotta Know." We blazed through the song, and then the next one, with all the energy and aggression we had, right back at them. They didn't know what the fuck hit them. When we ended, it was almost totally silent; they were dumbfounded.

We busted straight into "World Peace," "Show You No Mercy," and a few more, and the crowd started turning into a head-banging frenzy of freaks with their fists in the air. A few people were giving us the finger in the front row, so I knee-slid across the stage to this guy, and punched him dead in the face! Blood started gushing out of his nose, and I kept playing. He did it again, and this time John got him. The guy went from giving us the finger to giving us a thumbs-up. By the time we stopped long enough between the songs for them to react, we had totally won over the most hostile crowd. We had turned the place upside down.

Sometimes, when we'd do shows near the city, Chris Williamson would come along for the ride. Other times, he might use our gig money to fly himself to our shows. It's no wonder we never got paid. We'd be in the van, and Chris and John would be getting into it about Krishna consciousness; it was fucking hilarious. He'd be ripping into John, and John would be trying to debate with him about all kinds of stuff from the scriptures. And Chris would just tear into him. It always ended with John saying, "You're a demon, you're just a fucking demon. He's fuckin' Hiranyakashipu" (the demon killed by Narasimha on the cover of *Best Wishes*). Chris would always be like, "C'mon Harley, you're not buying into this, are you? I mean, I give you more credit than that. John I can understand, but you?" The rest of the guys would be giggling or smirking or straight-up laughing. As much as everybody fucked with each other, some of those van rides were hilarious.

We did some crazy gigs in Los Angeles. Our first two times there, Skinheads dominated the shows. It's funny 'cause at the beginning of the first show some Sui tried to hard-rock me before we went on. I just laughed. The first thing I said when I got onstage was, "I'd like to dedicate this gig to the L.A. Skinheads," so of course, the Skinheads went apeshit. It was some real violent, crazy shows. But the third time, people were getting stabbed and shit. The shows at Fender's Ballroom were really crazy. All the Skinheads would come out to see us, and gangs like the Suicidals would come out. Inevitably, there would be these massive fights between the two. Then on top of it, you'd get the Nazi Skinheads, the anti-Nazi Skinheads. Crews like SHARP, "Skinheads Against Racial Prejudice," and the LADS, "Los Angeles Death Squad." There were so many gangs. Almost every time we'd play in L.A., there was a riot.

Greg Hetson from the Circle Jerks was at one of our shows in L.A. At first, there were several fights. We were up in the balcony, and he was like, "Oh, that's nothing. This is L.A., it happens all the time." But within another 15 minutes, he was like, "Dude, I've never seen no shit like this before!" Our shows had a tendency to bring out so many warring factions.

At that same show, there was one huge Indian in the middle of the dance floor, knocking motherfuckers out left and right. He was going nuts, screaming, "Fuck you! I'm an Indian!" It was great; he was big like Chuck Billy of Testament or Chief from *One Flew Over the Cuckoo's Nest*. By the time we went on, half the crowd had been thrown out. There were fights breaking out everywhere, and bouncers would try to run over and stop them. They'd break out somewhere else, and then the bouncers would get caught in the middle of them, with fights going on all around them. They started getting fucked up, too.

By the time we came on, there was a massive wall of huge bouncers in red shirts standing in front of us across the stage. You couldn't even see the band through them! While we were playing, fights were still breaking out. There were still a few people in front of the pit trying to enjoy the show without getting dragged into a fight or hit by a fist or a chair. It was crazy as fuck. I don't remember how many songs we did before they turned the house lights on and chased everyone out, but it wasn't many. Outside, there were riot cops, helicopters, the whole shit.

There were a few other cities that were crazy for us, like Detroit and Chicago. I think it had to do with the fact that New York was the first city in the States to have a real Skinhead scene, and we represented New York at its "hardest." Some of the bad rep—maybe even a lot of it—was deserved, but a lot of it was exaggerated hype and bullshit. And that shit would follow us, and attract that type of energy, even though by *The Age of Quarrel* John and me were getting into Krishna consciousness. But my friends and me were known for fucking people up, and I guess that reputation and karma carried over into the reputation of the band.

Photographer Stacia Timonere remembers a show in Chicago: "The buzz was out not to miss this show and no one was disappointed. There was a lot of tension with some of the Skinheads at that time. They wanted to make punk about hate and most people in Chicago don't buy that stuff. I was expecting a fight, but I never thought the band would start it. I remember seeing Harley clock this guy with a follow-up from John, and I was thinking, 'Wow, I've never seen a band beat up their fans.' It was like, 'Shut up and listen!' Then they rocked so hard, the tension eased, and there was some kind of unity. Cro-Mags set it straight that night."

Sure, I've got a lot of great stories about those tours, but anyone who was part of it back then will tell you that there wasn't any money in it. We'd go on tour, come back, and there'd be no money. I remember one time we pulled up to Avenue A and Houston Street in the middle of the night at the end of the tour, and Chris would be like, "Well, there's the subway!" I'd be like, "What?! I just drove all fucking night, and now you're gonna tell me to get my bags and bass and jump on the train?" Needless to say, we started hating him pretty early on.

So, we had that tour with Motörhead all lined up, and Mackie quit right before it began. He was smart enough to know Chris was going to dick us over like he always tried to do when it came to money. After we did the GBH tour and didn't see any money, I guess he knew better. So we were getting ready for our first "big break" Motörhead tour and he wouldn't pick up his phone, wouldn't return calls, and made himself unreachable. That's when I approached Petey Hines from Murphy's Law. I told Jimmy Gestapo, "Bro, if it's all right with you, I need to borrow your drummer." I had no intention of getting him to quit Murphy's Law. I was just like, "Dude, you're the only drummer I know in town that's good enough to pull this off. If you bail me out here, I'll be eternally in your debt!" And Petey came out, and really pulled it off with just days of preparation. He was great.

The first show on that Motörhead tour was at the Orange County Pavilion. Megadeth was on that tour for a couple of shows. Motörhead's stage was set up and Megadeth's shit was in front of that. We had to set up our drums on the side of the stage, facing sideways. We just had the front of the stage to run around. We could barely hear 'cause we had no monitors but Petey saved the day. Even that show, with all those issues, was pretty great.

We did that tour in a van that was so run-down, dirty, and mangled. It was a 1969 Ford Econoline van our manager Chris bought from a plumbing company called Kendick in California, without ever looking at it. It said "Kendick" in big letters on the front and back; we wrote "We 'Kendick' U and WE Will" on it with a black marker in big letters. There was one row of seats in the back, so you had this empty space with a rusty floor for our gear and bags, and for our roadie Bleu, who could kick just about anybody's ass, but he always huddled up in a ball on the most uncomfortable spot on the floor 'cause he didn't want to take up space from the band members.

The Kendick van was in the "We Gotta Know" video, in the scene where we're all sitting in a van. Kendick started breaking down everywhere. We had no air conditioning, and there was an unbearable heat wave when we were in the desert in Texas. The engine was one of those ones that's inside of the van, with a cover over it. It was having problems, and it kept overheating so we had to drive with the cover off 'cause it kept breaking down. So the motor was exposed inside the vehicle, it was already hot, and only got hotter and louder. Then finally we broke down again, for the last time. We were done. We were in the middle of nowhere—Ozona, Texas, heading toward Corpus Christi. We thumbed a ride, and this Jeep pulled over with two Texas hippie-type dudes; one of them looked like a midget Willie Nelson! So, I shit you not: we cut the seatbelts out and tied our front bumper to their rear bumper and had them tow us like two hundred miles through the desert. The shit was insane.

We pulled into Ozona, pulled up to a red light, and John went up to a Mexican dude and asked, "You know where I can get any weed?" And the dude was like, "Well, I don't, but my brother does. He's a cop but he's cool though, he smokes." By that point, I was shaking my head in disbelief. I was saying to John, "Are you crazy? You can't be pulling this kind of shit in a place like this." He was giggling his ass off, spit flying everywhere. I looked at them and said, "I'm gonna walk into that store over there. When I come out, all y'all motherfuckers are gonna be handcuffed together." John was like, "Yo, I'm gonna get some killer shit. This dude's a cop, so you know he's got good shit!" I'm shaking my head like "This fuckin' guy can't be serious."

The night before, we were in some cheap-ass shitty hotel. Doug found a baggie of powder in the hotel room. Fake coke, it was talcum powder or some shit. So Doug, instead of leaving it, took it with him. When I asked him why, he said, "Maybe I can trade it for something with someone," and put it in his wallet. So, in Ozona, I go into the store, and sure enough, I come out, and those motherfuckers were cuffed together!

Those cops were total redneck cowboy fucks. They all had big white cowboy hats, custom engraved pistol grips, and pump-action shotguns. John looked up at me with a stupid look, grinned and went, "Guess what, Harley? You were right!" And the cops were like, "Are you with these boys?" So they handcuff me too. The only person who didn't get cuffed was Parris, I guess 'cause he looked like a big kid who didn't really belong with us riff-raff. One of them smiled and yelled, "Get some rope, we gonna have a lynching party! We got ourselves some Yankees!" and they all started laughing.

As it turned out, while I was in the store, John was going back and forth with this dude about his brother the cop who smokes weed who's cool like that. Dude, we're in a small town and we're the only rock 'n' roll motherfuckers, and we're from New York. So this dude is saying to John, "No, I don't want any money, I just want to trade something for it. You guys ain't got nothing to trade?" They're trying to entrap this stupid motherfucker's ass. So John and Doug are up trying to trade the fake coke for weed.

Now mind you, this all happened while I was in the store. So they were only able to arrest Doug and John. Although they weren't real drugs, for pretending that they were, it's the same crime. So they had them for possession of drugs, with intent to whatever the fuck; I don't even remember. They wanted $10,000 each to get them out! We were in this itty-bitty town where the precinct was connected to the courthouse where they did the sentencing. We knew we were fucked. They had Doug and John in a cell full of Mexican dudes just busted trying to sneak through something 'cause they were covered in mud; John claimed that they were covered in shit. It was like a fuckin' movie.

So we had to get in touch with our record company to bail out these dudes. We managed to get the money. Needless to say, we never went back to court for those guys, so I think probably to this day, John and Doug want to stay out of Ozona. So, we almost missed the show. Motörhead and their management were raising shit: "If these guys don't get to the show in time, they're off the tour." We got there just in time to play. All kinds of crazy shit went down on that trip; it could be a book in itself.

Our driver and main roadie on that tour was this guy Roger. We called him "The Horse." He lost his mind on that tour, and got committed after! He was this big, strong ex-Army motherfucker with long hair. He would always be looking at himself, fixing his hair, and he always wore a backwards baseball hat. He was like, "Fuck, I'll do five hundred push-ups, right now!"—and he'd drop and do five hundred push-ups right there, and then say, "I'll do another five hundred!" The guy was crazy but was mad cool. He'd do these long-ass drives, and talk and talk; a lot of times when it wasn't total nonsense, it leaned toward spiritual philosophy.

One day, I woke up, and Roger had this crazed look. He'd been vegetarian this whole time and was mad in-shape. He was inspiring in a lot of ways, but he wasn't buying our whole Krishna consciousness thing. At that point he was an atheist. So anyway, he'd been doing a crazy all-night drive and had this crazy look in his eyes. I asked, "Are you all right?" And he was like, "While you guys were asleep, I pulled over to a McDonald's and had a Big Mac." We were like, "What?!" Then he said, "Yes. And I found Jesus!!" We asked, "Where the fuck did you find him? At the McDonald's?!" He was stone-faced.

We started bugging. We were like, "How does Jesus condone hamburger? How does one thing have anything to do with the other? Eating meat, you might as well be murdering the cow—that shit is bad karma!" All of a sudden, Roger started swerving the van from one side to the other, and punching the roof of the van with his fist, real hard, going, "So you're saying you've got a murderer driving your van?!" And we were like, "No, that's not what we meant! Roger, what happened? Everything's chill, dude; you've been a vegetarian for years, what made you pull over and get a burger?" And he was like, "I don't know, man. I'd been driving and driving, I saw those golden arches, and Jesus told me to get a hamburger." So basically, he lost his motherfuckin' mind.

After the burger, Roger went on this fasting kick. All he consumed was warm water with salt. Now this fucker was jack-diesel; he was fuckin' big. He didn't eat for days, and his face became sunken in. By the time we got to Chicago, where he was from, they checked his ass into a mental institution! Chris Williamson later told me what had happened to Roger; it had something to do with his woman, another guy, a cat and the devil. I saw him years later, and he seemed normal, but who the fuck knows what's normal?

That tour was one crazy thing after another. Because Motörhead was headlining, they were mostly metal shows. There'd be other metal bands playing and then there'd be us, and we'd always have fans and friends showing up. One show in Texas with Motörhead was at the Longhorn Ballroom where the Sex Pistols played back in the day. It had all these big oversized cowboys and steers out in front. It was funny as shit. Anyway, Marc Dagger was living in Texas at the time and was in full-on Skinhead mode. By then, he'd been to prison and was even crazier than I remembered. He showed up with a whole crew of Skinhead buddies, and he was like the "big boss." Wendy O. Williams was also on the bill, who I knew from the old Max's days. It was a lot of fun, but I remember Marc and his boys went nuts during our set. By the time we were done, all the Skinheads had been kicked out by security. It was crazy. By like the second song, I saw Marc get in a fight, and three bouncers jumped on him. He punched one in the face, and put him down. The other one tried to grab him from behind, and Marc reached over, pulled the guy over his shoulder and onto the ground, and tossed the other one to the side. And then he started pounding. It took like five bouncers to get him out. I was trying to stop playing the song. All I could see was him getting dragged out, and layin' motherfuckers out the whole way.

All the other Skinheads followed his lead, and started getting in fights on the dance floor. So by the time we got off stage, they were all outside in the parking lot, drinking beer and waiting for us. Marc's like, "I'm sorry, bro. I just started dancing, and they jumped on me!" Which is pretty much what started it. Those Texas bouncers didn't know what to do when they saw that shit.

But anyway, we got invited to a party, so we loaded out and started driving. We got to within about two miles of the place, and we saw Marc and his girlfriend driving away. He pulled up to us, and said, "Yo man, you guys need to get the hell out of here; the cops are on their way!" I'm like, "What happened?" Well, the party was at this Skinhead chick's house. Her roommate was a college girl who hung out with all these jocks. So when all the Skinheads showed up, this girl already had a bunch of people over for a kegger. Well anyway, eyeballs were getting exchanged. The two girls got into a huge argument, and some jock said some shit about

Skinheads, and the shit hit the fan. Marc laid him out! The place erupted into a full-on brawl; people got stomped badly. People were running down these suburban streets, holding their heads with blood gushing out. Motherfuckers were passed out on lawns from the beatings. And Marc was like, "Y'all need to go, bro! I'll catch you guys next time you're in town. Love you man!" Yeah, good ol' Marc.

The first and one and only time Cro-Mags ever went to Europe on tour to support *Age of Quarrel* was in '87. It was me, John, Parris, Doug and Pete Hines. It was an incredibly short European tour and it would prove to be our downfall.

It only lasted from December 11th 'til December 21st. Our first gig on that tour was in London on the 11th. Then we played Leeds, Hamburg, Bochum, Mainz, Eindhoven, Katwijk, Antwerp, and ended in Paris.

We were in Motörhead's old tour bus. We also had their old driver, this old biker-looking dude. I loved seeing new places, and getting off the streets of New York. So for me, everywhere and every gig, I always put 110% into it; we really had intensity when we played. We didn't fuck around. I was proud of that.

We played a big festival in Leeds called Xmas on Earth. Megadeth was headlining, Nuclear Assault, Overkill, Virus, Kreator, Lääz Rockit; Voivod was supposed to play but didn't make it. It was a pretty historic event—all these thrash metal and crossover bands on the bill and then us. We were the only Hardcore band on the bill, and we were the first Hardcore band most of them had ever seen.

It was an insane gig. We pulled up at like noon and it was already nuts—people were already drunk and throwing up in front of the place. There was mud everywhere. The venue was huge; it looked like a big hangar. It was originally a tram and then a bus depot.

All the bands were all staying at the same hotel. It was total madness in the lobby, lots of fans running around, all the bands hanging out, press, everyone, milling around. I had never been in that type of environment before; it was my first show like that and the first big metal event or festival I had been to. That's probably normal for everybody into the big-time rock scene. But for me, that was a new thing.

I remember hanging out with Dave Mustaine, and everything was cool. There were mobs of adoring metalhead fans. We get on the elevator, the door shuts, and Mustaine goes, "Fuckin' assholes," shaking his head and laughing. I thought to myself, "What a dick." Those people are your fans! They may be acting like a bunch of groupie losers 'cause they were so over-the-top heavy metal, but I felt that he didn't appreciate the admiration of those fans. To me, that was always the big difference: Hardcore is "of the people," while metal is more of a "we think we're hot shit" type thing.

Then we had some crazy smaller shows after that: several in Germany, some of them full of Nazis, and a few in Holland.

One of the first gigs we played in Germany on *The Age of Quarrel* tour, Nina Hagen showed up at sound check with a bunch of Hare Krishnas and with a huge feast of vegetarian Hare Krishna food for us 'cause she had heard we were devotees. She didn't speak any English, we didn't speak German; it was funny as shit if you can picture the Cro-Mags, Nina Hagen and a bunch of Hare Krishnas having dinner.

That night the show was full of Nazi Skinheads. German Nazi Skinheads, in fuckin' 1987! They were serious about that shit; they were Sieg Heiling and they meant it. The club security was all U.S. Army guys, and most of them were black. So you knew the shit was not cool; these dudes were trying to pull the security guys off the stage, to beat them up. Going, "Nigger! Come on, fuckin' nigger!" It was so bad. Paul Thomas, one of our roadies, was black; he looked like Bob Marley in spandex pants, with a video camera, filming the shit. At one point, the shit got so hairy, John jumped into the crowd to pull one of the Army guys out of getting jumped. He was lucky he didn't get jumped himself. It was definitely an ugly situation.

I remember this one club we played at: "Club Scum" in Katwijk, Holland. It was this little place in the middle of what looked like farmland. It was this little square shack or bar in the middle of a field. The gig was jam-packed full of Skinheads. The owner was this big kickboxer. He wound up beating up several Skinheads throughout the course of the evening and throwing them out. He laughed and said, "I beat them up and throw them out every week, they come back next week, I do it again." It was a very funny gig. And the last gig on that tour was in Paris on December 21st with Motörhead.

Yes, that fateful gig…

The final *The Age of Quarrel*-era show with John was in France with Motörhead. Black Sabbath was scheduled to headline the show, but wound up not playing. It was around the time they'd played Sun City and had to cancel a bunch of shows due to boycotts and bad publicity. They never contacted the promoter or informed anyone that they weren't gonna show up; they just didn't show. So as the day progressed and it became obvious Black Sabbath was a no-show, they flew in Girlschool at the last minute. So there wound up being one or two opening bands, then we went on, then Girlschool, and then Motörhead. It was a great show—honestly, no one missed Sabbath not being there, because Motörhead just fuckin' smoked. I was so excited, because it was right after *Orgasmatron*, but Phil Taylor rejoined for a quick second, so he was playing with them that night. I remember playing our set and being super proud, with Lemmy and Phil Taylor watching our set from the side of the stage. Both of them were digging on us. There I was, a poor-ass Lower East Side kid playing in front of thousands of people, with Motörhead standing on the side of the stage, grooving, with me and John running all over the fuckin' place!

After that show, Doug Holland came up to me in the dressing room. He had a grin on his face, and he was looking all around to see if anyone else was in there. He goes, "Yo man, I found a wallet!" Now, Christmas was coming up. I'm like, "Yo nigga, hook me up—it's Christmas!" So he goes, "Come here, quick." So we went in the bathroom. Little did I know, Petey Hines was sitting in the stall, taking a shit. Doug looks at me and gets very serious. He pulls out the wallet, and he goes, "It's Chris' wallet." Chris Williamson, our manager. I was like, "Oh shit!" He opens it up, and it's $300–$350, plus his credit cards. Now mind you, Chris was sending us on tour in vans that were always breaking down.

We'd come home after two months of touring for no money at all, while he was living it up. Like I said before, I never forgot that time he dropped me off at Houston and Avenue A in the middle of the night after an eight-week tour, and was like, "There's the subway." He did such scumbag shit all the time. So my reaction was "Fuck that nigga, he's been ripping us off for years!" I know it was wrong, but we were young, we were broke, and we knew he was ripping us off. It was a bad move, but we were like two schoolkids that just found a wallet, and found out it belonged to the principal. So we split the money, and it wasn't much. I only got like $200. I knew I wasn't gonna make shit at the end of the tour. That was the last show on the tour, and I was gonna stay and visit my stepfather in Denmark, and the rest of the guys were going back to the States. So we said "Fuck it."

Anyway, the show ended and Doug and I split the money. Doug looked for a spot to drop the wallet, to make it look like it just "fell there." We didn't take any of the credit cards. By the time Chris found it, I'd already split. From what I understand went down, Chris freaked out, and knew that somebody stole his wallet because he never dropped it. Chris said it was taken out of his jacket. He said, "It was in the inside pocket of my jacket in the dressing room. Which means that somebody that was in the dressing room had to take it. Which means that one of you motherfuckers took my wallet, and I want it back, or else none of you are getting paid! That's that, cough it the fuck up!"

Well, Doug wouldn't cop to it. John started flipping the fuck out. Everybody was pissed. Then supposedly Pete took Chris aside and told him what he overheard in the bathroom. It was so fucked up. John was flipping; everyone was pissed off. This was such a downer for the last gig. And again, I'd already left the building; I missed the whole episode.

When I got back to New York, I heard the news that Chris had flipped, John had quit the band, and everything was in turmoil. From what I understand, John went apeshit, saying to Doug, "Motherfucker, I'll strip-search you right here!" Doug was scared shitless. I've heard, but I can't say for sure, that Doug rolled the money up, and stuck it up his ass! But as it turns out, there was $3,000 in the wallet but I only saw a few hundred. The whole band's tour money that everybody was supposed to get paid with was in that wallet. And I only knew what Doug showed me. I guess Doug went in the wallet, took the majority of it, left a bit in there—maybe to make himself feel a little less guilty, or maybe so he wouldn't get all the blame if he got caught. For whatever reason, he got me involved. But he sure as shit didn't split it with me; the motherfucker gave me a few crumbs off the loaf he just stole. And I never thought for a second it would turn into what it did. Damn, that must have been an uncomfortable plane ride home for Doug.

So anyway, now shit was all fucked up. I knew I was gonna be walking into some drama and chaos and shit. So I was like, "All right, fuck it." I went to Chris' office with my head all slumped down, and I'm like, "Chris, I just want you to know something. Me and Doug stole your wallet." He didn't know I'd already gotten wind that he knew the shit had hit the fan. I kept going, "I feel real bad about it." This motherfucker knew that I had no money and had nowhere to live—how fuckin' mad could he be at a kid, who has no money? Especially when we were playing all these big-ass shows, touring, and not getting paid. I mean I had nowhere to live. I was broke, and he had a phat pad on the Upper West Side and had money. I sure didn't think he was gonna take it out on everybody. So Chris forgave me. He was like, "Well, at least you're sorry." But that was the end of an era.

The only-ever Cro-Mags tour outside the States with John, Parris, Doug, Pete and me—ever. We never made it out of the country with Mackie. It was the end of an era and it was really the beginning of the quarrel. And as much of an asshole as Chris was with fucking us over, I do think he really did have some love for us in some strange ways. It's just that he was a promoter and a get-over. He was a hustler; he couldn't help it. But as much as he did to help us, he was also very responsible for turning us against each other, by ripping us off and creating a feeling of distrust that had never really been there before. He'd palm you a 20 in your hand, knowing you had no money and nowhere to live, and say, "Don't tell the other guys." Meanwhile, he had a houseboat and lived on Central Park West. And that was really the beginning of the end.

1984, BY KIM GRAF

Chapter Eleven

'BEST WISHES'
TO YOU

Our friend Crazy Dave just got out of jail. He started bangin' this chick that was staying with Roger Miret and some other friends of ours on St. Marks Place. John Bloodclot was there all the time.

Crazy Dave was a maniac. He called himself a "Skinhawk" 'cause he had a mohawk but hung out with the skinheads. He was a chaos punk, kinda like Wattie from the Exploited, as opposed to a hippie-punk or "crAsshole," as I called them; there was a big distinction between the two types of punks in NYC. He was always trippin' his balls off on purple mescaline. He'd be sitting on a stoop somewhere, just cackling to himself. And he'd be like, "You want some mescaline?" So you'd pop five or six hits, and sit there giggling with him all fuckin' night.

Around that time, John started doing blow on the sneak tip with Dave. John and Crazy Dave moved in with Roger on St. Marks Place. Dave's brother was sending Dave packs of coke in the mail from Florida, to sell and make money. I wasn't down with that shit, but it wasn't my business. I figured Dave's just trying to survive, and John's just chilling with him, they're smoking weed, living it up a little. I had no idea John had started doing that shit too. But then some crazy shit went down; John said someone ripped off one of those packages from Florida. He blamed our friends living there, and caused a bunch of drama.

One day, John came up to me looking all wild-eyed and crazy. He was like, "These motherfuckers stole one of Dave's packets that came in." He started going off, blaming a bunch of our friends. He was like, "I swear to God, bro, I know they did it." He even said he smacked Roger and called him out, which turned out to be total bullshit, of course.

Now, I didn't know John was doing that shit at the time. But still, I thought it was weird that he even cared or was even hangin' around that shit, being that he was all Mr. Hare Krishna. Never mind that he was throwing other people's names into the mix. As far as I was concerned, what the fuck was John even doing with Dave and blow, making it his business? It left a bad vibe with me. It just seemed shady. But looking back, it all makes sense, 'cause John then went on a crazy coke bender right afterwards. So I guess that was the very beginning of it.

Anyway, the point is that it fueled the tension both within the Cro-Mags and with a lot of friends of ours on the scene. A lot of people started getting the idea that John was a rip-off after that shit and a few other things he did. I was disgusted with the whole thing. I didn't like that John was involved with the coke situation; I didn't dig that at all. Soon after that, Dave split to Florida and John went with him. I was living with my girlfriend at her father's apartment in Chelsea.

About two weeks later, they called me at my girlfriend's house. They were like, "Dave's brother has mad loot, but we can't get no bud! Come down and stay with us at Dave's brother's house, just bring some weed. He wants you to bring some down." They were hyping us on how nice it all was. So we took a bus, and I brought two ounces of weed.

We got there, and the place was a dump—it was a fuckin' coke den! It was trashed, and Dave's brother was all fucked up on blow. He was dealing, and owed mad money to his connections. One night, people drove by and shot at the place. Crazy Dave's brother was just as fuckin' crazy as him! So we split, and wound up at a hotel. I mean, they were acting weird when I got there but I couldn't tell what was up. As it turned out, they were getting seriously fucked up on blow. I never really fucked with that shit; that was never my thing. All I knew was I gave them their bag of weed and I had my bag of weed, and they burned through their ounce bag within two days. They were just high as fuck on coke, smokin' through their weed, and not even feelin' it. Then they started sweatin' me for mine.

Once we figured out what they were up to, me and her split and left those guys to their madness. We found other people to stay with: this black Hardcore chick, her mom and her brother. They had a lot of money and a nice house with a pool and shit. I stayed with them for a couple weeks, and then came back to New York.

But yeah, that was the real start of the spiral down in John's and my friendship. A few things went down around that time that were fucked up, before and after that fateful Florida trip. I can't remember the exact order 'cause there was a lot of shit and it was a long time ago. But it's not like I'm talking shit or making it up or trying to play "Mr. Innocent." I've already said I was a fuck-up, and that I was just getting over having been a total Skinhead-street-thug-drug-casualty myself—none of which are admirable things—and it's not like my days of fucking up had come to an end.

I'm just giving you the other side of the picture 'cause I'm always being depicted as the bad guy or the fuck-up, and that's a bunch of bullshit. We all had issues; no one was innocent. Every one of us had our moments. Preachy, self-righteous "Mr. Hare Krishna holy roller" with neck beads on, spliff in his hand, was a total hypocrite on the sneak tip.

So we had our album out, *The Age of Quarrel*—the name itself came straight from *Bhagavad Gita*, and I was starting to get really on fire about the whole Krishna thing. I thought we were really on to something positive. I had been in Prabhupada's presence as a baby, so it all made sense to me. I felt it was like a karmic thing, and truth is, it was a good influence in my life. Even though it did at first alienate me from people on the scene, even some close friends, I didn't give a care. Fact is, I would've wound up dead or in jail if I hadn't gotten into that shit.

Around that time, the word was getting out on the scene that John had ripped off a few people and vandalized some people's apartments. John had been staying with this chick rent-free, eatin', and smokin' up everyone's weed. He said that 'cause he wasn't giving her no dick she wanted him out. Eventually she threw him out, and then he went off and trashed the place. He also stayed with these two chicks on like 23rd Street for a while. When they threw him out, he emptied the cat box in their lingerie drawers, pissed in their closets, and all kinds of crazy shit.

One time he was staying at some chick's apartment on St. Marks, right there between 1st and A where we'd all hang out and blaze spliffs and shit. When he was eventually asked to leave, he invited all the homeless guys from the block to use her showers and towels and shit. What a creative genius! What a mind. Imagine a bunch of homeless, crusty-ass bums taking showers in your apartment when you're not home! I mean, the filthiest ones on St. Marks, the ones that you'd see every day asking for change. It was funny, but it was completely fucked up.

After all that shit went down, this one chick Alexa, who was friends with some of the chicks John fucked over, went after his ass, and I wound up knocking her out.

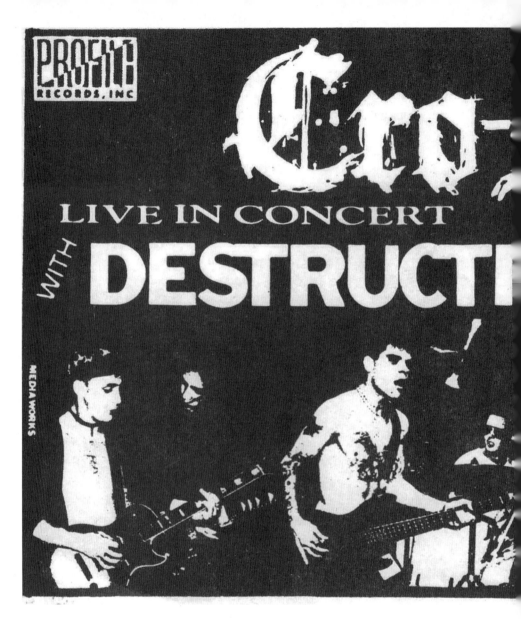

It happened right after the "NYHC" episode of the Phil Donahue show. Alexa was friends with Agnostic Front, Warzone and all of them—a "Warzone Woman." She was on the cover of a Warzone 45 crowd-surfing.

This one chick Brooke, who me and John used to stay with, and I had always been friends with up until that point, started talking shit to John during the taping of the Donahue show. Of course me and him, being the juvenile motherfuckers that we were, started

talking mad shit back to her and abusing the shit out of her like we were in fifth grade.

I didn't know at the time that John had ripped her off. We got outside the building and next thing I know Alexa comes running up on John and swings at him with a chain and a fuckin' padlock. He snatched it from her and grabbed her by her neck. I thought he was gonna fuck her up, so I grabbed her and held her back. I was telling him to get the fuck outa there 'cause he still had warrants for his arrest and she was making a huge scene.

He tried to walk away, but while I was still holding her back, she bit the shit outa me—sank her teeth right into my arm. I let go of her in disbelief and she punched me in the face. I was actually shocked! Then she went to hit me again, and on reflex I punched her in the face. And then I completely flipped out and went after her. I had to be pulled off by like four security guards from the building who came running out when they saw all the ruckus.

All these little fuckin' Hardcore kids were like, "Yo Harley, chill man, it's a girl—that's fucked up, she's a girl." I was like, "Yo, I don't give a fuck—you wanna fucking hit me? I'll fuck you up bitch, I don't give a fuck what's between your legs! I will fuck your shit UP! Who the fuck is next?"

I went off! She had a black eye for months.

I got a few dirty looks after that one, but no one said shit. I guess no one else wanted to get knocked the fuck out or fucked up. But for the record, she was a tough little Hardcore chick who was always getting into fights, starting shit, and always in the mosh pit—crowd-surfing, going off. It's not like she was some little girly girl, she was a scrapper; not to justify it, but whatever—it was a reflex.

Me and her are cool now, and we were cool before that shit happened. And to her credit she's one of the only people that ever went after Bloodclot; I give her props for that. A lot of people talked a lot of shit about him, but no one ever did anything. It's funny actually, 'cause a lot of the shit I got into was because of him. But that shit didn't win us no friends. The general consensus on the scene was that I was crazy and John was a scumbag.

We were pretty much friends with all the fuck-ups. Errol, our crazy black "rude boy" Skinhead friend, stayed there for a minute, too. His gig was he'd pick up chicks at bars and clubs, go back to their pad, fuck 'em, and then steal their money while they slept. He loved John and me 'cause we were such maniacs. He used to come to our gigs, hang out onstage, and pretend to do security. He'd pull people up onstage and they'd be thinking they were gonna stage dive. Then he'd punch them and throw them back into the crowd. I've seen footage of us at the Ritz with him standing there with a big grin, doing that. Me and him would always dine-and-dash at the yuppie restaurants that were opening on the LES.

We'd sit at the outside tables, order like 20 different things, eat, send them in for more stuff, and take off running into Tompkins Square Park, laughing our asses off.

John and me were fuck-ups, as were most of our friends like Bleu, Squint, and Stig, who had been beating the shit out of some of the new-jack Skinheads on the scene. So yeah, some people didn't like us, except for the old-school heads like the Bad Brains, so we didn't really give too much of a fuck. Plus, people still hadn't forgotten about the C-Squat Benefit. Some people were even trying to say me and John and me started the fire so we could keep the money! That shit was ridiculous, except for the fact that people actually died. I mean, after it burned down, we were out of place like everyone else. We didn't burn that shit down, but we did spend the money. Or really I should say "he" did, 'cause he controlled it. But hey, we both spent it—smoked it, ate it, whatever. John had the money in his waist pouch and basically we just smoked a lotta weed, drank a lotta milkshakes from Ray's on Avenue A, and stayed in hotels a few nights.

We'd be standing there in the rain, high as a motherfucker, stinking of Hawaiian bud, with this money, but nowhere to stay. John was like, "What are we supposed to do, split it up and give like $20 to every junkie and Skinhead and runaway that's crashing there? All those motherfuckers who are gonna just go spend it on drugs." He laughed and was like "I don't need that Karma," as we were standing there high as hell, drinking milkshakes.

We were like the bad guys on the scene even though we were trying to be religious. That's what made it all more ridiculous. I mean it was really just John and me. But as far as people were concerned, me and John and represented the Cro-Mags, and we were—I hate to say it—two of the worst fuck-ups I ever knew. And the funny thing was, we weren't nearly half as bad as we used to be before we got into Krishna!

I didn't intend to talk about half of this shit, but I feel like I have to, 'cause it's a preface for all the shit that was yet to come. Trust me, there was a lot of other fucked-up crazy things that went down. Some of it I won't get into 'cause it was too fucked-up. When John started doing blow on the sneak tip and I found out, I was really disillusioned with him. I felt like I was part of the fuckin' hoax, the farce. I felt like everything the Cro-Mags was representing was a joke. He was our frontman, and it was just shtick. At that point, it's not like it ended our friendship—he was still my boy—but I just couldn't take his shit so seriously anymore.

I don't think John ever forgave the band or me after he quit after *The Age of Quarrel* tour because no one in the band wanted him back. The fucked-up thing was I did want him back. But he quit. And that was that. He completely flipped out after that wallet shit in Europe—he threatened Doug, and freaked out on Chris, Pete, and Parris. He used to quit all the time, and everybody was just done with it. When I came back from Europe and dealt with Chris and the wallet, that's when I heard John quit. So, I went and found John, and talked him back into playing, like I always used to do. So I went to the next practice and told the guys, "John's back in, he's down to play again." And they were like, "We don't want to play with him anymore." So I was like, "Now what? I just talked this motherfucker back into playing!"

It was a fucked-up situation. We had all these songs that we were working on at the time. Parris and me had years of time and effort put in; I had been playing with Parris before I was playing with John. The whole shit was fucked up. We had bounced back from losing Mackie, and we were solid with Pete. Doug and Parris sounded great together. I mean, we sounded good. But they were done with John. It was just a bad situation. Ultimately, I think he resented the fact that I went with them instead of with him. He even said to me, "Dude, why don't you stay with me? We'll be the Cro-Mags, fuck those dudes!" I felt like, "Yo, this is a band, and you're the person in the band making waves. You quit like every other week, and I've got the rest of the band looking at you like, 'Dude, we're done with you.' What am I supposed to do? They don't wanna play with you anymore."

I was being put in the position of dealing with it 'cause he was my friend. I was never happy with the shit. But it was either that or the band was gonna fall apart then and there. They were done with him. At the time, I felt it was the right thing to do. It was "majority rules" as far as the band went, and one guy was quitting all of the time. What were we supposed to do? I hated telling him. But it was like, "Bro, you keep quitting all the time. What am

I supposed to do, form a band with you, so three-four weeks from now, you'll say you wanna go back to the temple?" Which he'd do all the time. Whenever shit got tough, he'd be like, "Fuck this, I'm going back to the temple. I'm going back to Hawaii!" That's where he was when he was with the devotees. It just became this thing where all that was more of a nuisance, and no one ever knew if he was gonna quit or not.

He left the band Bloodclot; he didn't stick it out when we tried to do M.O.I.; he didn't stick it out in the Navy; he kept leaving the temple and going back. You just never knew what he was gonna do from one instant to the next. He was always saying he was gonna quit, but when he left, we had no plans for that happening. It was just some shit that happened, and it exploded. Soon after John left, he started buggin' out on crack. He even started doing crazy shit like robbing people. I lived a few blocks away from him in Brooklyn, and I knew he was starting to bug out 'cause he sold everything in his house to a pawnshop down the street; he even ripped out the fridge that belonged to the landlord and sold that! We all came through a lot of struggles. It's hard to not lose your mind and go through crazy shit, especially when that's almost all you've ever been around. But fortunately, he pulled through that period of his life.

Then there was this empty spot—and the band, as well as Chris Williamson, wanted me to fill it. I guess in Chris' head, he wanted us to go more "crossover." The "frontman with the instrument" was more metal like Metallica or whatever. All I know is, I didn't want that position. I didn't even know if I'd be able to play bass and sing at the same time; I'd never done it. When I recorded *Best Wishes*, I didn't know what the fuck to do, but we were under the gun to do an album. In all honesty, I didn't trust anybody to take over that position and express my feelings. I felt John and I were on the same page lyrically, and that someone else would just be faking it, or might take it somewhere I didn't want it to go. It took John and me a while to find a lyrical direction, and I didn't trust that to just anybody. I reluctantly took charge of what was a runaway train; there was nobody behind the wheel, and I had to grab the wheel. But I never wanted to be a frontman or a vocalist.

We started writing a lot of the songs that wound up on *Best Wishes* when John was still in the band. In all honesty, no one was happy with John's vocal direction. The songs were becoming a bit more metal and John didn't have the ability to sing in any kind of key, not that I sang in any kind of key on that record. But some of the shit he was trying when we were writing those songs, everybody would just cringe. In his defense I'd always say, "We're still working on it, we don't have it down yet." But everybody, especially Parris, was like, "Oh man, what are we going to do about John?" It was a fucked-up situation.

Best Wishes was the end of an era and the beginning of something new. It was a metal-style album without the metal-style lyrics. Songs like "Death Camps" or "Age of Quarrel" were my straight-up versions of Judas Priest *Screaming For Vengeance*-type shit, but done by a Hardcore band. I was diggin' on metal, as was Doug, and Pete had been a metalhead before he got into Hardcore. Around then, you also had metal bands going in a Hardcore direction, like Crumbsuckers or even Leeway. That kind of started that next generation of NYHC. I don't know; I was doing my own thing.

As I said, a lot of it is a blur. There were only a few bands that stuck out. I was getting a little bored with that era of Hardcore. The shit had been going since 1980 and I had been hanging since the '70s. By now, it was nearing the end of the '80s. I didn't know most of the new kids; they all looked at my homies and me with awe, which to me was fucking ridiculous. Most of them only came in for the Sunday matinees or big shows. There were a lot of bands that were around then that people glorify now, and I couldn't hum you one song or give you one song title if I had to.

The Hardcore matinee new-school style was boring to me. It was no Bad Brains or Minor Threat, that's for sure. There were a few bands that stuck it out and earned their stripes over time but they were few and far between. But you're talking to someone who saw the birth of the shit, so I'm not easily impressed. I saw a book on New York straight edge, and I had to laugh. People seem to think straight edge had this huge impact on NYHC, when the fact is, most of the old-school people didn't notice or care.

To me, it was just a bunch of middle-class kids trooping into the city to play Hardcore on the weekends. And not to piss on anybody's parade, but it didn't change anything or contribute much. It just wasn't a significant time in Hardcore. It was an imitation. It was more or less during that era where Agnostic Front was temporarily on hiatus and the Cro-Mags weren't doing as many shows. John left the band and we were writing *Best Wishes*. Bad Brains were even kind of on hiatus.

So you had your most influential and strongest NYHC bands— besides maybe Murphy's Law, but they weren't as serious as we were—out of the picture around the same time. So it left room for kids that had caught the end of an era, and wanted it to keep on going. Sure, some of the band members were nice when I'd meet 'em, but what was happening wasn't too inspiring.

One night I was watching a gig at the Ritz from the balcony, and there was a group of Skinheads in the crowd slam dancing. But they were being really extra dicks, going after people and singling people out—back-fisting people not paying attention and throwing themselves backwards into people who were not looking, and being a bit too obnoxious. In my mind, I was thinking, "Who are these assholes?" I didn't even recognize them.

Anyway, I had recently gone to court for an assault charge—it was a justified assault, in my opinion—so I had grown out my hair for my court date. At the time, Skinheads were getting a bad rap in the media, so I felt it was a bad idea to show up for an assault case with my head shaved and tattoos on my head and shit. So my hair had grown in a bit, and I was sitting up in the balcony watching these guys be dicks.

I took a glass ashtray off the table and winged it into the crowd at them. It just missed one of them, and they started looking around like, "Where did that come from?" I got another ashtray, and whipped it at them again. I don't remember if I hit any of them or not, but one of them saw where it came from 'cause I was right near the spotlight in the balcony. So they all came running up the stairs. And those guys had jumped three people by that point if not more, and they'd been trying to intimidate people all night on the dance floor.

Back then, I didn't leave the house unarmed. You know the bar from a dumbbell that holds the weights in place? I had a short dumbbell bar with one of the bolts at the end up my sleeve. So these guys came up the stairs, and I jumped over the chain guarding the table, and punched the first one in the face that came rushing at me, and cracked another one over his collarbone with the piece of metal. I don't know if I broke his collarbone, but by the look on his face, I think I did. There were Hell's Angels at the table next to me and they all turned around. Everybody was taken back at the chaos that erupted. The bouncers came running up and were pulling everybody apart. As it was all going on, one of them had on a Cro-Mags shirt! They didn't recognize me 'cause my hair had grown in. For me, that was it. I was like, "Fuck these assholes! I'm not gonna represent this anymore."

Like I said before, when we started writing the songs for *Best Wishes*, John was still in the band. Some people may think that he left the band and the sound changed. Songs like "Crush the Demoniac," "Death Camps," and "Fugitive" had music written for them while John was still in the band. So, the music was already starting to change a bit. We were one of the first Hardcore bands to start leaning toward a metal sound and direction. It's funny 'cause at first, a lot of the bands and people were doggin' us for doing it and then, a lot of them kind of went metal themselves—or at least touched on it for a minute. Agnostic Front even enlisted metalheads and the guys from Carnivore to help them write songs.

But even though there were some metal influences going on, we didn't set out to write a metal album or a crossover album; we just started writing a new batch of songs. A lot of the late '80s and '90s bands praised *The Age of Quarrel* like it was the fucking Dead Sea Scrolls of Hardcore or some shit. I think a lot of '90s Hardcore was reminiscent of the riffs of *Best Wishes* but played with more of *The Age of Quarrel* attitude. *Best Wishes* wasn't the landmark album *The Age of Quarrel* was to Hardcore. But I think *Best Wishes* was as significant in the way that it changed things. *Best Wishes* influenced a lot of people, even if on a subconscious level. And it caused more metalheads to turn on to Hardcore. At least that's what people in bands that used to be metalheads who picked up on that record have told me many times over the years.

Doug had some shining moments on that album. He was going through some hard times. At that point unbeknown to me, he had developed a bit of a drug problem on the down-low that then had to be dealt with during that session. It was bad—he would freak out and go nuts, then we'd get him back to a mental place where he could play again, and he'd just tear shit up. It was crazy. If you listen to the leads on "Death Camps," they're awesome; they're like Tony Iommi on "Zero the Hero." But Parris was the rhythm guitarist on that album. I mean, as far as I was concerned, the riffs were still hard, and the words were still real. It was like a metal album played by Hardcore kids.

We were no longer a straight-up Hardcore band. So a lot of what they did with the sound mix was kind of experimental; a lot of it was Tom Soares' and Chris Williamson's ideas. We just wrote the songs and tracked the album; we were just psyched to be in a real studio. Normandy Sound had an upstairs apartment that we all stayed in while we were there. The place was kind of beat-up, but it was better than where I was used to staying.

Pete Hines started buggin' after a couple nights there, 'cause, well, Normandy Sound is haunted. Not everyone feels it, but some people do. He was freaking out, and of course, everyone started fucking with him worse, especially Chris Williamson. It was hysterical; motherfuckers were giving his ass a nervous breakdown. There was a living room in the upstairs apartment, and there was a door that was always closed. So they told Pete it's a room where someone killed themself. Of course it wasn't; it was actually a staircase that led out to the back entrance of the building, which they kept shut.

So after telling Pete the story, Chris Williamson snuck out the front and up those back stairs, and while we are all sitting there hanging out and watching TV, he came bursting through the door with a sheet over himself, screaming like a ghost. Pete just about shit himself—jumped screaming up into the air. We were all dying laughing. Pete was on the floor, practically crying. Chris was pissing himself. I gotta tell you, as much of a dick as Chris was, he was a funny motherfucker. The whole shit, the set-up, it was priceless.

In the studio, Chris would keep setting off the motion detector and moving shit to freak out Pete. He'd be down on his hands and knees in the live room, moving mics and shit, and Pete would be like "Yo, did you see that! You didn't see that shit? That mic just moved by itself!" Then Chris would sneak out that room, run around to the front of the building, and come walking through from the other side, so Pete would think he'd been in the other side of the building. It was hysterical. So, Pete tracked and left pretty quickly.

While recording, we did some crazy shit trying to get sounds, like surrounding the mics with guitar amps, literally boxing it in with Marshall stacks and JCM 800s. I played my Guild Pilot bass through like three heads. I used a vintage acoustic one on one track, and a nice vintage SVT on another. I had a direct one, the SansAmp—all that shit blending it all together—so I did get a really sick bass sound. Chris and Tom the engineer even did shit like slowly increasing the volume at the end of the song "Age of Quarrel" to build up dynamics at the end of the album. It just keeps getting louder and louder.

I don't know if they were buggin' or what, but it had some horrible shit too, like some of the effects they did on the vocal tracks. My vocal performance itself wasn't all that good, 'cause I was caught off guard by the whole situation. I had never thought about being the singer, and here I was, trying to figure out what the fuck to do. It was a lot of stress—I was having insane migraines and shit. I remember throwing up after doing some of those vocals from one of those fuckin' headaches.

While writing Best Wishes, I was living in Williamsburg, Brooklyn. The neighborhood was fuckin' insane. I lived in this little apartment on a serious dope-dealin' corner. I wasn't involved in any of that shit at that time, but I used to watch the madness going down outside my window. I once saw a full-on gang fight, where people were pulling out baseball bats, getting stabbed, and shooting at each other. Another time, I saw someone get shot four times, dive into their car while they were getting shot, and come out with a baseball bat, screaming, "You wanna get ill, motherfuckers? Let's get ill!" And the dude who shot at him turned and ran! It was a crazy fuckin' neighborhood.

There was a Good Humor truck on my corner that sold heroin, and there was a chick that used to sit with her baby in her stroller, and sell works—syringes—out of the stroller. I had a badass pit bull named Reigner at the time, and motherfuckers were always offering me money to fight him. It was like one of those movies that you see about New York in the '70s. And it was, except this was the late '80s. The area was mostly Puerto Ricans from the LES that got gentrified out of the LES, and ended up migrating to Williamsburg, because many of them already had family there. So naturally, I moved out there 'cause it was more my style, my rent and price range. It was what I'd grown up in. It was 'hood.

I was walkin' down the street late one night out there. I hear these dudes across the street. Some young Puerto Rican dude says to me, "Yo!" I'm like, "I hope they're not talkin' to me." "Yo! What's up?" I'm like, "Oh shit." They started to cross the street. Naturally, I had my knife in my hand. They come over and ask, "Are you in the Cro-Mags?"

Even though the Lower East Side had already started to get gentrified by the late '80s, a lot of people forget how crazy the neighborhood still was. I mean, we had Tent City in Tompkins Square Park. Bums and junkies everywhere, and scumbags living out of boxes, tents and makeshift shantytown shit. You could barely walk through the park, it got so bad. There were dope spots and coke spots every-fucking-where.

We had the Tompkins Square Park Riot in '88. I was walking down Avenue A with two pounds of weed in a K-Mart shopping bag, when all of a sudden, I see riot cops running straight at me! There were helicopters, the whole shit—a full-on riot on Avenue A! I walked into it, totally unaware that the shit was going on. The cops had been trying to get the squatters out of the park. They weren't even really squatters; they were just fucking bums, junkies, and scumbags. But it was crazy.

They were trying to enforce a new curfew on the park, and kick the homeless Tent City motherfuckers out. There were all kinds of protests going on, and all kinds of pseudo radicals jumped in. It turned into a big protest, and some asshole wound up throwing a bottle at the cops, who were already dying to fuck up some crusty punk rock squatters. And then the shit just erupted. The cops beat up a few friends of mine who happened to come around the corner at the wrong time. There were pictures of cops on the front pages of the papers with their nametags taped over with black tape, so you couldn't get their names. It was a major scandal.

It was totally planned; the cops wanted the riot more than the so-called anarchists. And the cops came prepared, with helicopters, riot cops, and mounted police on Avenue A! I was lucky I got the fuck away, especially with what I had in that K-Mart bag. But the city was still pretty grimy and crazy back then. There were still a few serial killer types like Joel Rifkin in the neighborhood. We also had that crazy motherfucker Daniel Rakowitz, who in '89 killed that chick and fed her to the homeless people in Tompkins Square Park.

Crazy Dave was the super in the building that Rakowitz did that shit in. That whole 'hood was insane. It's hard to believe it wasn't even really that long ago, and how fucking tame it is now. It's crazy how much shit can change in such a short time, really. I mean, shit had sure changed since the '60s, with Prabhupada feeding people in Tompkins Square Park, and chanting "Hare Krishna." Now, you had people shooting smack in bushes, scumbags everywhere, and motherfuckers feeding the homeless human soup!

BEST WISHES: THE MUSIC

The music was different on *Best Wishes*. I was digging Judas Priest when we started on those songs. John was still in the band, but he couldn't get past Rob Halford being gay. I was like, "Dude, listen to the fucking riffs!" Doug was into Mercyful Fate and shit. And we were both big Sabbath heads.

I remember when I came up with the idea for the lyrics to "Death Camps." Those were the first lyrics I wrote for that album. I was walking to a friend's house, who lived on the West Side over in the Meatpacking District. It was a disgusting neighborhood back then with all the meat warehouses and the transsexual hookers walkin' the streets.

I was humming the riffs to the song when I looked up and saw all these meat hooks and the conveyor belts over my head. It disgusted me. I looked around and all of the buildings had them, and of course the stink was unbearable. The Meatpacking District inspired all of that. I wrote the rest of the lyrics with my boy Doug Crosby. It may have been one of the first pro-vegetarian Hardcore songs.

"Days of Confusion": The chord progression was my version of a Discharge-type riff. I mentally just kinda bit off of one of my favorite Discharge songs, "Protest and Survive"—like many others did, Yeah, I admit it, I love those guys, but I changed all the chords. I just tried to attack it with that kind of feel, and then I tacked that Parris guitar intro on to the beginning.

"The Only One" was my first real Krishna consciousness song. I just tried to pour my heart into it from the feeling of someone in love with someone, or in this case, with "God" and the deities. It was very different from anything we'd done before. Glenn Danzig told me that was his favorite Cro-Mags song.

"Down, But Not Out" was written in Brooklyn, inspired by the night I saw that guy get shot in the gang fight, and by reflecting on my life growing up on the LES. But I was trying to be hopeful and inspiring, like, we are down but we're not out.

"Crush the Demoniac" was the first riff Doug Holland contributed to the band, that one main riff. I didn't know that it sounded like Iron Maiden's "Aces High"—that makes me laugh so hard, to this day. But it is fun to play. That was a song we started playing when John was still in the band.

"Fugitive" we did when John was still in the band. It was Parris' parts and one of my riffs. It was my least favorite song on the record, and it was the one that sealed John's doom with the other guys; Parris, Doug, and even Pete would be cringing. But really, Chris Williamson was always going off about John and his voice around that time. They hated the way he was trying to sing. In my opinion, I didn't do a much better job than he would have. I sang one note on the word "real" that was so unbearably bad, it hurts every time I hear it. I never knew the words John was starting to sing. We only did it live a few times with him, and his words never stuck.

The music to "Then and Now" is pretty funny. Listen to the first riff, the bass line; I was kind of doing my own version of the theme to The Exorcist. I switched some notes, and did it metal-style, then added those harmonic chords on the guitar.

The song "Age of Quarrel" is about the age that we are living in. Again, as a Hardcore kid from the LES, I have no problem saying that it was very Priest-influenced.

The name "Best Wishes" was kind of tongue-in-cheek. It was my way of saying "Fuck you" to some, but to others, it was really my way of saying "Goodbye to the past and best wishes to a whole era." Anyway, I wrote most of the riffs on that album and the words I wrote with Doug Crosby. Doug was a UFC judge and stunt man, among many other things. He's a great writer; those lyrics would not have come out that way if not for him and his help. He wasn't credited on the album and I have always believed that Chris Williamson took his name off the credits 'cause he didn't want it to look like there was anybody else behind or involved with the Cro-Mags besides him. Just like Eric didn't get credit on *The Age of Quarrel*—which I didn't even realize it until the record was out. I just want to make sure people get credit where it's due, now that I have the chance.

Chris was a bit nutty trying to "sculpt" us. When I started singing, I think he wanted to create a Metallica-type image, like the lead man on an instrument and vocals, with two guitarists on either side. Chris saw himself as the puppet master behind the band. He wanted to be like Malcolm McLaren. Chris would come to our practices and start trying to tell us what to play. He really saw himself as another member of the band, even to the point where we'd walk off the stage and Chris would be like, "We were great, guys!" He was completely nuts. I do think he believed in us, but he was a major part of all of the internal schism that began. Sure, he did help us get our first big gigs. But he also fucked us over. And really, people like him helped destroy the scene in many ways, and ultimately caused the business end of it to take over things and turn it corporate.

As usual, the artists—especially the original ones—get fucked over 'til the end. That is life. When I was in the studio doing *Best Wishes*, I used to draw this caricature of Chris' face everywhere, especially if I was bored. It used to drive him crazy. I spray-painted it on the street in front of his building. One time, I unraveled a half a roll of toilet paper, and drew him on every sheet, and rolled it back up. I was obviously very bored, but it was funny watching him unroll it. It was all made out of triangles. He was "triangle man"— always looking for an angle to screw ya.

The *Age of Quarrel* tour was still kind of during the early days of Hardcore. But by *Best Wishes*, the shows were a lot bigger.

Two days before the tour started, our first gig was supposed to be at L'Amour. I was on St. Marks Place on the corner by 1st Avenue with my girlfriend and two other girls I knew, when these rednecks come walking down, and they're shitfaced drunk. This was back in the day when the 'hood was still sometimes rowdy, especially on the weekends.

One of the rednecks turned to us and said some smart-ass shit. As I'm trying to walk away, he stepped up and threw a swing at me. I saw it coming a mile away, ducked underneath it, and nailed him with a left hook. All his weight was on his left leg from throwing the punch, so when I caught him with that punch, he just dropped. I stepped back, and was like, "What's up, motherfucker?"

He got up, smiled, wiped the blood off his lip, and came at me again. He threw another wild, sloppy, looping punch at me, and again I ducked underneath it, and nailed him, and put him on the floor. The guy was sloppy and I was lighting him up, the whole time telling him "Chill, I don't want to keep fucking you up, dude."

I put him to the ground twice, and as this is happening, his friend is circling behind me. He starts reaching behind him for a knife that he had on the back of his belt. One of the chicks tries to grab him by the wrist. He turned around and punched her dead in the face—her legs went up in the air and she dropped. At that point, I pretty much went ballistic.

It was the weekend, so there were bottles everywhere, garbage cans full of trash. Back then, everyone drank in the street—it wasn't like you really got in trouble for it. So I picked up a 40-ounce bottle and smashed it against the dude's face. Then I picked up two more bottles and smashed those against his face—from like three feet away! They were just exploding off his head. At that point, I was fucking both these dudes up so bad. Some bystander grabbed me from behind, in like a bear hug. I started reverse-headbutting the dude trying to get him in the face, figuring I'm going to cave in his nose and shake him off. I looked over my shoulder, and this dude was huge—my head was basically hitting him in the chest! He was an old guy, but like 6'5". He looked like an old Marine.

Meanwhile, one of the dudes was getting up off the floor. His face was mangled, it's just a mess—blood every-fucking-where. He's getting up off the ground wiping the blood with his arm and his sleeve and starts coming toward me looking all crazy. I shook the old man off me, right as this dude came charging at me. I picked up one of those square-shaped Jack Daniels or Jim Beam bottles, and the top of it was broken. So I held it by the bottom in my palm. As he came at me, I drove it into his face; I fed it to him. The dude's face just opened up in more ways than you can imagine, because it was nothing but sharp glass. That's what also opened up my hand—I cut my hand between my thumb and my index finger, and that shit was just spouting blood. I don't know if you've seen anyone cut a vein, but the blood pulses out. It was squirting like three feet in the air!

So by that point, I was still fighting. I went running inside the St. Marks Bar and Grill, and I was like, "Give me a fuckin' bat or something!" The guy goes to hand it to me, sees all the blood coming out of my hand, and didn't want to give it to me.

So I snatched two beer bottles off the bar and go running back outside, and while this dude was still wobbling with blood gushing out of his face, I came running out of the bar, and just, bam—nailed him with one bottle, and then, bam, the other bottle. And these were half-full beer bottles. Again, I dropped him, and at that point one of the girls I was with grabbed me by my arm and started dragging me away, because I probably would've bled to death if I didn't make it to the hospital.

It did cut a main vein in my hand. I was holding my hand over my head, because you're supposed to elevate the wound as high above your heart and head as you can. And the guys I fucked up were basically on their hands and knees, crawling around with blood coming out of their faces in fuckin' puddles on the ground underneath them. The fight started on 8th Street and 1st Avenue, and I fought these guys halfway down 8th Street to Avenue A, then back up to the corner of 8th Street and 1st Avenue, and then all the way to 7th Street and 1st, and then back over to that corner of St. Marks. The fight must have lasted a good ten minutes. No cops were around. They got me to the hospital, and I wound up with 20-something stitches in my hand. In the hospital, I was crying because I was like, "I fucked up the tour!" I called Parris, and he couldn't even understand what was going on, because I was crying, like, "I'm so sorry, I fucked it all up!" I felt responsible for wrecking it for everybody, not just myself, but for Parris, Doug and Pete. But luckily, the tour went on as planned, even though it probably shouldn't have.

To this day, I still have no feeling at all in my right thumb. I could stick a knitting needle through that area of skin and I wouldn't notice. There was a lot of nerve damage. I had to play L'Amour two days later! You'll see pictures from that tour: my hand was bandaged up, and I bled through it most of the start of that tour—the stitches were coming open, tearing, and popping. And then, coming home that night from the hospital, I got in a fuckin' car accident! Everybody was fine, but the car got totaled. It was a shitty night.

We toured with Destruction. That was when shit was still going good for us. But our fans used to fuck with them real bad, and I gotta say, a lot of metalheads got their asses kicked on that tour. Every night, the guitarist from Destruction would do a solo, and he'd be up there doing his Yngwie Malmsteen thing—or "Yanggy Shanggy" as we used to call him—all rocking out with his bullet belt and Flying V. One night, this Skinhead jumped up onstage, took the guitar cord, broke it off in his guitar, and skipped off the stage! He didn't just unplug the guitar—he broke the cord off in the guitar. It was so cold.

One time we played with them in Florida, and were parked outside this outdoor venue. We were sitting in the Winnebago, watching Skinheads pouring in from every-fucking-where. This is around the time when the Nazi Skinhead thing was starting to really jump off—and in Florida, it was out of control. I remember being onstage, and there was this insane circle pit going on, and you'd just see an occasional metalhead get sucked into it, disappear, and a few "circles" later, would get bounced out, looking all disheveled. A lotta crazy shit happened on that tour as far as brawls and stupid goofy shit.

After that tour, we kept at it. We were never making money, it didn't matter how big the show was or how many gigs we did in a row. There was always an excuse as to why we weren't making money. It's not like we were greedy; we were poor. We were unhappy with Chris and his Rock Hotel/Profile arrangement. He was keeping us in the dark about everything. He had this one clause in the contract, saying he could spend band money without accounting to us for it 'cause as he and his lawyer explained, "Well, say I can't reach you guys. I can't wait 'til I hear from you if I have to spend money out of the band fund to make arrangements, or rent vans, or gear, or flight, and do this or that. Nothing will ever get done if I have to okay everything with you guys." So as long as it was in the band's "interest," he could basically spend our money.

Do you know this guy was going to Hawaii on our expense, back when John was in the band? Telling us, "Hey guys, I may have us a gig in Hawaii. I'm working it out with a promoter over there. No one's ever done it before but I'm gonna bring you guys over there." He was spending our fucking money going there to do all this shit. And of course, those gigs were probably never even being booked at all—at least they never happened.

We were just dumb kids—some Hardcore kids from Avenue A he had totally fucking taken advantage of. We were young and dumb.

Not all was well within the band by this point. There were a few reasons the band split further after *Best Wishes*. First, we had signed such a shitty record deal with Chris and Profile. Chris had a subsidiary label under Profile; he had his lawyer represent us against Profile. But really, it was us against him. We didn't realize that's what his subsidiary label deal was: him locking us into a deal with him as the label and the management. The way he made it sound, "They're going to give me my own label and a budget, which means I'll be able to do everything you need." But he was just using us, along with bands like Leeway, Murphy's Law, and Wargasm, as a way of starting his own subsidiary rock label, Rock Hotel Records, under Profile. That's how we got bamboozled into that. He got us 'cause he was also throwing us some bigger shows. Things started going bad with Profile and Chris, and they in turn started taking it out on the Rock Hotel bands.

But before things went shitty with Chris, he introduced us to Michael Alago, who signed Metallica. Michael was a big fan of the Cro-Mags, and remained a big fan after John left the band. He started showing interest in signing us to the label he was working with at the time, which I think was Elektra. Anyway, after things went bad with Chris, Michael still showed interest in working with the band. So we got a hot-shit lawyer, who was quite expensive, but had worked with the Beastie Boys: Ken Anderson. He started negotiating with Profile to get us out of the deal, and they would not budge. The negotiating dragged on and on. We wound up running up a bill of over $100,000. There was not a shot in hell that we'd ever get the money to get out of that hole.

At that point, all kinds of other drama went down between Chris and Doug Holland. Doug started taking a turn for the worse with drugs, and he wound up out of the band. I don't think we fired him. He just kind of faded out of the picture—he didn't want to gig or tour. So Parris and me started looking at other guys, and wound up getting this young metalhead kid from Queens named Rob Buckley, who lived not too far from my grandmother. Parris didn't like the guy at first, but I thought Rob was a good guitarist. A lot of the songs that wound up on *Alpha Omega* came from Rob and me doodling at his house. He and Parris then bonded really tight for half a second. I stopped spending as much time with them, as I was hustling, trying to survive, sellin' weed in Central Park and shit.

So we had most of the *Alpha Omega* riffs together. But looking back, Rob's influence was definitely not good for the Cro-Mags. He was a great player but he was too metal. We did a tour with him on guitar and Dave DiCenso on drums. We still had our old road crew—Red, Squint, and Rich—but we were still trying to move forward. We hooked up with Dave DiCenso through Tom Soares, who was a great engineer. Dave came from Boston, and would come down to do gigs and practice. He was a sick fucking drummer, really versatile and could play just about any kind of music, but he was a metalhead at heart. He hit so fucking hard—one of my all-time favorite drummers I have played with.

Our fallout with Chris was bad, and the tension continued to increase—all the years of playing, line-up changes, the fucked-up management situation, and the record deal going south. Parris and me were worn out. That's basically what happened. We just got worn the fuck out. Parris was becoming a control freak. I guess he figured someone had to take charge, but he changed a lot. And I started to lose my mind. The band basically imploded and I started turning back to some of my old ways, like drinking and eating mushrooms. At that point, I had been disillusioned with the Hare Krishna movement. I had seen a lot of shady things go down in the movement. John's so-called guru had been kicked out of the movement for being a pedophile, and a whole bunch of other gurus had been kicked out for stealing money or being undercover homosexuals and pedophiles and whatnot.

John started accusing a bunch of devotees of being drug dealers and shit, but they were all his friends. He even claimed that he was getting weed from a few of them. They went on to say that he ripped them off. Then this one devotee, Vakresvara, a Prabhupada disciple, said he walked in on John fagging out with some other devotee at the temple in Puerto Rico—either giving or getting a blowjob, I'm not sure. And there were other people saying a lotta weird shit about him.

But there was all kinds of weird shit going on in the movement at the time. It started to feel just as fucked-up, corrupt, political, and full of shit as all the other religions. I found out about all kinds of supposed conspiracies too, people wanting to kill Prabhupada; it was just shady shit. Then John started doing blow; I was kind of like, "Where the fuck is all the faith?" And I guess I started to lose my faith and lose my way a bit in the process.

PART I: "ALPHA OMEGA" THE BEGINNING AND THE END — BLOODCLOT RETURNS

Chapter Twelve

ALPHA OMEGA TOUR – GERMANY, BY BERND BOHRMANN

s much as we tried to get out of our contract with Profile, they wouldn't release us. We were also trying to lose our manager Chris Williamson—which was a nightmare—and then the whole Elektra/Alago/legal debt fiasco exploded. It proved to be the end, or at least the end of an era. After a short tour with Wargasm, Parris and Rob abandoned ship.

At that point, my friendship and working relationship with Parris was worn the fuck out. I think we'd just been through too much shit, and he was ready to make a break from it and from me. So he was like, "I'm quitting, the band's breaking up. Rob and me are gonna do something else. I'm giving up on the Cro-Mags." I freaked! I was like, "What the fuck! I'm not giving up! We went through all this shit with members leaving, Chris fucking us over, and now you? What am I supposed to do? Get stuck with this $100,000 debt?" He looked at me, smiled, and said, "Well, all you have to do is not play as the Cro-Mags, and you won't owe that money." At that point, his intentions were to take all those songs that we'd worked on as a trio, and record them. So I was like, "Fuck these motherfuckers. I'm gonna record the goddamn songs myself."

They wanted to cut my throat and record the material that I wrote with them, and say, "Fuck you, you can have nothing. You can have a $100,000 debt, and fuck the name Cro-Mags"? At least that's how I felt at the time.

I know I can be a difficult person to deal with at times, and at that particular time I had a lot of pressure on me, not just from friends of the band, but from fans. I was fronting this "Hardcore" band that was getting further and further away from what we used to do, and from what our fans expected. And truthfully I was feeling the pressure. We still sounded good; the vibe was just changing so much.

I'd be looking into the crowd and some of the fans didn't get it, especially the diehard Cro-Mags fans. You had all of these people staring at us like, "Who the fuck are these metalheads up there with Harley?" A lotta people didn't recognize Parris, 'cause like I said, his hair had got real long. We didn't have Pete or Doug anymore. We'd be doing shows, and motherfuckers would be shouting, "Harley, Harley!" They weren't even screaming "Cro-Mags" anymore 'cause I was the only thing that they recognized left in the band.

We sounded good, but it sure as shit wasn't *The Age of Quarrel* or even *Best Wishes*, and the Cro-Mags fans knew it. That Hardcore vibe and look was long gone.

Rob and his guitar tech were total metalheads; so was Dave. It was cool, but I remember several occasions when Rob and his tech were kind of being dicks to some of the Hardcore Cro-Mags fans when they were drinking after the show. It was the first time they'd ever been on tour, so they didn't really know how to act, especially around Hardcore kids, Skinheads and diehard Cro-Mags fans. Our roadies Bleu and Squint wanted to beat their asses. And on more than a few nights, Skinheads wanted to serve them an ass-beating and they didn't even realize it 'cause they were all drunk and shit, and coming off like cocky smartasses. A few of those van rides got ugly after shit like that. It must've sounded like the Buddy Rich bus ride tapes—I went off on them.

It was fucked up 'cause I had been hanging with Parris since the early '80s, and I loved playing with him. He was a sick guitarist and he really was my boy; at least I thought he was. But he started to act like a snob. And I think that Rob rubbed off on him. Rob never fit in. The funny shit is, when he first joined, Parris didn't like him at all. But then they bonded, and that was it. Rob was never into Hardcore; he didn't know shit about it. The truth is, I'd lost interest in a lot of the people and bands on the New York scene. But I still had a lot of friends on the scene, not just in New York but through-out the States and worldwide. It had been my life, and I still considered it my home.

Parris was really moving away from it too. He got into hanging out at rock and Goth-type bars and trendy clubs—the "cool people" scene. All I know is, shit was changing, and looking back Rob should have never been considered for the gig 'cause he had so little in common with us, or our fans. We based our decision on his playing, and he was the best who tried out at the time.

When Hardcore kids came up to him at shows and asked him if he liked this band or that band, he'd be like, "I don't listen to Hard-core, I never did, and I don't like much of what I've heard." It might have been true, and that's cool. But the way he'd say it sounded really obnoxious, like, "Why is this fucking guy even here?"

A couple things happened on our short tour that completely

freaked out Rob and his guitar tech buddy. It freaked out Parris and Dave as well, but it was business as usual for me, Squint, Bleu, etc. As usual, there were several brawls and high-intensity situations. But there was one incident where some dickheads tried to rob our merch truck while my boys were on call. And let's just say that people were left twitching on the ground and bleeding, needing serious medical attention. The kind of bad shit that you don't want to see, be a part of, or be near—the van screeching out of town, running red lights, etc. And so, them metal boys that were rolling with us were fucking freaked. They weren't used to being around shit like that, or shit like that happening at shows. But this wasn't our first day at the beach. So anyway, after that tour Parris and Rob decided to break out. They thought I was a dick or whatever.

Well, whether that's true or not, I had no intention of going out like that. By the grace of God, the law firm we owed all that money to went out of business. So the debt no longer existed. I had also become friendly with Ken Anderson, the lawyer who represented us during the Profile bullshit, and he kept working with me.

Around that time, I talked with some German booking agents, Marc and Ute from M.A.D. They were like, "Harley, what's happening with the Cro-Mags?" They were all on fire about trying to bring the band over. I explained to them the situation and all the drama and that the "band" was really just me at this point. They told me, "Pull a line-up together and we'll bring it over." They introduced me to the guys from Century Media Records, and the label was interested in signing me as the Cro-Mags. At that point, I owned the name exclusively.

So I started negotiating a deal with Century Media, and jamming with an old friend, Gabby Abularach, who I knew since the early '80s. Gabby had been around the original NYHC scene. He lived at Westbeth and used to go see the Bad Brains, the Stimulators, and the Mad. He was friends with Frontline and Mackie and all of those guys; his brother was the guitarist for the Icemen. He didn't look like a Hardcore dude, but after playing with those other two, I'd play with this fuckin' guy in a second! He learned all the stuff with no problem.

At that point Century Media asked me if there was any way to get John on it. They said the kids would love it and it would sell records. I was a little hesitant. But they were like, "Come on!" The idea was that they would offer me a better record deal if it were the two of us, or possibly more than the two of us, together.

So I got Doug, and then approached John. I took the songs I had written while I was working with Rob and Parris, since they had planned on recording them without me, I said, "Fuck it," and recorded them with Dave on drums, Gabby on guitar, and Doug and John. That was the line-up that signed to Century Media. Since I owned the name and because I had written all the music, I got the majority of the money from the advance. But we all got part of it, and we all got put on salary from Century Media. And of course everybody knew the breakdown and agreed to it when they signed the record deal.

We recorded *Alpha Omega* at Normandy Sound in Rhode Island, where we had recorded *Best Wishes*.

Up to the point John came back in the band, I had been singing. So when he returned, we decided to sing the record together, kind of like a Hardcore version of what Glenn Hughes and David Coverdale did in Deep Purple, where Glenn did the high parts and Coverdale did the low parts—and it sounded amazing.

Unfortunately, there were parts of the record John couldn't pull off. That wasn't just my opinion; it was everyone's opinion. He tried and it wasn't cutting it. It was fucked up. The whole band and engineers were listening to John do these parts, and they're like, "Oh my God. This is fuckin' horrible. What are we gonna do?" He was doing all kinds of weird shit, almost like Cal from Discharge on the *Grave New World* album, but way worse—high-pitched ooohs and aaaahs and ohhhs trying to get all "vocal" instead of going for that *The Age of Quarrel* feel. It was just bad.

Now, this was before the days where everybody was digitally making singers sound like whatever they wanted to make them sound like. At least in Hardcore, people weren't doing that shit yet. And John just wasn't cutting it. Me and the engineers and the rest of the guys talked about it, and I wound up singing a lot more of the record than I had planned—and John really took that shit personally. He thought it was completely maliciously intended on my behalf, but it was the whole band and the engineers that felt that way. But since I was credited as producer, I got the blame. So I

tried my best to sound like him and mimic all the new "ooohs" and screams and shit he was doing at that time, and just did my tracks.

The record came out, and John was pissed off that I was all over it. I did my best to sing like him; that's why people can't tell who sang what part. But in the studio, it was everybody's call on that one, everyone but John.

You know how you can always tell when a heavy band is starting to lose their edge when they use a fucking keyboard? Yeah, we did that. We were working on the guitar sounds, and at one point we had just the guitar solo with the drums and we started bringing up the other tracks slowly. We all looked at each other and were like, "That sounds cool." So one thing led to another and yeah, we got a bit carried away. But hey, it was fun. We all drank mushroom tea during that session, so it mighta sounded better to us at the time.

Alpha Omega didn't feel like a real Cro-Mags album to me. Even though I love that freestyle jam at the end of the album, it didn't feel right. Some of those songs were written after I stopped playing with Parris and Rob, and some of them were parts I'd written years earlier. But most of it was from what we'd written together, and looking back, I don't think Rob's metal influence was good on my and/or Parris' style of playing. But I did what I had to do, 'cause in my mind, they were cutting my throat. They were gonna record the shit without me if I didn't record it first—bail on me and leave me with a big-ass debt. And I was trying to stay alive. That was that.

We did *Alpha Omega*, and when it was time to tour, Dave couldn't do it, so we got Amit Shamir, Gabby's jazz drummer friend—a really nice guy, but so not a Hardcore dude. He was a good drummer, but he wasn't used to hitting that hard, and there were parts he'd forget.

Doug only did one gig supporting that album. We flew out to L.A. for a record release party, and we played a great show at the Hollywood Palladium with Type O Negative, the Exploited, and Biohazard. We did songs from *The Age of Quarrel*, *Best Wishes*, and *Alpha Omega*. Parris was at that gig in the crowd, and I could see him while we were playing, which was really weird, I gotta say.

It was one of many shows over the years that I found myself up on top of PA stacks while playing my bass, going, "How the fuck

did I get up here?" Sometimes when you're playing, you don't realize what you're doing, you're just caught up in the moment, and
I guess I climbed the PA! People in the crowd were yelling, "Jump!
Jump!" What was I gonna do, crawl back down on my hands and
knees? I dove off the stack, between the PA and the stage. I was
15–20 feet up in the air. I have a clip of Wattie from the Exploited
talking about it, going, "I saw this crazy cunt jump off a 20-foot PA
stack, with his fucking bass on!" He was standing next to Glenn
Danzig when I did it. A few people caught me, but most of the people tried to jump out of my way! One guy in particular, God bless
him, jumped underneath me and took most of the impact.

After that, we went on tour to Europe. Doug decided that he
wouldn't join us, for whatever reason. We wound up going: Gabby,
John, and Amit, and me. It did start off fun. Marc and Ute were
tour-managing us and traveling on the bus along with a bunch of
other Germans; it was a lot of laughs. We played some sick shows
at these huge squats across Europe, and we did a big-ass circus
tent-like place in Berlin. We even played at the ETA's headquarters
in the middle of the fuckin' woods in Basque country.

We pulled up to this fucking abandoned factory with all kinds of
political graffiti spray-painted all over it, and dogs running around
barking. We pulled up in our tour bus, and all of a sudden, all these
punks and metalheads came out of the woods; it was funny as
shit! What a bizarre gig that was. We had no idea we were playing
at the fuckin' ETA's headquarters!

By that time, there was a clash in musical direction. I wanted to
bring the music back to *The Age of Quarrel* meets *Best Wishes*, while
John was trying to get the band to change direction, which was
crazy, 'cause he'd never written a song in his life. One night one of
our roadies, Bleu, came into my hotel room and he was like, "Dude,
you better get in there quick. They're having a band meeting without you, and it's fucked up what's going on in there." I walk in, and
I hear John saying, "We gotta start writing some shit that sounds
like Living Colour." And I just looked at them, like, "What?!" They
all stopped talking, and John was looking "busted." Living Colour?
Are you for real?

John's a real flavor-of-the-week type of guy. Whatever's popular
at that moment, he's into. When U2 blew up, he was all into U2,

and was trying to sound like Bono. When Living Colour blew up, it was all about them. When rap got big, he wanted to be a rapper. I listened to that Both Worlds record he did in the late '90s; that says it all. If left on his own, John will jump on whatever's current. But sadly the only music he can pull off is Hardcore.

So, after that European tour, shit started getting weird. Me and Gabby still laugh about it today.

When I look back at all of this shit now, it's so fucking Spinal Tap. But at the time it was just drama. If I was smarter back then, I woulda just laughed off all of the stupidity. But I was a knuckle-head-ass motherfucker my damn self, too.

John tries to say that I ripped off the band on that tour. But I never had the money, nor did I have access to it. Marc from M.A.D. and Ute had it. I didn't go through their pockets to steal my own money. I was making money; why the fuck would I rip the band off and fuck it up for myself? I had a girlfriend with me for a little while on that tour, and they even tried to say she stole it.

I asked Gabby if he had any stories he wanted to share about that time period:

"Around April 1992, when the whole break-up of the band happened, John called me up, talking about doing the band without you, and writing new tunes. He said something like, 'Yo, there's a new music out called grunge! They just had a grunge fashion show on Spring Street.' And then he followed it with the usual stuff about how we have to write music that is popular now, metal and Hardcore are dead, etc., etc. What about when he wanted us to sound like De La Soul or P.M. Dawn; remember him singing 'Paper Doll' on the tour bus? Amit's 'big-time producer' older brother had done some big rap and dance radio hits. When Amit introduced him to the band, John jumped out of the car, did a break dance move, and said 'I'm a devastatin' white rapper!' Or my shock when we began playing live, and he kept looking over to me to cue him in for his parts to songs that I had only learned a few months ago, and he had been playing since 1985? And we didn't even get into the fart and doo-doo stories. Don't you remember the time early on during the tour in Germany when he picked up his raw shit with his bare hands to write 'Fuck Off Nazis' in the bathroom of a truck stop? And when he came back on the tour bus, he gloated about how he dotted the letter 'i' in Nazis with a swazi?"

And now this brings us to the legend of the Doo-Doo Man.

Like Peter Parker is Spiderman, John Bloodclot is the Doo-Doo Man. Some people are gonna think I'm talking shit, but this is true and it's just hilarious. I couldn't make it up if I tried.

Back in the old days, Mackie used to call John "the Doo-Doo Man." He came up with that one. It started because John always would ride shotgun in the van, with his feet up on the dashboard, and you'd always know "it" was coming before you got hit, because he'd start giggling. He'd be sitting there farting his ass off, but he'd be farting at the vents up in the front, so the shit would be coming out of the A/C in the back. He loved doing it—he loved tormenting us with his ass. Over the years it turned into a monster. John started doing things that were pretty fuckin' disturbing.

Here's this guy who tries to carry himself as spiritual and all into cleanliness, as he does come off very clean and neat. But then he started doing things like taking a shit and not flushing it—walking out of the bathroom giggling and leaving it there. So whoever walked in next would be like, "Oh nooo!" And then he began to shit on the toilet seats – he'd come walking out giggling, and whoever would walk in after had to deal with shit all over the seat. And it just got worse from there.

In Canada, in like '84, I remember the freak climbed up on the sink in the bathroom, and used the revolving cloth towel over the sink to wipe his ass.

One time we were out west at Venice Beach and John comes waddling through the water—he's all grinning and laughing, saying "Yo, don't come over here... I just took a shit!" The motherfucker goes and shits, right there in the middle of every-fuckin'-body, and a fuckin' wave comes and his turd starts riding the wave toward a group of playing kids in the water, at which point John starts trying to paddle away from it! He's all laughing his ass off. And this was after we had been at a Hare Krishna temple, hung out there the night before and ate breakfast there. And then this dude is going and doing shit like that.

Another time, me and John were down in Florida, back in *The Age of Quarrel* days. Crazy Dave, this girl and me are all sitting on the bed in this hotel, and all of a sudden, blam! The bathroom door flies open, and John comes bursting out, giggling hysterically with a plastic plate—with a pile of shit on it! I'm screamin' "Yo, get that out of here! What the fuck is wrong with you?" He walked over to the hotel room door and wings it out into the parking lot. All of us were just in disbelief.

The first time he went really fuckin' crazy with it, we were on tour, and this guy at a gas station in East Germany was giving us a hard time. He wouldn't answer us in English, and his response was, "Learn how to say it in German." Our tour manager Marc and Ute from the booking agency M.A.D. were on tour with us. They are both German, and Marc was like, "They don't speak German, quit being an asshole!" And the guy said, "Well, they should learn." So I got back on the bus, and said, "Yo, John, do me a favor—go 'use' this dude's bathroom, all right?" And John's like, "Well, I don't know. I just took a shit not that long ago." He started giggling and rubbing his stomach real hard. He was like, "Let me see what I can do."

The motherfucker goes in there while we were out there fueling up our bus, then gets back on giggling hysterically. This mother-fucker took a shit in the middle of the bathroom floor, then took the shit and wrote in big letters on the wall: "NAZI," and drew a big swastika over it... in shit! Then he took all the toilet paper he had wiped his ass with and stuck it to the walls. And he was telling us this while laughing hysterically, tears running down his face. I started yelling at the bus driver, "Fuck filling up the tank, we got to go!" So we got going. But that was just one of many.

We'd be on tour in Europe, where you'd go to a club and the toilet would be just a hole in the floor and two spots for your feet. And you'd kind of stand there, hover, and aim for the hole. Well, this nigga would always shit in front of the hole. So you'd have no choice but to walk in and see it. And he'd leave dirty toilet paper everywhere. It was uncool for a grown man to do; it's not funny, and I don't get it. Shit is something to deposit and leave. You don't play with it, fuck with it, or decorate with it. And it got worse over the years.

What would inspire a grown man to be so involved with his doo-doo? There'd be a perfectly usable, functioning, clean bathroom in a club or in a dressing room, and he'd go shit on the roof of the club, in the stairwell of the club, or outside. And this ain't something that happened for a short period of time. Even during the 2000 reunion, John went in the dressing room and locked the door. The motherfucker came out of the dressing room, giggling, with a paper bag. He walked all the way through the club and up to the band standing in front of the van—me, Garry Sullivan, Doug Holland, and Rocky George. He walked up giggling and holding the bag out toward us. And I knew that look on his face. I was like, "No motherfucker, you fuckin' did not!" The smell started to hit us, everybody turned to leave, and John was just standing there giggling.

And the stories go on and on, all the way 'til the 2001 tour, and I'm certain must still go on today. I'm sure to this day the Doo-Doo Man still leaves his mark. Gabby used to call him "Swami Fudge Clot." Everybody knows about it, it's just that nobody wants to say anything, 'cause it's fuckin' embarrassing. Yeah man, Hare Krishna.

After all that 'let's write songs like Living Colour' shit in the hotel, it started going downhill. He got bitter about the record deal as time went on, and the fact that I got more money. That's part of the reason he started saying "Harley ripped me off." He knew I was getting paid more: I wrote the songs, I owned the name, and I got us the deal through my lawyer.

By then I had become increasingly disillusioned with the Krishna movement, Hardcore, and pretty much everything and everyone, including—and especially—John. I'd sit and watch John at the shows, and he'd have all these kids sitting around him in awe, like, "Oh wow, John Joseph!" And he'd be trying to impress them, talking all Hare Krishna this, that, and the other, and trying to be all philosophical. And then we'd go back on the bus, and he'd go right back to his normal/jive-ass self.

I started dressing completely not Hardcore or Skinhead. And it was on purpose. I was making a point, to go against the grain of what was cool on the scene. It was a definite choice I made. I was like, "I'm not going to go out and be what people expect, 'cause I am not what people expect." And I'm not going to be their fake-ass "spiritual advisor" like John 'cause my spirit is just as contaminated as everybody else's, whereas John really thrived off of that "guru" crap. He really loved the admiration. I found it to be more of a burden.

Part of my turn-off on the Hare Krishna thing in general came from watching John: from knowing him, seeing him preach, and seeing how he actually was when he wasn't playing that role. And really, the more I got involved with that movement, the more hypocritical I realized a lot of things about it and him were. I was almost embarrassed that I had been "had"—but at that point it was all a joke to me. I was still digging some of the philosophy, but I was done with people in general: skinheads, Hardcore, religion. All of it was sheep-like bullshit to me.

PART 2: THE DARK SWAMI — PRTHU PUTRA SWAMI A.K.A. "DEVIL MAN"

Speaking of the Krishnas, in the late '80s, I became friends with Patrick Geoffrois. Before I knew him, I used to jokingly refer to him as "Devil Man." He would sit on St. Marks Place, reading palms and doing tarot cards; he lived in the neighborhood, so I used to see him around all the time. He wore all black, lots of pentagrams, all kinds of snake bone necklaces and shit. One day, I found out he was a Prabhupada disciple from back in the day. So from that point on, whenever I'd see him, I'd whisper "Prabhupada" under my breath as I'd walk by him, to see if I'd get a reaction. The first few times, you could see his ears perk up, but he didn't say anything. Then one time I did it, he spun around with a big smile, and said, "All glories to Srila Prabhupada."

I laughed and asked him, "Yo man, I been dying to ask you how you got from being a Prabhupada disciple to where you are now." He explained that Prabhupada was the greatest magician he ever saw, and that he had seen him in France, when he was young and deeply involved with the magical arts. It turned out not only was he one of the real Prabhupada disciples, but he was a very close and personal servant to the man. Prabhupada gave Patrick the name "Prthu Putra Swami." Over the years of knowing him, I learned more about Prabhupada than I'd ever known.

I didn't realize at the time that I had met Patrick years ago when he had been in the band the Contortions, back in the '70s with James Chance. Although that wasn't my scene, I knew of all those people back in the Stimulators days. Well, me and Patrick became very close. He told me a lot about Prabhupada and about magic. Patrick freaked John the fuck out, and Patrick loved that John was such a simpleton.

As it turned out, Patrick had quite a following, not just on the Lower East Side within the magic community, but also in his native France, and with that necromantic freakazoid metalhead world. Unfortunately, he also attracted other freaks that were dabbling in the so-called "black arts"—one of them was the "soup killer" dude, Daniel Rakowitz.

The Daniel Rakowitz incident thrust Patrick into the news. They even went as far as saying it was a Satanic ritual killing that Patrick was involved with. It was such media-driven scapegoating. Of course, there was no connection other than this loser freak was fascinated with the fact that Patrick really knew his shit. Everyone in that 'hood knew each other; hell, I knew Rakowitz, I smoked a joint with him in Tompkins Square Park once. I just thought he was some hippie fuckin' loser. Anyway, Patrick freaked out John, and of course, I fed into it.

I felt like this was a guy who knew Prabhupada, but he also understood the world I came from. He wasn't a fuckin' sheep like those other motherfuckers. He was a Sanyasi and he wasn't trying to make money and milk Prabhupada's movement after his death. Patrick referred to them as "crime bosses." He said, "They wanted Prabhupada to die."

Patrick passed away after *Alpha Omega*—that was another thing that left me in a bad place. I miss him a lot.

He was a rebel, a rebel from the movement just like I was a rebel from the scene. Back in the day, people referred to me as a "Skinhead leader"; they used to write about me that way in fanzines like *Maximum RockNRoll*. People even spoke about me in that way, even though there was no such thing on the scene. But sheep always need a leader, and scenes always need people to mimic. I was no elected leader. I didn't have a "gang." I retaliated against all of that shit, I wasn't with it—just like I retaliated against Hare Krishna. I never liked being surrounded by sheep, wannabes and ass-kissing fucks. That is not my scene, never was, never has been and sure as shit never will be.

PART 3: NYHC NEW SCHOOL: "A STORY OF CREWS AND SHEEP"

In the late '80s, you had an influx of new kids on the scene, most of them bridge-and-tunnel; it seems like everyone started forming little crews or cliques. It was all teenage fantasy gang stuff, pretty tame. These were kids who hung out, went to shows, used to write their name on walls—whatever initials stood for their crew. They'd all troop into shows together, kind of in awe of the old-school dudes. This is back when bands like Sick of It All and all their friends used to wear necklaces with the little dragon thing on them. Before that, there had been the Agnostic Front "Skinhead Army" and the "Cro-Mag Skins" or "Krishna Skins" as people called us, who wore beads and shit—but it didn't really turn into gang-mentality shit in New York until maybe the late '80s or early '90s.

Prior to that point, my friends and me were kind of the hard-asses on the scene, the ones who used to fuck shit up. We'd get in fights at shows with people who didn't know what was up and would get outta line, or people from outta town who'd come to our shows and fuck around.

I don't know about the mythology that people want to pretend is true now, but when all that gang and crew shit started, those kids were Cro-Mags and AF fans, mostly from Brooklyn, Astoria, Queens, Jersey, Long Island or wherever—Sunset Skins and so on. I was cool with most of them. I didn't know all of them. Some of 'em saw Cro-Mags back when it was me, John, Parris and Doug, so I'd known most of them since they started coming around.

Sure, some of them were knuckleheads but most of them were good guys. They were no different than a lot of us had been when

302

we were their age, and they all knew and respected me and knew my rep from the old days. It wasn't 'til years later that more new kids got involved and shit started to change.

By the '90s you had people that just discovered the Hardcore scene, people who had never seen the Cro-Mags and thought Madball and Sick of It All were "old school"—kids who didn't know the history and hadn't been part of a scene before. And it kept going that way 'til you had the "new" new jacks thinking Skarhead and 25 Ta Life were "old school" bands.

Ironically NYC, a city that had once been known for violence and crime started to change, to gentrify and get more tame and less violent. The Hardcore scene started to get more violent, almost as if the new kids were trying to live up to the reputation that NYC once had. Now that "Hardcore kids," punks, and Skinheads weren't getting jumped on the streets by other groups, they turned on themselves, and it's kind of pathetic.

I think it's funny how some people now glorify the same dumbasses who started bringing hammers and chains and shit like that out on the dance floor in the late '80s and early '90s at Hardcore shows. Those kids were new jacks then and are now considered "old school" by the new jacks of today.

Now they say things like "DMS" started as a "graffiti crew." Maybe it did. Like I said, there were lots of little Hardcore crews writing their names on stuff around that time. To my knowledge, DMS originally stood for Doc Marten Skins. They were pretty much multi-ethnic Skinheads. Some of them had been late-'80s Hardcore/punks 'til they shaved their heads and became Skinheads; others were ex-metalheads who discovered NYHC. They were into Cro-Mags, AF, and Warzone. I guess Freddie from Madball was always in it. I don't really know. Roger started bringing him around once in a while when he was a kid, that's about it. I remember the first time he showed up with Roger but he didn't come around much.

People in bands started joining crews, or people in crews starting joining bands, and singing songs about it and hyping it up like it was larger than life, like it was some real "hard" shit instead of just a bunch of knuckleheads and kids in Hardcore bands. Some of the new bands started making it over to Europe where people didn't know what was what, and to them, New York still had this aura of toughness, and before you know it people started believing their own hype. And it started turning into some real soap-opera bullshit. The joke was that New York was no longer the hard city it had been. So now the imagery of NYHC "hardness" was now just that: image.

Hardcore started borrowing the worst aspects of hip-hop and metal and turning into some new mish-mosh crap and still calling itself NYHC; wannabe gangsta rap/speed metal bullshit. Hardcore became the antithesis of what it once was. And even in the guise of unity and New York Hardcore, everybody was talking shit behind each other's backs—all the bands that everybody thought were friends were all talking shit about each other.

Eventually, people started turning on each other, kicking people out of their "crews." When I heard that some of these motherfuckers started having meetings, like some kind of raccoon lodge or some shit and paying dues, etc., I thought it was fucking comical. What the fuck does this have to do with Hardcore or the Hardcore scene? When I heard SOB and others got kicked out of DMS, I was like "damn, he's been representing that shit since it started." I thought the whole thing was kind of ridiculous; I didn't get any of it.

Back in the '90s when John started talking shit about me, some of these dumbasses started siding with him. I didn't give a fuck. These people meant nothing to me. I always figured my old friends knew what was up. But by this point the "scene" was made up of a new generation of kids with no memory, and as it grew, even a lot of the old heads started pandering to the new jacks. I guess everyone felt that to maintain their "cool" status, they had to be down with the new scene. It all looked like a popularity contest to me. Hardcore was just life for me coming up. It's where I grew up; it wasn't some scene I joined.

This new scene was a circle jerk of assholes trying to rise to the top of some shit pile. It wasn't about the music; it was about the posturing. Where old-school NYHC had a direct connection to punk rock before it, now it was taking the worst elements of rap and metal and combining them with the worst elements of Hardcore.

Kids on the scene used to get jumped by the gangs in my neighborhood; sure, we started fighting back and we started getting harder, but we never tried to be them. We did not want to be like them. These days all they do is glorify drug dealing, do gang shit, jump people, and do blow.

Sure, when I was a kid I did a lot of drugs and got in a lot of fights and people thought I was tough. Me and my friends unintentionally ushered in that era of New York Thugcore/Hardcore. But time goes by and you grow up, and you learn things. You see friends die and go to jail and you learn from your mistakes, and from others. Years later when I started training Jiu-Jitsu with people like Renzo Gracie, Ryan Gracie and all the old-school MMA guys, I realized that, yeah sure, I'm tough, I can fuck someone up in a street fight, but yo, these guys are really tough. And at this point in life, all that "hard rock" tough-guy shit means nothing to me. Real tough guys are fighting in cages for money or in wars; they're not jumping people at Hardcore shows, ten against one.

A funny thing happened around the time of *Alpha Omega*. One night, I was hanging out with my friend Bags, who'd just gotten out of jail. He was the guy who bit off the dude's thumb while I was recording *The Age of Quarrel*. This is when I had my hair long. And once again—just like at the Ritz during the *Best Wishes* era—I almost got jumped by a bunch of Hardcore dudes that didn't recognize me and, ironically, grew up listening to my music. But as shit would have it, they fucked with the wrong people.

Me and Bags were both tripping on LSD; he had just got out of jail that week. These motherfuckers were following us, talkin' shit. There was some chick with them, she was some pseudo-Skinhead-looking bitch. I remember she was walking ahead of them near us; she could hear us talking and started to look a bit nervous.

Bags was like, "Yo Harley, I just got out of jail, I ain't takin' no shit from motherfuckers." I'm like, "Yo Bags, chill." I had a .38 snub-nose with hollow tips in my inside jacket pocket. Bags was like, "Yo, fuck that!"

One of them said, "Aww, look at the Skinhead," talkin' about Bags 'cause he had his boots and bomber jacket on (that he had been wearing when he got arrested for biting the guy's thumb off—he just got out of jail like two days before). He looked at me and said under his breath, "Harley, I'll kill these motherfuckers."

Then someone said, "Fuckin' punks!" So Bags said, "That's it," turned around, picked up a garbage can and threw it at them. He was screaming, "I'll kill you motherfuckers!" They looked like they were gonna piss in their pants; that's when I turned around and opened my jacket. I remember pulling out a knife and putting it to one of their eyeballs. I was later told I flashed the gun; I may have, I don't remember. One dude said something like, "We didn't know it was you, Harley." I was like "Fuck you motherfuckers!"

Bags was going off, I was talkin' mad shit, and by the end, me and him and were crying and hugging each other, screaming, "You motherfuckers don't even know what a real friend is!" We were all like, "I'll kill and die for you, bro, they don't fuckin' know, they don't get it." As I said, we were on acid; we were going totally fuckin' nuts. Looking back, I'm surprised that we didn't do something really crazy. They all backed down like big-time bitches, and me Bags and staggered off into the night. We were going to fuck them up, and they knew it. But these fools were gonna jump us 'cause they didn't recognize us. That's some pitiful shit.

In the old days we would never have jumped another punk rocker, Skinhead or Hardcore kid just 'cause we didn't know them or recognize them. In New York, we were glad to meet people and bands from out of town. People didn't get approached with this hard rock attitude; it was more unified. So that's when shit really started to turn against itself. Even in the day when I was a hard-ass, I didn't seek out people on the scene to beat down and prove myself. I had enough issues with outside people trying to fuck with us, and if I did have issues with someone on the scene, I didn't need other people to handle it for me. I handled my own shit.

The fact is Cro-Mags was a big part of what changed the sound, style and image of Hardcore; bands like us and Suicidal Tendencies were bringing a harder, tougher edge to Hardcore. It was a little more intimidating. It had thug-ness to it, "street-edge." My friend Steven Reddy who runs Equal Vision Records said, "There were some bands that were just scary to go see. You knew it was going to be crazy, and you knew shit was going to go down."

After the European *Alpha Omega* tour, Cro-Mags attempted one last tour, which completely fell apart. In fact, we were all sitting in the van waiting for him, and John didn't even show up! We wound up doing the shows as a three-piece with me, Gabby, and Amit. Bags came out on that trip with us a roadie. The shit was insane.

I knew people weren't gonna be happy. The posters had a picture with me, John, Doug, Gabby, and Dave, and here I was with Gabby and Amit. At that point, I was like, "Fuck it, the show must go on." And it did. But it wasn't the show people wanted to see. I got fucked up: shitfaced and tripping. I was like, "These people ain't gonna see what they came for—I might as well give 'em something altogether different that they'll never forget!" Now, as it turned out, Bags played a really mean flute—and no, I don't just mean skin flute, the motherfucker could play like some crazy Jethro Tull-type shit! So I brought a flute with us that was my grandfather's from the military, and we did an insane fucking Jethro-Cro-Mags-Tull freak show!

It was around this time I met the future mother of my sons, Harley and Jonah. It was one of the gigs that John didn't show up for, in Albany at the South Troy Community Center. I was losing my mind, tripping my ass off on LSD. I met her and her brother and their friends at the show. I wound up playing part of that show in nothing but Speedos and Saran Wrap from my ankles up to my neck!

I didn't hook up with her 'til a few years later. I became friends with some of the kids up there, and started going upstate to visit them from time to time.

After touring as a three-piece, I was no longer interested in going out on tour with John. I was like, "Fuck that asshole." He left us hanging. He was talking mad shit, so I was just like, "Fuck it." I kept living off the monthly paychecks from Century Media; they were trying to get me to go back out on tour with John. But there was no way that was happening—John and me would've been at each other's throats. But there was enough leftover material recorded from the *Alpha Omega* sessions to do a second album 'cause it was originally supposed to be an "epic"—like twice as long—but we ran over budget. So there were all these unfinished tracks that were ready to be finished and turned into an album. Either John approached Century Media or they approached him. I don't know exactly what happened, and I don't give a fuck anymore.

They took those leftover tracks from the *Alpha Omega* sessions, and turned them into an album. It was fuckin' horrible. They called it *Near Death Experience*, from a song title I came up with.

It wasn't "near death"—it was "death." I mean, *Alpha Omega* was not the greatest Cro-Mags album by any stretch of the imagination, but *Near Death Experience* is just fuckin' horrendous. It's embarrassing that it had the Cro-Mags' name on it.

Over the years, me and John had a few minor "incidents" that he blew way out of proportion. One time at CBGBs during the late '90s, I was just hanging out. I had just smoked two fat blunts, and he snuck up from behind me, hit me and ran. What a bullshit/cowardly thing to do! If the motherfucker had any heart, he woulda stepped to me like a man.

John has talked a lot about how tough he is. I've known John since I was about 13, and I've only known him to get into maybe three fights ever.

AFTER THE OMEGA AND BEFORE THE REVENGE

Chapter Thirteen

Before I get into this next chapter, I'm telling you that I had to lose a lot of stuff from this era 'cause I have kids now, and I don't want them to know exactly how insane things got or to think I'm a worse piece of shit than they already will or do. But again, this is proof that you can plummet to the bottom of the worst depths of hell and still come back and try to become a better person.

There was enough filth, drugs, orgies, violence and crime during this period to write a book about nothing else. As insane as it was, and as much fun as I thought I was having, deep down I was looking for a way out. I think that's why I took everything to such extremes. I don't think I cared if I lived. There were times I don't think I wanted to. I'm not proud looking back on it now. If anything, I'm surprised I survived.

In the early '90s, it became "fashionable" to be a heroin addict. People were glorifying Kurt Cobain and Courtney Love and the rest of the celebrity drug culture. Calvin Klein built an entire ad campaign around the strung-out, skinny bleakness of "heroin chic," but there was nothing chic about the real life of addicts. The MTV version of what was the Real World during those years was a distant stretch from anything resembling what the "real world" actually was.

That being said, after *Alpha Omega*, I started spiraling downward. I fell into some serious drinking and drug use. Every time I've fallen into drugs, it's been because I didn't have someplace constructive to put my energy and/or over chicks, or a combination of the two.

And it did get bad for a while. One night, actually one morning, I was fuckin' destroyed, and on the subway. I'd been partying all night; I was probably high on dope, pills, and alcohol. I had been wearing the same clothes for a week, beat-up looking, unshaven—I'd been partying for days. It was so late that it was early: morning rush hour. For those who don't know morning rush hour in Manhattan, it's so jammed on the trains that there's no room to do anything. You could be having the crack of your ass getting felt up or getting pickpocketed, and there's not much you could do about it. It's so crowded, people could have their hands in your pockets and you wouldn't even know.

I was such a mess. By that point, I was not feeling good. The last thing I'd eaten the night before was broccoli and tofu with black bean sauce, and brown rice. I was sitting on the subway bench next to the window, leaning all over. Well, you know how you can get that "projectile vomit" going? It comes up, you catch it in your cheek for a quick second, and then it just explodes out of your face? Well, it just filled up my mouth, and went *bwaaaaaaaaahhh*— all over the floor! Then it happened again.

I had a circle of people around me trying to get as far away from me as they could. But there was no room anywhere. I started heavin'. I got up, got to the door. The door opened for a quick second—it was too crowded on the train for anyone to get in, so the doors did one of those quick "open and shut" moves before anybody could get in or get out. But in that quick second that the door was open, I projectile-vomited straight ahead, right at the entire platform of people standing in front of me! I blasted them right in their fuckin' faces! It was in Midtown too, so everybody was dressed in suits. Everybody standing on that platform in front of the door got projectile-vomited on by this horrible, been-up-for-days mess of a burned-out rock 'n' roll loser. That door opened, and I just blasted them all, face-level, straight ahead of me! There was no way to escape, move, or avoid it, as the platform was packed. The door shut, and the train peeled out. I guarantee you that there were a lot of people who needed serious therapy after that shit. When this book comes out, somebody's probably going to track me down and kill me for being "that fuckin' guy that threw up on me at 8:00 in the morning on my way to work...in my mouth!"

I remember around that time, I somehow got word that P. Diddy was doing an audition for some rock project he was working on; it was supposedly a "black rock" project. I told a couple people I knew about it. One of them was Dr. Know from the Bad Brains; he said, "Why don't you go?" I said, "I ain't a brother!" He said, "Yeah you are," laughed, and said, "You might get the job!" So I went.

I showed up at some big rehearsal studio, I can't remember which one. Now mind you, this is back when I was smoking a lot of dust and shit—I was a mess, I had a scraggly beard going. So I get to the studio with a girlfriend of mine. There were all these people there. I don't remember why, but either my shirt was off or I was just wearing a vest or whatever, but I remember I was wilding out, all hyperactive and animated.

When P. Diddy, JLo and his entourage walked in, they looked at me, especially JLo, like I was nuts, but they tried not to react like anything was out of place. She couldn't stop gawking at my girlfriend and me. They were with some big gangbanger-looking bouncer, all in blue and some other rapper with tons of gold and diamonds and rings and gold teeth and shit. I guess they thought I was some crazy rock dude, which I was, but anyway…

The auditions started. He just sat there with her and his people and put different groups of us together to jam, no songs, just freestyle. I played bass and drums with a few different line-ups. Then at the end, he stood up and thanked us all for our time; he was very polite and courteous. Thinking about it now, the shit was comical: me wilding and freakin' the fuck out, with no shirt on in front of P. Diddy and JLo and all their crew—it was funny.

Around that time I was living in Fort Green, Brooklyn. It was still a bad neighborhood. I was down the block from Spike Lee, a few blocks from his store, "40 Acres and a Mule."

I'd started doing lots of psychedelics again. I was eating mushrooms, drinking mushroom tea, and smoking a lot of dust. One time, I really wanted to take it to another level and go deep inside my mind. So I filled my bathtub with hot water, turned on the cold shower, and aimed the fan at me. I turned off all the lights so I was in total darkness with the wind blowing, the hot steamy water from the tub, and the cold shower. I ate like an eighth of mushrooms, drank mushroom tea, ate acid, smoked a bag of dust, and got in the tub.

It was like sensory deprivation and stimulation all at the same time. I don't know how many hours I was in there, but when my girlfriend got home hours later, I looked like a fuckin' raisin. My mind was fuckin' out there; she thought I had lost it. I had one of the most insane and intense trips in my life, in the dark with just my mind to trip out on.

For a moment, I felt I could understand the mysteries of the universe and how everything worked. As I started to come back to Earth over the next few hours and days, I started to write it all down, all mixed with symbols and all kinds of crazy shit and it all made sense to me. I was like, "Wow! I figured out the mysteries of the universe!" Of course I lost the notebook a few weeks later with

315

all of the mysteries of the universe in it! Oh well. I'll never do that shit again. I'm lucky that my brain still works.

When I was at my worst, I carried a gun and was a bit of a dust-head. I think it was a paranoia thing. I was always in really shitty neighborhoods, and being a white dude in a lot of those neighborhoods was always a little sketchy. More than a few situations happened that were not so cool during that time—I'll just leave it at that.

So, I had an old Army issue .45 and a .38 snub-nose with hollow tips and fragmentation bullets that break into fragments when they hit bones and rip through you like shrapnel. But it wasn't even like I was "into guns," it was just the way I was living. I was bugging, doing crazy shit. There was a time in New York, in certain neighborhoods, where being armed may be the reason you got home at the end of the night—especially if you were dealing with criminals and drugs.

One time, I was so fucking high and stupid that I jumped the turnstile in a subway station, with that .38 full of hollow-tip bullets in it, and I got caught. I jumped it at the same time as these two other cats that I didn't know had jumped it, too. I had my gun and all my shit in a plastic bag with notebooks and this and that. As soon as I saw the cops come out, I dropped the bag—I let it slide down the back of my leg so they wouldn't see it. So if you were standing in front of me, you didn't really see me drop it. As I got up against the wall, I moved the bag over with my foot, and I stepped a little bit away from it. They start asking us, "Do you have ID?" I said, "I don't have ID, officer, but I've got my phone book in my pocket. There's a hundred numbers in here that you can call to verify who I am. Here's my mother's number, call her to verify who I am." The other guys had no ID, so the cops started cuffing them. Because I could at least try to prove who I was, they just wrote me a ticket. They're like, "All right, you can go now. Just make sure you show up on this date." I turned around, picked up my plastic bag, and fuckin' walked!

I was spending a lot of time in Central Park; I'd even hang out there at night, getting laid, getting high. One time, this fuck-up rich kid I knew had stolen a bunch of liquid Demerol and morphine from his dad, who had cancer or something. Anyway, we were getting fucked up in the bushes near Strawberry Fields, and I had never done liquid Demerol and morphine combined. I had no idea how much would be lethal or how much would be just enough to get high. I remember that right before I did it, I told the kid, "Just do me a favor, if I O.D., just call an ambulance before you split." Yeah, shit was pretty grim.

Another time in Central Park, it was the middle of the night and I was walking down one of those little paths; there was this staircase that went down a small hill and around to one of the side exits with lots of bushes and big rocks. It was on the Upper West Side of the park around 106th Street. On the path, there must've been thousands of empty crack vials with all the different colored caps scattered everywhere. The closer you got to this one spot on the hill, there were more and more of them. I was on dust so it was even more visceral. I was walking around the corner down the steps off in the bushes by this rock, and I see a pair of little girl's panties lying there in the bushes, and it sent a really bad feeling through me. I knew something fucked-up went down in those bushes. The whole shit was creepy and disturbing. This was New York back then; this is the way it was.

At one point I wound up in Albany, because I got a letter in my P.O. box from this band called Stigmata inviting me up there to see them play and maybe do a few songs with them. They said I could stay with them and they'd feed me, smoke me out, and get me drunk. I took them up on it; I had nothing else to do. I took another fuck-up friend of mine called O-Z with me. We were hanging out that day, and I figured, "Why take the ride alone?" We were both pretty dusted out at the time. He was a mess too, but not quite as "gone." He said, "Sure, fuck it," and we went up there on a Greyhound bus. I was smoking dust the whole way up in the bathroom of the bus, with one of those little metal blimps that people used to pack full of weed and smoke. At one point, I was so fucked up that I felt like I was in a spaceship and I'd forget I was in the bathroom. Every now and then, O-Z would come knock on the door and be like, "Yo, you been in there for a while. People need to use the bathroom, bro." I was like, "I'll be out in a minute," and I'd zone out, smoke some more, and breathe it out this little flap in the window.

I was so fucking zooted that I didn't know what the fuck was going on. I mighta been in there for hours, had he not got me out. I finally got to Albany, and there were a bunch of those kids waiting for me at the bus station. All of them were like Hardcore kids with their Jason Newsted of Metallica mohawks. Back then, everybody outside of Manhattan who was into metal had one of those haircuts. I showed up, and I was just a raging basket case, fucked up on dust. There were so many of them waiting for me, I couldn't even try to begin to remember all of their names. So I just made up nicknames for all of them and that was that. They didn't know what to make of me. There were a bunch of parties the week we got there, at people's houses in basements and keg parties in the woods. O-Z split back to the city after a few days and I stuck around to go to their gig.

When I originally got the letter and read it, I thought it said New York—I didn't realize they meant fucking Buffalo, New York! Damn, that's a hell of a drive. But I had nothing better to do, and I had no plans back home. I was kind of couch-surfing, crashing here and there. I had brought a bunch of dust up there with me, like a dozen bags or so. I was a mess, and I got that whole area's local fuck-ups fucked up out of their minds on Crazy Eddie. Anyway, I was smoking dust the whole drive to Buffalo with Stigmata, so I was fuckin' crazy. I was babbling all kinds of nonsense, singing songs, and playing acoustic guitar in their van, having a good old time, just being out of my mind. Those kids were all Cro-Mags fans—they must have all thought I was completely crazy.

So we got there and checked in to the hotel, pretty much in the middle of nowhere. All of a sudden, we see all of these Skinheads at the hotel. Not just your normal Skinheads that you might see at a Hardcore show, but straight-up Nazis with swastikas and Skrewdriver shirts, Hitler tattoos, and all that White Power shit. And they're walking around in groups outside the hotel with camcorders, talking "Nigger this, nigger that," and filming it. Then we started realizing there were other Skinheads at the hotel as well; they had a bunch of rooms. Some of the Stigmata guys were getting a little nervous; there were a few nervous giggles from our group. There was a black couple in the parking lot that got freaked out from all the shit they were talking. The hotel staff was black.

It was a really fuckin' ugly scene. There were a few black guests at the hotel, but besides that, the hotel was nearly empty; it was the Nazi Skinheads, the black staff, a few other guests, and us. The Skinheads pretty much outnumbered us all together. It was the middle of the night, and it kept getting weirder and tenser.

A couple of the Skinheads started making fun of the Stigmata guys 'cause they looked all metal. Anyway, we all got up to our room, and everybody was freaked out, trying to figure out what to do. The guys were all spread out, a few of us on each bed, some on the floor with sleeping bags and pillows. I was pretty high, but in my dusted state I was still very alert and aware of the situation and all of the potential outcomes. Having been in many violent situations and having been a Skinhead, I could see what might be around the corner. But I was so nuts at that point, I was reverting to crazy street mode and I was almost enjoying the tension, despite the chaos that might ensue. So I was in "ready mode." I had my Tanto knife with a 9" blade, which I kept in my inside jacket pocket, and my dust. I started looking around, assessing the group I was with. Despite most of these guys not seeming like fighters, there were a few in the bunch I felt would bang. I didn't know these boys well but I felt confident that if we stuck together, we'd be fine.

Bob Riley, the singer for Stigmata, was a big boy. One of the guitarists was a black belt; another guy, Caruba, was a big dude. He later joined the gang FSU and then became an outlaw biker. Plus there were a couple other guys that I thought would bang if shit went down—if nothing else out of fear. So, as I was sitting there looking around at this bunch and still wondering why all the fucking Skinheads were there to begin with, there was a knock at the door. Someone opened it, and about a dozen Skinheads were in the hall and started coming into the room. Most of them were like six feet tall and one of them had a camcorder filming. They were all Sieg Heiling at us, throwing their hands up in the air, going "White power!" They were all smirking, like, "Hmmm, what have we got here?" Immediately, the Stigmata guys got nervous and those guys could smell the fear, so they started trying to intimidate a little. Remember, there were very few people in the hotel.

At that point, I was recognized. Turns out pretty much every one of them had been a Cro-Mags fan at one point or another, and were all huge fans of *The Age of Quarrel*, and most of them had seen us play. Some of them had become Skinheads after having seen us play. So there was some respect there—but not much 'cause I was with all these "longhairs." I was looking all crazy and on drugs with long hair myself, hanging out with a bunch of hippie-looking metalhead motherfuckers and lookin' high as a motherfucker. So on one hand they were like, "Oh shit, Harley Flanagan from the Cro-Mags!" But at the same time they were like, "What the fuck happened to you?"

So they were checking me out, but they immediately started trying to intimidate the room. One of them said some shit to me about "What's up with the long hair?" They all looked at me to see the response. In one quick motion, I pulled my big-ass Tanto knife out from my inside vest pocket, and put it within an inch of his eyeball. Everyone froze. He started looking nervous. No one expected that shit; the room went dead silent; no one knew what to do. Everyone was frozen at that point. I was lookin' at him like "Yeah, what? My hair's a little longer, but I can still cut a mother-fucker's eyeball out!"

After a few tense moments, I smiled and put the knife away. They started telling me what fans they were, and how they'd seen me play. Turned out that some of them were in the band Bound For Glory. Pretty soon, some of the older ones began reminiscing about jumping people at our shows during *The Age of Quarrel* tour, with this look in their eyes like they were dreaming back to their best childhood memories, like they were talkin' about Christmas at their grandparents' home opening gifts or some shit. They were like, "Man, you guys were great!" They wound up leaving our room pretty quick after I pulled the knife on the one dude—and all the guys I was with breathed a sigh of relief. All the Stigmata guys were like, "What the fuck was up with that?" The guitarist Mike Maney or "3/5" as I called him, 'cause he had a S/E tattooed on his hand, and when I first saw it, it was upside down and I thought it said 3/5. Anyway, he was 3/5 from that point on. 3/5 and the rest of these guys were buggin' out. So I decided to go scout out the situation.

I walked around the hotel 'til I heard noise. I went and knocked on the door to one of the rooms full of Skinheads. I walked in as one of them was telling the rest all about his "Harley sighting," and that I had pulled a knife and what a mess I look like and shit. I was looking rather Charles Manson-ish at the time. I just walked in and was like, "What's up guys?" The room went silent. "How's it going?" They stayed quiet. I sat on the bed in the middle of them. One of them was looking at me all hard—grinding his teeth, trying to look crazy, like he wanted to jump me or some shit. I immediately stood up and went face-to-face with him and said, "What? You wanna do something? What's up?" I looked him dead in the face, and he looked down at the floor and kept grinding his jaw. He didn't say shit. I was like, "Yeah, that's what I thought." I sat back down and smiled. "So, how you guys doing?" I was still dusted out of my mind, so I didn't mind the whole tenseness of the situation. I was enjoying it and I was having fun fucking with them.

It turned out this one fat bitch who was with them was Canadian and knew Yob, Orbit, and some of them other dickheads from back in the day. So this gig that Stigmata had invited me to was a Skinhead White Power fest! This was in the middle of the blackest fuckin' ghetto in Buffalo, and this Nazi Skinhead band, Bound For Glory, was headlining, and playing along with all these other Skinhead bands. They had Nazi flags, rebel flags, and swastikas everywhere. And when I tell you it was an all-black neighborhood, I'm tellin' you, the shit was "'hood." The bar was small, and run by some crazy biker-looking dude. Turns out there were Skinheads coming from all over the country and Canada. I guess this gig was a big deal in the world of Nazi Skinheads—there were bands from all over the place, but it still only amounted to a small club full of about two hundred people at best.

Anyway, I was dusted out of my mind and still had a few bags left. The Stigmata guys completely freaked out when they saw what this gig was all about. Remember, most of the Stigmata guys were good kids; they weren't Nazis or Skinheads. One of them had a tattoo that said "Unity" with a black and a white hand. This was not their kind of scene. But they couldn't really leave, 'cause they needed to play the gig and get the money for gas to get home; it was a really long trip. It was a bad situation. So we were sitting there in their van in front of this shithole club in a black ghetto, with all these Nazi Skinheads running around Sieg Heiling, singing Skrewdriver songs, and making a lot of noise. Most of the 'hood wasn't really aware of what was going on yet, but as the evening progressed, people started noticing the racist energy that was projected. It started getting a little tense.

I was inside by this point. Me and one of Stigmata's crew got a few Skinheads dusted and left them fucked up and passed out on the floor in the back of the club. Every time the Skinheads would yell out "Sieg Heil," we'd yell out "Seagal!" or "Chuck Norris!" back at them! We were in ball-break mode, but still, the situation wasn't cool. There were all these Nazis and the neighborhood was starting to notice what was going on at the club. I remember two black teenagers, a guy and a girl, walked in the front door all pretending to rock out, laughing at all the Skinheads. At that point, there was no one at the door—all the boneheads were up by the stage going off to some whack-ass band, Sieg Heiling and stage diving and shit. The guy who promoted the shit immediately ran up, grabbed them and said, "Private party," and escorted them out the door before the Skinheads noticed. Then a few other neighborhood teenagers walked in and started looking around. At first, everyone on the block just thought it was a like a punk rock show or something. But by this point they were starting to notice it wasn't.

It was Stigmata's time to play, so they did. I remember when I was walking to the stage area, I saw the two Skinheads that I'd smoked dust with still all fucked up. One was still passed out on the floor, the other one was trying to figure out what was going on. They were totally fucked up. Stigmata did their thing, and I went up and sang "Life of My Own" and "Hard Times" with them, and all the Skinheads went crazy. Bound For Glory then played, we got paid and split. At that point the show was winding down. All the Skinheads were starting to scatter from the area and run back to their cars, just as bottles started crashing to the left and to the right of the club. It was about to jump off—we were ready to go so we got the fuck out of there.

I don't know if any of those Skinhead assholes got jumped or what happened after we left, but I was glad when we got the fuck out. And I was pissed at Bob 'cause I think he knew more about the gig than he told the rest of the band. To the rest of them, it was just a gig, they didn't fuckin' know. He knew Bound For Glory was playing and all that shit.

I had never heard of them or any of the other bands, and I thought they were all kind of whack. You know, the kind of bands where the guys are really struggling to play some real simple shit and they're just barely able to manage. It was funny after all the tough-guy shit, all the bravado, and then they get up there and try to do something, and it was just so musically unsound and technically weak—bad wannabe Skrewdriver-type bands, mixed with bad Hardcore, and childlike skills. These big guys struggling with their bar chords. These were guys more comfortable kicking someone in the face or goose-stepping at a Nazi rally. They were big oafish children, struggling to play some whack-ass shit that had zero musicality. It was as if they thought that screaming, "Nigger! Nigger!" or "Sieg Heil!" or "White Power!" through the lyrics of each song was enough to validate it. To them, it was serious. They were selling all kinds of swastika pins and Nazi paraphernalia at the merch table. To me, the whole shit was comical—except for the fact that if you were unlucky enough to be caught alone by some of those guys in the wrong situation, you might get jumped. But the whole thing was fuckin' ridiculous. There was even a midget running around Sieg Heiling and shit. A Nazi midget, I shit you not.

But that was the first time I saw Stigmata, and it was a very strange and fucked-up trip to say the least. From then on, Stigmata and me were pretty fuckin' tight. I wound up staying up there for a while at some friends of their parents' house. I bounced around that area for a while—couch-surfing, crashing in basements, and whatnot. After that, I wound up bouncing back and forth between the city and Albany. Around that time, I bumped into Parris on the street in NYC. We spoke briefly. It was a little tense at first. He was very standoffish but then seemed to share similar feelings about the whole turn of events. At the time I just wanted to know that I spoke my mind and I did consider him my friend and wanted him to know that, and clear the air. We did and it was cool.

When I went back out to the West Coast, I had over five grand in an envelope in my pocket, with a fucking rubber band around it. I flew back out and was staying with this chick in Santa Cruz for a little while, and then she kicked me out. So I hitchhiked to San Francisco with all my bags, my bass, and five Gs in my back pocket. Some hippie chick in a Volkswagen bus picked me up, blasting old

Sabbath, and we smoked kind bud the whole way to San Francisco. I was such a mess at one point, I showed up at my friend's house with everything I owned in a shopping cart, with a cow's skull tied to the front—like a Texas good ol' boy pulling up in a Cadillac with bull horns on the hood, except it was a shopping cart. I was real down-and-out. It was my friend Eddie's house; he and a few friends had a big-ass three-floor house right by Golden Gate Park, and they let me stay in the little room underneath the stairs where you'd normally keep your vacuum.

At one point, I was as broke as shit, and I got busted shoplifting food at a supermarket. I didn't have any ID, so the kids I was with ran back to the house and came back with three of my CD covers as ID! I was sitting in this holding area in the back of the store, and the store cops were looking at me all confused. They were like, "This is your ID?" I was holding up the pictures from *The Age of Quarrel*, *Best Wishes*, and *Alpha Omega*, and was like, "See? Look at the picture and my tattoos, this is me!" They were like "You're kidding, right? This is all the ID you got?" I was like, "Well, yeah. Look, you see what I stole. It ain't like I'm stealing jewelry, sunglasses, or some frivolous shit. I'm hungry and I'm broke; I'm stealing enough to eat!" One of the store cops was looking at the CDs and looking at me. It turns out her son was a metalhead. He had friends in bands, and she felt bad for me. She was like, "Why ain't you gigging? You got records out." I was just like, "Shit happens. The band broke up and I'm going through hard times now." So they said, "Just don't come back to this store, okay?" Then the last thing the lady cop said to me was, "What was the name of your band again? I want to see if my son's heard of them."

At one point I was staying at this apartment on lower Lower Haight, where there were just a bunch of fuck-ups crashing all over the place. Total mess/drug pad, fuck-ups living in every room, and me crashing on the couch. I had this meat hook that I used to carry at the time that I always kept inside my pocket. I was sleeping with my leather jacket over me as my blanket, and I woke up to this big lumberjack-looking dude in the apartment, swinging a fucking sword around! He was screaming I don't know what about. Everyone was pinned against the couches and walls, scared as fuck. I went into "defense mode," and put the leather jacket over my hands. At that point, I had the meat hook out underneath the jacket and I'm like, "Dude, what the fuck?" He was yelling, "Don't make me use this thing!" So I was thinking, when he swings the thing, I'm going to catch the blade with my leather jacket, I'm going to hook him, and pull whatever I fuckin' hook, whether it's his neck, face, or arm; I'm just going to grab something.

So I was heading at him like a matador, except the leather jacket was over my hands, because I didn't want to get cut by this straight-up cavalry sword. So he started backing away from me. We were on the second floor, and as I was backing him toward the stairs, I saw a baseball bat. As he got to the top of the stairs, I lunged at him, kicked him, and sent him down. I grabbed the baseball bat as I was chasing him down the steps, and then I just pounced on him with the bat. I started fucking this dude up real bad, and kicked him out the front gate. At that point, I let him get up, and he was like, "Motherfucker, give me my sword back!" I said, "Fuck you! You don't come in here and start waving a sword around!" Then he was like, "All right, I'm going to go get my gun, you wait right here!" And I was like, "What motherfucker?! Don't tell me you're going to get a gun 'cause you're not going to take two fuckin' steps away from here!" I started cracking him again and again, and a homeless dude, who was kind of big, grabbed my arm as I was getting ready to crack him in the head with the bat, and was like, "Stop! Enough's enough." So I went back inside and shut the gate. I went upstairs, and everybody else was still pinned against the walls, like, "What the fuck happened?!"

My boy Rex Everything—whose real name is Nick Oliveri, he played bass in the Dwarves and later Queens of the Stone Age—was one of the people that was in the apartment when that happened. He was a fuckin' mess too. I knew him through this mutual fuck-up friend of ours, Beau. Beau had "White Power" tattooed on the back of his arms from when he was in prison, and a dot tattooed between his eyes; he was an old-school S.F. Skinhead who was always in and out of jail. He actually went to jail the last time for running over a bunch of people at Burning Man. He got all fucked up on acid and crystal meth, stole a Jeep or some shit, and accidentally ran some people over. Beau was the one who got me back on the meth wagon. But I was a mess anyway. He didn't force me, he just offered...

So, back to the guy with the sword: I don't know if Rex was there for this, but the next morning I woke up, and the dude that I just fucked up real bad the night before was sitting in the fucking chair across from me! I was pretending to be asleep, but actually looking around and trying to assess the situation. There was no one else there, just me with him sitting there looking at me. I think someone walked into one of the other rooms, shut the door, and that's what woke me up. So I was looking at him, peeking from under my jacket that I used as my blanket. My eyes looked shut but I could see through my lashes. This was the same guy who was saying he was gonna shoot me last night, right before I beat the shit out of him with a bat! And here he was sitting across from me looking at me sleeping! I thought, "Well, I'm alive, he hasn't done anything to me yet, so I guess that's not why he's here." Because he could have snuffed me when I was sleeping, unless he was waiting for me to get up. So I got up, and was like, "So, what's up?" And he said, "I'm really sorry, I know I was out of line. Can I have my sword back?" And before I knew it, he broke out some kind bud, smoked a bowl with me and another dude who happened to walk in at that time, and took us out for breakfast! It was just one of the insane things that happened on Lower Haight. So I gave him his sword back.

Around the time, I briefly flew back to New York and produced a record for that Albany band Stigmata. This kid Bob Ocolinni had signed them—he had a rich family, so he started a record label as a pet project, Train Wreck Records. And basically, it was that: a train wreck. I was a train wreck, the label was a train wreck, the whole shit was a fucking train wreck. They flew me back for a minute, and paid me a decent chunk of change to produce the record. In all honesty, I was so fucked up on drugs when we were recording that album. One of the guys who owned the studio was also the engineer. I had his people delivering bundles of dope to the studio. I was popping pills all day, smoking dust—I was a fuckin' mess. But somehow or another, they will all tell you that I did help bring out a lot of good shit from those guys musically. I mean, they were already good, but I helped them shape their songs a bit, and edited a lot of parts. They were writing these songs with 20 parts; every song was an epic. But I was like, "Guys, you're trying to stuff 20 pounds of shit in a ten-pound bag, and it's just not going to work. You've got to trim some of these parts—less is more." I finally figured that out after doing *Alpha Omega*. It was Jason Bittner's first album, the drummer now in Shadows Fall.

So I finished that record, went back to California, and spent all the money I made on that trip on drugs. I basically O.D.'d a few times, and had all kinds of crazy shit go down, as I burned through all that loot. I was an ugly scumbag of a mess. Some time around when I was working on the Stigmata album, one of those dudes was in New York City with a friend of his, and I decided to take them to the Metropolitan Museum of Art, and "show them some culture." But first, we were up in the park walking around and I was getting high right there in public barely even trying to be discreet. I had my jacket hanging over my shoulder, I was shooting heroin under it while we walked near the reservoir, joggers jogging by us, people walking past us, pushing strollers, not even noticing.

See, that's the thing with drugs and me—when I was a mess, I was a blatant mess, and I really didn't give a fuck. I'm really amazed that I didn't end up in jail, just for my blatant disregard for law and common sense. It's embarrassing that I was that far gone.

So anyway, we got to the museum, and I was all fucked up and sick as a dog, vomiting everywhere; in the Metropolitan Museum of Art, I was puking in the trash receptacles! Trying to be discreet, when nobody was looking, I was like, "Blaaah!" You know the rooms with the knights on horses where they've got all the tapestries and banners? I was pulling tapestries and curtains over to the side and throwing up behind antique tapestries! We went through pretty much the whole museum, with me vomiting everywhere. And mind you, the two guys that I was with were straight edge. For all I know, I could have thrown up on Marie Antoinette's bedroom furniture or rug. Yeah, I've vomited in some great places.

When I got back to the West Coast, I burned through the Stigmata/Train Wreck money pretty fast. I'm not proud of it. In fact I'm amazed that I lived through it. I stayed with with crazy-ass Beau who was all into crystal meth, smack, and S&M. We had no electricity. Sometimes I'd come back to the house, and I'd be like, "Beau, you in there?" to the door of his room. I wouldn't hear shit, so I'd be hanging out, writing lyrics, drawing by candle-light, or whatever, just tweaking out. And all of a sudden, you'd hear a muffled whimper or some shit come from his room. Or you'd think you'd hear a slap, and you'd be like, "Did I just hear something?" Then you'd be like, "Nah, I'm imagining shit." Then like a half-hour later, I'd hear another one. Or a whimper and then a smack, and I'd be like, "Oh, Beau's home!" An hour later, he and his girl would come out of his room—he'd have a big smile on his face, and she'd be all embarrassed, and like not making eye contact with me. He was such a freak—we got into a lot of trouble while I was there.

I was a total mess at that point; every now and then, I'd pull myself together enough and find someone to take me in for a while. At one point, I was staying in this shitty crack house dope-den welfare hotel on Mission Street, I think it was called the Ho-tel Thor. These Pakistanis ran it. The fucking whole place stank of curry, crack, and brown tar dope getting cooked. It was such a pathetic existence of a life I was living at that point, I would have probably been better off dead—but then I wouldn't be here now or have my family or any of the good things that have happened in my life since then.

I was in a state of depression, and the drugs helped me stay in it. I was trying to get better, as far as wanting to get off drugs at least half the time. And I would, for a few days or a week or so here or there, but I was just too depressed, and one thing would lead to another, and then, back into the abyss, the death spiral into emp-tiness, nothing, nowhere-ness.

Of course, I was all into Alice in Chains and Nine Inch Nails, all that fucking depressed drug music. But even as fucked up as I was, there was this wheat grass juice stand on Mission, and I'd still make sure to get a shot of wheat grass juice every day, 'cause I figured, "Hey, at least wheat grass juice is equal to eating tons of vegetables," since I wasn't eating at all practically. I'd have lit-tle moments of clarity or inspiration; I'd go to music stores and pretend I was gonna buy shit, and just play instruments. I'd hang out as long as I could, and then leave. I actually got offered gigs while I was in stores playing—I got offered gigs doing sessions for different producers. But I'd be all fucked up and miss the session, 'cause I wouldn't know what day it was and I'd realize a day or two later, or I'd lose their business card or whatever.

It was around that time that I joined a band as the singer. It was with these kids I had met when I first rolled into town: Eddie, Rob, and Raif. Since they already had a bassist and a drummer, all they needed was a singer, so I said, "Fuck it, I'll sing." They didn't have a name for the band, so I came up with one: Naked Love Church! They had a few songs, and were actually good, in a crazy psychedelic meets Helmet/Melvins/Stooges even Doors-ish grunge-y weird way. We did a bunch of gigs and I did a lot of partying. We started to gain a little bit of local popularity. Two of the guys were college students, and one worked at a bar and a club, so they were pulling all their friends to see us, and it started to gain a buzz. I would never write lyrics; I just had themes and I'd go out and just freak the fuck out, and make shit up onstage. Some of those shows were fuckin' off the hook. I was just going crazy, running around the club, climbing the walls, running across bars, diving across shit, and fucking with people while we were playing. It was great; I'd make up the words as I was going. I was creating melodies and I'd base the lyrics on whatever theme I was on or whatever I was thinking of at that moment. That shit used to drive the other guys nuts, but free-styling was my thing. We were gigging with bands like Release, who were popular in San Francisco at the time. I kinda scared the other guys in the band with my erratic behavior. I mean, those guys partied, but I was nuts to the point of almost having a death wish. Some of them went on to start a band called Hetch Hetchy. Those were the guys whose room I lived in under the stairs. Great guys.

I stayed at like 20 different places while I was in San Francisco. At one point I stayed with this crazy crackhead fuck who had a big talking parrot, and his roommate made speed in his room, out of whatever the fuck you make speed out of. It was ugly. I even lived with Steve DePace from Flipper for a little while. He was one of the few people out there who had their shit together and wasn't all fucked up. We jammed, but it didn't pan out. I was winding up in some very fucked-up situations and places. Eventually, I got the phone number of my friend Joey, who used to be in Verbal Abuse, an old San Francisco Hardcore band. He was living in L.A., and I told him how I knew this one chick that was a bank teller, and was trying to get her to help me rob the bank. I had a map drawn, with all the cameras marked. I was off the deep end.

I was like, "I've got to rob this bank. Or join the Army. I've got to do something." Joey knew I was buggin' outta my mind. He said, "Well, the Army ain't no place for a crazy-ass white boy like you. So before you do something stupid, why don't you get your ass down to L.A.? You can stay with me for a minute. I've got a friend who's looking for a drummer. I know you still play the drums, and I'm sure he'll let you stay with him. You may even know him: Jerry, he used to sing for Legionnaire's Disease." Of course I knew about them from back in the day; they were one of the first Texas punk bands. Jerry was at that Sex Pistols show where Sid Vicious smacked that guy over the head with his bass. Jerry was crazy. He did like 15 years in prison in Texas, that's enough to fuck anybody up! He'd gotten busted for drugs several times. They have zero tolerance there. I think five years of that was for a roach in the ashtray of his car. He was a fuck-up, but a good guy. He was very political too, very much an anarchist.

So I got this chick that I was seeing to drive me to L.A., and stayed with Joey for a while. Within a few weeks, I moved into Jerry's house, and started drumming with his band, Anomie. I stayed with Jerry, and eventually wound up living with this other guy who was a pot-grower! He taught me how to grow weed. But the deal was I had to live at the house, guard the house, water the plants, and take care of the plants, 'cause he wasn't always around. He had a rehearsal studio in his house in one of the rooms. I used to jam with his band, and I even did a few gigs with them. And I was still playing in Anomie, and Jerry was taking care of me as well. I mean, I was still fucked up on drugs, but I was trying to wean myself off. Hell, I could play drums and grow pot? Sure, what the fuck!

Also by that point, I had been talking to Parris again on and off. I took his number when we talked that time in NYC. I was like, "You should come out here. There's a studio here, we can live here and work on material and try to do something." So Parris came out to L.A., and we worked on new material. We had a studio, a place to sleep, food and a room with a hundred pot plants in it listening to classical music all day long—'cause plants like classical music!

330

It was just Parris and me and this Mexican metalhead dude named Vinnie, the guy whose house it was. I started jamming with his band; they were kind of a rock-ish band with political overtones and a punk rock-type attitude. Which was funny, 'cause they were all dudes a lot older than me, like old hippie motherfuckers and shit; I was jamming with them since he needed a drummer. All I had to do was take care of the house and water the plants. It turned into "party central." There was all kinds of madness going on over there.

Around that time, I started slowly getting my shit together. It was a whole series of things that got me thinking and got me back on track, one of which was this chick that I used to go out with on and off before I split out West. She got in touch with me and told me she was pregnant and thought it was mine. Which it turned out not to be, but it did rattle me a little bit. The prospect of possibly being a father jump-started me cleaning up my act. Everything happens for a reason; sometimes we just don't know it.

I started running a lot, jogging every day and exercising. I was just trying to get myself over that hump, break that cycle of drugs. Up until that point, I would only go without getting fucked up for a few days, or maybe a week or two. Then I'd fuck up again. But finally, with some real motivation, I got through it. We were living in Sunland, California—it was beautiful and it was kind of in the middle of nowhere. Like I said, we were staying with the friend of mine and we had a studio. We were practicing a lot, and I had a ton of weed, so I was able to just work out, play music, smoke weed, or whatever. I was working out a lot again, playing drums in two bands, jamming, and getting back in shape. Parris was into running, so I started running with him. Within a short amount of time, I was jogging 10 to 15 miles a night. It really helped—that and playing music was what I needed. I decided to get my shit together, and had motivation, and somewhere constructive to put my energy. I really just pushed the button and went forward. And it was only really a matter of months before I was starting to get back to my old self.

We got in touch with Dave DiCenso and he flew out. He started working on songs with us: what would become the White Devil EP and the Samsara line-up of the Cro-Mags, which was me, Rocky

George, Parris, and Dave. We even had our old friend Rich Spillberg of Wargasm come out and jam with us for a while; it was a lot of fun but it didn't pan out, so he flew back to the East Coast. We stuck around for a little while—it was a nice place, a nice house, and we had the studio.

The girl I mentioned also told me that she had contracted HIV. I was floored; here was a girl I had been in love with and still loved. I kept it together and told her that it would be all right and that I would come back to NYC and that she would be fine. I of course went out and got tested and did every six months for years after that.

I remember going to get that first test—I was shitting in my pants. I was with my boy Jerry and this other friend of ours, an old Vietnam vet. We pulled up, Jerry looked at me, smiled and said, "Well, I guess we gonna find out if ol' Harley's gonna make it or not." We all laughed, but I was nervous as fuck. I paid the extra loot to get the immediate results back, and they came back negative—and again I thought, "Damn, I am a lucky motherfucker." I did a little celebration dance and that was that.

At that point I was already trying to clean up and just do music with Parris, but that was the reason I decided to come back to NYC really focused. As far as I knew at the time, that kid might be mine and even if she wasn't, she might need me.

So Parris, Dave, and me returned to the East Coast. We came back to New York, and wound up doing *Revenge*.

Chapter Fourteen

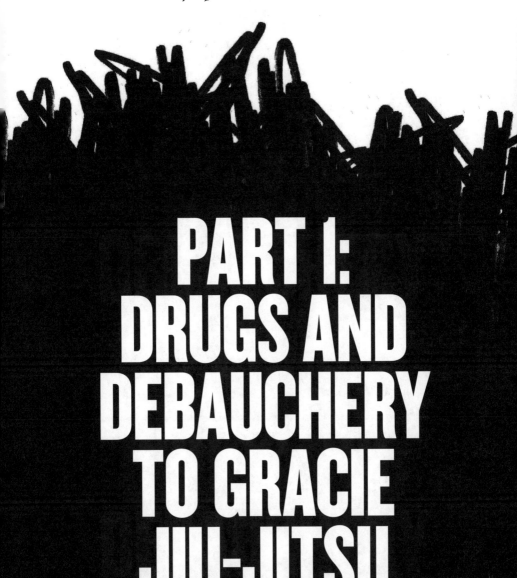

PART 1: DRUGS AND DEBAUCHERY TO GRACIE JIU-JITSU

UNDERGROUND COMBAT LEAGUE, BY ANIL MELWANI

When I first got back to NYC I was staying at this chick Aura's apartment. She had known me and John and everybody since *The Age of Quarrel* days.

At one point John found out I was staying with her, and he started calling her up talking shit on her answering machine. I was gonna flip, but she said, "No, fuck that, he's calling me at my house—I'm doing this." So she called him and went off, telling him how she had known us both for years and how dare he put her in the middle of this and call her house talking shit and how he should grow the fuck up and act his age and shit. She really laid into him, and I was proud of her for having the balls and the decency to do what so many other "friends" were too fucking cowardly to do. She never heard from him again.

Aura knew that I was going through some rough times and that I was trying to get it together. I hadn't been off hard drugs for very long, and it wasn't easy. I was under a lot of pressure. I started jogging a lot and trying to keep my shit straight.

I'd go for these long runs at night 'cause I couldn't sleep. She lived down by the Twin Towers and I'd run from there to Central Park and back. On the way I'd stop by Coney Island High on St. Marks Place and see who was hanging out for a few minutes, say hi etc., and then keep running uptown to the top of the park. I'd run a few laps around the reservoir, and then turn around and head back down. On the way back down I'd stop in at Coney Island High again and there would be the same people. Everyone was pretty much in the same place, just slightly more shitfaced. And I'd hang for a few minutes and then keep running. It was kind of good to see that, as I was getting my shit together—to see all these people really not doing anything but standing around getting fucked up as they got older and did nothing with themselves. It gave me motivation to keep my shit together.

Once I started making some money, I started helping out my ex and her daughter; then I moved in with them and started taking care of the kid. It soon became pretty obvious that she wasn't mine. But by this time I was already attached, and then the mother started falling back into drugs, so I felt I had to help the kid.

Me and Parris and started negotiating a deal with an old friend, Scott Koenig, who worked for Def Jam at the time. He used to manage Biohazard. He was starting a label called King Records. It was going to be Def Jam's "rock label." It was a subsidiary-type deal. They gave us a cash advance on the deal and we got a rehearsal space in the Music Building on 8th Avenue between 38th and 39th.

That neighborhood was crazy at the time, a lotta drugs. Crack was still a big problem back then, and the space was right there between Port Authority Bus Terminal and Penn Station—a hot spot for runaways, drug dealers, hustlers and all the crazy shit that goes along with it like peep shows, porn shops; that whole neighborhood was dirty. When they cleaned up 42nd Street, it all just moved down a few blocks and a little more out of sight—still in plain view, just not as much as when I was a kid.

That's where I lived in a 20x20 room with drums, amps, a PA, weights, and a heavy bag in it; bathroom in the hall, no shower, just the toilet and sink. I'd go on the roof in the morning and shower with four two-gallon water jugs and some soap; it was like the old days for me. I'd lift weights, hit the bag, play drums and listen to music all day and night. I mean yeah, I was going a little crazy living there. There were always people practicing and all kinds of madness—drugs, freaks, and crazy shit inside the building and outside on the street. I could write a whole book just about that building and that street.

With the Def Jam/King money, we got the rehearsal space with recording gear, ADATs (so we could do our own demos), amps, road cases, and we started making payments on a van. We got ourselves set up so that we could gig without any outside help. We had everything we needed—this was the first time we ever had that. I had never had an amp before. When we were kids, Parris used to play his guitar through a PA column. We had nothing growing up. We borrowed everything or our manager Chris rented it and charged us for it—that's part of why we never saw any money.

Around this time, two people came into my life that would change it forever. One of them, my teacher, mentor, and friend—one of the few people that I look up to and respect in this world—Master Renzo Gracie. With him, I began my journey into the "Gentle Art" of Jiu-Jitsu. The other—the mother of my sons, Harley and Jonah, who by giving me them would change my life forever...

I had been dying to learn Gracie Jiu-Jitsu ever since Sunland,

when I had accidentally stumbled across UFC 1 and 2 on VHS at
the local Blockbuster. They had only had two UFCs so far. I became
fascinated with it. I remember watching those first two UFCs on
VHS over and over for weeks. I was determined to learn Jiu-Jitsu.
And now that I was back in NYC, I was trying to find a place to
learn it. My interest in martial arts and fighting obviously goes
back to my childhood.

Anybody who was around in the late '70s was into Bruce Lee.
There were martial arts supply stores all over Forty-Deuce that sold
nunchucks, throwing stars, darts, swords and all kinds of knives
and weapons, Ninja suits and Karate uniforms and Kung Fu uniforms. They had the Bruce Lee outfits—the yellow and black one
from *Game of Death*, where he choked out Kareem Abdul-Jabbar—
and Bruce Lee posters everywhere. These stores were right there
on the Deuce with all the porn and horror movies, Kung Fu movies,
arcades, pimps, hookers, peep shows, drug dealers, pickpockets,
thieves, and whatnot. That was the Times Square I grew up with.

And it wasn't only up there. Of course in Chinatown there were a lot of Kung Fu movie theaters. On TV, there was *Drive-in Movie* and *Drive-in Theater*, and *Black Belt Theater* that used to show Shaw Brothers films like *The Four Assassins*, *Dirty Ho*, *Master Killer*, and *Return of the Master Killer*. All kinds of Bruce Lee movies, like at least two or three Kung Fu movies back-to-back on Sundays on Channel 5 or 11. Kung Fu was the shit back then. And then you had all the blaxploitation Kung Fu movies. It was just like the song, "Everybody was King Fu Fighting." That was no bullshit!

I used to joke that Bruce Lee musta had all kinds of illegitimate ghetto kids around the city 'cause everybody in my school used to hop around making cat noises acting like Bruce, like they knew some sort of Kung Fu. Eric Casanova had that "Bruce Lee Kung Fu Fever"—he was always doing Bruce. A lot of old B-boy break dancing moves came from cats that were into that. Some of the Spanish dudes in my neighborhood trained in different styles of Kung Fu and martial arts when I was a kid. This dude Jose, I saw him take on four dudes once—one of them pulled a knife on him. The guy tried to stab him and he caught the knife by the blade between the palms of his hands, held it, side-kicked the dude and continued fighting the other guys! He cut both his hands, but he still fucked the guys up.

When I was a kid, I did some "Northern Eagle Claw" with this Chinese master in the city. That didn't last at all. I just didn't have the patience, practicing all those uncomfortable stances, not really getting to hit anybody, grapple or roll full contact; no takedowns, nothing like that. When I was staying with those crazy fucks in Canada, we'd work out, and practice kick punches, combinations, and whatnot, lift weights and of course, we got in tons of fights.

I trained a little with black belt friends of mine who knew Karate and competed, like Bleu and Richie Stig who roadied and did security for us. They couldn't tune guitars or fix gear, but they could drive, carry gear, sell merch, and fuck people up. We didn't have tech tools to fix guitars or tuners and shit—we had like hickory wood axe handles and bats and shit in our road cases, just in case. We'd always work out, stretch, and practice kicks, strikes, and combinations, takedowns and some joint locks. When we got in fights, which was often back then, we got more hands-on training

342

HARLEY AND RENZO GRACIE — PERSONAL COLLECTION

than most people, 'cause we were Skinheads and, or I should say
ex-Skinheads or recovering Skinheads. But even when we were
getting out of it, we still had one foot in it and we still got in fights
all the time.

Richie recalled about me: "I remember over at C-Squat going up
on the roof one morning, one of the first times we hung out and
you were up there punching the brick walls with your bare hands,
and your knuckles were all bloody. You were up there working out,
doing push-ups, and stretching. I was like, 'Oh shit, this motherfucker's crazy!'"

My interest in martial arts had always been there. But I never had

343

any formal training or been enrolled in an academy or dojo. Until I met Renzo, most of my knowledge and experience came from street fighting. It wasn't until 1995 that I got really serious about training at a proper Academy.

I think at this point most people have heard of Gracie Jiu-Jitsu or Brazilian Jiu-Jitsu. And the Ultimate Fighting Championship, which is now one of the most popular sports in the world. The short version of the tale goes something like this: Renzo's grandfather Carlos Gracie, the son of Gastão Gracie, was the first to learn Jiu-Jitsu from Mitsuyo Maeda, a Japanese Judōka who arrived in Brazil in the early 1900s. His brothers, Oswaldo, Gastão Jr., Jorge, and Helio, also learned Jiu-Jitsu. In 1925, the brothers opened their first academy in Brazil, and that was the start of Brazilian Jiu-Jitsu. The Gracies worked on their style of Jiu-Jitsu for years, perfecting their art, proving its effectiveness in freestyle mixed martial arts matches with no rules, no gloves, no time limits, and no weight classes. And they continue to do so to this day.

In 1993 Rorion Gracie, son of Helio Gracie, brought the Ultimate Fighting Championship concept to America, and the rest is history.

I was lucky to get involved with Jiu-Jitsu and MMA in its early stages in America. There was nothing like it, with its freestyle rules. When I caught UFC 1 and UFC 2 that really re-sparked my interest in martial arts and fighting arts. I fell in love with mixed martial arts. I made up my mind that if I ever had the opportunity to meet any of the Gracies, I was going to get down with them.

So, there I was, it was '96, I was back in NYC, living at the Music Building. I started looking in every martial arts magazine I could find: *Black Belt*, *Kung Fu*, all of them. I was trying to find an advertisement for Gracie Jiu-Jitsu, or something like it. I was waiting for a school to open up in New York City. I knew it was only a matter of time. One day I found a little ad in the back of a magazine that said "Gracie/Kukuk Brazilian Jiu-Jitsu: Renzo Gracie, Craig Kukuk, etc.," and an address and number. So I went.

I'll never forget the first time I walked in there. It was this big loft space in the 20s. The place was empty except for wall-to-wall blue Jiu-Jitsu mats across the floor and a little desk with maybe three people. One guy was teaching a private lesson. I looked around and Renzo was standing by the desk next to the mats.

He walked up to me and smiled. I didn't know what the deal was with this fuckin' place. Was I supposed to walk in and bow to this guy? I didn't fuckin' know! I didn't even know if he was Renzo. I guess he could tell. He walked up to me with a big smile, put his arm around my shoulder and said, "Come in, my friend, you come to train." I'm like, "Damn, this motherfucker is cool as hell!" There was no pretentious bow-down-to-my-black-belt bullshit.

He was a real down-to-earth guy with a big smile—who could totally fuck you up if he wanted to, but with no attitude at all. I started training like two days later with his then purple belt Mito Pontual and his brown belt Vinnie Landeira, who at the time were his only assistants. He brought them over from Brazil to help. I started going like every fucking day, sometimes twice a day. I had Jiu-Jitsu fever! Besides the little bit that I learned from Vinnie and Mito in those early days, I pretty much learned almost every technique from Renzo himself.

The whole shit was still underground. There was only like one store on West 48th Street that sold real MMA and Jiu-Jitsu stuff on VHS, not DVD—MMA from Brazil and the Netherlands. I was so into the shit. If I didn't have a training partner, I'd find one, either a band member or a friend. Or I'd just sit and meditate on the moves. The people I knew who were into it, we'd share tapes, make copies, and circulate them among people who were down. Since then, everybody has incorporated Brazilian Jiu-Jitsu into their style. Back then it was still all relatively new in America.

I was fortunate to start training with him when it was in its early stages with just a handful of students, and I moved with him through several academies. The first one was at a Kung Fu school on 25th and 8th. Then we moved to 27th Street between 7th and 6th. Then we moved back to the Kung Fu school on 25th. It was funny, there'd be all these people doing Kung Fu in one end of the place, with all their staffs and crazy spears, and axes, and then on our side, people were getting mangled, choked, and arm-barred. I think the Kung Fu school lost a lot of students to Jiu-Jitsu. We went through several different places.

Then Renzo got a space on 37th and 8th right near the Music Building. That academy was crazy; the building was under construction, so most of the floors were empty. The only things in the building that were open was us and a methadone clinic on the second floor, so there were always all kinds of scumbags in the building and hallways. The elevator door would open, and there'd be like two or three junkies standing there, going, "We'll fight you guys!" and we'd just laugh, like, "Naaah, it's all good. You win, guys!" That was when Renzo started really putting together a team of fighters.

He had some crazy students back then. We finally moved to 30th Street, where we are now. And now, years later, he has legions of students and badass instructors—some of the most respected and decorated grapplers and fighters in the world. I can't even keep track of how many high-level guys roll through the academy today: GSP, Chris Weidman, and so many others.

Now Renzo has academies all over the world and an army of Black Belts! But I'm proud that I was a part of his team in the early days. I used to truck with the crew to see Renzo's fights, and compete with Team Renzo Gracie. In '96, when he fought Oleg Taktorov, a bunch of the guys and me piled into a car and went to Alabama. Oleg was a highly decorated Sambo Judo and Jiu-Jitsu fighter, and a former UFC champion. At the time, Renzo and Oleg were both undefeated; he outweighed Renzo by a good 40 pounds. Before the fight, there was a big press conference with all the fighters. Renzo was being interviewed, and Mark Coleman was in the crowd—and his manager was holding up a sign that said, "3 Gracies, one night: Renzo, Royce, Rickson!" At one point during the press conference, Renzo answered one of the questions, then smiled and said, "And my friend, there is no man alive on this Earth that can fight three Gracies in one night."

At that point, Coleman started to look a little uncomfortable. I was there ringside when Renzo knocked out Oleg. I was breaking Oleg's balls, saying, "Hey Renzo, what was that you got him with? Oh-LEG!" 'Cause Renzo knocked him out with an up-kick. Oleg gave me a dirty look, got up, and walked out. The funny thing was, he didn't even know he lost the fight 'cause he got knocked the fuck out. Sometimes it's like that when you get knocked out. You're like "Huh? What are you talking about? I'm fine, fuck that!" Meanwhile, your ass was just out cold.

I met Carlson Gracie at that fight; he was there with some of his fighters. Murilo Bustamante fought an insane match against this huge wrestler named Tom Erikson. It was brutal. This guy was like twice Murilo's size—there were no weight classes. Murilo took a murderous beating, but he never ever gave up and fought a valiant battle, to say the least. But it was ugly. I saw him backstage and I felt bad for him. There were a lot of big-name fighters there, but they weren't big yet.

Of all the people I've met, two of the people I respect the most are Renzo, and his brother, Ryan. I met Ryan back in the day at the old academy; it was his first time in New York. Within minutes he was breaking my balls and I was fucking with him right back. Even with a language barrier it didn't matter, it was funny as shit and we got along great.

I don't know why he took an immediate liking to me, but he did. He used to come to my house and hang with my family, and he always used to bring us gifts from Japan when he'd go fight. He gave me his gloves from Pride FC that he fought with and signed them for me. I heard there was a big freak-out over it at the event— the promoters and the people from Pride didn't want him to take them, but he didn't give a fuck. He promised me the gloves from his fight so he flipped out and took 'em. He gave me those gloves, and when he came back from Japan, after my son was born, he gave me like $2,000. I didn't want to take it, but he insisted. He said, "Shut the fuck up, it's for the baby." He was not someone to argue with. I tried but it was no use. He was a true brother.

I met a lot of his old homeboys back in the day: Nino Schembri and all kinds of crazy motherfuckers! Old-school MMA Fighters. I remember back then when Daniel Gracie, Fabio Leopoldo, Rodrigo Gracie, Ricardo Almeida, and all those cats first started rolling through New York City, former UFC champion Matt Serra, Nick Serra, and John Danaher were all just blue belts. Those were great times. I was at Rodrigo Gracie's first MMA fights, as well as Matt "The Terror" Serra and Nick Serra's, when they first started competing in MMA. I used to go to all their fights at the Copacabana and out in Long Island, before it was legal in New York State. They'd fight on Muay Thai cards and kickboxing events billed as "freestyle exhibition grappling matches," but it was MMA.

I always had a love for combat arts. I have competed in grappling tournaments and underground MMA-type shit. But most of my fights took place when I was young, on the street for free. I did some commentating for "Combat in the Cage" in Rahway, NJ, and at "World's Best Fighter" in Atlantic City: Team USA vs. Team Asia. It was a big deal 'cause it was the first time ever that an Asian team had fighters from Japan, China, and Korea. I also did a thing with Bodog; it was a blast. I have fought in NAGA and the New York State Grapplers Challenge—that was the first thing I competed in, back in 1999. I took third place. I also did some underground fight club stuff. I promoted seminars for old-school UFC fighters, like Mikey Burnett—fuckin' great guy. Most of them are nuts. But what do you expect? They get paid to fight!

MMA shit isn't sanctioned in New York State—at least not yet—but they're out there. It's basically underground MMA matches. Some of them are private; some, like UCL, Underground Combat League, sell tickets. They're held at boxing gyms and martial arts academies in different places across the city. The fights basically have the same rules as Ultimate Fighting. Some of them are rawer, like old-school "Vale Tudo." Anything goes-style: head butts, elbow strikes, and kicking downed opponents in the head. I've been to all that shit in the Bronx, Uptown, and Queens. The last one I went to was on 200-something Street. I don't want to get too specific about it. But they get pretty fuckin' raw, I'll say that much. I actually made it into a book about the underground fight circuit and several MMA magazines like *Full Contact Fighter*, *Fighters Only* and a few others.

PART 2: CRO-MAG REINCARNATION/ REVENGE

By the time we got back into the recording studio, I was training religiously. We had our rehearsal spot and we were doing pre-production for what'd become the White Devil *Reincarnation* EP and Cro-Mags *Revenge*. We went back up to Normandy Sound to start production up in bumblefuck Rhode Island. During the recording sessions, I had no training partners; all I had were my VHS Jiu-Jitsu tapes, which I'd watch all day and night.

One day I talked some local rednecks and ex-con white-trash wannabe Aryan Brotherhood-type fuck-ups that I met at the 7-11 one afternoon into training—or really, more like fighting. I bet them I could submit them in less than three minutes or I'd give 'em $20 and buy them a six-pack of tall boys. They thought they could take me, so I'd let them come after me and try to fuck me up. One after the other, I'd let them swing on me, and then take 'em down. So it only ever cost me like a six-pack just to keep them hanging out, and I'd just fuck these guys up and try out moves on them, while they'd sit and laugh at each other getting fucked up.

Anyway, we recorded part of the *Revenge* LP and released it as an EP; it came out under the name White Devil. The *Reincarnation* EP only came out in Europe. We decided to save the tracks that we did on that, re-do some of the guitar tracks, record a few more songs, and put them out as a full-length in the States. The White Devil EP had this dude Kenny Lee on lead guitar. He was a guitar teacher; the dude was nasty, but for some reason, Parris wasn't feeling it, so we got with Bobby Hambel from Biohazard, and we used that EP to get some dates. It actually went pretty well; it was Bobby, Parris, Dave DiCenso and me. I love Bobby—him and Dave are both great guys. We did a bunch of big festivals in Europe, and a bunch of club dates. That was when I broke Mackie's nose in London. That shit was funny, but unfortunate. It happened 'cause he was talking shit to me and then he put his hands on me, so I head-butted him in the face, broke his nose and left him rolling around on the floor, with blood bubbling out of his nose and face until the bouncers picked him up off the ground and helped him leave.

They asked me if I wanted him thrown out. I said no, but he left anyway. Then Bobby started freaking out and pulled a knife on—of all bands in the world—Shelter, who Mackie just happened to be playing with at the time, the nicest, most nonviolent guys. Bobby wanted to fight everybody! That was a crazy evening. We played some great shows; we did Dynamo with Venom, and we played with Ministry and House of Pain. We even played a festival with Biohazard while Bobby was with us.

A great Bobby story from that trip took place when we were on tour in Italy and we lost him in one of the airports. We were flying to a different part of Italy, and we lost him going from one gate to another. He just disappeared. Now, this was back when Bobby used to drink, and he was always meeting women everywhere he went. So we lost him because he started catching a rap with some chick in the airport, and we didn't know. We got to the gate and Bobby wasn't there. We boarded the plane and Bobby didn't show. We were waiting and waiting, but he never showed up. At that point, we were wondering if he even knew where the gig was, if he was gonna make another plane, how we were gonna find him—or he'd find us.

This guy was as unorganized as I am, and we lost him! It wasn't looking good. We showed up to this two-night festival, and there was no Bobby! We didn't know where he was, and we didn't know if he was showing. The next day, we still didn't know. All we knew was that he didn't know where he was going, he didn't have his guitars, he didn't have shit. Sure enough, that afternoon, after sound check, there comes Bobby, walking up the beach. It's hot as shit out, everybody's in shorts and no shirts, and Bobby's in his fuckin' leather jacket, army boots, black jeans, and wool hat! I was like, "How the fuck did you make it here?" And he was like, "Dude, I didn't even know what city the festival was in. I'm asking people, 'Do you know where this big rock festival is happening?'" Somehow or another he made it, and we played that night.

Bobby wound up leaving the band. I don't think he was getting along well with Parris, and he had some issues with Scott Koenig, who at the time was managing Biohazard. But I loved playing with Bobby. He's a brother for life. We signed with King Records, and they financed the recording of *Revenge*. But we were having a hard time finding the right new guitarist 'til we hooked up with Rocky George, the ex-Suicidal Tendencies guitarist, through our friend Mike Schnapp, who worked at Profile when we were signed with them.

The first time I met Rocky to play with him was at the Music Building. He'd just gotten off the plane and I met him at the rehearsal studio. He walked in with all his bags, his guitars, and dropped all his shit on the floor, with no sleep; just total disheveled madness. He looked around, saw my Billie Holiday CD next to the CD player, sighed, and said, "Thank God!" Then he looked around the room, looked at me and asked, "Anybody got a bong?"

So we instantly bonded. Rocky George and Bobby Hambel are two of the guys I had the most fun playing with onstage. You can tell when people are having a good time playing together, and we had that.

Rocky joined and we went back to Normandy Sound and finished the album. I loved working with Rocky, but those sessions were fucked. It was too much; we wore ourselves out. We did tons of pre-production, practicing the songs to a metronome, taping shit, and taking notes on what drum fills we liked best. Dave would chart out his drums. We were too meticulous. Then isolating ourselves at Normandy in Bumfuck, Rhode Island, staying at the studio for weeks, tracking endlessly—mixing, remixing, on and on. It turned into a nightmare of an album to make. But in the end, it sounded fucking great. And it really was me and Parris that produced it. We went through several engineers before we finished that shit.

We had several blowouts in the studio: I threw a chair at Parris once for talking shit, and one time he tried to make me flinch by rushing up in my face, so I swung on him. He was all, "I can't believe you swung on me!" But I was like, "What the fuck did you think I was gonna do? You rushed me!"

We wound up finishing the mix at Electric Ladyland in New York, the legendary home of Jimi Hendrix. But we were up in Rhode Island at Normandy for a long time working on that shit and we got fuckin' stir-crazy. Me, Rocky, Parris and were living at the studio in an apartment upstairs. Our buddy Alvin Robertson, who used to be in the band Bloodclot and roadied for the Bad Brains, was there helping out, kind of tech-ing, making us laugh, and being a freak.

Sean Kilkenny from Dog Eat Dog, who loaned us a bunch of amps that we were using in the studio, remembers: "I stand by my word by saying *Revenge* was the hottest f'n record they did since *Age of Quarrel*. And I had the pleasure of being there. I watched them write and rehearse the songs at the Music Building. It was like watching that machine that rips the asphalt off the street. Dave DiCenso was incredible! Then Rocky George shows up. Talk about insane! I remember loading gear out of the studio to bring to Normandy, a whole freakin' sound system! They set it up upstairs in the 'artist' apartment. These guys were ripping through

351

the rhythm tracks downstairs, and I'd bring a rough mix upstairs so Rocky could write the leads on the sound system they brought with them. During the recording of *Revenge*, Harley, Parris, and I were doing backing vocals and doubling them. Tom Soares or Phil said, 'Who's got that high girly voice in there?' Needless to say, Harley and I finished the backing vocals. At one point during the recordings, Harley was doing vocals. He asked for a drink of water. I brought him the water. I didn't know the motherfucker did his vocals naked with candles burning!"

Revenge is my favorite Cro-Mags album. Obviously the *Age of Quarrel* era meant more to me, but Parris' and my songwriting matured. I feel they were some of the best songs "musically" that we ever wrote together—all those years of playing together, separating, getting back together, the chemistry was still there.

In that respect, it was just like the old days; we'd both come up with riffs, then I'd play drums, throw riffs at him, he'd play them back at me, et cetera. The lyrics reflected what my life had become. It was brutal, fucked-up, raw shit. I mean, leading up to and during the recording of that album, I had been going through so much in my personal life that it did affect the direction of the lyrics. I just dug in and that's what I came out with. But that chapter was coming to an end, and a new one was beginning.

We called it *Revenge* because it was kind of inspired by the fact that I had "Revenge" branded into my chest, and also it was kind of "revenge" as far as the two of us playing together again. It was our way of saying "Fuck you" to the shit-talkers on the scene.

I remember at one point I actually suggested to Parris that we should get John in on it; his response was simple and cold: "Why embrace him when we can erase him." I thought, "Damn." That's kinda harsh, 'cause it would've been cool for the fans. But it didn't seem like it was even a possibility at that point, and things were sounding really good. But I knew it would be a bit of a musical struggle if John joined again.

One of the things I liked the most about *Revenge* was Rocky's leads, all the voicings and nuances throughout the songs and in between the vocal parts; he was into Mahavishnu Orchestra and all kinds of crazy shit. We were constantly turning each other on to cool music, and still do. I am lucky to have played with him on so many projects. He's a great guy and a great guitarist. I thought it was our best recording. Me and Parris were at the top of our game, and I was finally learning how to sing; I even took vocal lessons for that record. I was proud of how we sounded.

We finished recording, and I was back at the Music Building and bouncing around a few other places; shit was rough. At the time, I was coming out of several messy relationships, and that's when I hooked up with the future mother of my sons Harley and Jonah.

She asked to not be mentioned by name in this book, but it's impossible for me to tell my story without talking about our relationship because of how important it was, and how much it affected my life, especially by giving me my sons. So out of respect for her wishes I won't use her name.

I've had a lot of girlfriends, more than I can remember. The one thing most of them had in common was that they were nuts. I've gone out with good girls and bad girls, strippers, dominatrices, drug addicts, all kinds of freaks. I had to leave most of that shit out to make things fit into this book, but believe me, I could've easily written a book called "Crazy Bitches I Went Out With and Other Groupies and Sluts Along the Way." I have been in some real messy relationships: lots of drugs and madness, real Sid and Nancy shit. And I have been in love a few times. I've had my heart broken more than once. But the break-up with the mother of Harley and Jonah was the one that hurt the most and changed my life forever, because of my sons.

When I was young, I was always on the prowl. If I wasn't fighting, I was fucking or getting high or trying to do one of the above. I'd be on tour hunting, on Avenue A hunting, at the clubs hunting. Besides making music, those were my main pastimes.

But during those years there were a few significant relationships that stood out. When I was like 14, I started going out with this super-hot 17-year-old everybody wanted to get with. I took her cherry on her 17th birthday. When we broke up I was all fucked up. That was right before I hitchhiked to Cali; it may even have been part of the reason why. I can't remember anymore. And there was the chick I went to Canada with when I was 15; she was 18. But my first real knock-me-on-my-ass-love was the one who is tattooed on my arm, Kitty. I was like 18 and she was maybe 16. I met her in Washington Square Park. She was a West Side punk. There used to be a rift between the East Side and West Side punks; we kind of ended that. It was the Skinhead punk rock teen romance, and I was about as in love as you can be at that age. We were just kids. It was *Age of Quarrel* days. The first show I took her to was when the Cro-Mags played with the Bad Brains at the Rock Hotel on Jane Street.

Then there was the second "big one." That lasted from the late '80s into the '90s. We loved each other a lot, but we had a lot of problems. When I met her, I wasn't doing drugs, but she was struggling with a dope problem.

My main problem was that I was one of the "cool guys" on the scene and I was in a band, so I was fucking chicks left and right, and I guess I was kind of high on myself; looking back now I can admit it. She went out with one of the Dead Boys' roadies when she was like 14 or 15 and that's what got her all fucked up on drugs. The heroin scene in NYC was really ugly back then; she lived in squats like me. We had both been through a lot very young. We both lost our childhoods.

After we broke up, she had a kid with some crackhead. She continued with her drug use and I cleaned up and wound up taking care of her kid after rescuing the kid from a crackhouse. I took care of her for over two years until her grandmother stepped in, and at that point I knew it was time for me to let go.

Without the feeling of being needed, I didn't feel I had much purpose in my life, and I started falling back into fuck-up mode. I was seeing several different chicks around that time; one of them flew me to Amsterdam where I went completely bananas for a while. I wasn't using hard drugs like heroin or crystal meth anymore, but I was back in party mode: ecstasy, Special K, hookers, sluts, drinking, and smoking.

That's when I first started working on this book. This girl flew me to Europe, and I was staying in a hotel in the red light district in Amsterdam. The working title was "The Longest Suicide Note Ever Written." I was trying to document the madness from as far back as I could remember—until the end. The story was of my life as an insane suicidal joyride, of rock 'n' roll depravity and demise until the final crash-and-burn. It was gonna be the book that all the great fuck-ups never got to write 'cause they died first. So I began working on it. I figured the end would have to come sooner than later. But I was wrong.

Just after that, I hooked up with the mother of my sons. We were doing lots of club drugs like E, but not the hard shit I had been fuckin' with before. I remember one weekend in Amsterdam with her, I did like 16 hits of E and her little ass did 19, and we never left the room—we just fucked for the whole weekend.

I had known her and her family a few years. They were from a little town in upstate New York. I was friends with her brothers. They were both Cro-Mags fans. One of them was in a band.

I remember her brother asked me if it was all right for him to give her my number, that she had asked him for it, and I said sure. One day she came down to visit me, and then I started going up to see her. I'd go up and stay with her for days, sometimes weeks at a time. Finally, she came to the city for good, and moved in.

We went on some crazy trips to Amsterdam and other places. I took her all over the world with me on tour. She was with us when Parris, Rocky George, and Ryan Krieger and me went out on the Samsara tour of the States, as well as the final few Cro-Mags tours. I can't even tell you how crazy we were getting over there in Europe and Amsterdam, it's almost shameful. I don't want my kids to know how nuts me and their mother were, but let's just say we had a great time.

Before me, she had hung with a lot of criminals and scumbags like I had; she had lots of friends in jail. She'd been involved with dealing and so on: comin' to the city, troopin' shit from Hunts Point in the Bronx back upstate and movin' it. So I guess it was some kind of a step in the right direction for both of us. We were both getting away from some of the bad elements we had been around.

Looking back on it now, in some ways maybe we were too much alike, especially back then. She was 100% all the way, almost worse than I am—love, hate, or anything else.

And it was difficult at times, 'cause like me, she had a short fuse and a bad temper. She was young and jealous and pretty much ready to scrap with anyone at any given time. There were times she was ready to fight girls who were backstage or at a club—girls that were friends of the other band members, 'cause they were "hookers," as she called them. I used to get into beefs with her publicly over chicks all the time, even ones I had nothing to do with, or ones I had known years before we met. It was a little ridiculous at times. But at the time, I took it as her love for me.

We were a hard couple—hard on each other and hard to deal with. We loved hard, we fought hard, and ultimately the whole shit just got too fuckin' hard and ugly. Sometimes it was like the fuckin' UFC in our house. But I do believe that we loved each other, and for most of the years that we were together, things were good—crazy but good.

We smuggled shit across virtually every state in the U.S. and every border in Europe, smuggled in and out of the U.S. We grew weed together; we brought in all the most popular seeds and strains from Amsterdam. And you can thank us for some of the best kinds of bud that circulated NYC in the early '00s. We brought back a ton of E from Holland and sold most of it to her friends, and made a killing. I fought side-by-side with her when two-hundred-pound men would've run. She had been arrested for flipping on cops when they were arresting me—just goin' completely and totally ghetto nuts on them.

I remember one time I was upstate. I was out for a ride with an idiot friend of ours, and we got pulled over. He had no license on him, so they got him out of the car, and he had some pills on him. Meanwhile, I'm sitting in the back seat, and I had almost one hundred hits of E in my pocket that I brought back from Amsterdam and like two grams of weed!

I knew I didn't have time to hide both, so I took the E out of my pocket and put it inside my sock. The weed stank real strong, so I knew they'd find that. So I said, "Fuck it, I'll use it as a decoy." They pulled me out, and this fuckin' female cop, who was a total bitch, dug her hand in my pocket and found the weed. She started slamming me against the car, cuffs me, and throws me in the car without doing a thorough search. Right then, my girl happens to be coming down the street. She sees this and comes running over—and starts flippin' on the cops. I was in the car, and they had my idiot friend. I was the car like fuckin' "Harley Houdini." I had my hands cuffed behind my back, so I pulled my feet up through my hands, so my hands were in front of me. I got the E out of my shoe, stashed it under part of the seat. I had my arm wedged up under the shit, and tried to push the E as far up behind the seat as I could.

Meanwhile, they were out there arguing, and my girlfriend was flippin'. The cops were trying to control her and calm her down, and they had this idiot over the hood of the other car cuffed, while they went through his pills. No one noticed me in the car squirmin' around, trying to stash this shit, except for her—she totally saw it. At that point, I put my sock and shoe back on, trying not to get noticed while I'm like Houdini pulling my legs back over the handcuffs, to get my hands behind me again, so they don't notice.

So finally they got me to this little bitty precinct. By then, they had arrested her too, for disorderly conduct. Meanwhile, I had almost one hundred hits of E stashed in the cop car, and I was trying to play it cool, like it's no big deal—"Yeah, it's cool, you only got me for a bit of weed, I ain't sweatin' it." Meanwhile, I was shitting bricks, thinking that when they searched this fucking cop car they were gonna find that shit, and I'm fucked! So they took me in. They had me handcuffed to a wall, and she was in a different room, cuffed.

All I could hear was her screaming at the cops, talking mad shit. I was yelling, "Shut the fuck up, you're just gonna make it worse!" So I was still stressing, but I didn't want to show it. This one fuckin' dick cop strip-searched me, totally being a typical pig-fuck power-tripping, all trying to intimidate me. But I wasn't giving him any satisfaction. I was talking shit right back to him. Then they got another call, so the cop that arrested me ran out and took the car with them. I was lucky as fuck!

Usually, protocol requires a thorough search of the vehicle, but it was this shitty holding tank in a little precinct somewhere outside of Troy. There were no other squad cars there at the time, so this cop ran out, and took the car and the evidence with her. Who knows who eventually got busted for that shit. I'm sure someone must have eventually. So they only had me for a little bit of weed. I spent the night in jail, and I got out the next day.

But yeah, she was crazy. Maybe that was part of what I liked about her. But that's just how it was, if it was "on." I saw her hit people with big-ass Mag flashlights, beer mugs, and brass knuckles. When shit started going bad with Parris, she saw it coming before I even had a clue.

After we finished tracking the songs for *Revenge* and before it was released, we had the chance to do a short tour with this band Earth Crisis. It wasn't paying much, but it was a chance to get our feet wet with Rocky so we said, "Fuck it, let's do it." Dave DiCenso who drummed on *Revenge* and who toured with us as White Devil with Bobby Hambel from Biohazard was not available to tour. So we wound up recruiting Ryan Krieger, who was suggested to us by our old friend Billy Milano of SOD/MOD. Ryan was a sick drummer, and has since recorded and toured with me many times.

We still weren't sure about a name for the group. At that time we'd pretty much decided not to go out as the Cro-Mags, and "White Devil" had too much of a negative vibe. So we went out as "Samsara," which was one of the names we'd been considering. I liked the meaning—Samsara means "the eternal cycle of birth, old age, disease, death, and rebirth"—but I didn't like the name. We were opening shows and we weren't getting paid much 'cause we weren't being billed as the Cro-Mags. But we just wanted to play.

At the beginning of the tour, Earth Crisis were like, "Oh man, you guys are the best! If it wasn't for you, we wouldn't even be playing this type of music. Cro-Mags were such a huge influence... "

They were one of those "vegan-Hardcore bands," and they were giving me mad props for turning them on to vegetarianism. So at first, they started off being really respectful of us and of the Cro-Mags. They were all up Rocky's ass for his Suicidal-ness, too. I wasn't trippin' or lettin' it swell me up. I really didn't mind opening up for them, it was all good.

I thought they were cool at first, and the first couple days we were hanging. It seemed like we got along, but as soon as the tour got going, they launched into a whole different vibe, this "Now, you know we're not breaking down our drums or amps or anything else for you, right?" All stone-faced, and shit like, "you guys ain't the Cro-Mags anymore, we're headlining." Meanwhile, we were playing stages that weren't very big. It was kinda outta left field. It was like, that's the kinda shit you get from rock star bands, it's not what you're supposed to get from Hardcore bands—and especially not at small shows. And especially not when it's with people that just gave you all this horseshit about how much they love you, and wouldn't be doing what they're doing if it wasn't for you. You'd expect a little bit of respect, at the least.

Whatever, it was no big fuckin' deal. It's not the first time I've experienced that type of bullshit from other fake-ass motherfuckers. They get a little bit of juice and they think they're hot shit. They'll blow smoke up your ass privately one second, and then treat you like you're some bum the next second. But things just kept happening on that little-ass tour.

One night, their drummer got in some shit with some dude at a show. The guy was about to fuck him up, so I grabbed him and escorted him out before he fucked up the drummer or got jumped by the bouncers. The fuckin' dude then drove by the place, and threw something at what he thought was Earth Crisis' van, as he screamed, "Fuck Earth Crisis!" But it was our van, and he broke the window. But they just loaded up their gear and split. It was like, "I just jumped in a fight for you motherfuckers, and that's how you're going to act?" Not even a "Yo, sorry about the window." Nothing. So I developed a sort of dislike toward them. Then, a couple of times they showed up at shows and didn't want to play 'cause there wasn't a big turnout—but they still wanted to get paid. Just rock star shit that you're really not supposed to see on a Hardcore level.

Then one night, our merch money disappeared when their merch guy was watching our shit. It was just bullshit. He cried his fuckin' way out of it, and I wanted to kill him. After shit like that I was like, "Yo, fuck these guys." I'd piss in their ice buckets and coolers every night in their dressing room before they'd get there, where all their drinks and food were stored. So all night long, they'd be reaching into a bucket full of my piss! I'd dry the fuckin' sweat off my balls and out of the crack of my ass after my sound check and set those towels with their stage towels, and fold them back up neat again. I'd be watching them wiping their faces with their towels onstage all night, laughing: "Fuck you!" Anyway, I really didn't give a fuck again once it was over. It was old news to me.

After that little bullshit tour, we changed our name back to the Cro-Mags for the simple reason that no matter where we played, people would scream, "Cro-Mags! Cro-Mags! Cro-Mags!" at us as soon as we'd walk out onstage. It was obvious, we were Cro-Mags for life, no matter what. And people wanted to hear that music. We could play completely different music with a different name, and people will still want to hear the Cro-Mags' songs when they come to see us. And we were the main writers of the music—I did write a good majority of the lyrics—so it didn't really make sense to sell ourselves short or try to change the name. The way I saw it, bands lose members, families lose members, and you don't change your name; that's who you are. So we changed our name back to the Cro-Mags. We self-released *Revenge*; we put it out as "Cro-Mags Recordings," and piggybacked it with *Before the Quarrel*.

I was particularly proud of the production on *Revenge*. It was the first time we ever had a real budget, or spent lots of time working on something—and I thought Parris and myself were at our best, Dave was flawless, and Rocky's leads were amazing. But before King Records ever got up and running, the label folded, so that's why we wound up releasing the album. At that point, they had financed the album, and bought us recording gear, and even a van. But at the end of it, all we were left with were our masters, 'cause the label folded. I keep saying "folded," but really, it never happened at all. But we were lucky enough to be in possession of the masters and all our new gear when that happened. We also printed up the original cassette on CD, the one we had done when John first joined the band, which was *Before the Quarrel*.

So we did the tour under the name Samsara, and then changed our name back to the Cro-Mags. As soon as we changed our name back, we started getting some pretty hot gigs. People didn't care that John wasn't in the band—it was the two main songwriters and the lead guitarist from Suicidal. We were doing big-ass festivals, and playing all the big stages with Slayer and other big bands. It was all pretty impressive, considering that we released the thing ourselves. We did some cool Woodstock-type shit over in Europe. One time we played at this one festival with Destiny's Child on one stage, and Iron Maiden on another. There was a Death Metal stage. We were on the Hardcore/Punk stage, and there was also a huge circus tent with a fuckin' rave going on. The shit was nuts.

At one point, Ryan Krieger was unavailable to tour, so we got Garry "G-Man" Sullivan, who was recommended by our old friend Alvin Robertson. Garry was another kick-ass drummer who's played with just about everyone. We got right back out on tour. We went to Europe and did festivals. It was going well for a second. Then we did Europe again with Parris, G-Man, Rocky and me. Then we did another European trip with Ryan, Rocky, and me, and then one last tour with G-Man, me, Parris, and Rocky. But I'm getting way ahead of myself.

I gotta say, Parris was doing a lot of the legwork, and for that he deserves a lot of credit—making calls, and keeping track of shit. These were jobs he really shouldn't have been doing, but no one else was doing them, and we—especially he—didn't trust anybody after everything we'd been through with Chris Williamson and everything else. And as he felt more and more in control of shit, I guess it went to his head. It started to make him a bit nuts—and he broke under the stress. First, he was like, "Man, I just want to play music, I don't want to think about all this other shit." But we both knew I could never do that admin shit. It seemed like a good thing at first, but in the long run it would prove not to be a good thing at all.

The first of many things he did wrong was he didn't put a picture with Rocky on the CD cover; he even went as far as photoshopping Rocky out of the picture that was used. Here was a guy who sold more records than either of us, and Parris left him off the cover? I never got it. At one point, he said something along the lines of, "It's our band—he's just a guest player." That was just some ego thing that made no sense to me. I guess Parris didn't want to be overshadowed by someone he felt hadn't contributed as much or something. But it was a dumb decision.

A lot of shit happened that would cause Rocky not to dig him. He straight-up told me, "I really hate that guy. I try not to say that about people but I really don't like that guy at all." I was like, "Damn!" 'cause Rocky doesn't talk shit like that. But Parris wasn't the same kid I grew up with—the one we used to call "Kevin"—that's for sure. He'd changed a lot. Most people say the opposite about me. They say, "That asshole hasn't changed at all!"

I loved playing with Rocky and touring together. He always roomed with me, and whenever he was in town, he'd stay with me. But sometimes that motherfucker would get crazy drunk on tour and go wild.

One time, me and Rocky and got into a fistfight in our hotel room. We fuckin' went at it! It was one of those crazy/funny tour nights. He was being a belligerent madman that night, and I couldn't take it anymore. I was trying to get to sleep, and I tried to throw him out of my hotel room. He charged at me like a bull, and Rocky's a big man—he plays hockey and shit. He slammed me against the wall, and I was pinned with my feet dangling! I proceeded to grab him by the back of the head, pulled him down, kneed him in the face on reflex, and pounded on him.

But it wasn't doing shit, so I grabbed his arm and started cranking on it. Then my girlfriend and our roadie, Eric, jumped on me. They were like, "Harley, stop! You can't hurt his arms, he needs those to play!" So I put a "sleeper hold" on him, and put his ass to sleep, stomped out of the room, and found somewhere else to crash. The next morning, I went down to the hotel lobby, and didn't know what to expect. Rocky was looking all pissed off and mean. I said, "Rocky, no matter what happened last night, you're like a brother to me. I will always love you and respect you. If you feel like you gotta punch me in my face right now because of what happened last night, go ahead. I won't even take it personal, 'cause I hope that you'll still be my friend." And I put out my hand. He didn't even shake my hand, he picked me off the ground and gave me a big-ass hug! And then we laughed our asses off and kept hugging and walked off together. Parris was in shock, watching us make up after we had a straight-up fistfight the night before. But Rocky and me are brothers and always will be 'til the end.

Around this time, we ran into some jerkoffs we'd met before: Earth Crisis. At that point, we'd been touring and did this one festival where Earth Crisis played. I saw them there. I was with my girlfriend and every time they saw us, they'd all tense up, and I was just like, "These dicks were fuckin' sticking their hands in buckets of my piss all night." I don't give a fuck about them.

But Parris was "rock starring" them, being kind of arrogant. I don't know if he was drinking a lot, but he was with this chick that he was trying to impress, and he was talkin' a lot of shit. "Fuck you guys, you ain't shit. You're playing on the fuckin' small stage, we're playing on the big stage. Who's hot shit now?" He was rubbing it in their faces. I don't know, I wasn't there for the majority of it. I was off having fun with my woman. I kept hearing that he was going out of his way to be a dick to them. Anyway, we were eating breakfast in the hotel the next day, this fancy-ass hotel, and I saw them walk by. I didn't even look up. The next thing I know, they're outside, Parris is outside, and my girlfriend says, "Oh shit! Parris just hit Karl! Oh shit! They just jumped Parris!" It happened that fast, within seconds. I ran to the door—it was a revolving door, so it was moving slow. By the time it revolved and I got out, Parris was standing there walking like a zombie—all discombobulated, with his hand on his face. And there was blood gushing out of his face. I thought his nose was broken; I didn't know the extent of the damage.

It turns out that he punched the singer. Keep in mind, those guys were all pretty small, but it doesn't matter how small people are. The seven fuckin' dwarves will fuck you up if it's all seven of them! He punched the singer, and before he even had a chance to recoil his arm from the punch, he got cracked in the face with an apple juice bottle. That pretty much opened up the side of his cheek, to where you could stick your fingers through it. When he went down—I was still running to the door and trying to get through it, it was a big, slow revolving door and I couldn't get through it fast enough—they grabbed him by his hair, bounced his head off the cement a few times, kicked him around, and then started to walk away. The whole shit went down in a matter of seconds. They knocked out a bunch of his teeth; he needed his face completely stitched up. I started running after them. I didn't even have time to evaluate the damage because my instincts were "go to war."

They all jumped in their van and started driving away. As they were driving, I ran up and punched the side window as hard as I could, and the bass player laughed, like, "Yeah! What are you going to do?" I started chasing after the van, and unbeknownst to me, they were driving into what becomes a dead end. So, all of a sudden, the van turns around, and starts coming back at me. There I was thinking, "These motherfuckers think they're gonna come and fuck me up now? Bullshit, they just picked the wrong one!"

From being in so many street altercations throughout my life, I have a knack for finding a weapon when there are none. So, I picked up this metal pipe that was about three feet long, and it had another attached piece of metal at the end of it—it looked like some medieval weapon. So the van was coming, and it stopped in front of me. I faced off with the thing, like I was getting ready to take on the van. I was holding the shit back like an axe, I swung it and I sunk it into the hood of the van, and then ripped it out. Then I swung it again, and cracked the center of their windshield, right down the middle. At that point, everyone in the van was fuckin' panicking. Those motherfuckers looked like Godzilla was attacking them! You've never seen eight or nine people look like such pussies over one person. I've got no problem saying it: those dudes are fuckin' pussies, total bitches.

So I was like, "I better step to the side before the driver panics, steps on the gas, and runs me over." So I stepped aside, and whack! I hit the side of the window, and it shattered. Next I took out the back window, then "Pow," smashed the other back window. I ran to the other side and they started to screech off, so I took out another window. I was fuckin' killing this van. You'd think that these dudes who had enough balls to jump Parris—four of them on one—would at least have the balls to deal with me. But no, not one of them. Those motherfuckers ain't nothing but cowards. They can jump a motherfucker but they ain't got no balls.

They escaped. It was fucked-up. Parris had to go to the hospital and spend a few days. But I was so pissed at him for starting the shit that none of us were as sympathetic as we should've been. It was like, "Yo, how long are you gonna be a dick before something happens, dude? And now we're supposed to feel bad?" By that point, we were fed up. So while he was in the hospital, we all went to Amsterdam and Prague. We were like, "Fuck this shit." That didn't have to happen at all, and then we had to cancel shows. So yeah, we felt bad, but we were really pissed as well. There have always been fights at Hardcore shows, especially at our shows. It sucks, but it does make for some crazy stories. But that one did not start or end well. Parris was never a fighter, not back in the day, not in his life, ever. I'll never understand when it was he started thinking he was a tough guy.

While we're on the subject of tour brawls and riots, there's one that made the papers! We played with Pantera in Norway, and my girlfriend and I got into a bar brawl. That was funny: her, and me, and In My Eyes, this straight edge band. Phil Anselmo came up and sang "Down But Not Out" with us that night. I was hanging out in the dressing room before we were supposed to go on—I think Phil was there too—and all of a sudden, one of the guys from In My Eyes came running into the room, and said, "Harley, quick, your girl needs you, now!"

I went running downstairs, and I saw that dudes surrounded her and there was some shit going down, voices were getting raised, and she was in the middle of it. I ran up and was like, "Which one?" She pointed to the guy in front of her. I didn't even hesitate, I just punched him right square in his face, grabbed him by the back of his head, bounced it off the table, and began kneeing him in his face. Then the whole bar erupted. The guys in In My Eyes were skinny dudes. You don't look at them and think, "These guys are brawlers." But those guys were up on the table, breaking chairs over people's heads! It was impressive. My girlfriend, who was like five feet tall and 90 pounds, was up on the bar swinging a Mag flashlight, and cracked some dude's head open. That brawl made the papers the next day. I guess they're just not used to that kind of shit in Norway.

Garry Sullivan recalls: "We were playing with Pantera in Oslo. Harley and me were together on the side of the stage close to Dimebag, VIP area! I speak a little Japanese and understand the culture a bit. I lived for two years in Osaka. So we're watching Pantera tear some ass! Then they finish a song. Then Phil Anselmo looks directly at Harley and says 'Harley Flanagan is in the house! This man is my Senpai!' It's as if I got hit by a bolt of lightning what Phil said, because I knew this Japanese term well! This is called the Senpai and Kohai theory. I was like, 'Holy shit! Phil Anselmo just gave Harley the most highest honorable compliment a person, warrior can give!' Let me break down to you what Phil Anselmo meant. In Japanese history through the Samurai, Shogun era and to this day, Phil Anselmo explained that Harley is the higher warrior and he can never be as high as Harley, which makes Phil the Kohai, the lower rank. Making Harley the Senpai. But Phil is in his own right is a Senpai to many from Pantera, but never to Harley."

There was also one really bad incident in San Francisco, where me and my girlfriend took on a mob! I literally held off 20 or more cats with a "tire buddy," used for testing the air pressure in your tires. But it's really just for beating people up; I don't care what anybody says. Truck drivers don't buy those things to test their air pressure. It's a wooden stick with a piece of metal at the end of it, with a leather strap to put around your wrist. You can't tell me that's for testing anything except for someone's skull. Regardless, during that brief period of the tour we were playing under the name Samsara, we pulled into San Francisco after a long drive. We pulled up to this club that we were playing at; I think me and my girl had been arguing. Everybody was in a shitty mood. It was a long drive. Somehow, Parris wound up getting into some verbal conflict with a kid at the show. I never really got the whole lowdown because over the years, I've learned that everything that Parris told me was not always necessarily the truth. It was just to get me to react.

He came and said, "You see that motherfucker over there? That dude was trying to step to me in the promoter's office, saying how his boy's band has to go on after us." Parris was like, "I pretty much told him, 'Whatever you want. We're here just to play.' And he started to get all hard rock on me. So I just walked out of the room, and came to tell you." Anyway, that's what he told me. Now those guys were billed to go on before us, but that wasn't even the point. I didn't like the attitude that went with it. And I'm not someone who takes kindly to people stepping to me or to my friends. So I went up to the kid, who was about my size, a little taller, but maybe not as thick I guess. I was like, "Yo, fuck this dickhead. Who the fuck does he think he is, stepping to us and telling us when we are going on? When it says it right fucking there on the flyer and in the papers?" Besides all that, I felt like "Yo, San Francisco was like home away from home for me. I was hanging out on the San Francisco Hardcore scene back in the fucking day before this motherfucker was even floating in his daddy's nut sack."

This kid wasn't even a thought in his mom's brain when I was going to shows out there, living at the Vats, hanging at the Compound, going to the On Broadway, Tool and Die, and all that shit. I thought the shit was really disrespectful this punk-ass motherfucker was trying to flex on us. So, you know how when you smack somebody on the back of the neck, you give them like a "red neck," but then you grip them on the neck and walk off with them? So I walked him off and I'm like, "Dude, what the fuck bro? Why are you talking shit to my boy? You've got something you want to say?"

It turned out the guy was in some gang, unbeknownst to me. When I walked off with him, he started looking around and seeing all his friends, kind of eyeballing them. They were watching us. I guess this dude had a bit of a rep around there, so everybody was watching his next move. I could feel the tension and the vibe, so as soon as he started trying to run his mouth and start flexing, I immediately head-butted him in the face, picked him off the ground, and slammed him into the floor. I looked around at his friends—who at that point were big-eyed and didn't look like they knew what to do—and I started talking mad shit to them. I had him on all fours, so he was in the worst fuckin' position in the world, and I'm like, "You think you're some kind of badass? You look more like a bitch to me!" And I smacked him in the back of his head, and "humped" him in his ass to humiliate him, like Pele Landis did against Jorge "Macaco" Patino, in their first match back in 1996; some of you old-school MMA fans might recall that one. It was a classic bout, with a lot of trash talk, insults, and dirty shit. Then I kicked him in his ass, and smacked him in the back of the head as he ran out the door.

Hey, when motherfuckers step to me, I go ghetto on them. I don't give a fuck; don't fuck with me. Anyway, after the show, the buzz around the club was like, "Yo, that dude's in such and such gang, blah blah blah." So we're hanging in front of the club, we'd already loaded up our gear by this point. I was like, "Yo Parris, guys, let's roll." I'm ready to break out, the show was over, and we'd been hangin' out long enough. I had a feeling shit might still jump off, but Parris was standing around with his arms crossed, trying to look like a hard-ass, looking around all like, "We ain't going nowhere." And at that point, anything could still happen. I was aware of this from having been in enough shit to know.

So I had my good ol' tire buddy up my sleeve, and I was standing there talking to this dude between two vans in the parking area of the club, when all of a sudden, this mob of people came around the corner. I was only seeing 20 or 30 people coming toward the van; I had tunnel vision by that point. The tire buddy immediately pops out of my sleeve. One of them is like, "There he is!" They started bum-rushing me, and I started swinging this thing back and forth so fast that if anybody would have so much as stepped forward, their head would've gotten taken the fuck off. So nobody wanted to be that "first guy." The whole time, I'm going, "Who wants to die, motherfuckers?! Who wants it first?!" I went into barbarian mode. When your adrenaline gets pumping to that point, you really do feel like you can take on whatever's coming. There wasn't even time for fear.

So they weren't able to move on me at that point. In desperation, since they couldn't get at us, one of them spit, and it hit my girlfriend, who was right next to me. I was trying to hold her behind me, while swinging the fucking tire buddy like it's a sword. She fuckin' lunged past me, screaming, "Motherfucker!" and tried to run into the mob, swinging her fists! All of a sudden, an arm reached over my shoulder and just grabbed her and dragged her back. It was this mad fucking cool kid, "The Drunk Monk." He was trying to help us, even though all those motherfuckers were coming after us. And that was his hometown! But straight-up, either that kid from the club was in the wrong, Parris was lying, or there was just some kind of miscommunication, that turned into a misunderstanding, that turned into a little bit of abuse, that turned into a mini-riot!

Anyway, at that point, they noticed Parris. One of them who was holding a bat turned his head and yelled, "There goes the other one!" Parris was jetting up the hill, running away from the whole shit, even though he kind of set the whole thing off. They all turned and started chasing him, I guess 'cause they couldn't get at my girl and me. I ran around the van, and up the hill, got between them and Parris, and held them back temporarily, while Parris' ass kept hauling ass up the hill trying to get the fuck out of there. By then, there were like 30 kids behind me running up the hill. I don't know who's running after me to jump in, and who was running after us to watch—with the exception, of course, of the ones carrying weapons. They were obviously trying to fuck me up, and there were like eight guys or so in front of me that had been chasing Parris. So after I ran around the parked van, I cracked one of them and started running. Then they started chasing me up the

368

hill! I was running, and every time I saw one of them getting ahead of the pack, I'd slow down just enough for him to catch up to me, and then I'd try to take his fuckin' head off. I wanted to take out as many people as I could.

While all this shit was happening, one of our roadies, Nelson, saw the shit going on, and came running down the hill to jump in. Nelson was this older Chinese/Kung Fu dude, who'd been doing Fu Jao Pai—"The Tiger Claw system"—for like over 20 years, and he will fuck shit up. Motherfuckers didn't know if he was with us or what 'cause he kind of came out of nowhere. But every cat he approached backed the fuck away from him, weapon or not. You could tell that he meant serious "I will kill you" type of business. You could see it in his eyes. Anyway, more of them started coming, and it was a pretty big crew. And other people started gathering; people started coming out of their stores and bars. The street started filling up, because as I said, this was turning into a mini-riot.

Meanwhile, while all this shit was going down, our other roadie, Eric—I don't even know how he was able to jump in our van, but he did, and put the shit in reverse. It had a U-Haul trailer on it, and somehow, he got it out of the alley, and started cruising up the hill I was running up. At that point, they were smashing the windows of the van with bricks and bottles. They didn't even wanna fuck Rocky up just 'cause he was all Suicidal-down. They were yelling, "Yo, Suicidal, you're cool man, but you gotta quit that band." I guess they didn't want beef with Suicidal and V13 and whatever, but the whole shit was retarded. But I saw that Rocky was still out there. So I jumped out of the van, and went running back into the fucking mob to get him.

By then there was glass all over the inside of the vehicle. Believe it or not, we managed to come out of it completely unscathed. The only things that got busted up were the side windows of the vehicle. The kid I originally humiliated, his ego got damaged—and our vehicle got damaged. I guess he got even with us!

All I know is if it were any of my friends, and there were five people trying to hold us back, those five people would have gotten fucked up. That's why I'm saying Hardcore ain't what it used to be. Now it's like the jocks that people hated in high school, or the frat boys in college. It's all these little fucking stupid clique crews. I always handled my own shit. When I was a kid, I didn't need 20 motherfuckers to carry my balls for me.

Our drummer, Ryan Krieger, was away from the club when the shit went down. When we found him later, with the van windows smashed and glass inside it, he was all like, "What the fuck happened?" I started breaking his balls, telling him, "Man, they didn't like your drumming. They said you guys are all right, but your drummer sucks, so they attacked us!" Meanwhile, Parris was having a minor nervous breakdown. The rest of us were actually having a good time, all things considered. My adrenaline was so pumped that it took me a few days to wind down and for it to sink in just how close we came to getting fucked up by a bunch of motherfuckers. Of course, people out there tell the story a little differently, but the one fact that doesn't change, no matter who tells it, is that I held off a mob of motherfuckers by myself, and I didn't take no one's shit! It ain't the first time.

Needless to say, the next time we went out there as the Cro-Mags, it turned into a full-blown follow-up episode, because those guys had kinda looked foolish—five people and a chick had held off their whole crew! I knew it was coming; I just had that feeling. So I called the club in advance, and told them to get additional security. And they did. So at the end of the night, there was a big scene with all the Samoan bouncers, who were all gang bangers, plus there were Hell's Angels there. None of the dudes who had beef came into the show. It was a sick show; it was packed, but at the end of the night, a bunch of them tried to bum-rush the doors of the club. Well, the Samoans kept them out, but shit was getting crazy. And there were a bunch of those dudes outside the club across the street, waiting for us to come out.

I was hanging out inside laughing about the shit with some of the Samoans, they were all gang bangers/big fucking dudes. I don't know what set they were from; they all had guns. We were talking about the whole shit that was going down, and some chick who was all drunk walking around like she owned the joint overheard that there was some kind of beef going on with the band. She was related to Sonny Barger, so she speed-dialed the Angels and told them she needed some people to stand in front of the club.

So at the end of the night, we were walking out of the club with these Samoan bouncers, and there were all those Hardcore dudes from that crew standing on one side of the street yelling shit, and across the street from them, there were all these dudes with beards and trench coats on. This chick was all, "They're here for me guys, just stay close to me."

It was a fuckin' hilarious, insane, crazy, and highly volatile situation. I didn't know if the dudes in the coats were gonna start blasting if the Hardcore dudes were gonna try some dumb shit or what. The Samoans escorted us to our van while the bearded dudes in trench coats kept watch on the crew of dudes talking shit. We were in a big fenced-in parking lot next to the club that was connected to a much bigger parking area that took up the rest of the block. All of a sudden a bunch of the dudes from that crew ran around the block to try and bum-rush the parking lot. I guess they thought they were gonna bum-rush and climb the fence while we were fenced in and the Angels and Samoans were back in the club.

We cracked out a .357, fired off some rounds, and sent them scattering. I'd told my tour manager, "There may be an incident in California," so he brought his toolie with him. We didn't usually travel with shit like that; that wasn't our thing. We were musicians, not gang bangers. I mean, yeah, usually just bats, tire buddies, clubs, pieces of drum stands, ball-peen hammers or whatever, in case shit got crazy at a show. But people don't roll like that anymore; they have serious weapons. I never got in too many situations where it's like one person has a problem with me. I somehow manage to rile up whole crews!

I remember a different tour, when my drummer then was Garry Sullivan. He can tell you some hysterical tour brawl stories. One time, I fucked up this huge black dude. He was like 6'5", 6'6" and around three hundred pounds; I shit you not. I hate telling these stories myself, it sounds like I'm exaggerating. But I ain't making this shit up, bragging, or lying! I don't need to: G-man will tell you. We got into what seemed like a mini "race riot" in Texas, which was fucking ridiculous because two of the guys in our band were black; it was like these two punk rockers, me, Garry, and my roadie Ali, versus these three or four guys. But then shit started jumping off and more people started running up; in fact every brother in the parking lot started running up. Motherfuckers from down the block. Before we knew it, we were outnumbered. And it all jumped off over some stupid shit.

We were just standing there talking to these kids at the load-out at the back door to the club we just played, and these dudes walked up and started talking shit. They were like, "Anybody got weed? Yo, let me get that beer." Then they just started being total dicks. The one punk rock dude had a Rebel flag belt buckle, and one black dude started saying, "What are you, a racist? What, you don't like niggers?" He was totally revving himself up to hit this punk rock dude. Meanwhile this one chick was like, "Yo, what's your fuckin' problem, man?" And she got sucker-punched for it. Before you knew it, it was "the brothers" vs. "the punks"—two or three punks against these three or four big dudes. It got real fuckin' crazy in seconds. I picked up this 2x4, and I basically "fed it" to this dude that was running toward me. I pushed it into his face as he was running at me hard. Knocked his teeth the fuck out, and knocked his ass on the floor. The dude he was with was huge, a human I have no business even thinking about tangling with, nor do I want to. He hit one dude, knocked him the fuck out, hit another dude, put him down cold. He knocked our roadie out, and then punched him in the face three more times, when his face was down against the cement!

Then that big-ass motherfuckin' guy turned around, hit me, and I saw like "the flashbulb" that you see when you get hit real hard. But I came to instantly. I was starting to go down. I was already looking at his knees, 'cause I was on my way down. So I lunged forward, and did a double takedown on him. My reflexes kicked in, and I took him down with such an impact—because he was such a big man—that when he hit the concrete from the takedown, it discombobulated his whole shit. Yo, a strong takedown, especially on cement, can end a fight. And I took him down good.

Immediately, I rose up, put my knee to his stomach, postured up, and started pounding him in his face. Then, within seconds some other dude kicked me from behind. I rolled to my back, and started scooting away from him. Two people that I knew ran up, grabbed me, and started to pull me away. As they were pulling me, I got to my feet. Then, the cops started coming. By that point, I ran and hid in the van underneath some blankets. It turns out the big dude who was knocking everyone out was a corrections officer! So this motherfucker is yelling at the cops, "Yo, I'm a C.O.! These dudes jumped me!" So now all of a sudden, the cops were harassing all the punk rockers; I was under the blankets, and all I could hear is, "Where's the dude with the stick? Where's my teeth? He knocked out my teeth!" So they got out flashlights, and were trying to find the dude's gold teeth. The shit was crazy.

So, we went back to Europe on a second leg of the *Revenge* tour. The promoters advised against going back to Europe so soon, but Parris insisted that they book more shows. It wound up being a disaster for the band, but it was fun for me, my girlfriend, Garry and Rocky. I mean, despite the riots and brawls and whatnot, everyone had a good time except for Parris. Even the driver had a blast! But this tour was definitely the end of that era.

Let me just say that I'm not the only one who felt that Parris had started to become a bit of a dick at that point. And I loved the guy. I don't even like saying it like that 'cause it sounds like I'm just talking shit about him. But even his closest friends, everyone in the band, and most of the people who knew him, felt there was a change. He just wasn't the guy—or should I say kid—I knew growing up. He tried to flex on me a few times like he was some kind of a hard-ass, and I just laughed it off it as comical.

All this shit started to happen slowly over a period of a time. He even started getting into beefs with cats he used to get along with, cats like Biohazard, who he had done videos with; he almost got into a fight with them, and Type O Negative and Pete Steele, who he looked up to and also did some video work for. He got in some shit with a band called Merauder, who he produced a record for. He got himself into some shit with Sick of It All at some show, and got jumped or something; I don't know, I wasn't there. I think he even got into a scuffle with Mackie that ended with them rolling around on the floor like two girls. I heard Mackie broke his hand hitting Parris on top of the head or something.

I mean, look, I'll say it again: I admit that I'm not always an easy person to get along with. But the fact is I was getting along with everyone else in the band. I wasn't having problems with anyone or getting into any beefs with anyone at the time on the scene or otherwise. The only person I had issues with at the time was John and at that point I didn't even really give a fuck. He was a non-issue. We were all having a great time, pretty much—except Parris.

I don't know, he used to be a good guy; I loved the guy a lot. I think he was just under a lot of pressure and it got to him. But hey, that's the Cro-Mags; we all had problems and issues, not just him but John, Doug, Mackie and me. We were all difficult motherfuckers at times—a lot of the time. And I have to laugh when sayin' this 'cause I feel deep down all of us know that it's true.

That reminds me of how Parris used to say that Pete Hines was the one guy in the band that he got along with. But Pete hated Parris so much that one time on tour, when Parris always used to mark his food with a black Magic Marker so that no one would eat it, Pete jacked off in Parris' peanut butter, stirred it up with a fork, and then put it back in its place. You really gotta not like someone to do that shit.

Anyway, it seemed like Parris thought he could control the whole situation, control me, the rest of the band, the money and so on. I guess 'cause he was handling the business, he felt like he had that right or was entitled to, and he started doing some shady shit. At least that's how we all saw it. Up until that point, I felt me and him had really re-bonded after the whole *Alpha Omega* disaster. I loved playing music with the guy and I really didn't see it coming. Ever since he started managing our business, everything I thought he was doing for us and for the band, I guess he wasn't really doing for "us," he was really doing it for himself, with merch, CD sales, etc. He did stand to make a lot and probably has. He had all our bank info, all my personal info. But anyway, my dumb ass didn't realize how much resentment and bitterness was boiling inside of him. That was until one day, I accidentally opened up a Beatles book, of all things.

The Beatles book is what finally set it off. It was a book that he was always walking around with, and reading and writing in. He even mentioned a few times what a good book it was. To me it was just a "Beatles book"—full of stories and photos of the band. So one morning I woke up, I was still half asleep. I walked to the front of the bus, and there was the Beatles book. So I picked it up to thumb through the pictures, and… Boom! There was all kinds of shit written in the book, shit about the rest of us—little thoughts and shit, like a journal. Parris would sit there and scribble in the book, as he was either reading or pretending to be reading, when he was really just sitting there looking at everyone else on the bus having a good time, and him just being miserable. He wrote a lot of fucked-up shit. Not just about me, but everyone on that tour: Rocky, Garry, my girlfriend, her family, our road crew, tour manager, driver—everybody.

The more I read through it, the worse it got. I wanted to kick the shit out of him as soon as I saw him. He's lucky we all didn't. He had little notes to himself about all kinds of deals he was doing without my knowledge. I mean, why would he even write stuff like that down, and then leave it around? Did he want me to find it? It burned me the fuck up.

So I was like, "Fuck this." I went through his notebooks, and that's were I started finding out all the really fucked-up shit he was up to. It was as if he was trying to set me up to fuck me over; it was all in the book. It was some total backstabbing betrayal shit. After going through the book, I put it back; I guess I wanted to see what other shit he was gonna write about all of us. More so, I was interested in what kind of business shit he was up to behind my back and what else he was gonna write down like a dumbass. So I put the book back, and was gonna confront him at a different time. Now, I wish I would have saved the shit; I could have printed it here so you could see for yourself. But what would that solve? I wish none of it would've happened. It was a fucked-up way for it to end. He was a childhood friend and I don't forget the good times, but this was just fucked.

Before the tour, I kept hearing weird shit. Parris had been spending a lot of time with a friend of mine. One day he tells me, "Yo man, you need to keep an eye on Parris if he's handling all your business." I'm like, "Why?" And he's like, "Well, I mentioned to him that you guys should look into some publishing deals, and that we should talk about it, and he completely flipped and started yelling at me saying, 'Don't ever discuss business with Harley—ever! Don't put any ideas in his head!'" Now this was all stuff I had just heard right before the tour started, and I had other heard shit like this from other people, so I already had a bad taste in my mouth before we went on the tour. That shit stuck into my head. But when we were getting ready for the tour, Parris' dad got very sick. The guy was old and in the hospital. I knew Parris was a little freaked out about it. So I thought to myself, "OK, I'm gonna wait until his dad's out of the hospital, or until we get back from this short-ass European tour." I didn't want to jump on him and start flipping while his dad could be dying, that wouldn't be right. I figured I'd wait for when we got home and the time felt more appropriate. Then I was gonna get to the bottom of this shit—for real.

I mean, who was he to tell anyone not to talk to me? I was so mad. And I guess he could feel it, 'cause I remember even on the way to the airport, he was looking at me all nervous and shit. I don't know if he could just feel the tension, but I was definitely having a hard time looking at him and keeping my mouth shut. He came to me all trying to act concerned, saying, "What's the matter? Are you all right?" And I'm saying to myself, "You know what's up, motherfucker!" I tried to keep it in, but I'm just not good at hiding my feelings; maybe I should have talked with him about it then, I don't know.

Anyway, at least half of the shows were total bombs on that short European tour. There was zero advertising, so no one knew we were coming at all. Plus, we had just been there a few months earlier. The booking agent told us it was a bad idea, but Parris insisted that we go for whatever reason.

So, back to his fuckin' "Beatles book." I was shocked and pissed. Throughout the book, there were things about deals he was trying to do that I never knew about, with comments like, "I'm gonna milk this for what it's worth." I was never "the math guy" so this got me freaked. We had a joint bank account that I didn't have access to. We'd invested in gear together, plus recording gear and a van, and he kept the passwords to our bank accounts, PayPal account, our website, all my personal info, even my social security number! See, I was "the trusting type." I was his friend forever, regardless of our ups and downs and whatever had happened in the past. It's my nature. I wear my feelings on the outside, always have. That's why some people don't like me, but at least you know what you get.

But in that book, there was a lot of hate that had been brewing for a long time that was a surprise to me. To this day, I can't understand how someone can put themselves on a tour bus and sleep, eat, and be with people every day you have such bitterness toward. That's something that I could not do. It's crazy how people who used to get along can get so resentful. I mean, we all made some great music together, did great shows. It's fucked up.

So anyway, I just couldn't keep it in anymore, and I confronted Parris about the book. I was so pissed off that I taped up my knuckles, so I could beat on him more without wrecking my hands. Rocky and Garry thought I was gonna fucking kill him. They saw me taping my hands and left the bus. I walked up to him, and I was like, "Motherfucker!" He cowered and flinched, and I threw a punch at him. He crawled into a ball, and I stopped the punch right before it connected to his face. He's like, "What?! What?!" I'm like, "Motherfucker, you better start thinking about 'What'!" I didn't even want to tell him everything I knew, because if I did, then he'd know what I didn't know. Let me just keep him wondering, until I can get all the facts sorted out.

I told him, "When we get back, you've got two weeks or less to give me every fuckin' accounting of everything that's been sold. Every T-shirt sold through our website, every CD we've sold. I want to know every fuckin' thing, and I want to know what's left in our account." It was a very fucked-up scene. Like I said, Garry and Rocky really thought I was gonna kill him. Later that night, Garry saw Parris ripping up all his notebooks and throwing them in a canal.

Naturally when we got back from the tour, I never did hear from him. So I started calling him. It went from, "Parris, we need to talk" to "Motherfucker, you better get back to me!" Then, it progressed to, "You cocksucker, I'm going to fuck you up if you don't give me access to our bank account!" Basically, as I got more and more pissed, the more I went off; he recorded the phone calls, went to the cops, and got an order of protection against me. The funny thing was after I got busted, the cops were all sitting there with smirks on their faces, and they started giggling. They were like, "By the way, we heard the tapes." And one cop busted out laughing. He quoted me: "I'm going to grab you by your big-ass ears and skull-fuck your punk ass!" They couldn't believe that a man would go and have another man arrested over some business that went bad, that they should have just 'fessed up and dealt with. But nonetheless, they were cops, and they had to arrest me.

It was funny—when I went to court, Mickey Fitz from the Business was with me, and I had a friend of mine from Renzo's go with me who was a music lawyer. He wasn't even a criminal lawyer, but I just wanted to show up with someone in a suit, so I didn't look completely helpless. I got in there, and there's this bitch-ass judge, and she basically said if I went near, was on the same block or street, if I called him, e-mailed, contacted him through any third party, blah blah blah, I could get up to seven years in jail. Mickey Fitz was in shock. First off, he couldn't believe Parris did me like that. Secondly, he couldn't believe a man could get up to seven years in jail for threatening to kick another man's ass! He was like "That's American justice for you!"

Around that time, Pantera called me and invited me down to one of their shows. And Parris left a message on my friend's machine saying, "I'm going to be at the Pantera show, and if I see Harley there, I'm going to call the cops and they're going to arrest him, like they did to John." Parris had John arrested twice, maybe even three times, I'm not even sure anymore. I almost understand why he did what he did with John, because John was nearly stalking him, telling him he was gonna have him fucked up by other people. At one point, when Parris and I had started playing as the Cro-Mags again without John, John started threatening Parris on his phone a lot, and had other people threatening him.

John was playing some really fuckin' stupid games, trying to pump some fear into Parris—just basically being the bully he always was. Parris had gotten stabbed, I think back in the early '90s. It was in a bar-fight situation at the Spiral on Houston Street, and he got stabbed around the kidney area and it almost killed him. So John goes to Parris, "You think you got fucked up when you got stabbed? You're going to get fucked up a thousand times worse! And tell Harley he's not even going to know when it's coming, 'cause it ain't gonna be anyone he even knows."

So Parris was like, "Fuck John!" At that point, Parris went to the cops and filed an order of protection against John. But John, who

378

just can't help himself, kept fucking with him. One day—this is almost funny, but it's not just 'cause how it all turned out—John was jogging by him, Parris didn't see him, John snuck up on him and went, "BOO!" and Parris jumped! That's what led Parris to call the cops and say, "This guy that I have an order of protection against just threatened my life" or whatever the fuck it was he said.

John of course, who is always looking for an angle, took complete advantage of the whole situation and ran with it as far as he could. He threw himself a benefit, pretended he was in military prison and all kinds of bullshit. All in typical John form: blowing up bullshit into something it really wasn't. He threw the benefit, got everyone to play at it, and meanwhile, he was in D.C., chillin' at a friend of ours' house. The motherfucker was at a Bad Brains show in D.C. two nights before his benefit, when he was supposed to be "locked up." He knew it was all a bunch of bullshit, and at his benefit gig, his brother is up onstage reading a letter from John saying he's in jail, he can't believe his friends did this to him, blah blah blah. It was such a fucking hoax. All this fucking Cro-Mags drama, it just got so fuckin' pitifully ridiculous and fucking pathetic. I sometimes wish the band never existed. I really do have many regrets over ever having that band. Everyone just turned into such a bunch of bitches.

Here I am, getting accused of some shit I didn't even do, and here's Parris being a cop-calling motherfucker on people he grew up with. John took big-time advantage of it, and was up on every soapbox he could jump up on, going on about "Harley and Parris had me arrested!" But it's like, "No, Parris had you arrested, 'cause you kept fucking with him and he got sick of it." It was all such stupid, childish, immature shit for a bunch of grown-ass fuckin' men to even be involved in.

Meanwhile, I was dealing with a lot of family shit at the time. I didn't have time for his bullshit or all the fuckin' games. So I really wasn't even reacting or giving a fuck. I had real-life shit going on, not Cro-Mags bullshit drama. I was just like, "Fuck this asshole." I figured everybody back in the day knew John was full of shit. And most people who get to know him after a while figure that out. I mean, it's not to say he's not a likable guy when he wants to be. He's just full of shit, that's all. But to every new-jack motherfucker who don't know shit except "This is John from the Cro-Mags... wow!" They believe all his horseshit, not realizing what a history he has of being a jive-ass motherfucker.

But the thing that really pissed me off was when some people I thought would know better started feeding into that shit. So I became like the bad guy of NYHC, along with Parris simply because he acted like a little bit of a coward, and in the end, John took total advantage of it. Parris reacted the way he reacted. He wasn't a fighter; he never was. He was sick of being fucked with. He didn't want to get bullied. He did what most normal people do when they are getting fucked with or threatened. I mean, John should've known better and acted his fuckin' age, and Parris, the same thing.

My girlfriend was the first person to point out how underhanded Parris could be. Before I even realized things were going bad, he had me sign a partnership agreement with him, saying that he was now co-owner of the Cro-Mags even though, up until that point, I had been the owner of the name alone. He had me sign it without giving me a chance to go over it or have a lawyer look at it. He just handed it to me in front of the Music Building were we practiced one night when we were getting ready to go. We were standing in the rain and he said, "I need you to sign these papers" and he gave me some reason why he needed it done right then and there 'cause he needed to do something with registering some bullshit. So I did. Why wouldn't I trust him? I thought we had gotten past the whole *Alpha Omega* fallout. We were "friends." We were "partners."

She was like, "You're not gonna have a lawyer look at that?" He looked at her with this really pissed-off glare. I was like, "For what? He's my partner." Well, that was the start of a lot of bullshit. And of course from that day on, he had major beef with her—like she was getting in between him and me.

As always, I was too trusting, and at the end of it all, he wound up selling all our gear and emptying out our "joint business bank account"—and oh yeah, having me arrested.

He in turn started trying to undermine my relationship with her and break us up. He started talking all kinds of shit to her behind my back, telling her that I didn't really care about her and that I was cheating on her. And as it turned out, she was right. He did wind up fucking me over pretty bad, and ironically, so did she.

So, the "Parris era" officially came to an end in 2000, which is the last time I spoke to him. I don't even keep track of what he says about me—it's all just fucked-up that cats who really were friends when they were kids turned out to be such bitter... I don't wanna say "enemies," 'cause I still don't like to feel that he or any of the other guys are my enemies. But let's just say it's sad, and some of those things I can never forgive him for.

If I knew how, and if I could have, or if I could go back and keep that *The Age of Quarrel* line-up going, and avoid all the beef that arose over the years, I would have. But it wasn't up to me. Mack quit, John quit, and I just tried to keep going. And look at all the bullshit that followed. I guess everybody just got personally wrapped up in it: defensive, attached. When you get attached, pride and ego get involved. And when you don't have a lot, that's an easy trap to fall into. We all put a lot of time in, and we all got taken advantage of. I guess we lost the trust. Chris Williamson saw to that back in the old days. And it all just imploded from there.

WHY CAN'T WE ALL JUST GET ALONG

Chapter Fifteen

n 2001, me and John Bloodclot and started talking again. It happened 'cause Parris had me arrested. It was like we finally had something in common again, so we said, "Fuck it." Just for fun, we decided to do a CBs show, which wound up turning into two back-to-back shows under the name Cro-Mags NYC. It was John, Doug, Rocky George, Garry, and me. It was great.

Then we got offered a few shows with the Bad Brains. We were like, "Are you kidding?" Go on tour with Bad Brains, them and us, after all these years? It didn't take long to say yes. It was like, here's finally a Cro-Mags reunion, or the closest thing to it. But Parris, you can't be here 'cause you had us both arrested and have orders of protection against us. It was kind of funny. But I always had fun playing with John. It's just all the other competitive drama and ego shit that I couldn't stand.

But I wasn't interested in doing the Cro-Mags full-time, and neither was Doug. Rocky and me were in the studio laying down tracks for my new project called Harley's War. That was me, Rocky and a bunch of old friends like "Crazy Jay Skin" Vento from Warzone, Vinnie Stigma from Agnostic Front, and Mickey Fitz from the Business.

I was already working on it, and I wasn't 100% confident that John and me would keep playing together. It had never been a reliable thing in the past. As far as I was concerned it would've been great if we did some shows once in a while, did our *The Age of Quarrel* set—no pressure, no expectations. The fans would've loved it. And then the rest of the year, we'd go out and tour with our own bands, and still keep playing as the Cro-Mags.

But the motherfucker went nuts; he went ahead and booked an entire statewide tour as the Cro-Mags with A.J. Novello on guitar, as if he was ever in the Cro-Mags. And he expected me to jump on. It's like, yo, at first it was John, Doug, and Rocky and me. Those are four guys who had actually been on Cro-Mags records. But then Doug didn't want to tour, and Rocky went back out to California. So then, it was me with John, Garry, and A.J. We did a few shows together as a four-piece.

We weren't being billed as the Cro-Mags; we were billing it as "Street Justice." We also billed it as "Cro-Mags NYC" at one or two shows. But it really wasn't Cro-Mags—it was me and John and doing *The Age of Quarrel* songs.

My girlfriend was pregnant, and I just wasn't ready to leave and go on tour. I just had all those riots in Cali when I was out there and she didn't want me going back out. We were getting ready to have a kid, and the whole shit was too much. I was like, "Fuck this, I ain't doing it."

But John booked it anyway and went out and did the tour as the Cro-Mags, and let all the advertisements say "Featuring Harley and John," using old photos of the band in the ads. People paid money to see what they hoped was going to be the Cro-Mags. And then when they showed up, John's story was, "Harley couldn't make it. His woman is having complications with her pregnancy," which was total bullshit. What he was doing was touring as the band without me, and then lying about why I wasn't there.

I remember around the time I did those last few shows with John, I was sitting in the back of the van with my girlfriend, and he was up in the front talking about all the people he's friends with—literally, all of them, talking shit, laughing, making fun of them. And then he comes out of his face with, "Yeah, I think it's about time for me to do another one of my benefits." He and his friend Danny started laughing 'cause to them, it was a big joke. Every time John did a benefit, he kept all the money or at least most of it, and gave a little bit of chump change to whatever the cause was.

So I interjected real loud, "Yo motherfucker, if there's any benefits being done, it's for my unborn kid—not for some bullshit." And he was like, "Yeah, yeah, no—you're right. We should do a benefit and help you guys out a bit." That was supposed to be "the baby shower party," which John canceled. We wound up doing one anyway thanks to bands like Merauder, Candiria, Suicide Kings, All Boro Kings and others.

Then when John hit the road as the Cro-Mags and did interviews, he was like, "Man, they weren't shit until I joined the band. I made that band happen!" It's like, dude, we had already been gigging with Eric, performing almost the entire The Age of Quarrel album. All that was there before him.

It wasn't until the late '80s when a whole new generation of kids came on the scene that anyone even took John seriously. To them, whatever he said was gold. But to the people that knew him from the old days, it was like, "Oh, give me a fuckin' break! You're the

same guy that claims to have been a Navy SEAL." Todd Youth said, "Man, he used to tell me he was a Navy SEAL all the time. And I was just a little kid. What the fuck was he trying to impress me for? I was like 13 years old!" But that was John, bragging and lying.

John didn't get in many fights. That was never his thing. But he was kind of a jock and a bully. Like how he would try to intimidate Parris—he always called Parris "Casper" or "Dough Boy" or whatever—and made fun of his guitar playing, even though he's the best fucking guitarist he's ever played with. He always fucked with Doug and even Pete; he was just that way. He was always the guy who had to make fun of whoever was "the bottom man on the totem pole." You know how there is always a kid in school who is a dick to everyone? But for some reason, he's the cool kid, but also "the dick"? Well, that was John, 24/7.

The last time I played with John was 2002. But I bumped into him in 2003, at a Henry Rollins show at Irving Plaza. I was hanging out with Henry before the sound check, and then I went back for the gig. I was backstage, and I came walking out because I wanted to give Henry his space before they went out to play. I walked out, and John was standing there with some people around him. He smirked at me, and was like, "What's up?"—all being a smartass.

But I wasn't having it. I immediately got right up right in his face, and his eyes got all big. He was like, "Huh?" And everybody standing around him was like, "Oh shit!"—including Porcell from Shelter. Because there's "Big Bad John," who'd been talking all this shit about how he beat my ass. I stepped right to him and told him, "I'll crush that fuckin' pointy little bitch nose of yours like a fucking soda can." He was like, "You better back up out of my face." I stepped even further in his face, breathing in his fuckin' face, to where our noses were literally touching. I was like, "You want to do something, motherfucker? What's up?" He was trying to save face, like, "Let's take this shit outside. Let's take it down the block. Let's go to the park." Or like, let's take it anywhere that people can't see it. I was like, "Fuck you, do it right here. Who the fuck is holding you back, bitch?" And I body-checked him with both hands. He looked at me all crazy. And not like crazy hard, more like crazy shocked.

And that's when I was like, "Oh yeah, that's right. You only like hitting motherfuckers when they're not looking. Let me turn around so you can do what you did last time, you punk-ass motherfucker. You want me to smoke a blunt or two first?" I turned around, stood there for a few seconds then turned back around. He couldn't handle the abuse. I should have just punched him in his fuckin' face, but I was ridiculing him so bad that I think it was worse. I was just trying to get him to make a move, Mr. Big-Bad-Ass.

Henry Rollins was playing, and I was singing every lyric, yelling it in John's face. Shit like, "Revenge, to watch you bleed, Revenge, that's all I need!" It was so fucking funny. If this motherfucker had any nuts, he would have hit me, because I was humiliating him in front of all these motherfuckers who had just been jocking him.

At that point, I'd already made it clear that I would fight him in a fair one, not this sneak-up bullshit he pulled, or set up someone, or have someone jumped. Crap like he was claiming he was gonna do, saying I wasn't even gonna know who it was coming from or some bullshit like that. I was done with all the he said/she said bullshit. It was either put up or you simply don't mean shit to me anymore.

HARLEY'S WAR

Harley's War began in 2001, right after Parris had me arrested and right before me and John and got together with Doug and Rocky.

A friend of mine at the Music Building was going to the Institute of Audio Research at the time. For one of his projects he needed to record live drums. He asked if I could lay down some drum tracks for him. I said, "Sure, can I record some songs while you track drums, so we can both get something done?" He agreed, and that was that. So I wrote most of the first Harley's War EP that day in the studio on the spot, just so we could get some tracks done. I tracked drums and bass; it was Ryan Krieger and me. Then later I had Rocky and "Crazy Jay Skin" lay down guitar tracks at a different studio. That's how it began. I got my friend Mickey Fitz from the Business to sing on a track, and I got Vinnie Stigma to play guitar on that track with him. The song is called "Spirit of '77." So that was it, Harley's War: me, Ryan Krieger, Crazy Jay Skin, and Rocky George was the first line-up. But it wasn't a band in the sense that it was gonna be a permanent line-up or anything.

I never expected those guys to be there full-time. It wasn't about that; it was about getting together and trying to make some music that wasn't Cro-Mags. I got the name Harley's War from a band that the Cro-Mags played with in Germany on the *Alpha Omega* tour called Charlie's War. I was like, "Fuck it—if Charlie can have a war, then I can, too."

Ryan moved out West and was replaced by Garry Sullivan. Rocky George was still in NYC playing with me. We had just done a few Cro-Mags shows with John and Doug, with Garry on drums, and Rocky stayed around to do the recording with me, and some Harley's War gigs. But I knew Rocky was gonna split soon. I was just happy I played with him as much as I did, 'cause he is one of my favorite guitarists. In 2002, I had the honor of having Darryl Jenifer from the Bad Brains playing bass with me for a few gigs, and I just held down the vocals. That came about 'cause one day I was thinking, "If I could ever replace myself on bass, who would it be?" and Darryl immediately popped to mind. I gave him a call and asked him if he was down to do a few shows just for fun, and he was. So we did, and that shit was great—we even did a few Bad Brains songs.

This was when John Bloodclot and me weren't at each other's throats. We had just done those shows with the Bad Brains and he wasn't out pimping his fake Cro-Mags shit yet. So he came up onstage at those shows at the end of the set that Harley's War did with Darryl. I got on the bass and we did a bunch of *The Age of Quarrel* stuff. Those shows were great. Of course I knew playing with Darryl wasn't gonna be a full-time thing either. I just wanted to have some fun and play with some other cats that I respected. It was meant to be a good-time project.

I did a few gigs with just Darryl, Jay Vento, and Garry Sullivan. Then I briefly got that asshole A.J. from Leeway, or, that "scrawny, bald-headed motherfucker" as John called him. But when that happened, Jay bowed out; he wasn't feelin' A.J.—and looking back, "I hear ya." This was around the time that the whole new schism with John happened.

It was around this time that we booked the baby shower gig. It was gonna be big; it was at CBGBs with Cro-Mags, Harley's War, Candiria, Merauder, and a shitload of other bands. Rocky moved

HARLEY, PERSONAL COLLECTION

back to L.A., and Doug had opted out of doing any more Cro-Mags shows—but they were both gonna do that show. Rocky flew into town; he was working on the Harley's War recording with me.

I didn't want to go on John's Cro-Mags tour; I wanted to stick around for the pregnancy. So John pulled the plug on the baby shower gig without telling me. He called CBs and told them that the show was cancelled. So Harley's War played the gig at the Continental with Candiria, Merauder, and All Boro Kings—with Sean Kilkenny and some of the guys from Dog Eat Dog—and a bunch of other bands, instead.

That was the final straw for me. John went out and did his fake Cro-Mags, and I said "Fuck it," and kept gigging locally. In early 2003, I released the first Harley's War CD, *Hardcore All Stars/Cro-Mag*. It featured the tracks I'd recorded at the Institute of Audio Research, and it included the Cro-Mags solo recordings I did as a kid in 1982/1983, plus some Stimulators stuff. I pressed the CD myself. I saved up money from making VHS Cro-Mags videos of old gigs and selling them at shows. I'd be sitting there at the table, cutting out the covers that I had just printed at Kinko's, and putting them in the boxes. If that ain't Hardcore, I don't know what is. I made enough money selling those VHS tapes to print my first 1,000 CDs, which I sold right away, out of the box. So I printed another 2,000, and then another 2,000, and sold like 5,000 copies right away. I did pretty fucking well doing it out of my apartment, by myself with no label. The shit was totally DIY—and I still sold more CDs than Both Worlds or Bloodclot did with a real label behind them.

From there, Harley's War just kept morphing into different line-ups as different cats got involved. I kept gigging around the New York area. I didn't want to go on tour while my girlfriend was pregnant, but whenever I'd book a gig or two, I'd just call my boys, and see who was down. If one guy couldn't do a gig—most of them were in other bands as well—I'd just call another friend of mine to jump in and take their spot.

Around that time, this guy from the Netherlands called "Onno Cro-Mag," an old Skinhead who'd helped promote some of our shows when I had been there with Parris, was working on an Oi! tribute compilation CD with Roger Miret. So I went into the studio and recorded two of my favorite Oi! songs: "Bad Man" by the Cockney Rejects and "Freedom" by the Last Resort.

I've had most of the best players on the NYHC scene play with Harley's War. I've had Eric Arce, now with the Misfits, on drums. I also played with another monster drummer, Walter Ryan, Maximum Penalty guitarist Joe Affe, and like I said, Rocky George, Jay Vento, Gabby Abularach, A.J. played a few gigs with me; also Eddie Ortiz, Joseph James and Steve Gallo from Agnostic Front and Inhuman, Vinnie Stigma even jumped up onstage with us, and of course Sean Kilkenny, who has been my "go-to guy" for years. Will "Cave Man" Dahl played guitar with me and recorded with me in the studio; he's a great player and engineer. I've gone out with so many different guys; I even had Jorge from Merauder singing with me for a few shows. We played everything from Hardcore shows to big metal festivals to little bitty gigs in the woods in front of handfuls of people in the dark.

That one time in the pitch-black woods, they had to use a car with the headlights on to light the stage and dance floor. As it got darker, we couldn't see shit. I started yellin' for my boy, Tank. I'm like, "Yo, Tank, where you at?" He's like, "I'm right here." He was standing next to me and I couldn't see him! We played and we had a blast. Of course the kid who booked the "show" tried to dick out on the money. I dragged him to an ATM and made him empty his account, and that was that. As Sean Kilkenny said: "Harley always made sure you got paid. He never once promised something he could not deliver."

We did Europe, Scandinavia and Japan; we flew to fucking Norway for two days and did a two-day festival with GBH and came home. Sean Kilkenny: "Harley called me one day to ask what I was doing next weekend. I said, 'Nothing, why?' He said, 'We're going to Norway!' And off we went. We were only there for a few days; after the last show I left without my guitar. Nobody realized my guitar was there. Somehow, some way, a year and a half later, this guy shows up in Europe at a Dog Eat Dog show with my guitar! He said, 'This is from Harley and Ottar!' I couldn't believe it! But Harley came through again."

We played at CBGB so many times. I miss that place; it was like my home, my fuckin' living room for most of my entire life. We did the last Hardcore matinee there with bands from Agnostic Front to Sick of It All to Murphy's Law to Madball. It was insane! That was really a "goodbye to NYHC" in a lot of ways for me, the ending of an era. I actually gigged there a few times in the last few weeks of the club. The Stimulators did a reunion and played with the Dead Boys, and a week later with our old friends, the Bad Brains. I may have been the only person to play there three times in that last month of CBs.

The truth is, I don't have much in common with the new kids hanging out, besides that love for the music. They come from a different world than me. I don't know much about what's going on anymore; and that's cool. I think my kids know more about it than I do—they've grown up on music. I remember walking my son to school one day when he was five. It was 8:30 in the morning, and he looked up at me and goes, "Dad, Tony's really special." I looked at him and go, "Tony who?" He looks at me in all seriousness, and goes, "Tony from Black Sabbath!" I thought that was great.

But after I had my kids, it was like "pow"—the one kid in '02 and then "pow" again in '05. I was faced with the fact that while I was making okay money—I mean, it definitely pays better than it used to—it doesn't have any real kind of security, and it's always feast or famine. You go on tour, you make a little money, and then you rough it in between. Rock 'n' roll, and Hardcore in particular, doesn't always pay the bills, and when you have kids, you gotta make sure there's food in the fridge.

Because of the first pressings of the Harley's War CD, I had a little to float off of. My kids' mother decided she wanted to go back to school so she could get a job, and that was fair. So I took off two years from playing gigs—and it really was the best gig I could've had. Those were some of the happiest times of my life, being with my kids all the time. I loved it. But it put a damper on the gigging and touring. Sometimes you have to prioritize, and I have no regrets. At that point I became the kids' primary caregiver, looking after the kids every day.

In 2007 Harley's War made it to Japan. It was kind of bittersweet because that was something the Cro-Mags never did. And it was always a dream of mine. I had always wanted the Cro-Mags to be the first NYHC band to make it to Japan.

I've been to Japan three times. We've done the Magma Fest, a big Hardcore/Punk event, sponsored by Magma and Measure, a Japanese Hardcore/Punk label. It was us, Murphy's Law, Sick of It All, Madball, Hazen Street, H2O, Underdog, and a few other bands. It was like New York Hardcore took over Japan for a week! There were two stages, two huge skate ramps with pro skaters from all over the world doing tricks, big inflatable balloon dinosaurs, and Godzilla-type monsters—like a Warped Tour-type vibe. I got paid more to do a single show there than I'd ever been paid before. They must have spent hundreds of thousands of dollars. If that plane went down, more than half the NYHC scene would've died!

I remember Jimmy from Murphy's Law and me almost got into it on that trip. Everyone thought that we were gonna fight in the airport. It was funny. I've known Jimmy most of my life—neither of us are known for taking shit, and we both have bad tempers. When we first got to Japan he started flippin' that H2O, Madball and some other bands were acting like "rock stars," and somehow started yelling at me. Well, next thing you know, like half the

NYHC scene was standing there nervously while we were flippin' on each other.

At one point, I was chillin' over there with the old Cro-Mags drummer Mackie, who was with Hazen Street. I think we were in Okinawa, and he was all, "Man, it's too bad you and John can't work things out, man." I agreed with him. He was all, "We were some bad motherfuckers." I'm like, "It took you that long to figure that shit out?" And we both laughed. I gotta say it was good to see him and to hear that from him after all these years.

When we weren't gigging, me, Sean, and Russell and Matt from Underdog all went out swimming in the ocean in Okinawa. Like dummies, we were diving off the big cement breakers set up to stop big waves. We were diving into water known to be infested with not just sharks and poisonous fish, but deadly jellyfish, sea snakes, and all kinds of other shit that can kill you. Meanwhile, the beaches are all fenced off to keep all the dangerous shit away from swimmers!

There was a little drama at the end of the trip with the bands and money, but everything got resolved. I had no complaints. It was just that they were a new company and this was a huge event for them to try to pull off the first time around. But really, it was historic.

Then I recorded some new material and shot a video at an underground fight club in the Bronx. The CD itself didn't wind up coming out until after our next trip to Japan, but the video did. It was at the Underground Combat League (UCL), directed by B-boy legend Pop Master Fable. I lost the fight, but the video came out good.

After it was recorded, I went back to Japan, and then the CD and DVD came out in the States and Europe. So I had these new tracks, but due to some mishaps with the engineer, I didn't have enough material to release a full-length CD. So I released the new material along with the old Harley's War *Hardcore All Stars/Cro-Mag* EP, with the 1982/'83 Cro-Mag demos and some bonus live Harley's War at CBs, and a bonus DVD.

Mike Mahler is a fitness, strength coach, and motivational speaker. Initially, I had given him permission to use some Harley's War music for his DVDs on Kettlebell workouts, and then in turn, he helped me get back in the studio when I was unable to finance it myself. I got a distribution deal with MVD Audio, and I got in the studio thanks to Mike, who basically sponsored the recordings. I felt some of it was going to be the best stuff I ever recorded, but the engineer freaked out. At some point out of nowhere, he discovered a new "hobby"—crystal meth/coke. One thing led to another, and somehow in his mind I went from owing him $300 to $3,000 overnight! Go figure. Anyway, it turned into some drama with him flipping out, and I only got to walk with some of my tapes, and unfortunately, some of the best stuff got lost. Soon after, that engineer died. I tried to salvage what I could, but I really did lose some of the best stuff. The worst part is, some of it had HR of the Bad Brains on vocals. The shit kills me to even think about.

In 2008, I was contacted by Magma and Measure to do another Magma Fest tour of Japan. This time they told us we'd be playing with punk rock legends the New York Dolls, as well as the Bad Brains, Biohazard, Marky Ramone's band, and some Japanese bands. This time it was just a quick visit, a few gigs.

November 27, 2008, we were getting ready to go. It was me, Will "Cave Man" Dahl, Sean Kilkenny, and this time Ryan Krieger on drums. We brought along my friend Rich Von Mullen, a tattoo artist and guitarist as tech/roadie, and Steven Blush, author of *American Hardcore*, to film and document the trip. This time, the chaos started when they didn't get us our visas on time. They tried to talk us into re-routing through Seoul, Korea, to "try" to get our visas confirmed from there, which was completely nuts. So they re-booked our flights and we missed the first couple of gigs.

December 2, 2008, we had our flights booked and we were supposed to be on our way to Japan. My roadie got to my house at 5:00 in the morning, and my phone battery was dead. The motherfucker didn't know what apartment I was in, and sat there for three or four hours, and then I don't know what the fuck, but he split. Sean and Will stayed at the studio the night before, and made it to the airport. Ryan was flying to Japan from L.A.; that would be the guys' first face-to-face meeting. Steven Blush was in Florida and he made it to the airport. Everybody got to their airports.

Me, I finally woke up; I got my AM and my PM fucked up! So the guys were at the airport, the plane was getting ready to board and I was calling them up, flipping the fuck out, and leaving messages. Finally, I got through to them. I was like, "Where are you?!" They're like, "We are boarding the plane, where are you?!" It was almost kind of funny. So the boarding started and I was still in my house.

The whole band was on the plane but me! Anyway, after a bunch of phone calls to and from Japan, I would leave the next morning, land in Japan, get picked up at the airport, get driven to the gig, walk up onstage, and play.

The band had never actually met each other or played together! I had introduced them like two weeks earlier through an e-mail. It said something along the lines of "Ryan meet Sean and Will, Will, Sean meet Ryan," and that was that. I sent them the set list of songs I wanted them to know, and they all met up in Japan for the first time!

I knew individually they had it down, and that the band would sound great 'cause it was all guys I had played with before. Everybody knew what they had to do. I told them a few parts they needed to concentrate on and said, "When you get there, do sound check. Run through whatever songs you need to work on, and put together a set. I told them over the phone, 'I'll get picked up at the airport, and see you guys at the gig.'"

So I was doing a headlining gig the same night I would land, then one day off, then two shows with Biohazard and the New York Dolls.

Now, the madness begins—my drummer was in Tokyo 'cause he flew from L.A., my guitarists were in Nagoya, and I was in Detroit! My drummer would be arriving in time for sound check the next day, and I'd be arriving in time to get to the venue and walk onstage. I was cutting it very, very close. Also Steven Blush's flight was late arriving in Tokyo; he missed his connecting flight. But somehow he made it there.

I arrived at the airport, got through the gate, my ride was waiting, showtime was supposed to be 9:30. I pulled up at the club at 9:27! My guys were in the dressing room with their guitars on, strumming, trying to figure out, "What are we supposed to do if he doesn't show up?" I walked in the door, got handed my instrument, walked onstage, took off my jacket and started playing.

"We were onstage tuning and the intro was playing. We still haven't heard if he even made it to Japan! Harley walked onstage at the last second. The band killed the place, and no one even knew he just got off a jet just an hour earlier and traveling all day. That's a fucking rock star right there." —Sean Kilkenny

"The amazing part of that night was waiting by the airport gate in Nagoya, and seeing Harley escorted out of customs, in his wife-beater, a bag over his shoulder, and two kettle weights. We got into the car and the promoter handed over a huge sack of weed from Mount Fuji. And yes, he arrived moments before showtime." —Steven Blush

So that's how the trip started. And then it gets even weirder.

We got to the first of those big shows with the New York Dolls and Biohazard; the Bad Brains were on the bill, but didn't make it. We were playing at a venue that held about 5,000 people, but there was zero advertising. So it was more like a private party: a two-day party with the New York Dolls, Biohazard, and Harley's War, and a bunch of Japanese bands. It was the strangest thing I have ever seen. All the bands were confused as fuck.

By the end of the second evening, there were all kinds of crazy rumors buzzing around that it was some kind of gangster money-laundering scheme 'cause they had spent so much money on the event and it seemed like they had no expectation of trying to make it back. It was hysterical—besides all the bands that were playing, there were only a couple of hundred people there. The first time we had been to Japan, the festival shows had a couple thousand. This time, there were bigger bands but it was empty. It was crazy. But these dudes who looked exactly like the Japanese Ramones were there.

After we played, Biohazard pulled up the entire audience onstage—every one of them—and had a big Japanese mosh pit onstage! The Dolls did a great but strange set; they jammed for like two hours, doing reggae songs and shit. David Johansen's wife was walking around the stage, taking photos of all the shenanigans that were going on.

It was like a strange dream. Everyone got paid really well. Biohazard said they had never been paid that much in their lives.

The end of the last night in Japan, after smoking endless phatties, everyone was partied out. I'd been hanging with the Dolls and Biohazard all night long. I was wandering the hotel aimlessly; it was 4:00 in the morning and I bumped into David Johansen and his wife. We were hanging out. Now bear in mind, these are people from the generation that I started out from musically: this is Max's Kansas City royalty. They were the shit when I was a kid. So there I was, 30 years later, with David Johansen in Japan. We were riding up the elevator to our rooms at the end of the night. I was stoned as fuck.

The elevator door opened, they got off, and David and I just looked at each other and smiled, and I said, "When I say I'm in love," and he said, "You best believe I'm in love!" and we both said, "L-U-V." The door shuts, and you could hear all of us cackling. A very classic rock 'n' roll moment—a perfect end to a hectic week.

While on that trip there was one last Cro-Mags offer, and yet another failed attempt to re-group the band. We got offered more than any other Hardcore band I've ever heard of to play one show: 40,000 euros. I've always wanted to get the band back together and do a reunion, but after all the drama, I can honestly say at this point, the idea of being locked in a van or a bus with John is not really pleasant.

September 2009, we went back to Japan for Magma Festival with my old friends GBH, the Exploited, and one of my favorite bands, Discharge. Seeing my old homeboys was such a good time. It just reminded me what was real about the scene back in the old days.

Everyone was getting drunk and partying after the shows; I was running around the hotel outta my mind wired on like eight Red Bulls from the gig at 6:00 in the fucking morning. I was playing bass in the halls and elevators with a fake dog-head hat on that I bought on the street earlier that day for like four bucks.

People were up tattooing, drinking, and blazing phatties left, right, front, and center. Me and Wattie were up all fuckin' night talking about the old days; he remembers the first time the Exploited played NYC at the Ukrainian Hall by St. Marks Place. When they did "Fuck the USA," a bunch of my Skinhead buddies tried to pull him off the stage and were about to lay an ass-beating on him. I football-tackled him into the crowd. I just wanted him to know what was up. But then I pulled him back up onstage, and when my friends saw that, they left him alone for the rest of the night. He told me he was scared shitless—and that motherfucker doesn't scare easily!

Wattie gave me such a compliment when he told me, "Harley, you're my favorite bassist in the whole fucking world. I really mean that." His bassist later told me it was no bullshit, that he said it all the time. Wattie is one of the realest motherfuckers I know—I really respect that guy. And a compliment like that from him means a fucking lot to me.

We also bumped into Charlie Harper from the UK Subs on that trip. He later reminisced about their first U.S. gig, and meeting me when I was just a little kid: "The first time we met, I think that was 1979, you were maybe 12. We were in New York to play with the Police, and we were hangin' out to play with the Fall a few days later. You showed us around the city. But all the time, you wanted my Dr. Martens boots. I would have given them to you, but I was a size ten and you were a size six at the time! But we've been mates since."

That night when we played, Charlie came onstage and did a few UK Subs songs along with guys from GBH, Discharge and the

Exploited. Between us all there was over 1,000 years of punk rock up there!

I also got to connect on that tour with Rainy from Discharge. We spoke for hours about music, about all our old influences like classic shit blues and other shit. Growing up, he and Bones were such a huge influence on me and on my writing.

I met everything from Japanese punks and monks, to pro fighters and Yakuza gangsters: guys covered in tattoos with missing pinkies and all kinds of shit, serious motherfuckers.

On that trip, I was also invited to a Jiu-Jitsu dojo. At our first gig, a stocky Japanese guy, about 5'9", 180 pounds, came up to me backstage with our promoter and tour manager as translator, and told me his master had invited me to his dojo to "train" the following weekend. He added, "Everyone is looking forward to training with you." It was well-known that I train with Master Renzo Gracie.

My band members, especially Sean, got wind of it, and they started breaking my balls, preparing me for an ass-beating. So all week I was anticipating that this could be anything from a warm welcome to an ass-beating. I kept remembering when a Japanese fighter had come into Rickson Gracie's Academy back in the day, with photographers and all of that shit, and got his ass beat. So I couldn't help but laugh and wonder what was in store for me. And it didn't help that I hadn't trained in a couple of months.

Anyway, I was looking forward to training with some serious Japanese dudes. The week went by quickly, the gigs were great, but of course, I was out drinking with the promoters the night before I was set to go train. He took me to his family's restaurant, and we got drunk as hell on soju. It's like sake, but instead of being made from rice, it's made from potato, and they water it down. They add ice and a little green tea, and let me tell you, the shit is deadly! I am not a drinker and don't really party anymore, so it got me fucked up. But Sean, who is a very good drinker, got so fucked up he almost puked on the promoter!

So the next morning they booked me a car to get me to the dojo in time for class the next day. I kept remembering his words, "All of the guys want to train with you." We got there almost 20 minutes late 'cause of traffic. When I got there, the head instructor and Master Ippei Onuma were standing at the door with the student who invited me. They brought me into the academy and I saw about 15 guys sitting there waiting for me, and waiting for class to begin, which was being delayed until I arrived. I went to change, came out, and hit the mats, and warm-up began.

There was a student there who had lived in Queens, New York, who spoke perfect English—he was my translator. While we were warming up, a crowd started to gather. Word had got out that I was there; the promoter for Magma and some photographers gathered, as well as some video people, so the pressure was on a bit. I didn't want to embarrass myself and more importantly, I didn't want to embarrass Renzo. Despite being a little hung over, I did quite well, I trained with a bunch of guys, and had a great time.

After training, we all took photos together in front of the academy logo. The master gave me a belt with a message embroidered in Japanese, saying "Ground Control Family." He said from now on I don't need an invitation, just to come by and train with them whenever I'm in Yokohama. Then one of the students gave me a plaque with the name of the dojo, "RB Academy," in English and Japanese, and pictures of me and the guys from the academy. It says "Harley's War NY/YC"—for New York and Yokohama City.

I was honored to be there. And I walked out with a whole new level of respect from the Japanese promoters and the booking agents, who had all come down to watch me train.

The next day we headed home. Sean Kilkenny recalls: "We were headed to the airport to fly home. We drive for hours to the airport, at like 6 a.m. We get stuck in Japanese rush hour traffic. We are on the verge of missing our flight. Then we get pulled over at a traffic check-stop. Our Japanese driver has an expired license. Taka Kikuchi, our main man in Japan, explains the situation to the police—in Japanese. Next thing I know, we are put in the back of police cars! We thought we were going to prison! Turns out we got a full-on police escort—straight to the airport. We were given stickers on our shirts that let us run through security and everything. It was amazing. Like some Led Zeppelin-type shit."

After training in Yokohama, I was really inspired. I got right back to training at home in NYC with Renzo at the Academy. It re-ignited the fire in my training, and I trained five days a week, and I started to help teach classes. I had been teaching both of my sons at home since they were babies, but they started to train at the Academy and have been training and competing since they were five and seven years old. And I'll tell you, the first time I looked down at the other end of the mats and saw my boys training, it was one of the greatest moments of my life. My youngest son spent his birthday at the Academy with Georges St-Pierre and all the rest of the fellas. My eldest son had his birthday there with all the Gracies and about 30 kids, a full house, and a cake with the Renzo Gracie Academy logo on it.

My sons have grown up with Renzo like an uncle. Igor, Rolles, Gregor, Daniel, and Neiman—all the guys treat my boys like family. They've known their instructor, Magno Gamma, since birth; he came to the hospital to see them hours after they were born, and Renzo they have known since they were days old.

My eldest and I have been on Greyhound buses in the middle of the night, traveling hours away to represent RGA and Team Renzo Gracie. I have competed with my sons at nationally ranked grappling submission and Jiu-Jitsu events. One of my proudest moments was when we both competed at the same event—my son took first place in his division and I took second place in the Expert Masters division in the 30-to-35-year-old age bracket, although I was 44. Renzo joked when he first saw my son, "This is the proof that even though the fruit is rotten, the seed is still good!"

In 2002, when I had just put Harley's War together, we were playing the Continental and CBs just about every month. I was in the studio working on a record, and that's when I found out my father died—it was the same week I found out my girlfriend was pregnant with my first son Harley. I only saw my father once after my parents split up. It was at the Chelsea Hotel, when I was like four or five. It didn't go too well. I think I had maybe two phone conversations with him in my life. Anyway, he was dead. Granted, this was a guy I had no memory of, but nonetheless, it was a blow, especially since I was going to become a father myself, and I knew that I would never meet him.

When he died, his mother and his half-brother had no way to reach me. They didn't know anything about me or where I lived. But they did have copies of both *The Age of Quarrel* and *Best Wishes*, which I sent to his mother's for him back when they came out. So his half-brother, Sean, called the number on the back of the record, for Profile Records. Now mind you, Profile Records had not existed for quite a few years. But the phone line still existed, and it was still in the same office. There was a new record label in that office; I don't even know which label.

He called there looking for me. It was around the time that I was getting ready to sign with Equal Vision Records—which actually never panned out—but the buzz was out that I was getting ready to ink a deal with them.

The secretary he was talking to said my name out loud: "I'm sorry, I can't help you. I have no idea who Harley Flanagan is. I've never heard of the Cro-Mags." And as she says that, somebody in the office who happened to be into Hardcore walked by her cubicle and said, "Harley Flanagan? I think he just signed with Equal Vision Records." Crazy shit, like I said, as I never even signed the deal. The chances of such shit are way less than a million to one. So, that secretary called Equal Vision Records. Equal Vision got in touch with me while I was in the recording studio to tell me that my grandmother, whom I had never spoken to in my life, called to tell me that my father was dead.

This was a man that was never around, so I didn't have many feelings about him, bad or good. He was just this name that I heard. For some reason, one night, I got really angry with him. I was like, "Y'know, if that motherfucker wanted to, he could have found me. He could have tracked me down. If he ever would have tried or wanted to." That was the first time I felt anger toward him. Two days later, I got that call.

Telling the story doesn't have the same impact.

My father died from a fire that he set himself to keep warm. He was in a dumpster trying to keep warm on a cold night. He was drunk, and the smoke got to him. Unfortunately, he didn't die from the smoke. I managed to get his autopsy report, and he was still alive when they got him to the hospital. It was weird to fly all the way out to fuckin' Amarillo, Texas, to basically bury a cigar box. I never got to look in his eyes as a man.

I still have a cassette that he sent me in the '80s of him in a halfway house, basically telling me a bit about his life, and sharing his regrets and pain—in his words, over being "the ass" that he was back in the day, and hoping that now that I'm all grown up, I don't want to kick his ass for whatever rotten son-of-a-bitch he was back in the day. He'd start playing blues guitar and start singing little songs he'd written. It was kind of touching. So that's it, other than being handed the phone once or twice when I was young. I didn't even know his name was Harley until I turned 21—and that was another kick in the ass.

I don't remember what we talked about on the phone. What do you say when you're eight or nine, and your mom goes, "Harley, there's someone on the phone who wants to speak to you... it's your dad." It's not like there are any pieces to pick up, because I'd never been there. I was talking to a stranger.

But I don't have ill feelings toward him really, 'cause he simply wasn't ever an issue. The '60s fucked up a lot of people, including my folks. And here I am, "a product of the '60s." All that peace and love, boy, was that a failed experiment!

It's crazy though, 'cause over the years, my father would encounter Cro-Mags fans, and I would hear stories. People would be like, "Dude, I met this guy on Venice Beach, he said he was your father. I'm not trying to insult you, but he was kind of a bum—I mean, like, homeless. Real nice guy, funny as well, so I gave him a buck." He knew my band because I sent him those records. So whenever he saw Skinheads or punk rockers, he'd approach them. And he'd ask them, "Did you ever hear of a band called the Cro-Mags? That's my son!" And of course, nobody would ever believe him. One guy took a picture of him, and a few years later, gave me the picture of my father on the beach in California.

One time on the tour in support of *Best Wishes*, I tried to track him down to the one letter I'd gotten from him—to a halfway house; I believe it was in Oregon. We pulled up in our fancy Winnebago, and all the bums and scumbags on the block were like, "What the fuck is this?" It must have looked like the *USS Enterprise* or some shit to them. But he wasn't there. So I broke into his room, and left a picture of me on his bed—and I actually also left the *Bhagavad Gita*—with a phone number where I was going to be.

We did our gig, and the next morning, I was getting ready to leave, and the phone rang. I picked it up. They said, "It's Harley."

I'm like, "Yeah, this is Harley, who is this?" And they were like, "It's Harley." I'm like, "Shut the fuck up, who is it?" And then all of a sudden I'm like, "Oh shit, dad! I'm sorry—I wasn't thinking!" We only had like five minutes to talk, because it was checkout time and everybody was in the vehicle. I talked to him for a few minutes, and he said, "Well, where are you guys going to be playing? Maybe I'll try and hitch a train and try to run into you?"

It hurt in a way. As much as I wanted to meet him, on one hand, I was like, "What am I going to do, drag this old-ass vagabond motherfucker around with me on tour? This can't become my problem right now." In a lot of ways, I was probably better off growing up without him. I had a great stepfather in my life for a little while, and maybe that gave me the edge on trying to be a good father myself, or at least wanting to be. I don't know.

So that was my father. The only things I got from him were my name and my face, and maybe my temper. All I know is, unlike him, my kids changed everything for me.

My first son, Harley, was born in 2002. My second son, Jonah Odin, was born in 2005—both on the 18th, but in different months. 18 must be my lucky number. And I am so lucky, especially after the life I've had. They really did save me from myself. I've always been a maniac, and will probably be struggling with that side of myself until the day I kick the bucket. But they definitely keep me more focused, and out of a lot of trouble.

Even with little shit, like one day I was going to pick up my boys from school and some asshole nearly ran me down on Queens Boulevard. I yelled, "Watch where you're going," and this big Muslim dude got out, talking mad shit. He grabbed me and tore my shirt. So I swept him and he went down. I went to start pounding him out and then I realized my sons were getting out of school in minutes, so I backed off and kept walking. He started yelling, and I kept going. I couldn't be giving this asshole a beating. I'm a father, and I have responsibilities now that are greater than a torn shirt or my pride. I have to be there for my sons, not getting into fights or breaking some dickhead's arm. So I guess it's made me grow up a little; I don't act on every impulse like I used to.

I guess part of being a father is learning how to eat a certain amount of shit. You do it for your kids, 'cause they need you. You just throw on a little salt and pepper, and maybe some Tabasco, and smile 'cause you gotta be there for them.

One thing my father said was, "I've got all these years of experiences that I don't know what to do with." And that's kind of how I feel with my boys. How do I come in for a graceful landing after so much fuckin' turbulence in my life?

Hopefully, I can guide them better than I was guided, or at least maybe they will learn from my mistakes; God knows I have made enough for everybody.

Chapter Sixteen

'THE FINALE' — STABBING SLASHING BITING AT THE CBGB FEST

LAURA AND HARLEY FLANAGAN, BY FERNANDO GODOY

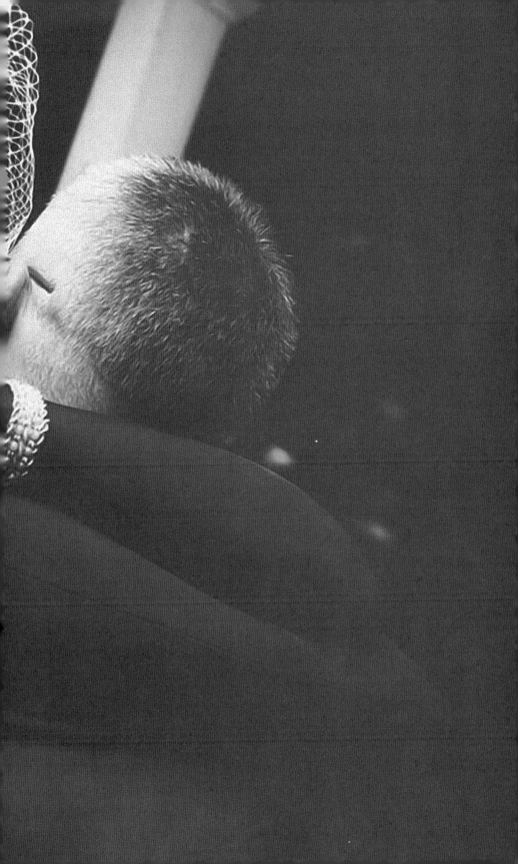

Even though I am now in a very different place in my life, I am a sentimental fool, and there has always been a part of me that still has attachment to my past, my old friends and what it all represented to me.

That brings me to where I am now, and to one of the most highly publicized events in my life and in New York Hardcore history: Stabbing Slashing Biting at the CBGB Webster Hall Fest!!!

After years of playing as Harley's War, years of Bloodclot touring as some version of the Cro-Mags, and after receiving countless e-mails, letters and requests from fans begging us to put the band back together, I made attempts to do so. And of course all attempts were shot down.

I thought that if I saw John in person, I might be able to talk to him without the phone calls or e-mails or other people's influence. I thought if we saw each other face to face there would still be something there from all those years of having been friends, and that maybe we could talk to Parris and Doug. I mean, the fans wanted it, and deep down I wanted it; my kids would have loved to see it. And like I said, I guess I am a sentimental fool. I always believed that it could happen.

As it turned out, the so-called Cro-Mags were playing in NYC at the so-called "CBGB" fest; the line-up featured them with Sick of It All and a bunch of other bands at the old Ritz (a place I had played many times back in the day), now known as Webster Hall. The CBGB fest was there and at several other clubs all over the city. It was a big event spanning several days.

Initially I had no intention or interest in going. They had played New York before and I hadn't gone. But this time I was a little curious.

I would get e-mails saying something like, "Just show up and bring your bass, what are they gonna do, say no to you jumpin' up and playin' with your band?" People kept encouraging me to do it, and well, I guess it got to me. And on top of it, my kids wanted to go.

Then, I got a call from Steven Blush and Paul Rachman, the writers and directors of the movie *American Hardcore*. They invited me to one of the days of the fest when they were showing movies relating to CBGB and/or punk and Hardcore music.

It happened to be the day before "Cro-Mags" were supposed to play. I went to the film part of the festival where they were showing the *American Hardcore* movie. They thought it would be a good idea to have somebody there who was in the film. I was taking my kids to Jiu-Jitsu as usual, and I had to teach class, so we stopped by on the way to help introduce the film. It went well—a lot of press asking questions and so on.

While I was there I spoke to Louise, Hilly's booker at CBGB. I hadn't seen her in a long time; it was good to see her, and we were talking about life, the old days, and how much has changed. We both have kids now, and I was telling her how my sons really wanted to see the "Cro-Mags" because it's their father's old band. So I asked her if she could hook me up with laminates so my kids could see the band and maybe some other bands, and she said absolutely. She gave me three passes and I asked if she could give me a fourth one if I decided to bring anyone else. She said sure and she gave me four VIP passes.

Of course we spoke about the Cro-Mags and I said, "You know, it's really a shame that John and me can't sort things out because it would be really awesome if we could," and she was like, "Yeah, I know." I said, "You know, it would be great if I could even jump up and do a few songs, just so my kids could see it and see what their dad was a part of," and she said, "If you want, I'll give John a call right now," and I said, "Yeah, that would be great." So she did, but he didn't answer. But she texted me before the movie screening and said that she spoke to John, and "John says no way."

I knew John a long time, and I know how he can change his mind about things real quick, so I still thought something good could come of it. Besides that, I had just signed a deal for my own music, and I thought that between doing the *American Hardcore* movie press event and then possibly getting onstage with them, even just for a few songs, would be a step in the right direction, in a positive direction—defusing some of the negativity between John and me that had been building up over the years.

That next day, July 6, I went to the Academy, taught my classes and a private class. I left and started walking downtown. I wasn't sure what time the show started or if I'd actually go. I called a few people to try and find out what time they were going on. I even called Louise. When I found out it was an early show, I realized I had no time to go get my kids and bring them, so I decided to keep walking downtown and check out the scene to see how many people were there. But I still wasn't sure I'd go in. I even called a friend and asked if he'd come to the show and to bring a bass, just in case I got to jump up and play.

So I went. We had sold out that place several times in the old days, and I was curious to see what kind of crowd was coming. And I guess part of my ego was hoping that there would be a lot of well-wishers and supporters rooting for us to make something happen as the old band. I was hoping it would be a positive thing.

As it turned out, I thank God my kids weren't there.

I had those four laminates with me, so I started walking around to the people on the line, saying, "Yo, I got these laminates, anyone want to grab one? I'll give you one for 20 bucks." I don't wanna say I was scalping them, but I guess I was. I figured I only needed one, so why just give 'em away when people were paying money to get in. After a minute or two I stopped 'cause it was a little embarrassing, selling fucking passes like a scalper in front of a show, especially a show my old band was playing.

During that moment, when I was walking around in front, several people said what's up to me; I shook a few people's hands, it was all chill. I sure as shit wasn't acting like the madman they said I was in the press.

So I went up the stairs, through the front door. I showed my pass, and they waved me through the line. The guys at the door made me open my Gi bag which had all my Jiu-Jitsu stuff from the Academy and they dug through it to make sure I didn't have whatever it is they were looking for. They patted my pockets like they do to everybody else and I walked in and it was kind of nostalgic in a way, walking through those doors and up that old staircase that I used to walk up all those years ago. It was like a flashback and I guess I kinda got sucked into that moment.

I walked upstairs to the first floor where the dance floor was and the big mosh pit and all that crap. I didn't really want to waste any time walking around there because I don't really give a fuck about mosh pits or want to mingle. I was there to see John and Mackie and I also thought there could be some people there that I didn't get along with.

So I went up the stairs and I showed my laminate, and I walked through. I was walking around and I looked over the edge to the dance floor just to see how big the crowd was, and I looked at the stage and the music was loud and I was feeling nostalgic and it was kind of cool.

I sat down. I was just looking around and this one guy with skulls tattooed all around his neck, "Rat Bones," came up to me. I had known him for years; he'd always been a huge Cro-Mags fan, pretty much an on-again-off-again crackhead but a pretty harmless guy. He came up, gave me a hug and said, "Bro, you know I always had love for you."

At that point, I saw Frank McGowan, Jr., John's nephew, and he kind of looked at me like he always does, all big and goofy. He grinned, and we pounded each other and he was like "Yo, what's up Harley." And then he walked over to the bouncer who was near the dressing room area and whispered something in his ear; the bouncer approached me. I couldn't really hear what he was saying underneath the volume of the music and I'm also half deaf from all the years in front of amplifiers, so I thought he said, "Empty the bag, empty the bag." I thought, "Didn't I just do this shit downstairs?' and I started pulling stuff out. But he said, "No, no, take the bag, take the bag." So now thinking back, that's probably what he was saying at first anyway: "Take the bag and go."

So I remember thinking to myself, "Damn, Frank, you're making me leave the fuckin' VIP area, who the fuck are you? You're John's fuckin' nephew." I'd known his punk ass since he was like four or five years old, are you fuckin' kidding? To me it was a joke. I laughed, took my bag and started walking away. Then this Chinese kid called Gook comes out and walks past me straight up to the bouncer and whispers something in his ear. The bouncer turns to me and says, "Yo, it's cool, it's cool, it's cool."

I'd known that kid vaguely for a few years. He's from some other city. I met him on tour when he was in whatever band he was in and he'd always shown me respect. He came up to me, gave me a pound and a hug, and said, "Yo bro, this shit has been going on for too long, we gotta squash this shit. Come backstage with me, we gotta talk to John and put an end to this shit." And so we started walking toward the dressing room.

I was actually looking forward to seeing John and talking to him before they went on. I wasn't even thinking that something was wrong.

As soon as I walked in, I literally walked into the room, took two steps, the door shut and I got punched from behind. Out of the corner of my eye I could see it was some big dude with tattoos; it was like *baaam.*

He hit me hard. I saw a bit of a flash bulb like you see when you get hit out of nowhere and you don't expect it and then it was a rain of fists and kicks that were just coming from every direction of the room. And this was a small room, it's a dressing room, and I started falling forward. I fell onto the couch and rolled to my back and started throwing up kicks, just instinctively to get people off me. I was getting jumped by at least four or five guys, probably more. There was a bunch of people in the room; I think I counted seven or eight although I couldn't really count in all the chaos.

I did not know that the Chinese kid was one of the guys hitting me. I did not know that the other punk-ass who came up to me earlier, "Rat Bones," was one of the guys hitting me. I only know it now 'cause I injured them both and they had Orders of Protection against me after I was arrested and then they sued me. I didn't know they were even in it. I thought it was just a bunch of motherfuckers jumping me.

At that point, I reached into my pocket. I had a little knife. I pulled it out, and it still had its sheath on, so I just tried to punch the first person that was in front of me to get them the fuck off me.

Everybody started screaming. I saw the door of the dressing room open and I started yelling "Security! Security!" and I then I saw somebody pull the door shut. And I thought to myself, "Fuck, these dudes, their intention is to fuck me up, they don't want no one to see it, they're trying to beat the shit out of me!"

And I have seen all these fucking dudes, in a pack, kicking people to the point where their brains don't fuckin' work. I knew right then and there that if I didn't get the fuck out of that situation I was not going to make it home in one piece.

So I started flailing the knife as furiously as I could, just to get myself the fuck out of that situation and toward the door. Everybody's screaming, "He's got a knife, he's got a knife" and I don't even know who it was or how they ended up in my face; I guess it was when they were lunging at my arm when I bit whoever it was in the face. I tore a nice big piece out of his cheek. I fucked up that kid who came up to me earlier, "Rat Bones," which I find disturbing now because he came up to me at the beginning of the evening saying, "You know I love you bro," and I was always cool to him.

They might think it's more "gangster" to get set up by a so-called friend, someone you know or whatever, but I think it's weak. They've been watching too many fuckin' mob movies, sniffin' too much blow, thinking they're some wannabe *Scarface/Godfather* bullshit. To me that's some real punk-ass shit. And I didn't know that Chinese kid "Gook" was in the mix either. He was the one that had come up to me with this fake love, bringing me backstage; total fuckin' pussies—and that's why they needed to jump me. God knows they couldn't handle that shit one-on-one.

It's funny, according to the press, one of the guys that I fucked up, the Chinese kid Gook, was supposedly in the Cro-Mags. They said he was playing bass, or so they claimed after it went down. But as I found out a few months later from Mackie the drummer, he wasn't really playing with the band; Craig from Sick of It All was playing. They just hyped it up like that for the press, to make it sound like I went after band members—it was all a set-up to make it look like I started it. And fucking John knew.

It was obvious that it was a set-up. When I saw that door get pulled shut, I was fighting for my life. These guys wanted to kick the shit out of me, stomp me out, and no one would see it. There would be no witnesses and that would be that.

But that shit was not going down.

I bit that one guy in the face. I just tore his fuckin' cheek open right below his eye. He was screaming. Blood was running down his face. I bit someone's wrist as they were trying to get the knife out of my hand—I didn't just bite it, I tried to tear a piece out.

That's when the bouncers broke into the room. At this point I was on the bottom of a pile trying to stab and kick up and everybody started trying to grab my hand; they're like "Give me the knife, give me the knife, I'm security." I ended up getting dragged out onto the balcony, getting kicked.

I got one good kick right in my face and I'm surprised it didn't knock my teeth out. One dude screamed, "Get on your stomach, get on your stomach, put your hands out in front of you!" And this one big guy stepped on my back with both of his feet, and another guy was looking in my face and squeezing my throat. I don't know who the fuck was who. One guy looked at me and said, "Motherfucker I'll fucking kill you. I will kick you in your fucking face until you are dead motherfucker if you don't stop moving!"

I saw Pete from Sick of It All in the crowd of people next to us, with a freaked-out look on his face. He was gesturing with his hands for me to calm down and stop resisting. He kept mouthing the words, "Harley chill, Harley stop please, chill Harley."

That's when one guy said, "Put your hands out in front of you!" I asked, "Are you a cop?" and he was like "Yeah." So I said, "Show me your badge!" and at just that point the boys in blue came running up the stairs. I was like, "Fine, I'm not moving anymore, cuff me." I stuck my hands out in front of me, face down on the floor.

I still didn't know that I'd been stabbed. I got 40 stitches in my leg. Thank God it was in my leg. The cops cuffed me, turned me over, and that's when I saw the wound in my leg—it was grotesque. The blood was bubbling out of it, the fascia and tendons were literally hanging out of my leg; that's why people started saying that it was a compound fracture. The cops cuffed me, put me on a chair, carried me down the stairs and put me in an ambulance. It wasn't until I got cleaned up in the ambulance that they realized it was a stab wound.

There had always been tension at my shows and fights with assholes, whether it was in New York or other cities on tour—people getting jumped and shit like that. It's been happening since the '80s.

Over the years, as shows got bigger, it got worse. As the scene started being more about crews and tough-guy imagery than about music and bands, Hardcore kids getting jumped by other Hardcore kids and fights became more commonplace.

Back in 2007, some of these assholes had jumped a guy in the crowd at a Harley's War show at Continental on St. Marks Place. It was actually the guitarist from one of the opening bands called EGH. I stopped them from pummeling the guy. I called them all out, and I remember them looking at me and looking at each other and looking at their one main guy who was there. He was some total new jack. It was a total stand-off; they didn't know whether to jump me or not, but then they backed off and split.

That put me at odds with a lot of these assholes. These guys are just one of the many Hardcore crews that popped up over the last 20 or so years. Most of them are nothing but nutless fucks when you catch them alone; I have seen it so many times.

I used to be friends with guys who started a lot of those crews. They were fans of the band and used to look up to us and me and bands like Agnostic Front. I knew a lot of 'em since they first found their way down to the Lower East Side and discovered Hardcore.

But after that shit went down at Continental, they made it very obvious that they were no longer down with me. And because most of 'em were Cro-Mags fans, they were now supporters of Bloodclot and whatever bullshit Cro-Mags band he'd gig with.

Not long after that gig, I put out the Harley's War *Hardcore All Stars* CD. It came out in Japan and eventually in the States. It had a song on it called "LES OG"—Lower East Side Original Gangsta. I made a video too, filmed by B-boy legend Pop Master Fable. We shot it at that underground fight club in the Bronx. Lyrically it was a play on the whole gangsta wannabe shit that the Hardcore scene had turned into.

When that song and that video came out, that was the final rift between me and the NYHC wannabe thugs. They took it as a direct jab at them, which it wasn't. But I guess when you sniff enough coke and look for beef hard enough, you'll find it. The irony is, in a lot of ways me and my friends started that NYHC thug shit.

I'm not proud of my own mindless stupid violence, but it is what it is. I can't go back and undo it. But I'm trying to move forward, and the difference between me and this new-jack shit is I didn't need a whole fuckin' crew to hold my own; I never did. I did what I did and that was that. If I fucked someone up or did whatever "wrong" shit I did, I didn't need a crew behind me to have the balls to do it. And when I was young, I might've had beef with most of the world, but I didn't prey on other Hardcore kids; that's just not how it was.

After that CD came out, some of these assholes put out a song where they made threats to me. I paid it no mind 'cause people

422

are always gonna use your name if you're anybody with any kind of a reputation or if you have credibility, to try and legitimize themselves.

Them going after me or giving me any kind of shit—as someone who helped create their scene and put it on the fuckin' map—is as ridiculous as them going after the Bad Brains or members of Black Flag, or like me going after members of the Clash or the Sex Pistols or Black Sabbath 'cause they don't agree with me or don't like me.

By going to Webster Hall that night, I had unintentionally launched myself into the most sensationalistic worldwide media frenzy in Hardcore history. Hardcore-Punk Rock-Stabbing-Biting-CBGB—the press had a field day.

So there I was, being carried out of Webster Hall by cops into an ambulance, strapped into a chair with my hands cuffed behind my back, but I was still reaching my arms around to the side, giving everyone the finger. I was screaming all kinds of shit: "You fuckin' punk motherfuckers! All of you pussies couldn't take me out. You bitch-ass motherfuckers! How's your fuckin' face motherfucker, you like that shit!..."

Those motherfuckers had gotten so used to jumping people at Hardcore shows—kids with no heart who'd just take the beating—but yo, you jump on me, you better know that shit's gonna get serious. And of course, my ol' buddy John was nowhere to be found.

He left down the back stairs that led to the stage as I was coming into the dressing room, just in time. He later told the press that he had armed himself with a metal pipe just in case 'cause he knew that I was gonna be there.

I have to laugh: big, bad John dipping down the back stairs with his pipe. I mean, I always knew he was a bit of a bitch, but this was straight-up embarrassing. He should be ashamed and embarrassed; I'm ashamed for him that he even aligns himself with a bunch of wannabe thugs, especially since he pretends to stand for Krishna Consciousness and righteousness. That's the guy I thought might still have some sincerity or love left. Boy, was I wrong.

I thought all those years and all the good times meant more than all the petty bullshit and beef, and that the positivity would outweigh the negativity—that what we did together mattered more.

I still believe in brotherhood, friendship, loyalty and forgiveness. I believed that growing up with someone and living on the streets with them and all that mattered. I believed that New York Hardcore had some sincerity and loyalty and honesty—or at least the old heads did—and that it was still a family. But I was wrong.

So many people decided to immediately point fingers at me and to jump on the "Harley's a loose cannon" bandwagon—even journalists that I know and people at labels that were supposed to be friends of mine for years started talking shit.

God forbid anyone has the balls to speak the truth or for that matter stick up for a friend or someone who's been on the scene since it began—motherfuckers would rather hide in the shadows than speak up 'cause everyone is a punk nowadays, and sadly the scene has deteriorated into some high school bullshit, where everyone is a kiss-ass so desperate to be accepted that they'll just suck each other's dicks to be a part of the cool crowd. I've been saying it for years, people: your New York Hardcore heroes and idols are nothin' but bitches.

The ambulance was outside Webster Hall, and people were all freaking out trying to take my picture. I had people coming up to the ambulance trying to get a look inside to see if it was me. I could hear people saying "Is that Harley?" Some chick looked in the window and said, "Harley, is that you?" I just smiled and shook my head.

On the way to the hospital in the ambulance, my arresting officer smiled at me and said, "Well, at least they know you ain't a punk!" Then he started laughing and repeating some of the things I had been yelling at the crowd. We both started laughing. I got to Bellevue Hospital and my leg was a bloody mess. There was blood all over my sneakers—some of it mine, some of it the punks' that jumped me. From that point on, it just got more and more surreal.

I was in a section of the hospital reserved for people either going to jail or who had been fucked up in jail and needed work on them that they couldn't do in the prison hospital. I could tell you a few funny stories from there: guys on stretchers high on dust flipping out, people with slashed faces talking shit to cops and hospital staff—total madness.

I was recognized by a few of the detectives who came to talk to me and see what was going on. By then, the incident was already all over the news and Internet. The punk-ass motherfuckers that I fucked up were in another section of the hospital ward getting stitched up—and that's when I found out that I was the so-called perpetrator and they were the so-called victims.

All these NYHC bitches were making it out like I launched myself into the dressing room like a wild man and just started stabbing people or some bullshit. I've known where John lives for years, so if I wanted to attack him wouldn't I just go to his apartment? No, I would go to a concert full of people and attack him in a room full of witnesses and all his friends and band members all by myself. Even a dumbass should be able to figure out that isn't what happened.

All these fake hoods were quick to point the finger at me to try to cover their own tracks, and all the rest of the sheep and the media just went along with it—the more outrageous and sensationalistic, the better the story, right? The best one I heard was Jimmy Gestapo smuggled the knife into the club up his ass and gave it to me.

From the hospital, I went to the 9th Precinct, where I had several cops come by my cell saying shit like, "Flanagan, what the fuck happened? What were you thinking?" To which I kept responding, "I got jumped. I got stabbed in the leg. Those motherfuckers are lying. This is bullshit." Then a detective interviewed me. He's interrogating me, trying to get all the details of the event, and he kept re-asking the same questions over and over in different ways, walking in and out of the room. I told him the same shit, and then they took me back to my cell. Time stood still from there on.

From there I went to "The Tombs" down by Centre Street. The sun was just coming up when I got out of the police van. There were photographers waiting for me. Who was I, John-fuckin-Gotti? Charles Manson? I couldn't believe the press was there, snapping my picture as the cops marched me in.

I got inside, the doors closed behind me and the whole process began, strip-searched and whatnot. And then I waited; and as I did, I tried to wrap my brain around what was going on. It was bullshit, and on top of all of it, it didn't help that me and the mother of my two boys were, to put it politely, going through a extremely ugly break-up. And all of this shit blew up around the same time. The worst part was that my kids were stuck in the middle.

I didn't handle it well. She was threatening to take my kids, and after the Webster Hall incident she started using it against me, trying to take them. I didn't see any of it coming.

At that point, the press was at my house interviewing my neighbors and trying to get comments from my family. I was being railroaded. The quotes from all the assholes at the show had painted me like I was some dust-crazed Charles Manson that just went berserk.

Eventually I got led to see the judge, and met my court-appointed lawyer from the Legal Aid Society. After a few minutes in front of the judge, he said some shit but all I heard was blah blah blah $25,000 bail! My jaw dropped and I was led back down the stairs and into a cell. Eventually I was taken with all the other inmates and we boarded the bus to Rikers Island.

The bus ride to Rikers was a trip. They had me in my own little cage up in front of the bus, me and this one big black guy. He was in a separate cage behind mine 'cause we were both going to PC (Protective Custody) since we both allegedly committed serious crimes, and mine in particular was so high-profile that they didn't want me or him in with the general population. We started talking, and I started mentally preparing myself for whatever might happen next. I still hadn't slept. I'd been awake for two or three days; I kind of lost track of time.

I got to Rikers, went through all the processing, endless strip-searches, body scans and bullshit. Every step of the way, I was meeting people, both COs and inmates, who knew who I was, either from the Cro-Mags or from all the press. I was sent to C-76. I had no idea how much media attention I had been getting. I was in every major newspaper, on almost every channel and the radio—like 1010 WINS, Channel 2, and Channel 5. I was even on Taxi TV. So by the time I got out there, everyone knew about me. I even met a few COs that were fans of the band. It was bizarre.

Anyone who knows Rikers knows how big the place is, and how much craziness goes on in there. There were helmeted riot cops with shields heading from one area to another. They were these big motherfuckers that you weren't allowed to look at. You had to face the wall whenever they walked by. I eventually got brought down to my cellblock and brought into cell 22. While in there, an inmate they called Smoke walked by mopping the floor. He looked at me and said, "I know you, what's your name? Are you Harry?" I replied, "Harley." He said, "Yeah, I saw you on Channel 2. They called you the white Mike Tyson," and smiled and kept mopping. A little later, he came to my cell and gave me a copy of the *New York Post* with a full-page picture and story about me on page 2.

The more I read, the more pissed I got. The lies were ridiculous. They claimed I was pacing around in front of Webster Hall with a serrated hunting knife, acting all crazy, singing the lyrics to Cro-Mags songs, talking about "Who the fuck do they think they are, playing my songs?" I was like, "What??? That didn't happen!!! What the fuck??!!"

Of course all the reports came from nameless sources, and then they had quotes from bitch-ass John talking shit. I was so fucking pissed. The guy in the cell next to me, Bam Bam, had shot two cops. The guy across from me ran a guy over three times; they called him a habitual violent offender. He was actually a nice guy. This other dude I met they called Knowledge, he had been in and out of the system for most of his life. He showed me around a little. One dude offered me some food 'cause I had missed dinner. I didn't want to take it; I didn't feel like owing any favors, but he was cool. I eventually took it. I was starving. I hadn't eaten in so long, I didn't even care that it was chicken. So for the first time in many years, I ate chicken. It was nasty but I didn't give a fuck.

I had no blanket, just two sheets and this thin plastic mattress on a metal bed in a little cell. There I was, and I had no idea for how long. When I came out and went into the main room with the TV where everyone hung out, they were all checking me out; they all knew who I was. I was still wearing my bloody T-shirt and bloody sneakers. There were also these two drag queens that pretty much just hung out by the TV shaking their asses as they watched and "vogueing," hoping to get some attention from the other inmates.

I almost got into a fight with some big Puerto Rican dude on the second day I was in there. He tried to hard-rock me but I stood my ground; nothing happened and that was that. From that point on, I kept my eye on him and didn't let him stand behind me. I was doing over 1,000 push-ups a day. I was skinny from not eating right, but I figured if I'm gonna be here for a while, I'm gonna need to get in shape.

It was as if my past and my present had collided; it was like some A *Clockwork Orange* shit. Just when things were starting to go well: I was working at Renzo Gracie Academy, I was a black belt, I had just signed a recording deal, I had my kids, and all of a sudden my past reached out and grabbed me. And I was really seeing who my friends were and who was full of shit.

I remember my man Knowledge saying to me, "Yo, you're high-profile, B. As many people are comin' up against you right now, watch, you're gonna have just as many people comin' for you soon from out of places you never expected. You wait and see, this is no bullshit. Your shit was all over the news, B. That's no bullshit."

Sure enough, he was right. As many friends I had that didn't want anything to do with it or with me—people who were chicken-shitting away from me and talking shit—I had people that I couldn't believe stepping up for me. I spoke to Renzo while I was locked up and he told me, "Don't worry, we'll get you out of there. Do you have a lawyer? We will get you one." I told him I was good and that it was self-defense. He assured me that he and everyone at the academy believed in me and had my back and knew it was bullshit.

At one point, I was in my cell and I was told I had a visitor: "legal counsel." I was like "Damn, this shit must be serious if my public defender is taking time from all his other cases and coming all the way out here to talk to me." I didn't have a jumpsuit, but I needed to wear one to go from one part of the jail to another, so they made me borrow one. They told an inmate to give me his—ironically, it was from the one guy I had almost had a fight with.

I get up there and bam, it wasn't my lawyer at all, it was Laura Hill, who I had met just a few months earlier. I had done an interview for her website *New York Natives*. After I did the interview, we stayed in touch via e-mail; she was going to help me do some editing on this book. I had sent her a few chapters and we had started going back and forth with it when all of this shit happened.

I was racking my brain thinking what the fuck was she doing here, and then I remembered her telling me that she was a lawyer, but not criminal law.

I was like, "What are you doing here, this isn't the kind of law you do???" I'd just spoken to her a few days earlier, and she was freaked out when she heard about what happened, so she used her legal credentials, got some sort of letter from her law firm, and was able to come in and visit me. I will never forget that shit.

It was fucked up. Here was someone who barely knew me coming out to see me, and the mother of my boys was hanging up the phone in my face and talking mad shit to me. I was heartbroken and pissed off as hell. And I had never felt so betrayed in my life.

All night, you'd hear people screaming and talking shit. The youth offenders were in the same building as us, right next store. So all night, you'd hear them screaming, "Suck my dick motherfucker! I'll fuck you up! Suck my dick!" Riot cops came in all fucking night. Then as the sun would start coming up and they'd finally shut up, the seagulls would start making noise. It was nonstop. Ironically, it was the best sleep I had gotten in a while—ever since I'd started going through the bullshit with my ex.

My life had truly become a nightmare.

I remember at one point, I was looking out my window through the gates. It was a beautiful sunny day and I could hear birds, and a butterfly flew past my window and I was like, "Damn." Right then and there that butterfly represented freedom. What I wouldn't do to be free right then. I had no idea what was gonna happen. My lawyer told me that I was possibly looking at two and a half years in jail.

The idea of being away from my kids and in jail, my woman leaving, losing my job, my apartment, my record deal—all of it— and for what? Defending myself? What the fuck! After a week I got bailed out by my uncle, so I knew I'd be on the street at least until my next court date, providing I could stay out of trouble until then.

During my stay in Rikers my stab wound had gotten really infected 'cause when I was in the hospital they stitched it up real tight instead of stuffing it and letting it drain out. I wound up with MRCA and a staph infection from all the filth in there, so I ended up back in the hospital for about a week after I got out, on an IV.

It was as if I was being tested in every way.

So many of my so-called friends turned their backs on me, all the motherfuckers on the scene were painting me out to be some insane freak—even though most of these fucks are nothin' but coke-sniffin' drug-dealin' scumbags at this point. Oh yeah, and of course I can't leave out all the straight-edge dweebs and wannabe Hare Krishnas.

I hadn't been to a show in years except for when I had a gig to play, and I hadn't been in a fight in years. I hadn't done drugs or drank in years; all I did was take care of my kids, train Jiu-Jitsu and teach. It didn't matter; I guess my reputation from the past still lingered in people's memories and in NYHC history—forget where I actually was in my life.

Because of all the people talking shit and trying to frame me, the record label I had just signed with was having second thoughts; everything was coming to a head. And now I had to prepare for a court date, facing four felony counts of second-degree assault and weapons charges—for biting and stabbing people

I shoulda stayed home that night.

I gotta laugh. If there was ever a time that I was about to lose my shit, I'd have to say it was around this time. If there was ever a time someone would relapse into drugs, alcohol or some self-destructive shit, it was a time like this. I actually went out and got drunk a few nights, which I hadn't done in a long time. I was really depressed. I was really at the bottom. I could have easily spun out of control, but I said to myself "Fuck that," I was not gonna let myself go and do that to myself or to my kids, or give in and give the satisfaction to my enemies. I'm a black belt—I have more control than that now. I am not who I once was, I am stronger than that.

I didn't know where to turn or what to do, but I was starting to see who my real friends were, and for the most part, they weren't who I thought they were. But I did have a few people who really came through for me, and I'll never forget that. A few people started trying to raise money for me to help with legal fees and such, but it was few and far between and nothing actually happened. And then of course there were the total fuckin' nuts reaching out to me as well.

But during this time Laura really came through for me; she literally took me in off the street. I had been couch-surfing, sleeping on my roof and in parks. If not for her being there, I would not have made it through those times.

As I waited for my court date, I started training and working at RGA again (thank you Renzo). I was amazed how much support I got at the Academy, not just from Renzo and all my friends, but from the parents of my young students. I was humbled by their faith and trust in me. I remember one of the mothers telling me that in the wake of all that had happened, her husband said to her, "At least we know that the person who is teaching our son martial arts isn't a pussy." I laughed my ass off. It was not what I expected to hear her say, and Renzo loved it. I started training again as soon as my leg healed enough to do so. It was exactly one month to the day of the incident that I started teaching again.

My first court date was September 27th. I was more than slightly nervous. I was facing four felonies and looking at a good amount of time in jail. It all would have amounted to nothing back when I was a kid, but in 2012, in the soft-ass city that New York has become and with all the media attention, it was a very big deal.

But the DA didn't have a case established. The 20-something witnesses they had were all starting to fall to the wind. All of the statements they made to the cops and to the press, including John's, were all contradicting each other; people's lies weren't matching up. John was giving interviews left and right and each time changing his story, so the DA started having a hard time putting a solid case together. It was as if John was helping me beat the case with his inability to shut up and with his nonstop lies. Each time he told the story it changed, and each time he told it he implicated himself more in having played a part in setting me up.

The whole thing makes me sick. Even at my worst hate for John or anyone else, I would never stand by and watch and knowingly turn my back on someone while they were getting jumped, especially a former friend or band member.

NYHC has become the antithesis of its former self. It's not about unity; it's about conformity. What is that Agnostic Front line? "You talk about unity, talk about conformity, you say that you support the scene, why don't you get the fuck away from me?" That shit is more true now than it ever was.

Another hearing got adjourned while the DA's office continued to try to build the case against me. It was a big case and they did not want to let it go. I was like Sid Vicious meets Charles Manson or some shit: a crazed knife-wielding, stabbing, slashing, biting, Hardcore Punk Rocker "attacking my former band" at a show with the infamous "CBGB" name attached to it. It was great media fodder and I think the DA wanted to make a name for himself.

Then at my next court date I wound up getting an adjournment again 'cause they still didn't have a case against me. And again it got pushed back while the DA continued to try to build it, until finally in December of 2012 they contacted my lawyer and said to appear in court on Friday, December 14th, when the entire case was dismissed.

Over the next year there was more fallout in my personal life, not just from the mother of my two boys, but also I was sued by some of the punk-ass motherfuckers who attacked me at Webster Hall. Bitch-asses jumped me, then try to turn me into the "bad guy" 'cause they got fucked up—ain't that ironic? Anyway, it all slowly started to level out.

After all that, I was walking around with so much anger and rage inside me, I was ready to explode; I felt like a fucking bomb. I wanted to go hunting, get some payback, unleash some hate. My thoughts would go from angry to hostile to murderous. And I realized that if I didn't remove myself from all of the things that were bringing me to that point, that bad things were gonna happen. So I made a conscious decision to separate myself from the people and things that were bringing me to that kind of negative place.

I have a hard enough time dealing with anger and violence; it has been a lifelong struggle. There has been enough of it in my life, and in order to maintain some level of calmness and control I have had to move away from it. It wasn't about giving in or giving up, it was about knowing what I had to do and surviving.

Since then, I have left the majority of the people I once knew behind—not all, but the majority. People that bring negative energy and anger out of me and into my life, I'm done with it. Maybe one day I will look back without the feelings I have now. One day it won't matter to me so much, but either way, I am in a different place now.

But even with everything that's gone down, I would still gladly get together with all of those guys: John, Parris, Doug, Mackie, all of us together in a room, and do one last show. Not because of the scene, not for the money, not for the fame, not for NYHC, but because the time that we spent together meant something to me. Those guys and the songs that we played together meant something to me. It meant more to me than the beef, it meant more to me than all the bullshit, all the ego, all the drama and everything else. I would do it for free in a heartbeat just to share that moment with those guys again and then walk our separate ways and know that it ended right. 'Cause I don't like ending things on a bad note. I know that once one of us is gone it's over. There will never be a chance to do it again and no chance to end the quarrel. Either way, I won't hold my breath. I'm in a great place in my life.

The hardest thing I ever faced in my life was losing my kids; it hurt more than anything else ever has. I suffered through serious depression over it, but I tried to learn from it as well. I have two great kids from that relationship who I love with all my heart; they mean more to me than anything, and for that I am grateful. I have always done the best I can for them and I always will. And despite all the craziness I've been through in this life, I still have love and hope in my heart.

As I finish this book I am shedding my past and looking to the future.

I am in the best relationship I have ever been in, I am in love with a beautiful, educated woman; she is a doctor and a lawyer, who treats me better than anyone ever has. In fact the only thing wrong with her is that she loves me.

I am teaching Jiu-Jitsu at one of the most respected martial arts academies in the world alongside world-famous MMA and Jiu-Jitsu legends, people who I truly respect; writing, traveling, being a father, spending as much time as possible with my kids and the people that I love. Every day I know how lucky I am and I am grateful. I hope my kids can learn from me and from my mistakes and not have to make as many as I have.

Not too long ago, I walked through the Lower East Side with my sons. We didn't plan it, it just happened. I showed them the building I grew up in, with my mom, Simon, Allen Ginsberg, Richard Hell and a ton of other now famous people that lived there back in the day when the neighborhood was nuts.

I have so many memories of that building and that block. They tore the church down across the street from my building where the Hitmen used to hang out at night and blast their radios when I was a kid, and the funeral home. I didn't even know they were allowed to tear down churches. So much has changed and yet it still looks kind of the same—kind of. It's just so busy, so safe and so white now.

My eldest wanted to know all the crazy stories, so I told him a few. I showed them where I used to hang out and where I went to school, where I went and got ice cream at Ray's. I can't believe he's still alive. The place looks relatively the same, just messier: the small counter, barely any room to move, and all the handwritten signs in Magic Marker, and the best milkshakes and egg creams on the LES.

I only saw three people that I knew. I ran into Dick Manitoba from the Dictators, and his wife, and I saw this martial arts dude Jose that I knew when I was young.

I spoke to a couple of neighborhood people who noticed me on Avenue A, and I walked by the old C Squat and the new one. What used to be a crazy and dangerous neighborhood is now full of tourists, yuppie bars, restaurants, coffee shops and stores; it's so bizarre.

Life goes on.

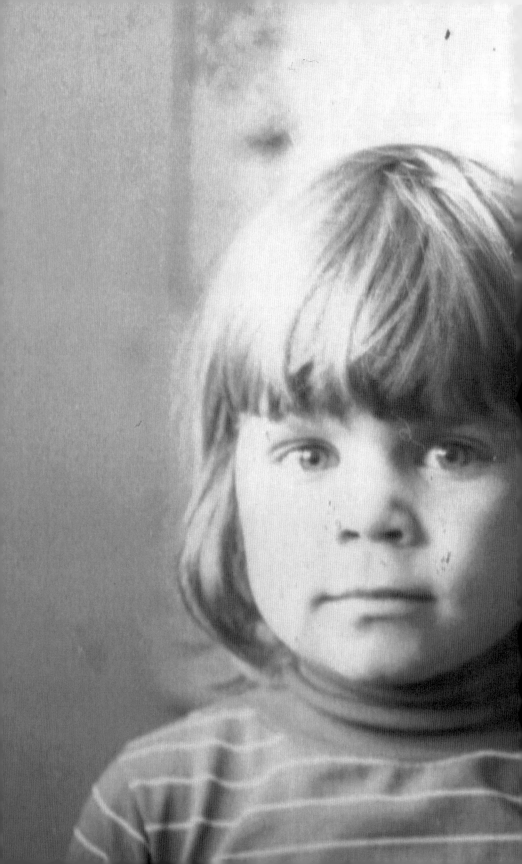

Epilogue

After all the madness in my life and the recent drama surrounding Webster Hall, my arrest, losing my kids, starting a new relationship, getting my kids back in my life, and dealing with all the drama of family court, my mom was stricken with terminal cancer.

After a major operation and what seemed like a recovery, things took a turn for the worse. And through it all, she remained supportive in my battle for my kids, and I started spending a lot more time with her.

It's fucked up when you know your mom or your dad is dying. You go through your life with all the baggage and shit that they put on you, and all the shit the world and your friends put on you, and then there comes a time when you realize you have to put it all down, just let it all go.

I remember just a few days before she went into hospice that Patti Smith called her 'cause she had heard she was sick. They had only met a few times. Obviously my mother must have made an impression on her. It meant a lot to my mom that she called. My mother had always admired her. They knew each other through Ginsberg and they had both been with him when he died.

I was with her as much as possible during her last few months. We spent more time together than we had in years. We even left the city one day just a month before she died to spend some time at a horse stable. She loved horses, and she hadn't been around them since she was a child. She said it was the most beautiful day of her entire life; and later she spent the night, and then the next three nights at my apartment. We had such a good time that she completely forgot to take her pain medication.

I hope I can face death with as much dignity. The way she has handled it, I have never seen a braver person in my life. She makes all the "men" I know look like cowards.

Sadly she only saw my kids twice during her last few months. But the time that they spent together was amazing and very meaningful, and picked up her spirits; and I know that she took great comfort in the fact that I am finally in a place in my life where things are coming together in a positive way. I just wish she could've been here with us longer.

After she was admitted to hospice, I still had two good days of conversation with her before she slipped into a deep sleep. She had looked so tired and worn out when she first got there, but then just a day later, she looked so peaceful. In just days she had gone from looking like my mother to looking more like my grandmother to looking like herself but as a child—her skin so smooth, all the stress gone from her face. While she lay there breathing, I held her hand.

She had a constant flow of visitors, quietly coming and paying their respects and giving her love.

She died Monday, June 15, 2015.

I was at home getting ready to go see her, when I got the call that she had passed. I went to Bellevue hospice where she had spent her last few days and there she was looking beautiful and peaceful. My Aunt Sophie's rosary lay out across her chest; it was surreal.

There was my mother dead, the one who brought me into this world. I cried. I sat with her. I kissed her goodbye even though I knew she was already gone. She was still warm. Even though her heart had stopped and her breathing had stopped, her cells were still alive. Then it was as if I could hear her voice in my head saying, "Go now, don't stay here with my body, I love you my son." I spent just a few more moments with her and then I left.

Over the next few days came the calls and e-mails from old friends, friends of hers—some I knew, some I didn't, calls and e-mails from people from the Stimulators days, people from the old Cro-Mags days, people who knew her from when we lived in Europe, and people who knew her in the '60s.

It's so surprising the people you hear from at a time like this. But even more surprising is the people you don't hear from. The only member of the Cro-Mags that I heard from was Doug Holland.

Her funeral was beautiful. She didn't want a service in a church and she wanted to be cremated, so we did as she wished. The father of my girlfriend, now my wife, gave my mother a plot to be buried in at Woodlawn Cemetery, a beautiful place where lots of writers and musicians like Miles Davis and many historic figures are buried.

It had been raining all morning on June 20th, but it stopped as soon as we arrived at the cemetery. I was there with my boys, my girlfriend, my family and hers, close family friends, some going back to my early childhood and even to my mother's childhood.

My mother's second husband, my stepfather Karsten, flew in from Denmark. And her third husband, Simon Pettet, flew in from Toronto with his wife. Friends flew from Scandinavia; a lot of the people I knew from 12th Street in the building that I grew up in showed up, like the author Luc Sante, famous artists like Carol Bove who was with my mother up 'til the end, Allen Ginsberg's longtime friend and assistant Bob Rosenthal, Steve Taylor from The Fugs and many other old friends. Her boyfriend of nearly 20 years, Kirt Markle, who is the same age as me, was so devastated that he did not attend.

Her ashes were carried out and placed on a table. They were in a box not meant to be buried, a beautiful statue of a crying angel. There was an awning set up for the rain, but as if on cue, the rain had stopped. There were three chairs sitting by themselves right in front but strangely no one sat in them. It was later that day that I thought about it: I felt that those seats were for my grandmother, my grandfather, and my Aunt Sophie sitting right there in front, and I cried again.

The priest who did the service was a childhood friend of my mother. He had my youngest son light incense as he smiled, and said how my mother always loved incense. He did a blessing with holy water, and then gave my son the flask to hold for him as he then continued with the service.

We all took part in reading from Bible verses; I held on to my son Jonah and he cried quietly. My son Harley stood behind me with my girlfriend, trying to keep his composure as tears rolled down his face.

At the end of the service, a drizzle of rain started again. When everyone was done consoling each other and people started walking away, I looked at the box sitting there on the table surrounded by flowers with the hole in the ground beside it. Two cemetery workers arrived with shovels and a rake, and I walked back and asked if I could cover her with the soil myself, as I had done for my father 13 years earlier.

I explained that I didn't feel right about someone who didn't know my mother covering her with dirt. They understood. I thanked them. I took the box with the angel off the table. I kissed it, my sons kissed it, and I got down on my knees and put it in the ground.

One of the cemetery workers handed me a shovel and I started to fill the hole. My youngest son, who'd been crying, came over next to me, got on his knees, and started to help me fill in the hole with his hands, grabbing pieces of soil and putting them in, picking out rocks so none would damage her box as we filled it. And his tears stopped.

I put down the shovel and we both finished by hand, and then I raked the soil over, and we patted the earth down with our hands and it was done. It was so sad and so beautiful.

The next day was Father's Day.

When I started writing this book I didn't know what the end was going to be or what I wanted to say besides telling the story of my life, and setting the record straight. But now it's so obvious what it's about: closure.

###

SECOND EDITION
AMERICAN HARDCORE
A Tribal History by Steven Blush

American Hardcore: A Tribal History
SECOND EDITION
STEVEN BLUSH

The Second Edition of the "definitive work on one of rock's most important eras" (*Juxtapoz*), has over one hundred new pieces of artwork, hundreds of new band bios and a radically expanded discography. The first edition, which became the Sony Classics–released documentary of the same name, was 328 pages; the new edition clocks in at 408 pages.

According to the *Los Angeles Times*, *American Hardcore* is the "definitive treatment of hardcore punk," changing the way we look at punk rock. And according to *Paper* magazine, *American Hardcore* sets the record straight about the last great American subculture."

7 x 10 | 408 Pages | Hundreds of photos and illustrations
ISBN: 978-0-922915-71-2 | $22.95

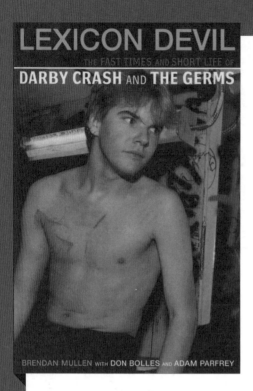

LEXICON DEVIL

THE FAST TIMES AND SHORT LIFE OF

DARBY CRASH AND THE GERMS

BRENDAN MULLEN WITH DON BOLLES AND ADAM PARFREY

Lexicon Devil: The Fast Times and Short Life of Darby Crash and The Germs
BRENDAN MULLEN, DON BOLLES AND ADAM PARFREY

LEXICON DEVIL, an oral history that probes the brains of over one hundred characters, and contains 140 never-before-seen photos, goes beyond early punk rock into secret regions of suicide, mind control, suppressed sexuality, corrosive humor, self-abuse, and addictions to rock celebrity, drugs and cults.

"This book is an important oral history of a person, a band, a time long past that will never be repeated."
— Trent A. Reinsmith

"This book scared the shit out of me. It's amazing, it's great ... I can't believe how good it is."
— Pat Smear, Germs guitarist, and later a player for Nirvana and the Foo Fighters

6 x 9 in, 296 Pages | ISBN 0922915709 | $16.95

Violence Girl: East L.A. Rage to Hollywood Stage, A Chicano Punk Story
ALICE BAG

"Alice Bag...paved the way for an entire generation of female musicians inspired by her ferocious performance style, her confrontational, provocative attitude and of course, her great and powerful music."
— Network Awesome

The proximity of the East L.A. barrio to Hollywood is as close as a short drive on the 101 freeway, but the cultural divide is enormous. Born to Mexican-born and American-naturalized parents, Alicia Armendariz migrated a few miles west to participate in the free-range birth of the 1970s punk movement. Alicia adopted the punk name Alice Bag, and became lead singer for The Bags, early punk visionaries who starred in Penelope Spheeris' documentary *The Decline of Western Civilization.*

"*The book's slices of punk life from thirty-five years ago also document a flashpoint for a city rich with talent and anger, erupting into something completely oppositional to the feel-good, pastoral, and often saccharine Laurel Canyon melodies and glistening surf music of the preceding decade.*"
— City Watch LA

"*Bag is inspiration, Bag is power, Bag's words fuel. While the world can feel so very separated in terms of language, religion, race, gender, class, and the violence these things sometimes bring, there is universal power in someone just speaking their truth. I'm just thankful that Alice Bag did it.*"
— [E]coco Papy, *Persephone Magazine*

6 x 9 | 384 Pages | Paperback | ISBN: 978-1-936239-12-2 |$17.95

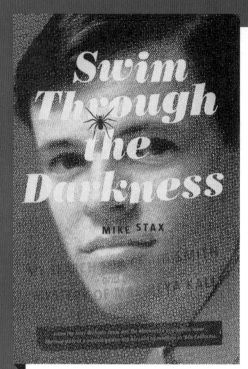

Swim Through the Darkness: My Search for Craig Smith and the Mystery of Maitreya Kali
MIKE STAX

Craig Smith was a 1960s golden boy: good-looking, charismatic, outgoing; a preternaturally gifted musician and songwriter whose songs were recorded by some of the biggest names in entertainment — Andy Williams, Glen Campbell, the Monkees. His future success seemed assured, until an unexpected turn of events plunged him into a terrifying darkness. Clean-cut Craig Smith became Maitreya Kali, the self-proclaimed psychedelic Messiah. He laid out his poignant, disturbing schizophrenic vision on a sprawling self-released double album before disappearing completely. Author Mike Stax spent fifteen years piecing together the mystery of Maitreya Kali, uncovering one of the strangest and most tragic untold stories of the 1960s and '70s.

Swim Through the Darkness reveals author Stax's fifteen-year quest in tracking down this strange saga of American pop culture. Included in the story are Smith's close ties to the Monkees, particularly Mike Nesmith, who produced and promoted Smith's band, Penny Arkade. Also covered are the bizarre self-released albums he made as Maitreya Kali, which now command thousands of dollars among psychedelic music collectors.

6x9 | 232 pages | Paperback | 978 – 1-934170-65-6 | $19.95